Behold the Man

Behold the Man

Essays on the Historical Jesus

Peter S. Williams

FOREWORD BY
Craig L. Blomberg

WIPF & STOCK · Eugene, Oregon

BEHOLD THE MAN
Essays on the Historical Jesus

Copyright © 2024 Peter S. Williams. All rights reserved. Except for brief quotations in critical publications or reviews, no part of this book may be reproduced in any manner without prior written permission from the publisher. Write: Permissions, Wipf and Stock Publishers, 199 W. 8th Ave., Suite 3, Eugene, OR 97401.

Wipf & Stock
An Imprint of Wipf and Stock Publishers
199 W. 8th Ave., Suite 3
Eugene, OR 97401

www.wipfandstock.com

PAPERBACK ISBN: 978-1-6667-3606-9
HARDCOVER ISBN: 978-1-6667-9388-8
EBOOK ISBN: 978-1-6667-9389-5

VERSION NUMBER 06/07/24

Scripture quotations marked (ESV) are taken from The ESV® Bible (The Holy Bible, English Standard Version®), © 2001 by Crossway, a publishing ministry of Good News Publishers. Used by permission. All rights reserved.

Scripture quotations marked (NIV) are taken from the Holy Bible, New International Version®, NIV®. Copyright © 1973, 1978, 1984, 2011 by Biblica, Inc.™ Used by permission of Zondervan. All rights reserved worldwide. www.zondervan.com. The "NIV" and "New International Version" are trademarks registered in the United States Patent and Trademark Office by Biblica, Inc.™

Scripture quotations marked HCSB are taken from the Holman Christian Standard Bible®, Used by Permission HCSB © 1999, 2000, 2002, 2003, 2009 Holman Bible Publishers. Holman Christian Standard Bible®, Holman CSB®, and HCSB® are federally registered trademarks of Holman Bible Publishers.

Scripture texts in this work taken from the New American Bible, revised edition © 2010, 1991, 1986, 1970 Confraternity of Christian Doctrine, Washington, D.C. and are used by permission of the copyright owner. All Rights Reserved. No part of the New American Bible may be reproduced in any form without permission in writing from the copyright owner.

Scripture quotations from New Revised Standard Version Bible, copyright © 1989 National Council of the Churches of Christ in the United States of America. Used by permission. All rights reserved worldwide.

Scripture quotations marked MSG are taken from The Message, copyright © 1993, 2002, 2018 by Eugene H. Peterson. Used by permission of NavPress. All rights reserved. Represented by Tyndale House Publishers.

Scripture quotations marked (NLT) are taken from the Holy Bible, New Living Translation, copyright © 1996, 2004, 2015 by Tyndale House Foundation. Used by permission of Tyndale House Publishers, Carol Stream, Illinois 60188. All rights reserved.

Scripture taken from the Holy Bible: International Standard Version® Release 2.0. Copyright © 1996–2013 by the ISV Foundation. Used by permission of Davidson Press, LLC. All rights reserved internationally.

Scripture taken from The Voice™. Copyright © 2012 by Ecclesia Bible Society. Used by permission. All rights reserved.

This book is dedicated to
Dr. David and Mrs. Rachel Butler,

with thanks for over two decades
of friendship and pastoral care.

"The story of Jesus . . . is not just an epiphany—a revelation of glory and no more—and it's not just a commandment or a set of instructions dropped down from heaven. It's a manifestation of radiant beauty that lands in our world in the form of a profound moral challenge, because it's a revelation of active love that dissolves fear. . . . a revelation of an action of love into which you are invited to come, with which you are invited to cooperate."

—Rowan Williams, *What Is Christianity?*, 36

Contents

Foreword by Craig L. Blomberg | xi
Author's Preface | xvii

Chapter One: A Skeptic's Guide to the Historical Jesus | 1
Chapter Two: The Epistle of St. James vs. Evolutionary Christology | 88
Chapter Three: An Interdisciplinary Inquiry into Dating the Fourth Gospel, Part I: John 5:2 and Papyrus 52 | 113
Chapter Four: An Interdisciplinary Inquiry into Dating the Fourth Gospel, Part II: Other Evidence | 140
Chapter Five: *Resurrection: Faith or Fact?* Miracle Not Required? | 156
Chapter Six: Scientific Rebuttals to "Ancient Aliens" as Popular Alternatives to Biblical History | 189

Appendix I: Addendum to *Getting at Jesus*: The Deceptive Demon or Daemon Hypothesis | 231
Appendix II: How Far Can We Trust the Gospels? | 237
Recommended Resources | 243
Bibliography | 255

Foreword

NOT ONE OF THE topics discussed in this book is likely to be among the top ten issues people think about when they discuss "the historical Jesus." Made famous and popularized by Albert Schweitzer's *Quest of the Historical Jesus*, published early in the twentieth century, historical-Jesus scholarship tends to ask and attempts to answer questions like: "if we didn't begin by assuming everything in the Bible's four Gospels was true, which parts of them could pass the historian's criteria of reliability or trustworthiness?" or "what do we know about Jesus of Nazareth from sources outside of the four Gospels?" or "what kind of man was Jesus—a prophet, priest, king, sage, warmonger, pacifist, chauvinist, feminist, advocate for the disadvantaged of his society, proto-capitalist or . . . ?" or "can we determine if Jesus grew in his self-understanding and, if so, how?" The list of questions could be multiplied.

Every one of these questions is legitimate. Curious minds want to know, and to know if we can know. Lurking behind each of these and related questions, however, is another set of questions that are not always explicitly stated. Can miracles really happen (and what is a miracle exactly)? Can historians even assess if a person was truly divine? Can they weigh in on claims about a resurrection? What are our sources for the historical investigation of these questions and how do we decide what they are? What are the criteria for historical authenticity and how do we determine what they are? To what extent are scholars' reconstruction of the historical Jesus already determined by their presuppositions? Can committed Christians really examine the evidence dispassionately or will they, however unconsciously, skew the evidence in their favor? Can committed atheists or skeptics engage in historical investigation any better, or will they assert *a priori*, with the famous eighteenth-century philosopher David Hume, that the chances that claims of the supernatural are in some way mistaken will always outweigh the probability of them being correct? Here Peter S. Williams tackles quite a few of these issues.

The most formative fifteen-year period for my intellectual education spanned 1967–82. During those years I attended and completed junior high school, senior high school, college, seminary and graduate school (with one year of teaching high school math in the middle of it all). I began that period as a seventh grader; I ended it as a newly minted PhD in New Testament studies. Not once did I have anything like the internet; to my knowledge, no one whom I ever knew during this period even imagined it. For good or for ill, there were strict filters through which authors had to pass their material if they wanted to see it published. Of course, there were always outliers who managed to privately publish materials, usually leaflets or tracts of various kinds, but they rarely fooled anyone into thinking they represented serious scholarship. Beginning in the 1990s, with the proliferation of the internet, all this began to change, and today the boundaries are so blurred between fact and fiction, real news and fake news, and all the gradations in between those ends of a spectrum. In short, the guardians of scholarly guilds can no longer dictate what is and isn't fair game for academic conversation, or any other kind of conversation for that matter. Often this is good and furthers what has been called the democratization of knowledge. But it makes critical thinking skills more crucial than ever, skills which often seem to be in short supply in contemporary society.

Peter S. Williams profoundly understands all this. To an extent that I have rarely come across, his expertise spans not only the multiple disciplines of philosophy and biblical studies, but he is equally at ease researching and interacting with the highest, most vetted, and peer-reviewed levels of scholarship and with the most popular, recurring, and sometimes outlandish views put forward online in blogs, podcasts, YouTube videos, and personal websites. Often the two domains overlap in interests; occasionally, they do not. Sometimes, scholars learn how to influence sizable portions of the world that most do not know how to, by taking to cyberspace, along with older media, and even personal speaking engagements. More commonly, masters of the digital world make a much bigger impact on society with fake news or semi-fake news than masters of scholarship do with world-class printed material read by the comparatively few.

I say all this to explain the unusual combination of topics that this book contains, and contains under the rubric of the historical Jesus. Williams's long first chapter may be his most important. What does studying Jesus look like under the rubrics of premodernism, modernism, postmodernism, and metamodernism, and what do those categories even mean? How much can having textually reliable manuscripts, for which we can have a high level of confidence we know what the original authors wrote, aid us in historical research, and what can it not do? What kind of criteria of historicity help us in the remaining tasks? Can they be applied to debates about Jesus's divinity and, if so, why and how? What do we learn about Jesus as a result?

Chapter 2 turns to a quite different part of the New Testament than the Gospels. It is not new to ask what we can learn from Acts or the letter writers about the historical Jesus, especially when something emerges tangentially or incidentally from the major topics at hand. There is an entire cottage industry of determining how many of the sayings and deeds of Jesus the apostle Paul, author of as many as thirteen of the New Testament letters, knew. Books on New Testament theology regularly discuss what comes from Paul's seven undisputed letters, all of which were written between 49 and 62 CE, at most a scant thirty-two years after Jesus's death. Vigorous claims for Jesus's divine identity emerge from these letters, including in creedal or confessional material that considerably predated Paul's own writings. In comparison, almost no one looks at comparable material in the letter of James, as Williams does, even though James may predate all of Paul's writings. If we find "high Christology" there, it becomes all the more telling.

It has only been in the last twenty years that what is increasingly being called a "fourth quest" for the historical Jesus has started to recognize that the Gospel of John has quite a smattering of texts and themes that can compete with Synoptic Gospel material for acceptance as historical by the standard criteria. But questions about the dating of the Fourth Gospel further complicate its use. If it were, say, a second-century document, it could not have been written by the apostle John and, more to the point, it would be less likely to preserve historically credible information. In a two-part study Williams deftly takes readers through this debate and notes how he has modified his own views when new evidence was brought to his attention (an exemplary model for more people to emulate). The Fourth Gospel emerges, nevertheless, as containing old enough material to be credible.

Just a few years ago, Williams and I collaborated together with two atheist scholars to produce a point-counterpoint conversation that was published as *The Resurrection: Faith or Fact?* by Pitchstone in Durham, North Carolina, in 2020. The main presenter of the perspective opposite my own, Carl Stecher, ranged widely enough in his views that the subsequent, shorter responses from other participants left numerous questions still to be addressed in more detail. Williams fills some of those gaps here. Little needs to be said to justify inclusion of discussion of the resurrection of Jesus as central to any claims about him as being more than a mere man, and central to any claims that he was not uniquely special in this fashion.

But what about the last chapter? Surely Jesus as an alien brought to earth by what today we would call a UFO is the stuff of science fiction, not of worthwhile historical research? At the most fundamental level of discussion, the answer is "of course." Still, when polls disclose the number of people who claim to believe that aliens visited Earth in ancient history, one realizes the need for at least some *bona fide* scholarship to weigh in on the topic. Here is where Williams is most adroit in his interdisciplinary study, spanning numerous media or delivery formats in his research as well.

Appendices deal first with the epistemological question that potentially burdens any area of historical research. How do we know that our apparent perceptions of reality are not faulty, indeed so faulty as to mask reality from us because of some malignant power that has the ability and desire to do so? Second, Williams deals with the main thesis of Bart Ehrman, today's foremost popularizer of one skeptical wing of historical Jesus research, that in the minds of his followers Jesus became God only slowly, over a lengthy period of time.

There is a sense in which this book resembles anthologies of much more well-known and prolific scholars, in that it gathers together previously authored and/or published materials in comparatively obscure sources, reworked and edited, and combined together for more widespread distribution. Williams may not be as well known or prolific as many, but he has previously published several books and numerous articles, with his most important work in this field arguably being *Getting at Jesus: A Comprehensive Critique of Neo-Atheist Nonsense about the Jesus of History* (from Wipf & Stock in 2019). When I first saw the table of contents to *Behold the Man*, this present work, I wondered about the book's relevance. When I finished I no longer doubted it! Enjoy the fruits of Peter's labor.

Craig L. Blomberg
Distinguished Professor Emeritus of New Testament
Denver Seminary, Littleton, CO
February 2024

Preface

THIS IS THE FOURTH book in a series of themed "Essays on . . ." volumes designed to showcase different facets of my work as a Christian philosopher and apologist over the past few decades. At the insistence of Professor Blomberg, the bulk of what was the preface in an early draft of this volume has become chapter 1: "A Skeptic's Guide to the Historical Jesus." The subsequent chapters were originally papers published in *Theofilos*, a Nordic journal devoted to the study of theology, philosophy, culture, and neighboring disciplines.[1] They are re-published here with various revisions, updates, and expansions. Appendix 1 is a revised version of a short "addendum" to my book *Getting at Jesus: A Comprehensive Critique of Neo-Atheist Nonsense about the Jesus of History* (Wipf & Stock, 2019), originally published on my personal website, www.peterswilliams.com. Appendix 2 is a revised version of an article commenting on the discussion between New Testament scholars Bart Ehrman and Peter J. Williams hosted by Justin Brierley's "The Big Conversation" video series, and was originally published online by Premier Christian Radio.[2]

I'd like to offer the following notifications of thanks:

- Professor Craig L. Blomberg, for his foreword.
- Professor Lydia McGrew, for detailed feedback on, and valuable correspondence about, draft manuscripts of this book.
- Everyone who provided an endorsement.

1. *Theofilos* was established in 2009 as a popular journal of apologetics, and then re-established and officially recognized as a peer-reviewed academic journal from 2012. It was transformed into an *open access* journal in 2020. *Theofilos* publishes papers written in Norwegian, Swedish, Danish, or English. See https://theofilos.no/.

2. Williams, "Was Jesus' Claim to Be God."

- Everyone at Wipf and Stock, including copyeditor Elisabeth Rickard and typesetter Calvin Jaffarian.
- Justin Brierley, for commissioning my article on the Big Conversation between Bart Ehrman and Peter J. Williams.
- My colleagues at NLA University College in Norway.
- My church small group, for their encouragement and prayers.
- Last but not least, thanks go to my parents for their constant love and support.

Peter S. Williams
Spring 2024.

Chapter One

A Skeptic's Guide to the Historical Jesus

PHILOSOPHER AND ATHEIST BRADLEY Monton recognizes that:

> a key part of Christian doctrine is that God became flesh in the form of Jesus Christ, and that Christ acted in the world in such a way that we can get evidence of his existence, and of his divinity.[1]

The truth or falsehood of this doctrine is something that matters, and which therefore deserves to be the subject of some skepticism.

The central concern of this book is what a properly skeptical historical investigation has to contribute to our thinking about this key part of Christian doctrine.[2] To undertake such an investigation, we need to think critically about (a) collecting relevant historical *evidence*, (b) choosing the best *explanation* of that evidence, and (c) considering the worldview *expectations* that impinge upon these tasks.

Thinking critically about our worldview "expectations" (that is, our worldview beliefs and/or assumptions) is the most fundamental aspect of this project. We not only need to ensure that our investigative "expectations" will help to reveal, rather than to obscure, the historical truth about Jesus; we also need to allow the possibility that historical

---

1. Monton, *Seeking God in Science*, 71.

2. For philosophical explorations of this doctrine, see Moreland and Craig, *Philosophical Foundations for a Christian Worldview*; Morris, *Our Idea of God*; Swinburne, *Was Jesus God?*

inquiry might lead us to adjust elements of our worldview, even to the extent that we end up holding a different worldview. Depending upon the reader and their current worldview, this may be an unsettling prospect, or an exciting one, or both. In any case, it is of paramount importance that our investigation is not aimed at any predetermined result, besides *discerning the truth*. (Any reader who chafes at the notion that "discerning the truth" is a goal to be held in high esteem might profitably consider the perilous state of democracy when those who possess or seek political power routinely flout the truth in its pursuit, especially when much of the electorate are taken in by their lies.[3])

A growing dissatisfaction with "modernism," and its "postmodern" terminus, is currently stimulating a quest for a "post-postmodern" or "metamodern" worldview more in line with human experience and more conducive to human flourishing. Many of those engaged in this quest are deeply reticent about the idea that any contemporary "pre-modern" worldview, such as Christianity, might have the key answers they are seeking. Nevertheless, there's an acknowledged existential hunger for things that modernism and/or postmodernism reject but which a Christian worldview can supply.[4] In this context, a properly skeptical historical investigation into the truth of the Christian doctrine "that God became flesh in the form of Jesus Christ, and that Christ acted in the world in such a way that we can get evidence of his existence, and of his divinity"[5] may be seen anew as a matter of both cultural and personal consequence.

Pre-Modern Skepticism

As the website of *Skeptical Inquirer: The Magazine for Science and Reason* reminds us:

> The word "skepticism" comes from the ancient Greek *skepsis*, meaning "inquiry." Skepticism is, therefore, not a cynical rejection of new ideas, as the popular stereotype goes, but rather an attitude of both open mind and critical sense [that requires] . . .

---

3. See Williams, "President Trump and Nationalism" (YouTube playlist); Cheney, *Oath and Honor*; Karl, *Tired of Winning*; Kessler et al., *Donald Trump and His Assault*; Rucker and Leonnig, *Very Stable Genius*; Osborn, *Assault on Truth*; Sider, *Spiritual Danger of Donald Trump*; Woodward, *Rage*.

4. See Williams, "Reading Culture in 3D."

5. Monton, *Seeking God in Science*, 71.

mindful cultivation of critical thinking, and an honest attitude toward intellectual inquiry.[6]

Hence, to say that Christian claims about Jesus deserve to be the subject of some skepticism is to say that they deserve an attitude of both open mind and critical sense, and should be the subject not of cynical rejection but of an honest attitude of critical thinking.[7]

Of course, one person's "critical sense" can be another's "cynical rejection." As Egyptologist James K. Hoffmeier observes:

> "Critical" biblical scholars are averse to speaking of possibilities or probabilities when it comes to the Pentateuch [the first five books of the Old Testament] as a witness to history, owing to modern and postmodern skepticism.[8]

Clearly, what goes for the Pentateuch goes for *any* literature that has been gathered into the Bible, including the New Testament literature referring to Jesus.

The mere fact that the pre-modern concept of "skepticism" can now be qualified as being either "modern" or "postmodern" highlights the fact that different scholars bring different worldview expectations into their pursuits. Indeed, as Hoffmeier points out, while so-called "critical" scholars "often believe that [so-called] conservative scholars err because of flawed philosophical or theological assumptions,"[9] it is only fair to recognize that "everyone interprets texts, especially the Bible, through their political, theological, worldview, and experiential lenses."[10] Philosophical expectations *per se* are a necessary component of scholarship; but the cannons of "modern" and "postmodern" skepticism should be just as open to skeptical review as the assumptions of so-called "conservative" scholars.[11]

---

6. *Skeptical Inquirer*, "What Is Skepticism?," §1, 5.
7. See Williams, "Critical Thinking" (YouTube playlist); Sinnott-Armstrong, *Think Again*; Williams, *Faithful Guide to Philosophy*, chs. 2 and 3.
8. Hoffmeier, "Hoffmeier Rejoinder," 133.
9. Hoffmeier, "Hoffmeier Rejoinder," 133.
10. Hoffmeier, "Hoffmeier Rejoinder," 133.
11. On the Old Testament as a witness to history, see Williams, "Christianity and Archaeology" (YouTube playlist); Williams, "ELF 2023: Evidence for Old Testament History"; Hoffmeier et al., *"Did I Not Bring Israel Out of Egypt?"*; Kitchen, *On the Reliability of the Old Testament*.

Worldview Expectations

> Historical judgement exercises itself within a framework of faith...
>
> —Scot McKnight[12]

In the words of Hanzi Freinacht, fictional political philosopher and author of *The Listening Society: A Metamodern Guide to Politics* (2017):

> A lot of people think that philosophy is a certain activity: that you write books about it... or discuss with friends. But philosophy is more than that—it is: How you view the world (ontology, "what is really real" and epistemology, "how to know stuff"); and your place in it (your idea of a "self"), and what is right and wrong (ethics or ideology). So everybody has a philosophy. When someone prays, or doesn't pray, or saves money, or helps a stranger, or works to end animal slavery, all of these things are rooted in the philosophy of that person.[13]

The philosophy that underpins a person's actions is their "worldview."[14] As Tawa J. Anderson, W. Michael Clark, and David K. Naugle explain:

> The English term worldview is derived from the German Weltanschauung, a compound word (Welt = world + Anschauung = view or outlook) first used by Immanuel Kant to describe an individual's sensory perception of the world.... German philosophers used Weltanschauung increasingly for the concept of answering pivotal questions regarding life, the universe, and everything. Very quickly, other German thinkers—von Ranke (history), Wagner (music), Feuerbach (theology), and von Humboldt (physics)—applied Weltanschauung to their own disciplines. Furthermore, Weltanschauung was quickly adopted in other European countries, either as a loanword or translated into the local language.[15]

---

12. McKnight, "Jesus of Nazareth," 161.

13. Freinacht, *Listening Society*, 15. As Jules Evans explains: "Hanzi Freinacht is a made-up character invented by two people—Emil Ejner Friis, a Danish philosopher and activist in the Danish Alternative Party; and Daniel Gortz, a PhD student in sociology at Lund University in Sweden" (Evans, "New World of Metamodernism," §5).

14. See Williams, "Understanding Worldviews" (YouTube playlist); Sire, *Universe Next Door* (6th ed.); Williams, *Apologetics in 3D*.

15. Anderson et al., *Introduction to Christian Worldview*, 9.

While Freinacht draws attention to the link between worldview assumptions and actions, he overlooks the connective role of motivating attitudes. Properly functioning humans develop a "spirituality," a "way of life" that aims to ingrate their worldview *assumptions* (i.e., the philosophical "expectations" they believe and/or act upon), *attitudes* (a term that here includes commitments as well as emotions), and *actions*. In other words, a spirituality is a way of life that tries to coherently combine your head, heart, and hands.[16]

Worldview assumptions ground spiritual attitudes to jointly sustain spiritual activities. Spiritual activities are part and parcel of a positive feedback loop. This is obvious when one thinks of the practices involved in liturgical worship, for example, but "spiritual activities" encompass the whole of one's practical life *insofar as it is coherently lived out of one's worldview assumptions and accompanying attitudes*. Our attitudes not only reflect our worldview expectations, they can restrict the range of propositions we will even consider believing or assuming. Spiritual practices are not just the practical outworking *of* faith, but positive aids *to* faith.[17] In light of this fact, it is appropriate to represent spirituality as a dynamic loop:

---

16. See Williams, *Apologetics in 3D*.

17. Following philosophers Daniel Howard-Snyder and Daniel McKaughan (see their article on "Faith" in *Encyclopedia of Philosophy of Religion*), I would suggest that for X to have faith that *p* or in *p* is for X to have a positive doxastic ("relating to belief") or non-doxastic cognitive stance toward *p* (e.g., for X to *believe* that *p* is more probably true than false; or to *assume* that *p* while neither believing nor disbelieving *p*), and for X to have a positive conative posture toward *p* (as the worthy subject of X's choice and/or admiration), such that X is disposed to live in light of their cognitive stance and conative posture towards *p* (e.g., trusting and/or giving allegiance to *p*, making commitments and choices on this basis, and being disposed to virtuous resilience in the face of challenges to their positive dispositions towards *p*).

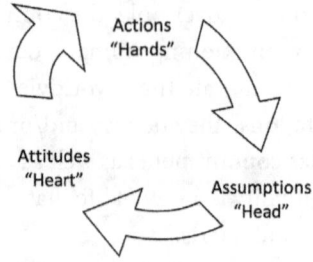

Fig. 1. Spirituality as a Loop.

As theologian Mark Earey observes:

> It is not just that we express with our bodies or voices what we think in our minds or feel in our hearts: on the contrary, what we do with our bodies or say with our mouths can change or influence how we feel and what we think, as individuals and communities.[18]

That said, spirituality is more firmly rooted in worldview than in attitudes or actions, for as philosopher Dallas Willard argues: "Thoughts determine the orientation of everything we do and evoke the feelings that frame our world and motivate our actions."[19] In general one "can't evoke thoughts by feeling a certain way. However, we can evoke—and to some degree control—our feelings by directing our thoughts."[20] Hence: "what we think, imagine, believe, or guess sets boundaries to what we can or will choose, and therefore to what we can create."[21]

Spirituality is intimately bound up with the sort of people we see ourselves as being and/or becoming. As psychologist Joanna Collicutt explains:

> Our idealized self-image . . . is expressed in terms of certain principles, which are in their turn expressed in action programs. A less technical way of describing this is as who I want to be;

---

18. Earey, *Liturgical Worship*, 65.
19. Willard, *Renewing the Christian Mind*, 4.
20. Willard, *Renewing the Christian Mind*, 4.
21. Willard, *Renewing the Christian Mind*, 4.

rules for living this out; and what I actually try to do in order to keep to those rules.²²

That is, our worldview includes a vision of the sort of people we want to be (a matter of both "head" and "heart"), and this vision leads us to make commitments to various "rules for living," commitments we translate into actions that, over time, can become habitual or "second nature." Generally speaking, it's easier to find a different way of acting upon a given rule for living than it is to commit to a different rule, and harder still to change our idealized self-image. This aspect of spirituality must be diagrammatically represented in a hierarchical manner:

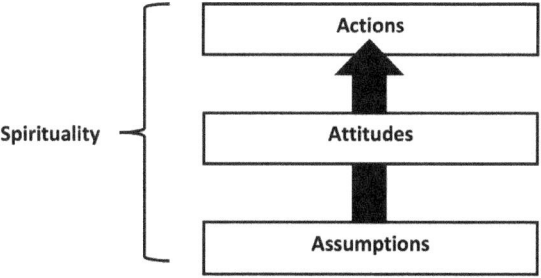

Fig. 2. Spirituality Is Rooted in Worldview.

When a spirituality is shared, it sustains a "culture." In the words of Professor Walter Leirman:

By culture we mean three related aspects:

–a culture contains a vision of man and society, with a set of values and norms

–a culture is a living community of people with a certain identity

–a culture is a social and institutional practice which reflects to a certain degree the vision and the community.²³

Leirman's "vision of man and society, with a set of values and norms" is grounded in the worldview concepts of philosophical anthropology and axiology. In the words of British philosopher C. E. M. Joad:

---

22. Collicutt, *Psychology of Christian Character Formation*, 16.
23. Leirman, *Cultures of Learning and Education*, 4.

> Civilization . . . is bound up with the development of those qualities and the practice of those activities which distinguish us from the animals. . . . Our reason, our perception of the difference between right and wrong, our sense of beauty.[24]

The notion of "a culture" may be captured by Raymond Williams's phrase "a structure of feeling,"[25] or Charles Taylor's concept of a "social imaginary":

> our "social imaginary," that is, the way that we collectively imagine, even pre-theoretically, our social life. . . . What I'm trying to get at with this term is something much broader and deeper than the intellectual schemes people may entertain when they think about our social reality in a disengaged mode. I am thinking rather of the ways in which they imagine their social existence, how they fit together with others, how things go on between them and their fellows, the expectations which are normally met, and the deeper normative notions and images which underlie these expectations . . . this is often not expressed in theoretical terms, it is carried in images, stories, legends, etc. . . . the social imagery is that common understanding which makes possible common practices . . . . It incorporates a sense of the normal expectations that we have of each other; the kind of common understanding which enables us to carry out the collective practices which make up our social life.[26]

I agree with Freinacht that "spirituality has little or nothing to do with specific religious content or belief."[27] Spirituality *per se* is a matter of having *some content or other* that fills out the generic spiritual structure of assumptions, attitudes, and actions. A spirituality may be Muslim or Hindu; it may be Marxist or Secular Humanist. However, content does matter! Assumptions can be true or false, attitudes can be beautiful or ugly, actions can be good or bad, and a specific spirituality can have a more or less integrative or disintegrative effect upon its adherents, depending upon whether or not it tends towards the virtuous and coherent integration of their assumptions, attitudes, and actions.[28]

---

24. Joad, *Joad's Opinions*, 120.
25. See Akker and Vermeulen, "Periodising the 2000s," 6–7.
26. Taylor, *Secular Age*, 146 and 171–72.
27. Freinacht, *Listening Society*, 265.
28. See Williams, "Reading Culture in 3D"; and *Apologetics in 3D*.

Freinacht lays out the historical sequence in which different spiritualities have become culturally prominent:

> very roughly: First you have pre-modern society, like in medieval Europe. Then you have modern society. Then you have a postmodern criticism of modern society.[29]

Freinacht is a major voice in the contemporary quest to establish a "metamodern" worldview, spirituality, and culture.

Pre-Modernisms

There are a wide variety of "pre-modern" spiritualities in the contemporary world. Many—notably those rooted in classical and/or historic near-eastern cultures—celebrate the existence of objective truth, goodness, and beauty (in their axiology), believe in a cosmos of both material and spiritual realities (in their ontology), and think (in their epistemology) that humans can have and communicate knowledge (albeit in an often limited and fallible way) about those values and that cosmos, because (in their anthropology) they view humans as embodied but fundamentally immaterial selves with capacities for rational thought, reliable perception, and morally significant choice.[30]

Most contemporary pre-modernists are monotheists, including (as of 2022) "at least 3.8 billion . . . followers of Abrahamic religions."[31] According to philosopher Charles Taliaferro, in addition to "philosophical theists" with no religious affiliation:

> Hindu tradition includes important strands in which ultimate reality is described in theistic terms and there is an acknowledged distinction between Brahman (conceived of as the creator of the cosmos) and the cosmos itself.[32]

That said, comparative religions scholar Gavin Denis Flood cautions that:

---

29. Freinacht, *Listening Society*, 361.
30. See Holmes, *Contours of a Worldview*; Williams, *Faithful Guide to Philosophy*.
31. Koch, "How Many Monotheists Are There?" On Abraham, see Kitchen, *On the Reliability of the Old Testament*, ch. 7. On Islam see Williams, "Islam" (YouTube playlist); Craig, "Concept of God in Islam and Christianity"; Beverley and Evans, *Getting Jesus Right*; Licona, *Paul Meets Muhammad*; Qureshi, *No God but One*.
32. Taliaferro, *Philosophy of Religion*, 147.

If by monotheism we mean the idea of a single transcendent God who creates the universe out of nothing (*creatio ex nihilo*), as in the Abrahamic religions, then it is open to question whether or not that idea is found in the history of Hinduism. But if we mean a supreme, transcendent deity who impels the universe (whether created from nothing or not), sustains it, and ultimately destroys it before causing it to emerge once again, who is the source of all other gods who are her or his emanations, then this idea does develop within that history.[33]

As Keith Ward explains:

> *Creatio ex nihilo* (Latin for "creation from nothing") refers to the view that the universe, the whole of space-time, is created by a free act of God out of nothing, and not either out of some preexisting material or out of the divine substance itself. This view was widely, though not universally, accepted in the early Christian Church, and . . . is now almost universally accepted by Jews, Christians, and Muslims.[34]

Interestingly, a substantial percentage of religiously unaffiliated people (known to pollsters as "nones") say they believe in some sort of God, "even if they largely dislike organized religion."[35] In a 2023 poll of American adults:

> Forty-three percent of all nones professed belief in God or a higher power—including 61% of nothings in particular, 40% of agnostics and 4% of atheists. Overall, 79% of U.S. adults professed faith in God.[36]

The existence of an uncreated, personal God who created the cosmos *ex nihilo* and conserves it in being is a key element in the ontology of Abrahamic forms of monotheism, and one that arguably offers the best overall explanation for the other pre-modern worldview claims (about axiology, ontology, epistemology, and anthropology) enumerated above.[37]

33. Flood, "Introduction," 3.
34. Ward, "Creatio Ex Nihilo." See Craig, "Creation Ex Nihilo."
35. Smith, "Highlights from AP-NORC poll."
36. Smith, "Highlights from AP-NORC poll."
37. On the existence of God, see Williams, "Natural Theology" (YouTube playlist); "Debating God" (YouTube playlist); Beck, "God's Existence"; Copan, "God, Naturalism, and the Foundations"; and "Hume and the Moral Argument"; Craig, "Theistic Critiques of Atheism"; and *Five Arguments for God*; Evans, "Mystery of Persons and Belief in

However, the "pre-modern" label encompasses a plethora of different worldviews. While space precludes a comprehensive treatment of pre-modern worldviews here, I will pass some comment about a selection of non-Abrahamic perspectives.[38]

Polytheism postulates the existence of multiple "gods" who come into existence from the cosmos.[39] Like naturalism, polytheism lacks an adequate explanation for the existence of the physical cosmos,[40] especially one whose physical laws and initial conditions exhibit an organic life–permitting "fine tuning,"[41] within which the gods are said to emerge. Polytheism also faces the same problems as naturalism with respect to accounting for the existence of rational, conscious minds,[42] and to providing an adequate grounding for objective moral and aesthetic values.[43] Moreover, as Norman L. Geisler observes: "The idea of an eternal universe posited by polytheism has . . . serious philosophical and scientific objections."[44]

The pantheistic identification of divinity with the cosmos has stark axiological implications, as C. S. Lewis observed:

God"; Plantinga, "Two Dozen (Or So) Theistic Arguments"; Swinburne, *Evidence for God*; Baggett and Walls, *Good God*; Beck, *Does God Exist?*; Copan and Moser, *Rationality of Theism*; Copan and Taliaferro, *Naturalness of Belief*; Craig, *Does God Exist?*; Craig and Moreland, *Blackwell Companion to Natural Theology*; Craig and Moreland, *Naturalism*; Evans, *Natural Signs and Knowledge of God*; Holder, *Big Bang, Big God*; Meyer, *Return of the God Hypothesis*; Moreland, *Consciousness and the Existence of God*; and *Scaling the Secular City*; Moreland and Craig, *Philosophical Foundations for a Christian Worldview*; Ruloff and Horban, *Contemporary Arguments in Natural Theology*; Sennett and Groothuis, *In Defence of Natural Theology*; Walls and Dougherty, *Two Dozen (or so) Arguments for God*; Williams, *Universe from Someone*; *Faithful Guide to Philosophy*; and *C. S. Lewis vs. the New Atheists*.

38. See Williams, "Pantheism/New Age Spirituality" (YouTube playlist); "Buddhism" (YouTube playlist); Collins, "Eastern Religions"; Geisler, *Christian Apologetics* (2nd ed.); Pemberton, "Are We Really All Hindus Now?"; Sire, *Universe Next Door* (6th ed.).

39. See Geisler, *Baker Encyclopedia of Christian Apologetics*, 602–6.

40. See Beck, "God's Existence"; Williams, *Faithful Guide to Philosophy*, ch. 4.

41. See Holder, *Big Bang, Big God*; Holder, *God, the Multiverse, and Everything*; Meyer, *Return of the God Hypothesis*.

42. See Craig and Moreland, *Naturalism*; Goetz and Taliaferro, *Naturalism*; Moreland, *Recalcitrant Imago Dei*; Williams, *Faithful Guide to Philosophy*.

43. See Williams, *Faithful Guide to Philosophy*.

44. Geisler, *Baker Encyclopedia of Christian Apologetics*, 605. See Copan and Craig, *Kalam Cosmological Argument*, vol. 1, *Philosophical Arguments*; and *Kalam Cosmological Argument*, vol. 2, *Scientific Evidence*.

> If you do not take the distinction between good and bad very seriously, then it is easy to say that anything you find in this world is a part of God. But, of course, if you think some things really bad, and God really good, then you cannot talk like that.[45]

The problems with "absolute pantheism" (i.e., idealistic monism) are particularly severe. As philosopher Robin Collins explains:

> As traditionally interpreted, the Sankara school [of Hinduism] claims that there is ultimately only one reality, *Brahman*, with which each of us is absolutely identical. Moreover . . . Brahman is pure consciousness, without any internal differentiation or characteristics whatsoever. . . . Since Brahman comprises all of reality, and since there are no internal distinctions within Brahman, it follows that ultimately the world of separate entities, distinctions, and characteristics is an illusion [*maya*].[46]

However, if there's "a unity of all things," the distinction between true and false must then itself be "*maya*," and statements such as "Brahman comprises all of reality" and "the world of separate entities, distinctions, and characteristics is an illusion" *cannot be advanced as being true rather than false*. Hence:

> Sankara's philosophy . . . seems to be self-contradictory. As advocates of other Hindu schools of thought have pointed out, if the only reality is Brahman, and Brahman is pure, *distinctionless* consciousness, then there cannot exist any real distinctions in reality. But the claim that this world is an illusion already presupposes that there is an actual distinction between illusion and reality.[47]

A related problem is that, since Brahman is supposedly pure and complete knowledge:

> ignorance cannot exist in Brahman. But, since nothing exists apart from Brahman, ignorance cannot exist apart from Brahman either. Thus, it follows that ignorance could not exist, contrary to the assertion that our perception of the world of distinct things is a result of ignorance.[48]

Therefore, as Collins observes:

---

45. Lewis, *Mere Christianity*, 33. See Beckwith, "Why I Am Not a Moral Relativist"; Beckwith and Koukl, *Relativism*; Lewis, *Abolition of Man*.
46. Collins, "Eastern Religions," 187.
47. Collins, "Eastern Religions," 188.
48. Collins, "Eastern Religions," 189.

> It seems that one could never have any satisfactory experiential basis for believing in Sankara's philosophy. . . . even if we assume that the entire material world does not exist, but is merely a dream, experience would still overwhelmingly testify against Sankara's claim: for, within our dream itself there are innumerable distinct experiences.[49]

Mahayana Buddhists fall foul of the same problem, because they likewise "deny that any distinctions exist in reality."[50] On the assumption that there is "a unity of all things," it follows that no distinction between good and evil (or between beauty and ugliness) can truly exist, and that no statement about good or evil (or about beauty and ugliness) can be advanced as being either true or false.

James W. Sire presents the following *reductio ad absurdum* argument against any claim that there is a unity of all things: "the One is beyond duality. . . . language requires duality; several dualities in fact (speaker and listener, subject and predicate); ergo, language cannot convey truth about reality."[51] Sire's point is that this deduction, from the supposed "unity of all things" to the conclusion that "language cannot convey truth about reality," is made using language, and is thus self-contradictory.

According to *The Upanishads*: "The ignorant think that Brahman is known, but the wise know him to be beyond knowledge."[52] However, as philosophers Norman L. Geisler and William D. Watkins argue:

> The very claim that "God is unknowable in an intellectual way" seems to be either meaningless or self-defeating. For if the claim itself cannot *be understood in an intellectual way, then it is a meaningless claim. If the claim* can *be understood in an intellectual way, then it is self-defeating, since it affirms that nothing can be understood a*bout God in an intellectual way.[53]

According to the Madhyamika school of Mahayana Buddhism: "anything that can be spoken of or thought about is empty of content or substantial reality; indeed . . . all statements are empty of meaning."[54] Likewise, Yogacara and Zen Buddhists alike:

---

49. Collins, "Eastern Religions," 189.
50. Collins, "Eastern Religions," 210.
51. Sire, *Universe Next Door*, 155.
52. "Kena," in *Upanishads*, 31, quoted in Geisler and Watkins, *Worlds Apart*, 80.
53. Geisler and Watkins, *Worlds Apart*, 104.
54. Collins, "Eastern Religions," 211.

> assert that human reason, thought, and language are ultimately invalid and indeed self-contradictory. . . . After all, Zen Buddhists argue, if we are to experience the absolute oneness (or emptiness) of all things, we must get beyond language and reason, for the business of thought and language is to make distinctions and is thus directly opposed to the experience of enlightenment.[55]

In each case, these views are self-refuting, for "if, as they claim, all statements are empty of meaning, then the statement that all statements are empty of meaning is itself empty of meaning, and thus does not assert anything about reality."[56]

If a worldview excludes the idea that reality can be rationally understood *to any extent at all*, and/or denies that there are any real distinctions in reality, then that worldview cannot differentiate between fact and fantasy, between the objectively good and evil, beautiful and ugly, or between personal and impersonal realities. As anthropologist David Burnett explains, for Sankara Hinduism:

> Individuality and human consciousness are just a part of the total illusion of Maya. The individual soul, atman, is in fact the divine self, which is identical with "Brahman." The focus of human achievement therefore becomes world-denying rather than world-affirming. . . . To realize one's true oneness with the cosmos is to pass beyond personality.[57]

Likewise, "The Mahayana Buddhist's stress on loving others . . . is inconsistent with their overall worldview, because ultimately their worldview implies that there is no one to love."[58]

By contrast with these (broadly) pantheistic worldviews, the world and human affirming idea "that God became flesh in the form of Jesus Christ"[59] underpins Christianity's pre-modern, Trinitarian form of monotheism,[60] and its call to embrace a spirituality of inter-personal love

---

55. Collins, "Eastern Religions," 212.
56. Collins, "Eastern Religions," 213.
57. Burnett, *Clash of Worlds*, 72.
58. Collins, "Eastern Religions," 214.
59. Monton, *Seeking God in Science*, 71.
60. On the doctrine of the Trinity, see Williams, "Trinity" (YouTube playlist); and "Understanding the Trinity."

that virtuously influences and integrates our assumptions, attitudes, and actions *through faithfulness to Jesus as Lord* (Mark 8:34; Matt 11:29).[61]

As suggested by its earliest self-description as "The Way,"[62] Christianity is *a way of life* (a spirituality) *centered upon following Jesus Christ as* "the way, the truth and the life" (John 14:6; see 1 Cor 4:16–17 and 1 Pet 3:16). The fact that Christian spirituality is a Christocentric spirituality, grounded in historical claims about a historical person, opens the door to confirming or disconfirming the Christian "way" (including the Christian worldview) through historical investigation, an opportunity that does not arise with respect to spiritualities that are not dependent in this way upon historical events. As theoretical physicist turned theologian Sir John Polkinghorne commented, as "a historically orientated religion," the "foundational stories" of Christianity "are not simply symbolic tales," but are "mediated through particular persons and events."[63] Consequently, "there is an evidential aspect to what we are told in the Bible."[64]

Caveats about Pre-modernism

It is important to note that recommending a Jesus-centered spirituality, or recommending the basic ontology, axiology, epistemology, and anthropology of monotheistic pre-modernism, is *not* the same thing as rejecting everything that comes under the labels of the "modern" or the "postmodern." To borrow some words from sociologist Christian Smith:

> While I adhere to many modern ideas, I also find certain pre-modern ideas insightful and illuminating. In fact, I believe that some of them are true. Our criterion for adjudicating ideas should not be whether they are modern or premodern, but rather how well they seem to illuminate and explain reality for us.[65]

---

61. On the nature of Christian faith and spirituality, see Williams, "Nature of Faith" (YouTube playlist); "Discipleship and Spiritual Formation" (YouTube playlist); "Discipleship in 3D"; "Faith and Rationality"; Howard-Snyder and McKaughan, "Faith"; McGrath, *Mere Discipleship*; and *Passionate Intellect*; Moreland, *Love the Lord with All Your Mind*; Williams, *Apologetics in 3D*.

62. "Christian" was originally an outsider term of abuse meaning "Christ-slave." See Acts 11:26 and 22:4.

63. Polkinghorne, *Encountering Scripture*, x–xi.

64. Polkinghorne, *Encountering Scripture*, xi.

65. Smith, *To Flourish or Destruct*, 15.

The same goes for anything the monotheistic pre-modernist may coherently consider to be "genuine insights of postmodernism."⁶⁶

We can certainly grant that Danish economist and philosopher Lene Rachel Andersen (who describes herself as "a practicing, doubting"⁶⁷ Jewish convert) has a point when she warns:

> Pre-modern cultural code is the source of fundamentalism, authoritarianism, totalitarianism, and institutionalized violence, torture, oppression, persecution of minorities and freethinkers, violent enforcement of obedience and conformity, and the creation of order out of chaos through patriarchy, dogmatism and narrowmindedness.⁶⁸

However, one cannot assume that every pre-modernist endorses everything that comes under the expansive label of "the pre-modern cultural code." Even if one focuses upon Jewish, Christian, or Islamic pre-modernism, one finds plenty of "in-house" disagreements about the specifics of their cultural code! Moreover, Andersen's examples seem to be "cherry picked." On the one hand, the "modern" and "postmodern" cultural codes are obviously able to produce their own share of social ills (including authoritarianism, totalitarianism, etc.).⁶⁹ On the other hand, the Judeo-Christian "pre-modern cultural code" is the source of many socially beneficial outcomes, including such cultural institutions as hospitals, universities, experimental science, and human rights.⁷⁰ In the words of atheist philosopher Jürgen Habermas:

> Universalistic egalitarianism, from which sprang the ideals of freedom and a collective life in solidarity, the autonomous conduct of life and emancipation, the individual morality of conscience, human rights and democracy, is the direct legacy of the Judaic ethic of justice and the Christian ethic of love. This legacy,

---

66. Dempsey, *Metamodernism*, 8.
67. Rutt, "Lene Rachel Andersen on Polymodernity," 30:12–14.
68. Andersen, *Metamodernity*, 106.

69. See Carson, *Intolerance of Tolerance*; Kramer, *Black Book of Communism*; Weikart, *Hitler's Ethic*; and *From Darwin to Hitler*.

70. See Williams, "Is Christianity Good for Society?" (YouTube playlist); and "Theological Roots of Science" (YouTube playlist); Hannam, "How Christianity Led to the Rise"; Brierley, *Surprising Rebirth of Belief in God*, ch. 3; Cavanaugh, *Myth of Religious Violence*; Chamberlain and Hall, *Realized Religion*; Chapman, *Slaying the Dragons*; Dickson, *Bullies and Saints*; Hannam, *God's Philosophers*; Hill, *What Has Christianity Ever Done for Us?*; Holland, *Dominion*; Mangalwadi, *Book That Made Your World*; Scrivener, *Air We Breathe*; Ward, *Is Religion Dangerous?*

substantially unchanged, has been the object of continual critical appropriation and reinterpretation. To this day, there is no alternative to it. And in light of the current challenges of a post-national constellation, we continue to draw on the substance of this heritage. Everything else is just idle postmodern talk.[71]

One may question whether this egalitarian legacy can be coherently sustained once it has been extracted from the ontology, axiology, epistemology, and anthropology of the Judeo-Christian pre-modernism that gave it birth. A contemporary worldview that embraces at least *some* pre-modern assumptions is actually a prerequisite for any robust critique of the social ills listed by Andersen.

Modernism

> Nearly all that I loved I believed to be imaginary;
> nearly all that I believed to be real I thought grim and meaningless.
>
> —C. S. Lewis[72]

The cultural dominance of worldviews that are "pre-modern" in the sense explored above waned with the growth of agnosticism and secular atheism in the (self-described) "modern" era of the nineteenth and twentieth centuries.[73] Ironically, as Alvin Plantinga points out, the "modernist" worldview has "pre-modern" roots stretching back:

> to Epicurus, Democritus, and others in the Ancient world and finds magnificent expression in Lucretius' poem, *De Rerum Natura*. . . . it is also to be found in the medieval world, perhaps among some of the Averroists, for example. It was left to modernity, however, to display the most complete and thorough manifestations of this perspective.[74]

Broadly speaking, modernity embraced an ontology of materialism/physicalism or metaphysical naturalism,[75] an epistemology of (either

---

71. Habermas, "Conversation about God," 150–51.
72. Lewis, *Surprised by Joy*, 197.
73. See Walker, *Seven Atheisms*; McGrath, *Twilight of Atheism*; Spencer, *Atheists*.
74. Plantinga, "Augustinian Christian Philosophy," 296–97.
75. See Rosenberg, *Atheist's Guide to Reality*, ch. 2.

"hard" or "soft") scientism,[76] and an axiology that ejected moral and aesthetic value from the realm of facts.[77] As philosopher Jonathan Rowson explains, modernism has generally been opposed to the pre-modern, transcendental triad of objective truth, goodness, and beauty[78] as such:

> it . . . broke them apart—so you have a . . . scientific truth severed from the . . . ethics and aesthetics of the good and the beautiful.[79]

From a pre-modern perspective, the resultant modernist anthropology is dehumanizing. As Plantinga explains, according to the typical worldview of modernism:

> there is no God, nor anything else beyond nature; and we human beings are insignificant parts of a vast cosmic machine that proceeds in majestic indifference to us, our hopes and aspirations, our needs and desires, our sense of fairness or fittingness.[80]

True, a number of thinkers who are "modernists" in the sense of being agnostic or atheistic reject scientism and/or make philosophical arguments for objective moral values, and/or for a non-materialistic anthropology (e.g., David Chalmers, Donald Hoffman, Mary Midgley, Thomas Nagel, Russ Shafer-Landau, Eric Wielenberg). Nevertheless, the culturally dominant strand of "modernism" remains that summed up in Richard Dawkins's assertion that:

> The universe that we observe has precisely the properties we should expect if there is, at bottom, no design, no purpose, no evil and no good, nothing but blind, pitiless indifference.[81]

To quote Freinacht: "'Modernism', in this sense, is the standard worldview we get in secular Western societies today."[82]

---

76. See Williams, "Scientism" (YouTube playlist); Moreland, *Scientism and Secularism*.

77. See Baggini, *Atheism*, ch. 3 (especially p. 51); Mackie, *Ethics*; Rosenberg, *Atheist's Guide to Reality*.

78. On this triad, see Williams, "Thinking in 3D"; Wattles, "C. S. Lewis, Peter Kreeft,"; Adler, *Adler's Philosophical Dictionary*; and *Six Great Ideas*; Cowan and Spiegel, *Love of Wisdom*; Lewis, *Abolition of Man*; Turley, *Awakening Wonder*; Williams, *Faithful Guide to Philosophy*; and *Apologetics in 3D*.

79. Quoted in Perspectiva, "What Is Metamodernism?"

80. Plantinga, "Augustinian Christian Philosophy," 296.

81. Dawkins, *River out of Eden*, 133. See Baggini, *Atheism*; Rosenberg, *Atheist's Guide to Reality*. See also Williams, "Sorting the Chaff from the Wheat."

82. Freinacht, *Listening Society*, 372.

Outlining the ontology of modernity, C. S. Lewis explained that "some people believe that nothing exists except Nature ... a vast process in space and time which is *going on of its own accord*."[83] He noted that, according to materialism, the process which is "going on of its own accord" is a "meaningless play of atoms in space and time."[84] To put this more formally, what we might call "standard modernism" says that:

- *The physical world is an uncreated, and therefore unintended, closed system* (i.e., every effect within the system has a cause within the system).
- *The fundamental elements of the physical world are "blind"* (i.e., they lack conscious awareness or intentionality).
- *If anything exists that can't be described in the terms used by the naturalistic physical sciences* (something denied by the strict naturalism described by Lewis), *then it "supervenes" on* (i.e., depends upon and is wholly determined by) *something that can be so described* (and it is thus causally *effete*).

A classic statement of the standard modernist ontology and anthropology was laid out by British philosopher and mathematician Bertrand Russell (1872–1970), in a famous essay published under the title "The Free Man's Worship" in 1903:

> That Man is the product of causes which had no prevision of the end they were achieving; that his origin, his growth, his hopes and fears, his loves and his beliefs, are but the outcome of accidental collocations of atoms; that no fire, no heroism, no intensity of thought and feeling, can preserve an individual life beyond the grave; that . . . the whole temple of Man's achievement must inevitably be buried beneath the debris of a universe in ruins—all these things, if not quite beyond dispute, are yet so nearly certain, that no philosophy which rejects them can hope to stand. Only within the scaffolding of these truths, only on the firm foundation of unyielding despair, can the soul's habitation henceforth be safely built.[85]

As for the axiology and epistemology of modernism, Russell affirmed elsewhere that:

---

83. Lewis, *Miracles*, 4–5.
84. Lewis, "On Living in an Atomic Age," 73–80.
85. Russell, "Free Man's Worship," 2.

> While it is true that science cannot decide questions of value, that is because they cannot be intellectually decided at all, and lie outside the realm of truth and falsehood. Whatever knowledge is attainable, must be attained by scientific methods; and what science cannot discover, mankind cannot know.[86]

More recently, atheist philosopher Alex Rosenberg presented a modernist creed in his book *The Atheists' Guide to Reality*:

> Is there a God? No. What is the nature of reality? What physics says it is. What is the purpose of the universe? There is none. What is the meaning of life? Ditto. Why am I here? Just dumb luck... Is there a soul? Is it immortal? Are you kidding? Is there free will? Not a chance. What happens when we die? Everything pretty much goes on as before, except us. What is the difference between right and wrong, good and bad? There is no moral difference between them.[87]

With respect to the axiology leading Rosenberg to affirm that there is "no moral difference" between right and wrong, philosopher Nancy Pearcey comments that:

> The strict separation of facts from values is the key to unlocking the history of the modern Western mind.... people have always known that there is a distinction between is and ought ... between descriptive statements and normative statements. In earlier ages, however, people thought both types of statement dealt with questions of truth. If you made a moral statement about what someone ought to do, it was either true or false.[88]

The strict separation of objective facts from subjective values is entailed both by modernism's ontology and by the epistemology of "hard scientism" expressed in Rosenberg's statement that "we trust science as the only way to acquire knowledge."[89]

Of course, the philosophical claim that "science" is "the only way to acquire knowledge" is self-defeating. In the words of philosopher of science Del Ratzsch:

> science cannot validate either scientific method itself or the presuppositions of that method.... Those who claim either that

---

86. Russell, *Religion and Science*, §27.
87. Rosenberg, *Atheists' Guide to Reality*, 2–3.
88. Pearcey, *Saving Leonardo*, 25 and 27.
89. Rosenberg, *Atheists' Guide to Reality*, 20.

science is competent for dealing with all matters or that science is the only legitimate method for dealing with any matter are seriously confused.[90]

Moreover, the claim that science is either the only way to acquire knowledge ("hard scientism"), or even that it is the best way to acquire knowledge ("soft scientism"), is refuted by counter-examples concerning intuitively known, properly basic truths, such as our knowledge of modal logic, or of certain ethical and aesthetic values (e.g., "the holocaust was evil," "rainbows are beautiful"). As atheist Sam Harris rightly observes:

> "intuition" . . . denotes the most basic constituent of our faculty of understanding. While this is true in matters of ethics, it is no less true in science. When we can break our knowledge of a thing down no further, the irreducible leap that remains is intuitively taken. Thus, the traditional opposition between reason and intuition is a false one: reason is itself intuitive to the core, as any judgement that a proposition is "reasonable" or "logical" relies on intuition to find its feet . . . . The point, I trust, is obvious: we cannot step out of the darkness without taking a *first* step. And reason, without knowing how, understands this axiom if it would understand anything at all. The reliance on intuition, therefore, should be no more discomforting for the ethicist than it has been for the physicist.[91]

To quote atheist philosopher Mary Midgley: "Physical science . . . is not a separate, supreme champion outclassing history or philosophy. It has no private line to reality."[92]

However, once we widen our epistemology beyond the self-contradictory confines of hard scientism, we come face-to-face with metaphysical realities that refuse to fit within the parameters of modernism. As William Lane Crag and J. P. Moreland explain, using terminology that originated with philosopher Frank Jackson:

> given that naturalists are committed to a fairly widely accepted physical story about how things came to be and what they are, the location problem is the task of locating or finding a place for some entity (for example, semantic contents, mind, agency) in that story.[93]

90. Ratzsch, *Science and Its Limits*, 93.
91. Harris, *End of Faith*, 183.
92. Midgley, *Are You an Illusion?*, 6.
93. Craig and Moreland, *Naturalism*, xii.

The apparent existence of realities including consciousness, intentionality, rational thought, libertarian free will, objective values, and complex specified information in nature pose "location problems" that many philosophers and scientists argue constitute location problems that break the strictures of the modernist worldview.[94]

Modernism and History

When the modernists at *Skeptical Inquiry* say that "proper skepticism promotes scientific inquiry, critical investigation, and the use of reason in examining controversial and extraordinary claims,"[95] you may be tempted to simply nod in agreement. However, there are questions about what it means to say an inquiry is "scientific,"[96] how some truth-claims are and others are not assigned the label of being "controversial and extraordinary," and what all of that might imply when it comes to critically assessing the key Christian doctrine about Jesus, questions that are themselves matters deserving proper skepticism.

It is all too easy for the modernist skeptic to build their conclusion into their method of inquiry. For example, many modernists are persuaded by David Hume's skepticism about miracles, but as William Lane Craig writes: "those who are familiar with contemporary philosophy . . . know that Hume's arguments are today widely rejected as fallacious."[97]

---

94. For critique of the modernist worldview, see Williams, "Problems with Materialism/Metaphysical Naturalism" (YouTube playlist); Hedin, "Information and Life's Origin"; Koons, "Incompatibility of Naturalism and Scientific Realism"; Lewis, "Cardinal Difficulty of Naturalism"; Menuge, "Dennett Denied"; Plantinga, "Evolutionary Argument against Naturalism"; "Content and Natural Selection"; and "Against Materialism"; Reppert, "Argument from Reason"; Willard, "Knowledge and Naturalism"; Craig and Moreland, *Naturalism*; Goetz and Taliaferro, *Naturalism*; Moreland, *Recalcitrant Imago Dei*; Moreland and Rickabaugh, *Substance of Consciousness*; Menuge, *Agents under Fire*; Midgley, *Are You an Illusion?*; Nagel, *Mind and Cosmos*; O'Hear, *Philosophy in the New Century*; and *After Progress*; Reppert, *C. S. Lewis's Dangerous Idea*; Taliaferro, *Consciousness and the Mind of God*; Ward, *God, Chance and Necessity*; Williams, *Informed Cosmos*; *Universe from Someone*; *Faithful Guide to Philosophy*; *C. S. Lewis vs. the New Atheists*; and *I Wish I Could Believe*.

95. *Skeptical Inquirer*, "What Is Skepticism?"

96. See Monton, *Seeking God in Science*; Ratzsch, *Science and Its Limits*; Williams, *Informed Cosmos*.

97. Craig, "Christ and Miracles," 142. See Williams, "Miracles" (YouTube playlist); Beckwith, "Theism, Miracles, and the Modern Mind"; and *David Hume's Argument against Miracles*; Earman, *Hume's Abject Failure*; Geivett and Habermas, *In Defence of Miracles*; Houston, *Reported Miracles*; Larmer, *Legitimacy of Miracle*; McGrew,

A key point worth making here is that Hume wrote before probability calculus was well understood. As philosopher Angus Menuge explains:

> That Hume is mistaken in applying the probability of frequency to historical cases is clearly shown by Bayesian probability theory. According to Bayes's theorem . . . even if an event initially seems unlikely, new evidence can rationally convince us that the event occurred. . . . As applied to miracles, Bayes's theorem shows that even if the prior probability of a miracle (M) is low based on our background knowledge (B), there may be evidence (E) that is very unlikely if no miracle occurred (Not-M) but very likely if there was a miracle (M). This is the relative likelihood. When multiplied by the prior probability, this is sufficient to give a high posterior probability for M.[98]

As a case study in modernist assumptions predetermining the conclusion historical investigation is allowed to reach, consider the approach taken by atheist philosopher Daniel Dennett, who says of his naturalism that: "It's defeasible. I could learn to abandon it if I encountered insuperable difficulties in carrying out the naturalist program."[99] Despite this apparent openness to falsification, Dennett rejects the possibility that evidence for a miraculous act of divine revelation might pose an "insuperable" difficulty to "carrying out the naturalist program," on the *a priori* basis that: "historical arguments simply cannot be introduced into serious investigation [of God], since they are manifestly question begging."[100] Yet, far from begging the question of God's existence, historical arguments for miracles need only presuppose *the possibility of* God's existence. Moreover, miracles might play a part in a cumulative case for theism, or for a particular revelation claim (such as Christianity) once other arguments have already established a measure of plausibility for the proposition that God exists. Hence, it's actually *Dennett* who is begging the question here. Indeed, Dennett invokes "the scientific method, with its assumption of no miracles"[101] as a bulwark against considering evidence for miraculous defeaters to his "naturalist program." According to Dennett: "saying something is a miracle is a failure of imagination."[102] On the contrary, saying

---

"Arguments from Providence and Miracles"; Williams, *Getting at Jesus*, ch. 1.
98. Menuge, "Justified Belief in the Resurrection," 131–32.
99. Dennett and Spencer, "Mounting Disbelief," 13.
100. Dennett, *Breaking the Spell*, 240.
101. Dennett, *Breaking the Spell*, 26.
102. Dennett and O'Malley, "Q&A."

that naturalism "is defeasible," while simultaneously rejecting evidentially motivated arguments for miracles on *a priori* grounds, is an exercise in smuggling the modernist conclusion into one's investigative method. All of which highlights the importance of Richard Dawkins's call for making "disciplined precautions against personal bias, confirmation bias, pre-judgement of issues before the facts are in."[103]

An Enlightened Understanding of Jesus?

Many people (including academics) have modernist worldview commitments that preclude a pre-modern understanding of Jesus. For example, according to New Testament scholar Helen K. Bond:

> modern *academic study* of the historical Jesus only really began in the wake of the eighteenth-century Enlightenment, with . . . its rejection of a God who intervenes in history in supernatural ways. The emergence of historical criticism in the nineteenth century allowed distinctions to be made between the "Christ of faith" and the "Jesus of history," distinctions that have underpinned the Quest [for the historical Jesus] ever since.[104]

This received, modernist "wisdom" deserves some skeptical unpacking.

First, "the Enlightenment" was not the monolithic movement portrayed by Bond. According to historian Helena Rosenblatt:

> The term "Christian Enlightenment" no longer raises eyebrows. . . . A widespread consensus used to exist that the very essence of the Enlightenment . . . was its attack on religion. . . . Many scholars . . . described the Enlightenment as being—by its very nature—anti-Christian, anti-Church and even anti-religious. We now know, however, that the relationship between Christianity and the Enlightenment was far more complex and interesting. We realize that these previous interpretations were overly focused on France, and erroneously tended to posit a single Enlightenment. . . . we now see it not so much as a unified and Francophone phenomenon, but rather as a "family of discourses" with many regional and national variations across Europe and in America. It has become clear that earlier

---

103. Dawkins, *Science in the Soul*, 7.
104. Bond, *Historical Jesus*, 7.

interpretations were based on an impoverished view of religious traditions and perhaps even an outright disdain for them.[105]

As historian Rodney Stark explains:

> The single most remarkable and ironic thing about the "Enlightenment" is that those who proclaimed it made little or no contribution to the accomplishments they hailed. . . . Voltaire, Rousseau, Diderot, Hume, Gibbon, and the rest were literary men, while the primary revolution they hailed as the "Enlightenment" was scientific. Equally misleading is the fact that although the literary men who proclaimed the "Enlightenment" were irreligious, the central figures in the scientific achievements of the era were deeply religious. So much then for the idea that suddenly in the sixteenth century, enlightened secular forces burst the chains of Christian thought and set the foundation for modern times. What the proponents of "Enlightenment" actually initiated was the tradition of angry secular attacks on religion in the name of science. . . . Presented as the latest word in sophistication, rationalism, and reason, these assaults are remarkably naïve and simplistic—both then and now. In truth, the rise of science was inseparable from Christian theology, for the latter gave direction and confidence to the former.[106]

Likewise, many of the Enlightenment's leading philosophers were Christians (e.g., Immanuel Kant, Gottfried Leibniz, John Locke, Thomas Reid, Mary Wollstonecraft, etc.). Hence Terry Eagleton observes both that "the Enlightenment . . . was not especially anti-religious"[107] and that "the Enlightenment was deeply shaped by values which stemmed from the Christian tradition."[108] As historian Allan Chapman concludes, in the skewed sense that modernists often attach to the phrase, "the Enlightenment" turns out to be "the creation of scholars with their own cultural and usually anti-Christian axes to grind."[109]

Second, and more importantly for our present purposes, the Enlightenment did *not* draw a line of demarcation between scholars whose rejection of miracles left them free to engage in a respectably critical, properly skeptical historical study of the "Jesus of history," and un-critical

---

105. Rosenblatt, "Christian Enlightenment," 283.
106. Stark, *Triumph of Christianity*, 252.
107. Eagleton, *Culture and the Death of God*, 5.
108. Eagleton, *Reason, Faith, and Revolution*, 68.
109. Chapman, *Slaying the Dragons*, 67.

scholars whose religious beliefs condemn them to blind adherence to the "Christ of faith." Indeed, the rejection of the supernatural expressed in the traditional, anti-religious conception of "the Enlightenment" does not *allow* the distinction between the "Christ of faith" and the "Jesus of history" as Bond says. Rather, it *requires* that distinction, and does so *regardless of the evidence*! Philosopher C. Stephen Evans calls out the modernist critics on this game bait and switch:

> Critics . . . raise objections to historical religious knowledge that are apparently empirical in nature, and thus should presuppose [a] conception of religious knowledge that is open in principle to such historical knowledge. When we look more deeply, however, we find that these empirical objections are a smokescreen for covert [philosophical] presuppositions. . . . Why should we assume that whatever religious knowledge takes as its object . . . can't manifest itself in the natural world at all? While it may be a genuinely empiricist claim to say that empirical religious knowledge is difficult to attain or can only be attained under certain conditions, empiricism provides no real support for the thesis that empirical religious knowledge is impossible.[110]

Being open to the evidence means being open to whatever theory is best supported by the evidence. A miraculous explanation should never be our *first* port of call (even people who believe in miracles think they are exceptional events); but neither should our theory of knowledge preclude accepting a miracle *regardless of the evidence*. Hence, when it comes to claims about miracles, there's no avoiding the need *to examine and explain the evidence*.

From Modernism to Post-Modernism

> What then is the postmodern? . . . It is undoubtedly part of the modern.
>
> —Jean-François Lyotard[111]

Modernism's main claim to superiority as a worldview is that it offers the supposed explanatory simplicity of a monistic ontology.[112] However, the monism of modernism forces it to deny the existence of apparent realities

---

110. Evans, *Historical Christ*, 176 and 177.
111. Quoted in Rudrum, "Note on the Supplanting," 337.
112. See Gage, "Is the God Hypothesis Improbable?," 59–76.

(ontological, epistemological, axiological, and anthropological) that most people think they are warranted in acknowledging. At the turn of the twenty-first century, British philosopher Anthony O'Hear articulated the incongruity of this situation:

> There are key aspects of human life and experience which cannot be seen in purely materialistic terms. Our search for knowledge, our moral sense and the appreciation of beauty all extend our horizons beyond those of survival and reproduction. The phenomenon of consciousness is hard to even describe in terms drawn from the physical sciences. So central is consciousness to our life that it is impossible to see it as a mere by-product of physical forces and events. . . . In the past these intimations of value have typically been expressed in and understood religiously. . . . with the advance of materialism, formal religion has declined. But the intimations of value survive, and they are resistant to being explained away in materialistic fashion. . . . Together, consciousness and our attitudes to logic and knowledge suggest that seeing ourselves as biological survival machines is woefully inadequate. Similarly, the moral sense which permeates our lives . . . suggests the limitations of naturalistic accounts for human existence. . . . And so does our aesthetic interest.[113]

Orthodox modernists recognize that their worldview commits them to a form of nihilism that ejects pre-modern notions of objective goodness and beauty from their axiology, and pre-modern notions of personhood from their anthropology.[114] They profess this a metaphysical price worth paying, because they believe modernism to be both grounded in, and a royal road to, objective truth about reality discovered through naturalistically defined sciences. Postmodernists argue that modernists have not taken their ontological commitment to naturalism seriously enough, and that the logical outcome of this commitment is a deeper form of nihilism that forces objective truth into the outer darkness formerly reserved for objective goodness and beauty. Hence postmodernism has its roots deep within modernism and belongs "to a long post-Nietzschean tradition of despair about reason."[115] As philosopher Douglas Groothuis comments:

---

113. O'Hear, *Philosophy in the New Century*, 146, 153, and 159.

114. See Baggini, *Atheism*; Rosenberg, *Atheist's Guide to Reality*. See also Williams, "Sorting the Chaff from the Wheat"; *C. S. Lewis vs. the New Atheists*; and *I Wish I Could Believe*.

115. Butler, *Postmodernism*, 115.

> Postmodernism is so often presented as a radical departure from modernism that it is easy to miss the insight that postmodernism is, in many ways, modernism gone to seed, carried to its logical conclusion and inevitable demise.[116]

Taking the Darwinian Saw to the Modernist Branch

> If philosophy is to have a future in the twenty-first century, it must not sacrifice rigour. But to retain relevance and significance, it must turn away from scientism and cultural nihilism, the philosophical dead-ends of the twentieth century.
>
> —Anthony O'Hear[117]

Postmodern philosopher Richard Rorty (1931–2007) wrote that "keeping faith with Darwin" means realizing that "our species, its faculties and its current scientific and moral languages, are as much products of chance as are tectonic plates and mutated viruses."[118] Why trust the cognitive capacities of a creature cobbled together by "chance" events winnowed by the axiomatic restriction that the results of those events must work with respect to survival?[119] As Steven Pinker observes, according to philosophical Darwinism: "Our brains were shaped for fitness, not for truth."[120] Following this logic, atheist John Gray argues that modernists should *not* treat science as a quest for truth:

> Now and then, perhaps, science can cut loose from our practical needs, and serve the pursuit of truth. But to think that it can ever embody that quest is pre-scientific—it is to detach science from human needs, and make of it something that is not natural but transcendental. To think of science as the search for truth is to renew a mystical faith, the faith of Plato and Augustine, that truth rules the world, that truth is divine . . . . Modern humanism is the faith that through science humankind can know the truth—and so be set free. But if Darwin's theory of natural selection is true this is impossible. The human mind serves

---

116. Groothuis, *Truth Decay*, 40.
117. O'Hear, *Philosophy in the New Century*, viii.
118. Rorty, "Untruth and Consequences."
119. See Dennett and Plantinga, *Science and Religion*; Plantinga, *Where the Conflict Really Lies*, part 4; Williams, *Faithful Guide to Philosophy*, ch. 12; and *C. S. Lewis vs. the New Atheists*, ch. 4.
120. Pinker, *How the Mind Works*, 305.

evolutionary success, not truth. To think otherwise is to resurrect the pre-Darwinian error that humans are different from all other animals. . . . Darwinian theory tells us that an interest in truth is not needed for survival or reproduction . . . Truth has no systematic evolutionary advantage over error.[121]

Hence Rorty argued *on modernist grounds* that:

> The idea that one species of organism is, unlike all the others, oriented not just towards its own increased propensity but toward Truth, is as un-Darwinian as the idea that every human being has a built-in moral compass.[122]

Again, it was on the basis of the *modernist* philosophy, "which denies that we are related to the world in anything other than causal terms,"[123] that Rorty concluded he had to explain "rationality and epistemic authority by reference to what society lets us say, rather than the latter by the former."[124]

David Rudrum hits the nail on the head when he comments that postmodernism:

> is not an epoch that follows the modern, but a moment of crisis, fissure, or rupture within it, and it is part of the very fabric of modernity that such moments will come back up again (and again).[125]

This being so, it follows that to deviate from postmodern skepticism about reality we must simultaneously deviate from the core commitments of modernism. Fortunately, this is a deviation urged upon us by reason itself, for as atheist philosopher Thomas Nagel recognizes: "Evolutionary naturalism provides an account of our capacities that undermine their reliability, and in doing so undermines itself."[126]

---

121. Gray, *Straw Gods*, 20, 26, and 27.
122. Rorty, "Untruth and Consequences," 36.
123. Ramberg and Dieleman, "Richard Rorty."
124. Rorty, *Philosophy and the Mirror of Nature*, 174. See Koons, "Incompatibility of Naturalism and Scientific Realism"; Menuge, "Role of Agency in Science"; and "Libertarian Free Will"; Willard, "Knowledge and Naturalism"; Lewis, *Miracles*; Reppert, *C. S. Lewis's Dangerous Idea*; Williams, *Faithful Guide to Philosophy*, ch. 12; and *C. S. Lewis vs. the New Atheists*, ch. 4.
125. Rudrum, "Note on the Supplanting," 337.
126. Nagel, *Mind and Cosmos*, 27.

Incredulity towards the Postmodern Metanarrative

Oxford University literary scholar Christopher Butler (1940–2020) explains that "the basic attitude of postmodernists was a scepticism about the claims of any kind of overall, totalizing explanation."[127] French philosopher Jean-François Lyotard "argued in his *La condition postmoderne* (published in French in 1979 . . .) that we now live in an era in which legitimizing 'master narratives' are in crisis and in decline."[128] Lyotard famously commented that: "simplifying to the extreme, I define postmodern as incredulity towards metanarratives."[129] For postmodernists:

> This heralded a pluralist age, in which . . . even the arguments of scientists and historians are to be seen as no more than quasi narratives which compete with all the others for acceptance. They have no unique or reliable fit to the world, no certain correspondence with reality. They are just another form of fiction.[130]

To quote metamodern writer Brendan Graham Dempsey:

> Postmodern theories divorced language from reality, positing signs as arbitrary abstractions whose meaning only derives through contrast to other abstract signs in a linguistic system. In this way, language never quite refers to the world, only to other signs, which are always pointing elsewhere, leading to an infinite deferral of meaning.[131]

As Butler wryly observes, postmodernism "is certain of its uncertainty, and often claims that it has seen through the sustaining illusions of others," so that it "has grasped the 'real' nature of the cultural and political institutions which surround us."[132] Butler critiques the way in which French philosopher Jacques Derrida and his followers:

> seem to be committed to one fairly clear historical proposition: that philosophy and literature in the Western tradition had for too long falsely supposed that the relationship between language and world was . . . well founded and reliable. . . . This is Derrida's own grand metanarrative. . . . However, it is logically obvious

---

127. Butler, *Postmodernism*, 15.
128. Butler, *Postmodernism*, 13.
129. Butler, *Postmodernism*, 13.
130. Butler, *Postmodernism*, 15.
131. Dempsey, *Metamodernism*, 125.
132. Butler, *Postmodernism*, 2.

that you can't demonstrate how language always "goes astray" without at the same time having a secret and contradictory trust in it. For without a pretty confident notion of the truth, how can we show that any particular stretch of language has "gone astray" or fallen into contradiction?[133]

Literary scholar and cultural theorist Terry Eagleton likewise skewers the self-referential incoherence of postmodernism with respect to political (and hence moral) discourse:

> Who needs to launch a detailed critique of left-wing thought when you can argue, much more grandiosely, that all social discourse is blinded and indeterminate, that the "real" is undecidable, that all actions beyond a timorous reformism will proliferate perilously beyond one's control, that there are no subjects sufficiently coherent to undertake such actions in the first place, and that there is no total system to be changed in any case, that any apparently oppositional stance has already been pre-empted by the ruse of power, and that the world is no particular way at all, assuming we can know enough about it to assert even that? But in seeking to cut the ground from under its opponents feet, postmodernism finds itself unavoidably pulling the rug out from under itself, leaving itself with no more reason why we should resist fascism than the feebly pragmatic plea that fascism is not the way we do things in Sussex or Sacramento.[134]

Postmodernism and History

As Christopher Butler observes, postmodern deconstruction: "supported a general move towards relativist principles in postmodernist culture. It left postmodernists not particularly interested in empirical confirmation and verification in the sciences."[135] Naturally, this "deconstructive" attitude carried over into the study of history. However: "there is such a thing as a more or less adequately descriptive narrative. A large amount of correspondence between language and reality is possible."[136] It is an eminently reasonable form of (pre-modern) skepticism that cautions us to be more aware of "the theoretical assumptions

---

133. Butler, *Postmodernism*, 17–18.
134. Eagleton, *Illusions of Postmodernism*, 27–28.
135. Butler, *Postmodernism*, 28.
136. Butler, *Postmodernism*, 35.

which support the narratives produced by all historians;"[137] but "if anyone says that everything is 'really' just constituted by a deceiving image, and not by reality, how does he or she know? They presuppose the very distinctions they attack."[138]

Historian Richard J. Evans reckons that:

> the most far-reaching, comprehensive and explicit challenge to history as a discipline . . . has been mounted by the French linguistic theorist Roland Barthes and the philosopher Jacques Derrida. As early as 1968 Barthes charged that historians' claim to reconstruct past reality . . . was . . . "an inscription on the past pretending to be a likeness of it, a parade of signifiers masquerading as a collection of facts." Objectivity was "the product of what might be called the referential illusion." . . . Historians' own understanding of what they did remained, as Jacques Derrida noted, stubbornly "logocentric," that is, they imagined they were rational beings engaged in a process of discovery. But this too was an illusion, like all forms of "logocentrism."[139]

Of course, when Barthes wrote about the claims made by historians, he did so with reference to claims that historians *had* made, and he was therefore acting as a historian offering his readers a reconstruction of past reality (albeit the recent past). Hence, Barthes' critique of historians was self-referentially incoherent. Likewise, Derrida's objection to the idea that anyone can engage in a rational process of discovery has no force unless it is itself offered up as the conclusion of a rational process of discovery, in which case it contradicts itself.

Evans explains that, according to Derrida:

> the meaning of a text changes every time it is read. Meaning is put into it by the reader, and all meanings are in principle equally valid. In history, meaning cannot be found in the past; it is merely put there, each time differently, and with equal validity, by different historians. There is no necessary or consistent relationship between the text of history [i.e., the past] and the texts of historians.[140]

---

137. Butler, *Postmodernism*, 35.
138. Butler, *Postmodernism*, 118.
139. Evans, *In Defence of History*, 94.
140. Evans, *In Defence of History*, 95.

Of course, if Derrida is correct, then reading Derrida doesn't enable anyone (including Evans, and including Derrida himself) to correctly understand what Derrida wrote!

In his famous essay "The Death of the Author" Roland Barthes issued a self-contradictory rejection of the link between authorial intent and the meaning of a text, both with respect to literary texts and to "the world as text" authored by God:

> We know now that a text is not a line of words releasing a single "theological" meaning (the "message" of the Author-God) . . . Once the Author is removed, the claim to decipher a text becomes quite futile. To give a text an Author is to impose a limit on that text, to furnish it with a final signified . . . writing ceaselessly posits meaning ceaselessly to evaporate it, carrying out a systematic exemption of meaning. In precisely this way literature (it would be better from now on to say writing), by refusing to assign a "secret," an ultimate meaning, to the text (and to the world as text), liberates what may be called an anti-theological activity, an activity, that is truly revolutionary since to refuse to fix meaning is, in the end, to refuse God and his hypostases—reason, science, law.[141]

The obvious question here is: Did Barthes *intend* or *mean* to communicate this philosophy to his readers?! If the "death of the author" renders any claim to decipher what a text signifies "quite futile," it necessarily renders "quite futile" any claim—even a claim on the part of a text's author—that one has *mis*interpreted what a text signifies. But as William Lane Craig wryly comments: "nobody adopts a Postmodernist view of literary texts when reading the labels on a medicine bottle or a box of rat poison!"[142]

Responding to postmodern scholars who reject the very possibility of historical knowledge, Evans comments:

> The fundamental problem with this kind of extreme relativism is . . . that it inevitably falls foul of its own principles when they are applied to itself. Why, after all, if all theories are equally valid, should we believe postmodernist theories of history rather than other theories? If all knowledge is relative, if it is impossible to give an accurate summary of a discourse without at the same time projecting one's own reading on to it, then why should we

---

141. Barthes, "Death of the Author," 146.
142. Craig, "Resurrection of Theism."

not give to the work of Barthes, or Derrida . . . any significance that we wish to give it?[143]

As theologian D. A. Carson remarks:

> I have never read a deconstructionist who would be pleased if a reviewer misinterpreted his or her work: thus in practice deconstructionists implicitly link their own texts with their own intentions . . . in the real world, for all the difficulties there are in communication from person to person . . . we still expect people to say more or less what they mean (and if they don't, we chide them for it), and we expect mature people to understand what others say, and represent it fairly. The understanding is doubtless never absolutely exhaustive and perfect, but that does not mean the only alternative is to dissociate text from speaker, and then locate all meaning in the reader or hearer.[144]

If denying God's existence means denying that "the world as text" has an objective meaning (the kind of meaning that is discovered rather than invented), it follows that the only way to coherently affirm that the world has an objective meaning is to affirm the existence of God as its "Author." In other words, as many atheist philosophers recognize, the question of God's existence is not a question of merely academic interest, but a question of existential import.[145] Indeed, if we embrace a properly basic rational intuition of the meaningfulness of reality, we can reverse Barthes's argument into an argument for theism.

Of course, "Postmodernists are right to say that readers bring to history . . . their own beliefs and purposes. The point, however, is that these no more completely shape their reading of the book than do the intentions of the author."[146] Hence: "The first prerequisite of the serious historical researcher must be the ability to jettison dearly-held interpretations in the face of the recalcitrance of the evidence."[147] In other words, *contra* postmodernism, historical "interpretations really can be tested and confirmed or falsified by an appeal to evidence."[148] The past:

---

143. Evans, *In Defence of History*, 231.

144. Carson, *Gagging of God*, 101–3.

145. See Evans, *Despair*; Nietzsche, "Parable of the Madman"; Russell, "Free Man's Worship"; Sartre, "Existentialism Is a Humanism"; Williams, *I Wish I Could Believe*.

146. Evans, *In Defence of History*, 107.

147. Evans, *In Defence of History*, 120.

148. Evans, *In Defence of History*, 128.

really happened, and we really can, if we are very scrupulous and careful and self-critical, find out how it happened and reach some tenable though always less than final conclusions about what it all meant.[149]

While "modernist" skeptics all too often succumb to a question-begging failure to seriously engage with the historical case for the Christian picture of Jesus, "postmodern" skeptics all to often slide into an "extreme relativism"[150] that expects us to take their texts seriously when their texts assert that texts don't assert anything. But as Evans complains: "even the most extreme deconstructionists do not really accept that their own theories can be applied to their own work."[151]

Culture in Flux

In the assessment of Lene Rachel Andersen:

> modernity is not complex enough to handle our inner spiritual needs.... Postmodernism is good at deconstructing culture and society, but it is terrible at bringing people together; it is only good at taking things apart.... The postmodern world with its deconstruction of almost everything and constant relativizing, has prevented a lot of honest, deep emotional connection to cultural heritage and other people. There is always this "distance." It has left many morally alone, as Fromm called it; we are massively in an existential vacuum, and it feels horrible.[152]

Likewise, literary theorists David Rudrum and Nicholas Stavris protest that postmodern "scepticism about reality is not a strategy that is conducive to a sense of respect for others' identities or for the planet at large."[153] As eminent literary critic and writer Ihab Hassan (1925–2015) warned: "If truth is dead, then everything is permitted—because its alternatives, now more than ever, are rank power and rampant desire."[154]

---

149. Evans, *In Defence of History*, 253.
150. Evans, *In Defence of History*, 231.
151. Evans, *In Defence of History*, 231. For a further critique of postmodernism, see Groothuis, *Truth Decay*; Köstenberger, *Whatever Happened to Truth?*; Moreland, "Postmodernism and Truth"; and "Four Degrees of Postmodernism"; Scruton, *Intelligent Person's Guide to Culture*, ch. 11.
152. Andersen, *Bildung*, 90 and 152.
153. Rudrum and Stavris, "Introduction to Ihab Hassan," 13.
154. Hassan, "Beyond Postmodernism," 20.

Fortunately, truth is not dead, and postmodernism is a culturally waning force. As Brendan Graham Dempsey comments:

> the cultural vanguard has long since moved on from the played-out tropes and predictable strategies of "postmodernism." That story is old, and there is, by now, over a decade's worth of academic literature devoted not just to postmodernism's decline but to what has arisen to succeed it since the early 2000s. While the legacy of postmodernism will of course live on and continue to permeate society, it is hardly the spearpoint anymore of cultural innovation. Something new is afoot.[155]

In his 2002 introduction to postmodernism, Butler wrote that "the period of its greatest influence is now over. Its founding fathers are in their turn encountering the scepticism of a new generation."[156] In 2006, British cultural critic Alex Kirby commented:

> Buy novels published in the last five years, watch a twenty-first-century film, listen to the latest music—above all just sit and watch television for a week—and you will hardly catch a glimpse of postmodernism. Similarly, one can go to literary conferences . . . and sit through a dozen papers which make no mention . . . of Derrida, Foucault, Baudrillard.[157]

In 2007, John McGowan (professor emeritus of English and comparative literature at the University of North Carolina at Chapel Hill) noted that:

> The term "postmodernism" is still with us as a vague reference to French theory, historical meta-fiction, and eclectic hybrid forms in architecture and art. But the theoretical debate represented by "postmodernism" has, for better and worse, passed from the scene.[158]

In 2015, Rudrum and Stavris cautioned that while "postmodernism is in decline . . . calling time on postmodernism is still a work in progress."[159] The "work in progress" nature of postmodernism's "decline" reflects the fact that, having followed modernism through to its nihilistic terminus, and having "deconstructed" deconstruction itself, "it is not clear whether the 'present history' of the early twenty-first

---

155. Dempsey, *Metamodernism*, 7.
156. Butler, *Postmodernism*, 127.
157. Kirby, "Death of Postmodernism and Beyond," 52.
158. McGowan, "They Might Have Been Giants," 63.
159. Rudrum and Stavris, *Supplanting the Postmodern*, xiii and xviii.

century actually has a 'general sense of a cultural dominant.'"[160] The so-called "New Atheism" was big in the 2000s, but crumpled under the weight of external critiques and internal divisions.[161] The quest to define a "post-postmodern," "metamodern," or "polymodern" worldview and spirituality with the capacity to supplant both modernism and postmodernism as a new "cultural dominant" has become an increasingly prominent part of both academic and popular culture.

What has this growing disenchantment with modernism-cum-postmodernism, and its concomitant search for a new "cultural dominant," have to do with the quest for the historical Jesus? Despite the overwhelming evidence for the historical existence of Jesus of Nazareth,[162] our culture's worldview expectations have led to a cultural moment in which an astonishing 46 percent of the UK population are either uncertain of, or even actively refute, Jesus's status as a historical figure![163] The quest to transcend the modern-cum-postmodern worldview could create a space within which to reinvent the quest for the historical Jesus along more evidential and truth-oriented lines. If so, we may find that historical investigation can, in a partial yet adequate way, put us in touch with a Jesus whose historical life and teaching invites us to reshape our spirituality and culture in fruitful ways.

Metamodernism

> The word metamodernism is basically a term that describes that which comes after modern society (and after the "postmodern" critique of it).
>
> —Hanzi Freinacht[164]

---

160. Rudrum, "Note on the Supplanting," 344.

161. See Brierley, *Surprising Rebirth of Belief in God*, ch. 1. For an assessment of the New Atheism, see Williams, "'New Atheism'" (YouTube playlist); Craig, "Dawkins' Delusion"; Craig and Meister, *God Is Great, God Is Good*; Gilson and Weitnauer, *True Reason*; Ganssle, *Reasonable God*; Glass, *Atheism's New Clothes*; Hart, *Atheist Delusions*; Rasmussen and Vallier, *New Theist Response to the New Atheism*; Williams, *Outgrowing God?*; *Getting at Jesus*; and *C. S. Lewis vs. the New Atheists*.

162. As Craig L. Blomberg observes, by combining evidence from first- to third-century Greco-Roman writers: "one can clearly accumulate enough evidence to refute the fanciful notion that Jesus never existed" (*Historical Reliability of the Gospels*, 251). See Williams, "Existence of Jesus" (YouTube playlist); Casey, *Jesus*; Ehrman, *Did Jesus Exist?*; Habermas, *Historical Jesus*; Holding, *Shattering the Christ Myth*; Williams, *Getting at Jesus*.

163. Talking Jesus, *What People in the UK*.

164. Freinacht, *Listening Society*, 361.

Hanzi Freinacht lays out three different meanings for the term *metamodern*:

> the most commonly used in other sources thus far, is metamodernism as a certain cultural phase in matters such as art, architecture, media, philosophy and politics. . . . In that sense "metamodernism" is comparable to things such as the Romantic period . . . the Enlightenment . . . and postmodernism. If you ever studied arts, philosophy or literature you are familiar with this way of thinking in cultural phases.[165]

The second meaning, which relates to political philosophy:

> is metamodernism as a developmental stage. This is very different from a cultural phase. The idea of a phase, like Romanticism, which came after the Enlightenment . . . simply states that this phase came after that one (for instance, because the German idealists wanted to distance themselves from French rationalism). Stage theories are different. They claim, for instance, that adulthood comes after childhood. . . . Or that industrial civilization comes after traditional, agricultural civilization.[166]

The third meaning is: "a philosophical paradigm . . . a fundamental worldview."[167] A philosophical paradigm or worldview underpins the shared spirituality of a culture and finds expression in that culture's architecture, art, institutions, etc.

In Search of a Worldview

Little appears to be settled about metamodernism as a worldview. Different academics offer different definitions of what they think metamodernism is and/or should be, and whether *metamodern* is the best term to use for it. Nevertheless, one central metamodern theme seems to be the need to take personhood, and those things which make personhood existentially meaningful, with a seriousness that is undermined by modernism and postmodernism. As literary critic and intellectual historian Patricia Waugh observes:

---

165. Freinacht, *Listening Society*, 361.
166. Freinacht, *Listening Society*, 362.
167. Freinacht, *Listening Society*, 362.

In the current cross-disciplinary quest to recover from what Raymond Tallis calls "neuromania" and "Darwinitis" as well as from postmodernism, there seems to be a renewed interest in retrieving the self.[168]

Indeed, according to cultural theorist Greg Dember:

> the essence of metamodernism is a (conscious or unconscious) motivation to protect the solidity of felt experience against the scientific reductionism of the modernist perspective and the ironic detachment of the postmodern sensibility.[169]

Thus literary theorist and poet Alexandra Dumitrescu defines metamodernism as:

> the struggle to find meaning, and in searching for meaning, it is the tendency to re-establish that connection or those connections that would render life and creation, love and expression meaningful.[170]

This resonates with Freinacht's call for a metamodern spirituality that takes "philosophical, cultural and aesthetic matters very seriously, as they are seen as inherent dimensions of reality, not just 'additional woo-woo' on top of physics."[171]

Hollow Metamodernism

Unfortunately, Freinacht's proposals concerning the content of a metamodern worldview "that is not yet established, but we are trying to establish,"[172] are an incoherent mixture of beliefs grounded in the debatable proposition "that God is dead and humanism dying."[173] On the one hand, Freinacht affirms a need "to take ontological questions very seriously, i.e. to let questions about 'what is really real' guide us in science and politics."[174] On the other hand, he affirms a need "to be anti-essentialist, not believing in 'ultimate essences' such as matter, consciousness,

---

168. Quoted in Stavris, "Anxieties of the Present," 354. See Tallis, *Aping Mankind*.
169. Dember, "After Postmodernism," §8.
170. Dumitrescu, "Interconnections in Blakean and Metamodern Space," §69.
171. Freinacht, *Listening Society*, 367.
172. Freinacht, *Listening Society*, 362.
173. Freinacht, *Listening Society*, 363.
174. Freinacht, *Listening Society*, 365.

goodness, evil."[175] Indeed, Freinacht affirms a need "to accept and thrive in the paradoxical, self-contradictory."[176] Accepting paradox is one thing. Accepting self-contradiction is quite another.

According to an influential essay by cultural critic Timotheus Vermeulen and philosopher Robin van den Akker: "Metamodernism . . . oscillates between a modern enthusiasm and a postmodern irony, between hope and melancholy."[177] Cultural theorists Linda Ceriello and Greg Dember describe metamodernism in similar terms, using a different image:

> "metamodernist works" engage the conflicts between modernist conviction and postmodern relativism, in part by embodying an aesthetic that braids the various epistemic perspectives with an emphasis on felt experience.[178]

However, one cannot escape the problems inherent within modernism and postmodernism merely by oscillating between them, or by braiding them together.

Metamodern writer Brendan Graham Dempsey proposes a unifying account of metamodernism in the idea of "going meta,"[179] arguing that just as "Postmodernists come after, objectify, reflect upon, critique, and transcend modernism," so "metamodernists come after, objectify, reflect upon, critique, and transcend postmodernism."[180] Dempsey illustrates the idea of "going meta" by describing a series of nested perspectives:

> Going meta never means diminishing one's scope of perspectives, but always increasing it. By definition, it is what allows one to step outside a given frame to see more of the picture. It's like a person in a painting climbing out of the painting and then looking back at where they had been encased. Now they can see the whole context of their former position: it was just a painting! They can also see their old context within the broader context of their new vantage: an art gallery![181]

Dempsey describes the process of "going meta" as "iterative," such that:

175. Freinacht, *Listening Society*, 365.
176. Freinacht, *Listening Society*, 363.
177. Vermeulen and Akker, "Notes on Metamodernism."
178. What Is Metamodern? "About the Authors."
179. Dempsey, *Metamodernism*, 7.
180. Dempsey, *Metamodernism*, 7.
181. Dempsey, *Metamodernism*, 8.

> before long it becomes clear that the "reality" in which they currently stand is also limited. Transcending again, imagine the person now climbs out of a television, and can see that the art gallery was itself just in their TV as the painting was in the art gallery! . . . The context of the TV "contains more" than the context of the painting, allowing one a broader view of (provisional) reality. In short, higher vantages provide more information than lower ones.[182]

The principle problem with Dempsey's portrait of metamodernism is that, unlike the coherently nested perspectives of "the picture" of painting, gallery, and TV show, modernism and postmodernism *contradict each other* on various matters. Dempsey asserts that "the modern and the postmodern need not be antagonistic opposites,"[183] but in light of the contradictions between them, the best one could say along these lines is that they are both partially true perspectives with something to contribute to a "broader" meta-perspective on "the picture" of reality. To assert with Dempsey that "the metamodern perspective . . . contains the postmodern, as well as the pre-postmodern, as enduring modalities available to it,"[184] is incoherent. This incoherence pervades Dempsey's description of the "metamodern sensibility" as:

> a multi-perspectival one, able to move through the various levels of reflection it contains. So, while the postmodern has foreclosed the possibility of idealism in reaction to the modern, the metamodern can toggle between both, holding modern aspirational enthusiasm one minute, then checking this with a more reflective awareness the next.[185]

If modernistic "idealism" and "aspirational enthusiasm" was something "foreclosed" by postmodernism, is it "foreclosed" by metamodernism, or is it not? Either it is, or it isn't. The proposal of a meta-perspective that contains multiple *compatible* perspectives is one thing; the proposal of a meta-perspective that "toggles" between *incompatible* perspectives is quite another. Toggling between incompatible perspectives does not synthesize them into a more informative perspective. According to Dempsey:

---

182. Dempsey, *Metamodernism*, 8.
183. Dempsey, *Metamodernism*, 15.
184. Dempsey, *Metamodernism*, 14.
185. Dempsey, *Metamodernism*, 14.

While postmodernism had recognized plurality, metamodernism recognizes the nested nature of this plurality, the Russian doll structure that allows the metamodernist to relate multiple perspectives to each other and to its own vantage.[186]

Russian dolls are able to nest one inside of the other because they have compatible forms. This doesn't apply to the contradictory aspects of pre-modernism, modernism, and postmodernism.

Fig. 3. Russian Matryoshka Dolls.[187]

Another problem with Dempsey's theory of metamodernism is his assertion that: "like all theories and all knowledge, it is provisional."[188] One has to ask, Is *this statement itself* presented as a "provisional" claim? Is "all" knowledge, or are "all" knowledge claims, really "provisional"? What about the reader's first person knowledge of their own existence? What about our knowledge of the basic laws of logic?

Moreover, according to Dempsey, "going meta" is not an epistemological movement towards an increased knowledge of the way things are, but "towards a continually receding horizon."[189] In his view:

---

186. Dempsey, *Metamodernism*, 18.

187. Credit: TanTanika, https://pixabay.com/photos/matryoshka-souvenir-russia-toy-879751/.

188. Dempsey, *Metamodernism*, 21.

189. Dempsey, *Metamodernism*, 11.

> There is no final Absolute, rendering all gains relative. . . . This sort of paradoxical advance I call infinitesimal progress (movement by means of infinitely diminishing strides). . . . How does one reach a destination when the ground one must cover is recursively divisible into smaller and smaller parts? The metamodernist, appeasing both modernists and postmodernists, assures: "All progress is relative." Progress is real, but it lies in the going.[190]

Presumably, this will appease neither the modernist nor the postmodernist! As for the Abrahamic pre-modernist, they would reply that while humans lack the omniscience of God, they do have a God-given ability to know truth and to make genuine progress in their knowledge about reality, a progress that doesn't merely lie "in the going" because it isn't merely a matter of "never-ending approximation."[191] Dempsey appears to confuse genuine knowledge with *comprehensive* knowledge; but knowledge is knowledge, even if one knows one can always see one's knowledge in the context of additional knowledge. One can know (absolutely!) that one's present knowledge is partial, without this knowledge devaluing or contradicting what one presently knows (just as one can know that one's claims to knowledge, or to warranted belief, often remain open to sufficiently warranted challenge without thereby opening the door to the epistemological despair of postmodernism).

Nothing Matters Anywhere at Any Time, but All You Need Is "Love"?

The problem with these attempts to present metamodernism as a worldview is exemplified by the message of the 2023 multi-Oscar winning metamodern film *Everything Everywhere All at Once*,[192] summarized here by critic Calum Russell:

> Refusing to deny nihilism outright, *Everything Everywhere All at Once* argues that the feeling of worthlessness and apathy that comes with the philosophical concept can be combatted by embracing absurdity . . . and finding empathy in this shared mortal connection. In such a meaningless universe, the love Evelyn shares with her daughter and husband is the source of true

---

190. Dempsey, *Metamodernism*, 11.
191. Dempsey, *Metamodernism*, 28.
192. See Dember, "Everything Metamodern All at Once."

meaning, finding mutual understanding and acceptance in their shared experience of the absurdity of modern life.[193]

Everything Everywhere All at Once is a prime example of a metamodern attempt to "protect the solidity of felt experience against the scientific reductionism of the modernist perspective and the ironic detachment of the postmodern sensibility"[194] that ultimately rings hollow. Faced with the postmodern, nihilistic entailments of its modernistic worldview assumptions, the film advocates a knowingly absurd choice to focus upon love.[195] Of course, love is a paradigm example of something that *seems* to matter (not only in a subjective, "to us" sense, but in an objective sense). However, if one believes that, objectively speaking, "nothing matters,"[196] and that the way love subjectively *appears* to matter is an illusion one has seen through, can choosing to love really allow one to "transcend" the despair of nihilism *even as one continues to affirm the nihilism that evacuates love of all objective meaning*? Doesn't such an absurd act of "let's pretend" undermine itself? How is this any better than Alex Rosenberg's resolutely modernistic advice that:

> human life is meaningless, without purpose, and without ultimate moral value. . . . So, what should we scientistic folks do when overcome with *Weltschmertz* (world-weariness)? Take two of whatever neuro-pharmacology prescribes.[197]

Humans have an innate desire for meaning, and nihilism renders this desire "absurd" in the technical sense defined by Albert Camus when he wrote in *The Myth of Sisyphus* that: "the absurd is born of this confrontation between the human need and the unreasonable silence of the world."[198] The innate desire for meaning is rendered absurd by the modernist assumptions that underpin nihilism, such that trusting that desire would entail overthrowing those assumptions. Indeed, the very existence of that desire arguably constitutes a reason for doubting those modernist assumptions.[199] At the very least, isn't it worth keeping an

---

193. Russell, "Everything Everywhere All at Once," §5–6.
194. Dember, "After Postmodernism," §8.
195. See Breedlovecraft, "Absurd Philosophy"; Films Prophet, "Everything Everywhere All at Once."
196. Hup, "Everything Everywhere All at Once."
197. Rosenberg, *Atheist's Guide to Reality*, 18 and 282.
198. Camus, *Myth of Sisyphus*.
199. See Williams, "Argument from Desire" (YouTube playlist); Hoyler, "Argument

open mind as to whether there might be a more viable way to "protect the solidity of felt experience" than engaging in an absurdist act of pretense? As Marcelle Couto writes:

> In the case of "Everything Everywhere All at Once," love itself, particularly the choice to love, serves as the ultimate weapon against despair. While this perspective may seem liberating . . . what is love in a meaningless universe? . . . . why should I sacrifice my desires for the sake of another (which I will do if I truly love someone) in a meaningless universe? Why should I choose suffering, and vulnerability, when egoism offers a much greater reward under utilitarian arithmetic? Yes, I can feel affection toward my friends and family, but why in the world would I choose to forgive, to love persistently amidst failure and disappointment? In [a meaningless] universe, love is an empty attitude.[200]

However, maybe love itself is a sign that nihilism is mistaken about reality:

> But I think love . . . is never a vain thing. I would dare say we all know this, intuitively. "Everything Everywhere All at Once" knows this, too, and therein lies its tremendous influence. Audiences have frequently been left in tears—and not without reason—after observing the mother-daughter reconciliation central to the plot. This very scenario contradicts the movie's philosophy because it calls for an unspoken understanding of what true love should actually look like. Love is an inherent good, and an inherent good cannot exist under nihilism no matter how much we attempt to fabricate it. In other words, "Everything Everywhere All at Once" has not earned the right to use the word "love." Its philosophy does not allow for there to be anything remarkable about whatever combination of atoms consists of "love," or any other neurological phenomenon for that matter.[201]

---

from Desire"; Kreeft, "Argument from Desire"; Simek, "Bayesian Exploration of C. S. Lewis's 'Argument from Desire'"; Williams, "Beginner's Guide to the Theist Argument"; "C. S. Lewis as a Central Figure"; and "Re-Defending Arguments from Desire"; Bassham, *C. S. Lewis's Christian Apologetics*; Boethius. *Consolation of Philosophy*, book 3; Buras and Cantrell, "C. S. Lewis's Argument from Nostalgia"; Haldane, "Philosophy, the Restless Heart"; Puckett, *Apologetics of Joy*.

200. Couto, "Reflecting on the Philosophy," §3–4. See Mavrodes, "Religion and the Queerness of Morality."

201. Couto, "Reflecting on the Philosophy," §5 See also Gospel Coalition Australia, "Love."

Such "hollow metamodernism" is a doomed attempt to have one's cake while eating it.[202]

Knock, Knock . . .

Timotheus Vermeulen describes metamodernism as a response to the combination of what he calls a postmodern "claustrophobia of the chest," and the perception of "a knocking sound" from an unknown source that could, possibly, be "something out there"[203] beyond the confines of our currently dominant modern-cum-postmodern worldview. In a fascinating lecture entitled "Knock, Knock," Vermeulen diagnoses the human condition of life lived within the precincts of the modern-cum-postmodern "mall," or worldview, as one in which "we suffer from a kind of 'asthma of the soul,'" (i.e., those who live within this worldview feel is too constricting to accommodate "the solidity of felt experience"[204]) and in which there is consequently "this feeling of dissatisfaction . . . with the world around you."[205] This sense of suffocating dissatisfaction awakes within us a desire for *something more*. Since the 1990s, says Vermeulen:

> we're hearing knocks . . . on the walls of the mall . . . and we begin to think . . . what if there are still big questions, what if, even if we shouldn't believe in grand narratives . . . the mess that has left us in necessitates us to reimagine the possibility of an outside, the possibility of an alternative, the possibility that things could be different; and so people begin to run for the doors, to find that there are no doors in this mall, that they have been barricaded with all those books . . . that my [modern and postmodern] philosophy teachers at university used to speak about . . . and so we look for windows and there aren't any windows, and so this is the metamodern situation, the moment that we realize . . . that this shopping mall, this end of history . . . may not be the end state; and how do you create an alternative, how do you start from there, how do you begin to think, how do you kick start history . . . when you only have that inside, when you only have that enclosed space?[206]

---

202. For those who have seen *Everything Everywhere All at Once*, perhaps I should say it is a doomed attempt to have one's bagel while eating it!
203. What Is Metamodern?, "Talking Metamodernism with Tim Vermeulen."
204. Dember, "After Postmodernism," §8.
205. Vermeulen, "Knock Knock."
206. Vermeulen, "Knock Knock."

One way to answer Vermeulen's question is to suggest exploring the possibility that we might be able to critically dismantle that barricade of books his modern and postmodern philosophy teachers used to speak about, thereby clearing a path that allows people to journey outside the mall. Might it not at least be worth reading some of those books on the dustier shelves of the university library, the ones written by philosophers (ancient and contemporary) with a pre-modern worldview? Vermeulen laments:

> We have no idea what the alternative looks like, because I grew up in a generation that was told there is no alternative, and I grew up in a generation where if in school I would say "But this is the truth" then my teacher would say "Yeah, come on, this is *your* truth, right, the other kid has also his own truth." And so you think, "Ah, shit, there is no truth." And so how do you think the alternative when all your options, all the tools . . . which we used to create alternatives, have been taken away from you? When all the horizons have been wiped out, then how do you begin to think about how stuff could be different? And I think this is the difficult moment that metamodernism as a vernacular, as a heuristic label tries to capture.[207]

However, as British philosopher Roger Scruton once commented, anyone "who says that there are no truths, or that all truth is 'merely relative,' is asking you not to believe him. So don't."[208] The only coherent response to Vermeulen's woes rests in recovering the concept of truth denied to him by his teachers. Without the pursuit of truth, as Vermeulen observes:

> what is happening now . . . is that we are both trying to create new narratives . . . like those moderns (especially here "moderns" as a system of thought, as a philosophy) used to do, but of course because of all the postmodern knowledge . . . you are also stuck in that postmodern doubt, in a postmodern reflective stance. . . . I would say this is the ontological state of our present moment.[209]

The "ontological state" of this simultaneously modern and postmodern "present moment" both drives and undermines the quest for a better worldview. The result is an existential tantalization that breeds a desire it can never satisfy. But what if that presumed "postmodern knowledge" is

207. Vermeulen, "Knock Knock."
208. Scruton, *Modern Philosophy*, 12.
209. Vermeulen, "Knock Knock."

not actually knowledge, but only *falsely perceived to be knowledge*? What if we ditch the self-contradictory doubt of the "postmodern reflective stance," while embracing a properly (pre-modern!) skeptical reflective stance aimed at discovering the truth about reality?

The metamodern quest to retrieve the self requires what Nicholas Stavris describes as "a realigned focus on truth which deviates from postmodern scepticism about reality."[210] Ironically, as we have seen, postmodern skepticism about reality is driven by modernist worldview commitments. Hence, the metamodern quest to retrieve the self requires us to ditch those commitments.

The only hope for a better worldview lies in a willingness to doubt Vermeulen's assumption that "all the tools" for creating alternative worldviews have "been taken away" by "postmodern knowledge." At the very least, we have the critical tools to know that anything "outside" of the "mall" cannot be a replica of the inside. Nor can it be an oscillation, or braiding together, or toggling between its key modernist and postmodernist worldview "architectures." Furthermore, we know what the philosophical tools of critical thinking, and the classical concept of truth at which they aim, look like.[211] And we have good reason to believe that the "outside" has to be a worldview that can accommodate those experienced realities that pose serious "location problems" to the worldviews that delimit "the mall."

Hungry Metamodernism

> Metamodernism is a return to fundamental questions that define our being in the world.... It is a search for the meaning and beauty of the present.... Metamodernism is a bold assertion of the human being as a spiritual entity, rather than a forlorn person inhabiting his or her detached island of individualism.... Metamodernism is the expression of the self's search for home.
>
> —Alexandra Dumitrescu[212]

---

210. Stavris, "Anxieties of the Present," 353.

211. See Williams, "Critical Thinking" (YouTube playlist); Alston, *Realist Conception of Truth*; Audi, *Epistemology*; Cowan and Spiegel, *Love of Wisdom*, chs. 1 and 2; Geisler and Feinberg, *Introduction to Philosophy*, chs. 3, 4, and 16; Groothuis, *Truth Decay*; Köstenberger, *Whatever Happened to Truth?*; Sinnott-Armstrong, *Think Again*; Moreland, "Postmodernism and Truth"; and "Four Degrees of Postmodernism"; Williams, *Faithful Guide to Philosophy*, chs. 1 and 2.

212. Dumitrescu, "Metamodernism."

To successfully "protect the solidity of felt experience," escape the modern-cum-postmodern "claustrophobia of the chest," recover "the connection between the good, the true and the beautiful," and free ourselves to respond to the perceived "knocking" of transcendent reality upon the walls of Vermeulen's worldview "mall," we must reject both the destructive essence of postmodernism *and* its distinctively modernistic roots. This is *not* to say our culture needs to reject *everything* that comes under the multivalent labels of modernity and postmodernity. Nor is it to say that we need to uncritically embrace everything associated with pre-modernism. It is to say that we should keep an open but appropriately skeptical mind as we ask whether some form of pre-modernism might provide the core worldview concepts and tools for sifting and integrating the good aspects of modernism and postmodernism into a coherent contemporary spirituality and culture.

In this cultural moment, says Jonathan Rowson: "metamodernism is called for because we need to wake up to being in a time between worlds."[213] The cultural world we will eventually settle within after the present moment of cultural flux is ours to shape. In Rowson's judgment:

> We're not going to go back to pre-modern religion, but nor are we going to stay stuck in a kind of flatland postmodern context where the notion of the sacred struggles to be heard . . . where arguably there is a meaning crisis . . . We have to question the entire meaning and purpose of life.[214]

The phrase "meaning crisis" was coined by psychologist John Vervaeke to describe:

> the sense of alienation people experience as they move through life feeling disconnected from each other and the world. Most especially they feel disconnected from a purpose to live for, or a story that makes sense of who they are. . . . Vervaeke sees a range of symptoms to this crisis, including "the rise in suicide, even suicide independent of clinical depression right now, which is a very telling sign. A loneliness epidemic, the mental health crisis . . . depression and anxiety disorders, the addiction crisis, the opioid crisis."[215]

---

213. Quoted in Perspectiva, "What Is Metamodernism."
214. Perspectiva, "What Is Metamodernism."
215. Quoted in Brierley, *Surprising Rebirth of Belief in God*, 192.

Rowson talks of "the mystic beyond,"[216] and recognizes that:

> modernity [arguably] severed the connection between the good, the true and the beautiful—it . . . broke them apart—so you have a . . . scientific truth severed from the . . . ethics and aesthetics of the good and the beautiful; and one of the things metamodernism has to do is to take the responsibility of bringing these back together . . . The truth that I'd be looking for is one that contains goodness and beauty as a kind of integral part of it.[217]

Of course, a divine truth "that contains goodness and beauty as a kind of integral part of it" is at the core of every monotheistic pre-modern worldview! Isn't it possible, then, that a contemporary version of monotheistic pre-modernism might turn out to *be* the post-postmodernism our culture is longing for? Isn't it possible that solving the "meaning crisis" requires us to recover "the connection between the good, the true and the beautiful," to protect "the solidity of felt experience," and to escape the modern-cum-postmodern "claustrophobia of the chest" by allowing the "sacred . . . to be heard" thorough a contemporary version of a monotheistic spirituality?

Metamodernism and History

If there might be "something out there"[218] in "the mystic beyond,"[219] don't we have to be open to the possibility that, far from being content to knock at the borders of our perceived reality, it might be the sort of thing that can take, and could have already taken, the initiative, even in a historically accessible act of self-revelation?

Simone Stirner argues that whereas "postmodernism announced the death of the subject"[220] metamodernism heralds "a paradigm shift. The subject reappears and it comes with other dismissed categories such as trust, belief, coherence and even love."[221] Such a paradigm shift seems to imply we should be prepared to exercise trust (albeit a duly skeptical trust, alert to any indications of unreliability) in the apparently sincere

---

216. Quoted in Perspectiva, "What Is Metamodernism."
217. Perspectiva, "What Is Metamodernism."
218. What Is Metamodern?, "Talking Metamodernism with Tim Vermeulen."
219. Perspectiva, "What Is Metamodernism?"
220. Stirner, "Notes on the State of the Subject," §1.
221. Stirner, "Notes on the State of the Subject," §5.

testimony of our fellow humans. And that includes the testimony that reaches us through the documents that were subsequently gathered together into the New Testament.[222] To strike the appropriate critical combination of trust and skepticism in examining and explaining such evidence is the task of the historian.

Can such a critical combination of trust and skepticism be achieved? Gregg Henriques, Marcia Gralha, Brendan Graham Dempsey, and Layman Pascal jointly affirm that:

> While the metamodern sensibility embraces the modernist ability to ground knowledge in true claims about reality through empirical methods, it also acknowledges its limitations due to social and subjective elements of human culture.[223]

Note that acknowledging these "limitations" does not mean rejecting the reality of "knowledge" grounded "in true claims about reality" gained through "empirical methods." Note, too, that the philosophical assumptions held by a culture or an individual needn't be assumptions that encourage gullibility or that obfuscate truth. Instead, they can be properly skeptical assumptions that discourage gullibility and disclose truth. Acknowledging and addressing the limitations of searching for "true claims about reality through empirical methods" is the province of a properly formulated skepticism that critically considers the criteria by which we collect *evidence*, the criteria by which we choose the best *explanation* of that evidence, and how our worldview *expectations* impinge upon these tasks.

If everyone brings worldview expectations to the task of historical inquiry, does this mean that we are doomed to talk past each other from hermetically sealed scholarly silos? I don't believe so, because at least some of us are able to agree on a common commitment to critical standards such as: rejecting internally incoherent theories of knowledge, refusing to use less than indubitable worldview expectations as the basis for begging the question against a historical claim regardless of the evidence in its favor, and revising our historical beliefs under the weight of sufficient counter-evidence according to carefully formulated criteria of evidence and explanation. Commitment to scholarly standards such as these does not mean that historical arguments will always, or even usually, be resolved;

---

222. On why various writings made it into the New Testament, see Williams, "New Testament Canon" (YouTube playlist); Comfort and Driesbach, *Many Gospels of Jesus*; Hill, *Who Chose the Books of the New Testament?*; and *Who Chose the Gospels?*

223. Henriques et al., "What Is Metamodern Spirituality?"

but they do at least mean that scholarly arguments can be engaged in and that progress, even resolution, is possible.

Getting at the Jesus of History

If we use "the historical Jesus" as a phrase designating the flesh and blood person who was born in Israel under the auspices of the Roman Empire circa 5 BC,[224] and who was killed by crucifixion[225] and buried[226] near Jerusalem in 33 (or perhaps 30) AD,[227] in all of his feeding-trough-to-borrowed-grave particularities, then we may use "the Jesus of history" as a phrase designating the somewhat vague and more or less approximate "picture" of the historical Jesus that we believe the application of a "properly skeptical" process of historical inquiry warrants.[228]

Once upon a time (from 1936–67 in the UK), televisions displayed moving pictures in "black and white" at a resolution of 405 lines;[229] but that was and is enough to let people witness the coronation of Queen Elizabeth II in 1953.[230] Likewise, for all that the above description of "the Jesus of history" highlights the gap between past actuality on the one hand and the present-day results of historical research on the other, even a vague and approximate "picture" can be enough to reliably bring us face to face with significant realities.

---

224. See Humphreys, "Star of Bethlehem"; Maier, "Date of the Nativity."
225. See Bishop, "Historical Problems with Islam's View"; Williams, *Getting at Jesus*, 257–68 and 310–14.
226. See Craig, "Historicity of the Empty Tomb"; Evans, "Resurrection of Jesus."
227. See Köstenberger, "April 3, AD 33"; Köstenberger et al., *Final Days of Jesus*.
228. See Craig, *Reasonable Faith*, 296–97.
229. Baird, "Beginning of the End."
230. See Archive of Recorded Church Music, "BBC TV Coronation."

Fig. 4. Philip, Duke of Edinburgh, giving allegiance to his wife, Queen Elizabeth II, during her coronation ceremony in 1953.[231]

Of course, we are surrounded by many different and often mutually exclusive portraits of Jesus (for example, Jewish, Christian, and Islamic portraits of Jesus overlap but are fundamentally incompatible); and many of these portraits, including the incompatible ones, lay claim to historical warrant. Much of the difference between attempts to offer a historically warranted description of "the historical Jesus" can be explained by: (1) the worldview *expectations* that are brought to bear in this venture, (2) the methodological approach taken to establishing what will count as *evidence* that needs to be taken into account, and (3) the methodological approach taken to establishing the best *explanation* of that evidence.

Establishing Evidence

> A historical fact is something that happened in history and can be verified as such through the traces history has left behind.
> —Richard J. Evans[232]

In his signature work *Christian Apologetics* (second edition, Baker, 2013), Christian philosopher and apologist Norman L. Geisler (1932–2019)

---

231. Credit: https://en.wikipedia.org/wiki/Coronation_of_Elizabeth_II#/media/File:Philip,_Duke_of_Edinburgh,_giving_allegiance_to_his_wife,_Queen_Elizabeth_II,_during_her_coronation_ceremony.jpg.
232. Evans, *In Defence of History*, 76.

exemplifies what we might call the "traditional" approach to establishing the evidence to be taken into account by any historically warranted description of the historical Jesus. According to Geisler:

> The reliability of the New Testament records is a crucial link in the apologetic argument . . . if the New Testament records are historically reliable, then we can examine them to see if Jesus claimed to be . . . the Son of God.[233]

What Geisler means by "historically reliable" here is clearly something like "generally speaking historically reliable"; which we might take as an affirmation that the New Testament's historical testimony is truth-preserving to such an extent that we have *prima facie* reason to believe any historical testimony contained therein in the absence of a sufficient counter-argument.

The Traditional Approach: Textual Reliability

> The earliness and the number of manuscripts for most of the Christian documents, is unusually great. . . . [That's] very good authority for the accuracy of the text that is provided in translation in the New Testament.
> —Antony Flew[234]

Geisler's case for the general historical reliability of the New Testament has two steps. First, he argues for the *general textual reliability* of the New Testament, on the basis that:

> there are (1) more manuscripts, (2) earlier manuscripts, and (3) better copied manuscripts for the New Testament than for any other book from the ancient world. This [establishes] beyond reasonable doubt the reliability of the New Testament writings as an accurate copy of the original text.[235]

The text of the NT currently comes to us through about 23,980 manuscripts, including some 10,000 Latin manuscripts, 975 Coptic manuscripts, 350 Syriac manuscripts, and 5,700 Greek manuscripts:[236]

---

233. Geisler, *Christian Apologetics* (2nd ed.), 371.

234. In Habermas et al., *Did Jesus Rise from the Dead?*, 66.

235. Geisler, *Christian Apologetics* (2nd ed.), 363. On the *textual* reliability of the New Testament, see Williams, "Textual Reliability of the New Testament" (YouTube playlist); Mounce, *Why I Trust the Bible*; Williams, *Getting at Jesus*.

236. See Geisler, "Updating the Manuscript Evidence"; GreekNewTestament,net;

The number of Greek New Testament manuscripts (fragments or complete) as of October 2023 is 5,700. There are 135 papyri, 283 majuscules, 2,860 minuscules, and 2,422 lectionary (i.e. the New Testament text is divided into separate pericopes) manuscripts.[237]

Theologians Andreas J. Köstenberger, Darrell L. Bock, and Joshua D. Chatraw jointly comment that: "in almost every case even the most widely accepted works from ancient philosophers and historians are considered verifiable with only a small handful of available sources to vouch for them."[238] According to Geisler (writing with Frank Turek), many ancient works survive "on fewer than a dozen manuscripts [and the average is about twenty manuscripts], yet few historians question the historicity of the events those works describe."[239] Homer's circa eighth-century BC *Iliad* provides the closest comparison to the New Testament on this score, with recent discoveries pushing the number of manuscripts from the oft-quoted 643 up to about 1900.[240] However, classical literature only offers a very rough point of comparison, as unlike NT scholars (who count every manuscript), classicists don't count any manuscript that's clearly copied from another member of the same textual family tree. That said, the point stands that "there are a good number of manuscripts that attest to the text of the NT compared to classical authors."[241]

Of course, the New Testament manuscripts are spread across a wide range of dates, from the second to the sixteenth century (with numbers dropping off after the fifteenth-century invention of the printing press). However, as Don Stewart and Joseph M. Holden observe: "The entire New Testament text is accounted for in manuscript from within 300 years of the original writing."[242] Major early witnesses to the NT text include:

- *Codex Alexandrinus*, contains almost the entire Bible ca. AD 400

Fernandes and Larson, *Hijacking the Historical Jesus*, 73; McDowell and McDowell, *Evidence That Demands a Verdict*, 46–68.

237. GreekNewTestament.net, §9.

238. Köstenberger et al., *Truth Matters*, 112.

239. Geisler and Turek, *I Don't Have Enough Faith*, 225.

240. See Geisler, "Updating the Manuscript Evidence"; Jones, "Bibliographical Test Updated"; McDowell and McDowell, *Evidence That Demands a Verdict*, 56.

241. Potter, "Revised Approach to Defending," 9.

242. Stewart and Holden, "Were the New Testament Manuscripts Copied," 193.

- *Codex Sinaiticus*, contains the whole NT (and about half of the Old Testament) ca. AD 350
- *Codex Vaticanus*, contains complete copies of the four Gospels (along with most of the rest of the Bible) ca. AD 325–350
- *The Chester Beatty Papyri*, contains major portions of all four Gospels and Acts ca. AD 250
- *The Bodmer Papyri*, contains several pages of Luke and most of John ca. AD 200

Whole pages of Gospels appear within about 100 to 150 years, and there are Gospel manuscript fragments from within about 50 to 200 years of the autographs. Indeed, "paleographers have documented at least 120 Greek manuscripts that date to within three centuries of the original composition of the New Testament."[243] Since we know "a manuscript could survive [in use for] 150 to 200 years as a norm,"[244] some of these could be first generation copies of the autographs!

Consider the temporal gap between the original autographs and the earliest surviving *complete* manuscript in the following representative cases from ancient literature:

Fig. 5. Temporal Gap until Our Earliest Complete Manuscript of Ancient Literature.[245]

Ancient Literature	Temporal Gap until Our Earliest Complete Manuscript
Homer's *Iliad* (epic poem composed in the 8th century BC)	ca. 1800 years
Roman poet Gaius Valerius Catullus	ca. 1,500 years
The plays of Sophocles	ca. 1,500 years
The works of Aristotle	ca. 1,400 years
The histories of Herodotus	ca. 1,350 years

243. Holden, "Were the New Testament Manuscripts Copied?"

244. Mounce, *Why I Trust the Bible*, 131.

245. Data taken from various sources including: Geisler, "Updating the Manuscript Evidence"; Collins, *Defendable Faith*, 98; Köstenberger et al., *Truth Matters*, 115; McDowell and McDowell, *Evidence That Demands a Verdict*; Moreland, *Scaling the Secular City*, 135; Morrow, *Questioning the Bible*, 96.

Ancient Literature	Temporal Gap until Our Earliest Complete Manuscript
The works of Plato	ca. 1,300 years
Thucydides's *History of the Peloponnesian War*	ca. 1,300 years
The plays of Aristophanes	ca. 1,200 years
Josephus's *Jewish War*	ca. 900 years
The poetry of Horace	ca. 900 years
The histories of Suetonius	ca. 800 years
The surviving books of the *Annals* of Tacitus	ca. 800 years
The writings of Pliny the Younger	ca. 750 years
Pliny the Elder's *Historia Naturalis*	ca. 400 years
Gaius's *Institutes of Roman Law*	ca. 300 years

Note that whereas Homer's *Iliad* was the closest textual comparison to the NT in terms of the sheer number of available manuscripts, it fares poorly in terms of this "time gap" metric. Apologist David Cloud reports that "the oldest entire manuscripts of Homer's writings are from the 10th and 11th centuries AD, at least 1,800 years later."[246] Moreover, according to Lynnette Wofford: "Our earliest extant papyrus fragments of the *Iliad* are from the Ptolemaic period (fourth and third century BC) and thus reflect some degree of editorial intervention by Alexandrian scholars."[247]

Figure 6 compares the gap between the autograph and *the earliest extant complete manuscript copies* for both the NT Gospels and a dozen representative ancient literary examples.

---

246. Cloud, "Illiad vs the New Testament," §2.
247. Wofford, "When Was Homer's Iliad Written?," §4.

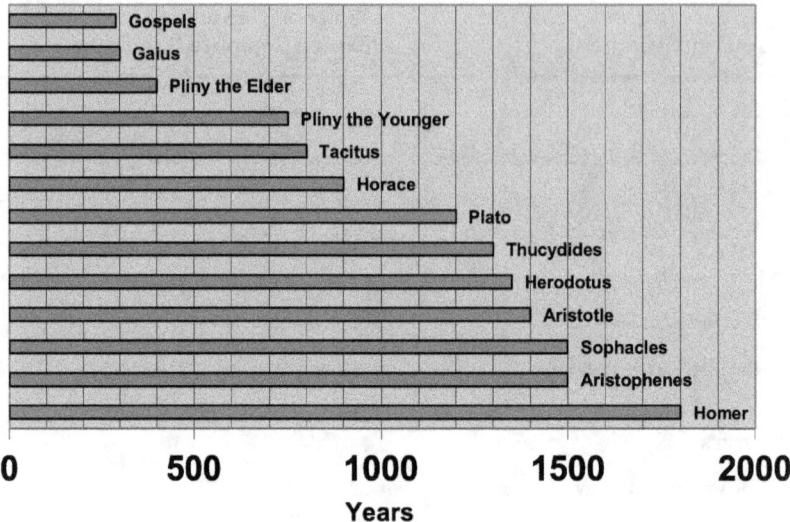

Fig. 6. Temporal Gap between Autographs and Earliest Extant Complete Copies.

As Geisler notes: "The average time span between the original and earliest [complete] copy of the other ancient texts [those outside the New Testament] is over 1,000 years."[248]

In sum, there is a wealth of manuscript evidence that allows textual critics to reconstruct the original wording of the New Testament with a high degree of confidence:

> the abundance of manuscripts and the antiquity of manuscripts, when run through the mill of text-critical methodology, allows us to know with a very high level of probability what the evangelists and other New Testament authors wrote.[249]

As theologian Timothy Paul Jones explains:

> The 5,700 or so [Greek] New Testament manuscripts that are available to us may differ from one another in as many as 400,000 places—and there are only 138,000 or so words in the Greek New Testament in the first place.... [However] Most of these 400,000 variations stem from differences in spelling, word order, or the relationships between nouns and definite articles—variants that are easily recognizable and, in most cases, virtually

---

248. Geisler and Bocchino, *Unshakable Foundations*, 257.
249. Roberts, *Can We Trust the Gospels?*, 37.

unnoticeable in translations . . . . Most important, *none* of the differences affects any central element of the Christian faith.[250]

Hence, as Bart Ehrman concludes: "Scholars are convinced that we can reconstruct the original words of the New Testament with reasonable (although probably not 100 percent) accuracy."[251]

The Traditional Approach: Testimonial Reliability

> The New Testament is a basically reliable source of information about the life of Jesus.
>
> —Richard Swinburne[252]

Having established the *general textual reliability* of the New Testament, Geisler proceeds to argue for the *general testimonial reliability* of the New Testament:

> As for the reliability of the New Testament writers as conveyers of the truth of the events of which they spoke . . . we have more writers, whose accounts are based on more eyewitnesses . . . which possesses more internal evidence . . . supported by more archaeological evidence, and attested by more non-Christian writers than any book from ancient times that the world has ever seen![253]

As William Lane Craig comments:

> Radical critics still get a free pass from the press today for their sensational assertions, but they are being increasingly marginalized within the academy, as scholarship has come to a new appreciation of the historical reliability of the New Testament documents.[254]

---

250. Jones, *Misquoting Truth*, 42, 43, and 44.

251. Bart Ehrman, *New Testament: Historical Introduction to the Early Christian Writings* (3rd ed.), 481, quoted in Stewart, *Reliability of the New Testament*, 31.

252. Swinburne, *Was Jesus God?*, 99.

253. Geisler, *Christian Apologetics* (2nd ed.), 363–364. On the *testimonial* reliability of the New Testament, see McGrew, *Testimonies to the Truth*; and *Hidden in Plain View*; Williams, Peter J., *Can We Trust the Gospels?*; Williams, *Getting at Jesus*.

254. Craig, *On Guard*, 183.

As philosopher Lydia McGrew observes, this appreciation comes from simply "holding the Gospels [and other NT literature] up to the standards that are applicable to other ancient works."[255]

McGrew sorts evidence for the reliability of any source of putatively historical testimony into two categories: internal evidence and external evidence. Applied to literature such as the New Testament Gospels, internal evidences mostly concern:

> ways in which the books look truthful by corresponding to what we know about how truthful people talk and write. They include undesigned coincidences, unnecessary details, unexplained allusions, reconcilable variation, and unity of personalities.[256]

External evidences concern the use of:

> information from outside the canonical books of the Bible to support factual statements made within the biblical books. These include information about geography, archaeology, customs, and rulers.[257]

The tight connection between the NT Gospels and their testimonial sources is confirmed by research summarized by Cambridge New Testament scholar Peter J. Williams in his book *Can We Trust the Gospels?* (Crossway, 2018), which documents "a plethora of ways in which the Gospel writers show that they are clearly familiar with the times, places, and customs of Jesus' day, including the local geography."[258] In short, the NT exhibits a historical verisimilitude that would in all likelihood be lacking in material written by authors informationally detached from the life and times of Jesus.

Again, the New Testament's testimony has been the subject of extensive *archaeological* confirmation.[259] In my own research into the currently available archaeological evidence, I have been fascinated to discover material evidence able to demonstrate and/or confirm (with varying degrees of plausibility) that:

---

255. McGrew, *Testimonies to the Truth*, ix.

256. McGrew, *Testimonies to the Truth*, vii–viii. See Williams, "Undesigned Coincidences in the Gospels" (YouTube playlist).

257. McGrew, *Testimonies to the Truth*, vii.

258. Brierley, *Surprising Rebirth of Belief in God*, 117.

259. See Evans, *Jesus and the Remains of History*; Evans, *Jesus and His World*; Williams, *Digging for Evidence*.

- *Jesus, son of Joseph and brother of James* (who was buried in Jerusalem in the middle of the first century), *existed* in the early-middle first century.
- Jesus *was crucified* (which probably killed him).
- Victims of Roman crucifixion *could be buried*.
- Jesus *was buried* (and thus probably dead) in a *now empty* Jerusalem tomb that was just outside the first-century city walls.
- Grave robbery was an offence that may have been particularly associated with Nazareth, where the NT says Jesus lived, by the middle of the first century AD (lending credence to the empty tomb).
- Despite his culturally shameful crucifixion, *Jesus was considered divine* by some people in the near east within *about 50 to 200 years* of his execution.
- Despite his culturally shameful crucifixion, Jesus was held to be divine *in the Judeo-Christian sense* in the early third century, ca. AD 200–230 (over a century before the Council of Nicea).
- The New Testament Gospels have been *repeatedly verified* by archaeological discoveries relating to places, people, culture, and beliefs, which encourages us to trust them on matters we can't independently verify in this way.[260]

Of course, historians may well use a combination of internal and external data to determine something like the date and/or authorship of a historical document (and the strongest argument for the historical reliability of a document is the cumulative case made by all of the internal and external evidences taken together).

The internal and external evidence taken together indicates that the canonical Gospels compare favorably with other ancient works of history in terms of the temporal interval between their date of publication and the events they claim to report (see figure 7). The average gap between a historical event and a published report of that event for the non-biblical sources listed in figure 7 is about eighty-eight years. Even if we exclude Plutarch's *Lives*, the average temporal gap for the remaining non-biblical texts is about fifty-nine years. The average lapse between the four Gospels and the events they report is (on the dating I assign to them) just over

---

260. See FOCLOnline, "Archaeological Evidence for Jesus"; Williams, *Getting at Jesus*.

forty-five years. This drops to about thirty-eight years for the Synoptic Gospels, and less if we exclude Matthew and Luke's stories about Jesus's infancy. Indeed, one can see that even on a "liberal" dating of the canonical Gospels (which would place Mark ca. 60–75, Matthew 65–85, and Luke ca. AD 65–95[261]), they would still count as relatively "early" sources by the standards of ancient historiography.

Fig. 7. Temporal Interval between Events and Reports.[262]

Author/ Work	Reported Events	Report Published	Lapse between Events & Report	Average Lapse
Mark	ca. AD 30–33	ca. AD 49	ca. 16–19 yrs	ca. 17.5 yrs
Luke	ca. 6 BC–AD 33	ca. AD 60	ca. 27–66 yrs	ca. 46.5 yrs
Matthew	ca. 6 BC–AD 33	ca. AD 65	ca. 32–71 yrs	ca. 51.5 yrs
John	ca. AD 30–33	ca. AD 98	ca. 65–68 yrs	ca. 66.5 yrs
Pliny, *Letters*	AD 97–112	AD 100–112	0–3 yrs	1.5 yrs
Thucydides, *History*	431–411 BC	410–400 BC	0–30 yrs	15 yrs
Xenophon, *Anabasis*	401–399 BC	385–375 BC	15–25 yrs	20 yrs
Polybius, *History*	200–120 BC	150 BC	20–70 yrs	45 yrs
Tacitus, *Annuls*	AD 14–68	ca. AD 100–110	ca. 32–96 yrs	ca. 64 yrs
Heroditus, *History*	546–478 BC	430–425 BC	48–121 yrs	84.5 yrs
Suetonius, *Lives*	50 BC–AD 95	ca. AD 120	ca. 25–170 yrs	ca. 97.5 yrs
Josephus—*War*	200 BC–AD 70	ca. AD 80	ca. 10–280 yrs	ca. 145 yrs
Plutarch, *Lives*	500 BC–AD 70	ca. AD 100	ca. 30–600 yrs	ca. 315 yrs

Much more could be said along these lines, but in sum: "the available evidence from a variety of angles confirms the strong foundation on

261. See Roberts, *Can We Trust the Gospels?*, 58.

262. For a justification of the Gospel dates used in this table, see Williams, *Getting at Jesus* on the Synoptic Gospels, and chs. 2 and 3 in this book, on the Fourth Gospel. Some data in fig. 7 sourced from Newman, "Miracles", 443.

which we can base the general reliability of the New Testament reports of the historical Jesus."[263] A plethora of standard tests for historical authenticity find application to the New Testament's historical testimony and warrants an inference to the conclusion that this testimony is, at least generally speaking, historically reliable.

Geisler's "traditional" approach constructs a historical argument for the *general* textual and testimonial reliability of the New Testament before using the New Testament's testimony to warrant a historical portrait of Jesus as someone who both laid claim to divinity and provided miraculous confirmations of that claim. Again, the case for this historical portrait has two parts.

The Traditional Approach: Evidence That Jesus Promulgated a "High Christology"

First, according to Geisler:

> After reviewing these historically reliable documents for what Jesus actually taught concerning his own origin and nature, we find both indirect implications and explicit statements that Jesus claimed to be God Almighty, the Creator of the universe in human flesh.[264]

Indeed, the New Testament testifies to a variety of ways in which Jesus laid claim to divinity through a combination of his words and deeds. N. T. Wright summarizes this data by stating that "Jesus was aware of a call, a vocation, to do and be what, according to the scriptures, only Israel's God gets to do and be."[265] As theologian Michael F. Bird explains:

> Jesus identified himself as a divine agent with a unique authority and a unique relationship with Israel's God. In addition, he spoke as one who speaks for God in an immediate sense and believed himself to be embodying the very person of God in his mission to renew and restore Israel.[266]

---

263. Habermas, "Recent Perspectives on the Reliability," §13.
264. Geisler, *Christian Apologetics* (2nd ed.), 391.
265. Wright, *Simply Christian*, 101.
266. Bird, "Did Jesus Think He Was God?," 46.

Hence, as J. P. Moreland concludes, "a high Christology goes back to Jesus himself."[267]

A separate line of argumentation that supports the same conclusion comes from considering the view of Jesus formed by the first generation of Christians. The New Testament letters "date mainly from the period AD 49–69, and provide confirmation of the importance and interpretations of Jesus in this formative period."[268] These letters prove that "a concept of a divine Jesus was already present, at the latest, within sixteen to twenty years after the crucifixion."[269] For example, Paul's mid-century epistles contain creeds and hymns (e.g., Rom 1:3–4; 1 Cor 11:23 ff.; 15:3–8; Phil 2:6–11; Col 1:15–18; 1 Tim 2:8) that had become "standard, recognized creeds and hymns well before their incorporation into Paul's letters."[270] These creeds and hymns "consistently present a portrait of a miraculous and divine Jesus who rose from the dead."[271]

In short, belief in the divinity of Jesus stems from the first generation of Jesus's followers, and this belief is indirect evidence that Jesus himself "claimed to be God Almighty, the Creator of the universe in human flesh."[272] As Paul Copan observes: "Orthodox Jews considered worshipping a mere human blasphemous and detestable (Acts 10:25–26; 14:11–15), so the church's without-controversy acceptance of Christ-worship is stunning."[273] The most plausible explanation of this early belief in the divinity of Jesus is that Jesus himself encouraged people to relate to him in these terms, and did so in a manner sufficiently compelling to convince them that this theological innovation was warranted. As philosopher Anthony O'Hear observes:

> We should remember that [Jesus's] first followers were pious Jews, to whom the claims being made would have seemed blasphemous had they not been given strong reason to believe them—and where better than from Jesus himself?[274]

---

267. Moreland, *God Question*, 111.
268. McGrath, *Jesus*, 69.
269. Moreland, *Scaling the Secular City*, 148.
270. Moreland, *Scaling the Secular City*, 148–49.
271. Moreland, *Scaling the Secular City*, 149.
272. Geisler, *Christian Apologetics* (2nd ed.), 391.
273. Copan, *True for You but Not for Me*, 167.
274. O'Hear, *Jesus for Beginners*, 84.

The Traditional Approach: Evidence for Divinity

Second, Geisler seeks to verify Jesus's claim to divinity on purely historical grounds, arguing that the best explanation of the relevant evidence is that Jesus's claims were genuinely verified by a convergence of miracles:

> Miracles associated with Christ's claim to be God are acts of God that confirm him to be the Son of God . . . . And in Jesus's case there is a convergence of three great miraculous happenings—prophecy, his sinless life and miraculous deeds, and his resurrection—that lead forthrightly to the conclusion that he alone is the unique Son of God.[275]

As Michael F. Bird affirms: "Jesus made extravagant claims about himself as to his authority, mission, and origin, and the resurrection was a divine affirmation that those claims were good."[276]

Secular philosopher Michael Ruse says he can "agree on the fairly uncontroversial claim that if the miracles of the Gospels did occur, then we have some pretty strong evidence for the truth of Christianity."[277] In particular, Ruse affirms that "if Jesus was really dead on Friday and really alive on Sunday, then I for one will be satisfied."[278] I submit that the principle obstacle in attempting to satisfy someone like Ruse as to the truth of Christianity is not historical, but philosophical. As R. T. France observed:

> At the level of their literary and historical character we have good reason to treat the gospels seriously. . . . Beyond that point, the decision as to how far a scholar is willing to accept the record they offer is likely to be influenced more by his openness to a "supernaturalist" world-view than by strictly historical considerations.[279]

Assessing Geisler's Traditional Approach

As a "classical" apologist,[280] Geisler explicitly constructs his historical case for a Christian understanding of the historical Jesus within the context

---

275. Geisler, *Christian Apologetics* (2nd ed.), 393. On Jesus's other miraculous deeds and his fulfilment of prophecy, see Williams, *Understanding Jesus*, chs. 4 and 6.

276. Bird, "Did Jesus Think He Was God?," 67.

277. Ruse, *Atheism*, 161.

278. Ruse, *Atheism*, 161.

279. France, "Gospels as Historical Sources for Jesus," 86.

280. For a discussion of apologetic methodologies, see Boa and Bowman, *Faith Has*

of a theistic worldview for which he has already argued on philosophical grounds. Geisler outlines his overall argument as follows:

> We have shown the following: (1) truth is knowable . . . (2) the opposite of true is false . . . (3) in opposition to all other views of God . . . a theistic God exists . . . (4) in a theistic world, miracles are possible . . . (5) miracles can be used to confirm a truth claim within a theistic worldview . . . (6) the New Testament documents are historically reliable . . . (7) those documents report that Jesus claimed to be God in human flesh. . . . Now we will show that (8) those documents provide multiple lines of miraculous evidence that Jesus is God, as he claimed to be.[281]

Geisler's approach to the historical Jesus has much to recommend it. However, while the historical case for Jesus is undoubtedly at its strongest within the context of a theistic worldview, historical argumentation for a Christian understanding of Jesus only requires the assumption that miracles *might* occur in a knowable way because God *might* exist and *might* perform miracles.[282] Moreover, having established the *textual reliability* of the NT, one can sidestep Geisler's focus on the *general testimonial reliability* of the NT by using various "criteria of historical authenticity" to argue directly for the *particular testimonial reliability* of various historical facts about Jesus.

The Criteria of Authenticity Approach to Testimonial Reliability

While the historical criteria of authenticity used by "Tradition Criticism"[283] cannot *guarantee* the historicity of data to which they apply, they do provide reasons to take such data with greater seriousness than would otherwise be the case.[284] All things being equal, the more criteria

---

Its Reasons; Cowan, *Five Views on Apologetics*; Morley, *Mapping Apologetics*; Williams, *Apologetics in 3D*.

281. Geisler, *Christian Apologetics* (2nd ed.), 391.

282. See Evans, *Historical Christ*; Williams, *Getting at Jesus*, ch. 1.

283. Bock, *Studying the Historical Jesus*, 199.

284. On historical criteria of authenticity, see Williams, "Historical Criteria of Authenticity" (YouTube playlist); Craig, *Reasonable Faith*, 298; Habermas, *On the Resurrection*, ch. 2; Stein, "Criteria for the Gospel's Authenticity"; Williams, *Getting at Jesus*, 242–48.

of authenticity a saying or event passes, the more seriously we must take it. As William Lane Craig explains:

> It is somewhat misleading to call these "criteria," for they aim at stating sufficient, not necessary, conditions of historicity . . . what the criteria really amount to are statements about the effect of certain types of evidence upon the probability of various sayings or events . . . all else being equal . . . the probability of some event or saying is greater given, for example, its multiple attestation than it would have been without it . . . these "criteria" . . . focus on a particular saying or event and give evidence for thinking that specific element of Jesus' life to be historical, regardless of the general reliability of the document in which the particular saying or event is reported.[285]

Thus, as theologian Darrell L. Bock observes: "One should remember that failure to meet the criteria does not establish a text's inauthenticity, because the criteria cover only a limited amount of assessment factors,"[286] such that "these criteria serve better as a supplemental argument for authenticity."[287] After all: "The Gospels are prima facie evidence for what the historical Jesus said and did."[288]

Then again, the criteria of early sources may find application to a whole document and/or to sources within a document. The New Testament connects us to multiple early sources that can be dated to within two decades of the crucifixion. For example, on the basis of internal evidence, most New Testament scholars infer the existence of a written source of some 250 verses shared by the Gospels of "Matthew" and "Luke," a source that therefore pre-dates both Gospels (which are themselves relatively "early," first-century sources). Named after the German word for source/spring (*Quelle*), "Q" may even have been written during the lifetime of Jesus, perhaps by Matthew the tax collector.[289] As Paul Barnett notes: "'Q' texts are cited or echoed in letters of Paul written in the mid-fifties."[290] Indeed, Dale Allison "concludes that Paul knew material from Mark,

---

285. Craig, *Reasonable Faith*, 298.

286. Bock, *Studying the Historical Jesus*, 202–3.

287. Bock, *Studying the Historical Jesus*, 202–3.

288. Wenham and Walton, *Exploring the New Testament*, 139. For a discussion of the epistemology of testimony in relation to the New Testament, see Williams, *Understanding Jesus*, ch. 2.

289. See Williams, *Getting at Jesus*, 204–205.

290. Barnett, *Birth of Christianity*, 147.

material common to Luke and Matthew ("Q"), material unique to Luke "L," and perhaps material unique to Matthew ("M")."[291]

Several early sources are to be found in Luke's Gospel sequel, known as "Acts." As James Dunn explains: "Luke has sought out much earlier material and has incorporated it into the brief formalized expositions which he attributes to Peter, Stephen, Paul, etc."[292] Hugh Montefiore comments:

> These speeches have been examined in considerable detail, and there are indications that the author did use sources for them ... there is the presence of Semitisms in the speeches. ... It is held by many that these speeches represent the primitive *kerygma* (preaching of the Gospel in the early Church).[293]

Bart Ehrman concurs that:

> the speeches in Acts are particularly notable because they are, in many instances, based ... on oral traditions ... these speeches incorporate materials from the traditions about Jesus that existed long before Luke put pen to papyrus.[294]

Moreover, remember that Paul's letters contain creeds and hymns (e.g., Rom 1:3–4; 1 Cor 11:23 ff.; 15:3–8; Phil 2:6–11; Col 1:15–18; 1 Tim 2:8) that had become "standard, recognized creeds and hymns well before their incorporation into Paul's letters,"[295] and which "consistently present a portrait of a miraculous and divine Jesus who rose from the dead."[296] A prime example of this material is the list of resurrection appearances in 1 Cor 15.[297] Jake O'Connell comments that:

> the pre-Pauline material of 1 Corinthians 15:3–8, which surely dates to within years of the resurrection, and is nearly universally regarded as summarising extremely early material, ensures that the appearances enumerated there cannot be legendary.[298]

Jewish NT scholar Pinchas Lapide writes of the 1 Cor 15 creed that:

---

291. Barnett, *Birth of Christianity*, 125.

292. Dunn, *Why Believe in Jesus' Resurrection?*, 22.

293. Montefiore, *Womb and the Tomb*, 134. See also Habermas, *On the Resurrection*, 418.

294. Ehrman, *Did Jesus Exist?*, 109 and 111.

295. Moreland, *Scaling the Secular City*, 148–49.

296. Moreland, *Scaling the Secular City*, 149.

297. Habermas, "Tracing Jesus' Resurrection," 202–16.

298. O'Connell, "Jesus' Resurrection and Collective Hallucinations," 75.

this unified piece of tradition which soon was solidified into a formula of faith may be considered as *a statement of eyewitnesses* for whom the experience of the resurrection became the turning point of their lives.[299]

Atheist New Testament scholar James Crossley concludes that in the 1 Cor 15 creed we have "reliable reports"[300] from "eyewitnesses"[301] that "must be taken very seriously."[302]

The canonical Gospels alone provide four sources relating to Jesus's death, burial, empty tomb, and resurrection appearances. Adding information from Peter and Paul in speeches from Acts, from Paul in his own letters, and from the creed quoted by Paul in 1 Cor 15 gives us *seven early sources* of testimony about the death, burial, and resurrection of Jesus. This testimony is presented in *multiple forms* and includes *several eyewitness sources*.

Fig. 8. Seven Early Sources on the Resurrection.

	Peter in Acts	1 Cor 15 Creed	Mark's Passion Source	Paul in Acts & Letters	L	M	John
Death	2:23 & 36; 10:39	15:3	15:37	13:28–29	Luke 23:46	Matt 27:24	19:30
Burial		15:4	15:46	13:29	Luke 23:53	Matt 27:64	19:42
Empty Tomb			16:6		Luke 24:2, 10, 12, 23	Matt 27:59	20:2, 6
Appearances	2:32; 10:40–42	15:4–5	16:7	13:31, 22:6–9 & 26:13–14; 1 Cor 9:1 & 15:8; Gal 1:13–17	Luke 24:12, 15, 36	Matt 28:9–10 & 16–17	20:14–29 & 21:1–25

---

299. Lapide, *Resurrection of Jesus*, 99, my italics.
300. Crossley, *Date of Mark's Gospel*, 140.
301. Crossley, "Against the Historical Plausibility," 171–86.
302. Crossley, "Against the Historical Plausibility," 186.

Fig. 9. The Earliest Sources on the Resurrection.

Acts 2:23–32 Peter's Pentecost Sermon from AD 33	1 Cor 15:3–5 Early Creed ca. AD 33–34	Mark 15:37—16:7 Pre-Markan Passion Narrative ca. AD 33–37	Acts 13:28–31 Paul's Pisidian Antioch Sermon ca. AD 45
You . . . put him to death by nailing him to the cross.	Christ died . . .	Jesus breathed his last.	They asked Pilate to have him executed.
	he was buried . . .	Joseph bought some linen cloth, took down the body, wrapped it in the linen, and placed it in a tomb . . .	They took him down from the tree and laid him in a tomb.
God has raised this Jesus to life . . .	he was raised . . . [which implies an empty grave or tomb]	He has risen! [The empty tomb is thereby implied]	But God raised him from the dead . . . [which implies the empty tomb]
We are all witnesses of the fact.	he appeared . . .	He is going ahead of you into Galilee. There you will see him . . .	For many days he was seen . . .

Hence a historical case for Jesus's claims,[303] and his miracles,[304] including his resurrection,[305] can be made by "arguing from a critical perspective,"[306] on the basis of evidence gathered using standard historical methods,

---

303. See Williams, "Christology" (YouTube playlist); and "Defending an Early High Christology"; Craig, "Who Was Jesus of Nazareth?"; Bird et al., *How God Became Jesus*; Bock, *Who Is Jesus?*; Bowman and Komoszewski, *Putting Jesus in His Place*; Craig, *Reasonable Faith*, ch. 7; Grindheim, *Christology in the Synoptic Gospels*; Gruneler, *New Approaches to Jesus and the Gospels*; Habermas, *Risen Jesus and Future Hope*, ch. 3; Komoszewski et al., *Reinventing Jesus*; Loke, *Origin of Divine Christology*; and *Studies on the Origin*; Overman, *Case for the Divinity of Jesus*; Williams, *Getting at Jesus*, ch. 2; Witherington, *Christology of Jesus*.

304. See Habermas, "Did Jesus Perform Miracles?"; Williams, *Getting at Jesus*, ch. 5.

305. See Williams, "Resurrection of Jesus" (YouTube playlist); and "Debating the Resurrection" (YouTube playlist); Craig, "Jesus' Resurrection"; *Did Jesus Rise from the Dead?*; *Reasonable Faith*; *Son Rises*; and *Assessing the New Testament Evidence*; Dunn, *Why Believe in Jesus' Resurrection?*; Habermas and Licona, *Case for the Resurrection of Jesus*; Habermas, *Risen Indeed*; and *On the Resurrection*; Licona, *Resurrection of Jesus*; Swinburne, *Resurrection of God Incarnate*; Williams, *Getting at Jesus*; Wright, *Resurrection of the Son of God*.

306. Habermas, *Risen Jesus and Future Hope*, 96.

such as making arguments using data from multiple early sources. For example:

> Of the five independent sources often recognized in the Gospel accounts—Mark, the Q sayings, the material unique to Matthew (M), the material unique to Luke (L), and John—Jesus's miracles are reported in all five layers, with some specific miracle claims being included in more than one of the sources. Jesus's crucial "Son of Man" statements are also confirmed in all five Gospel sources . . . . the story of the empty tomb is reported in at least three . . . of the Gospel sources.[307]

As historian Paul L. Maier observes: "Many facts from antiquity rest on just one ancient source, while two or three sources in agreement generally render the fact unimpeachable."[308]

The Criteria of Authenticity and "Minimal Facts" Approaches to the Resurrection of Jesus

In his PhD thesis and subsequent related research, philosopher Gary R. Habermas sets aside questions about the *general testimonial reliability* of the New Testament by using standard criteria of historical authenticity to argue *directly* for a set of *specific historical facts* about Jesus that can underpin a case for his resurrection.[309]

To construct what he calls "the minimal facts argument" for the resurrection, Habermas additionally sifts and categorizes these facts in terms of their acceptance by critical scholars in relevant academic fields:

> The Minimal Facts Argument proposes that even by using only those few historical data that are attested by many evidences each and that are therefore accepted as historical by a high percentage of scholars in the field, we have enough of a basis to show that Jesus' resurrection happened.[310]

Habermas explains that:

---

307. Habermas, *On the Resurrection*, 46.
308. Maier, *Genuine Jesus*, 264.
309. See Williams, "'Minimal Facts' Approach to the Resurrection" (YouTube playlist); Habermas and Licona, *Case for the Resurrection of Jesus*; Habermas, *On the Resurrection*; and *Risen Indeed*.
310. Habermas, "My Magnum Opus on the Minimal Facts Argument."

> My Minimal Facts Argument in favor of Jesus' resurrection . . . has two requirements for the historical facts that are used: each must be confirmed by several strong and independent arguments, plus the vast majority of even critical scholars must recognize the occurrence's historical nature. The critical scholars can be liberal, skeptical, agnostic, or even atheist, as long as they are specialists in a relevant field of study, such as New Testament. Of these two requirements . . . the initial standard concerning strong evidential back-up is by far the most crucial.[311]

Habermas uses his secondary requirement as a rhetorical move to deflect accusations of bias by showing that even scholars with non-Christian worldviews accept the "minimal facts," presumably due to the strength of the historical arguments for them. Indeed, Habermas describes his twin requirements for "events . . . established by an abundance of strong evidences,"[312] and accepted by "the vast majority of published contemporary scholars with credentials in relevant fields of study"[313] as "methodological moves" that "have the benefit of bypassing much of the often-protracted preliminary discussions which frequently take place regarding which data are permissible by beginning with a sort of 'lowest common denominator' approach."[314]

Habermas insists that well supported data beyond those admitted by the "vast majority" of relevant scholars can and should be taken into account as part of a supplementary argument, or as a tiebreaker between otherwise evenly matched hypotheses. So, in Habermas's "minimal facts" methodology, while a high level of common consent is *desirable*, good evidence marshalled by the criteria of authenticity is *essential*.[315] As Habermas observes: "If the case for historicity already has been resolved, this is an independent conclusion that stands regardless of whether any particular head count of scholars agrees."[316]

In his balanced and broadly sympathetic critique of "Habermas's Minimal Facts Argument," philosopher and theologian Robert B. Stewart comments that:

---

311. Habermas, "Minimal Facts on the Resurrection."
312. Habermas, *On the Resurrection*, 91.
313. Habermas, *On the Resurrection*, 91.
314. Habermas, *On the Resurrection*, 94.
315. See Stewart, "On Habermas's Minimal Facts Argument."
316. Habermas, *On the Resurrection*, 91.

> In historical investigation, one should take note of all the relevant data.... [The "minimal facts"] method, with its insistence upon 90-percent or higher consensus, may be too clever by half. By requiring at least 90-percent agreement, it may force historians to ignore facts that are potentially even more helpful in discovering the truth than those that Habermas accepts as minimal facts.... Habermas's method demands that he ignore propositions for which he has good reasons to believe—indeed, propositions that he does believe. I think this is why Habermas and Licona insist on mentioning ... "Second Order" facts.... Having more true beliefs rather than fewer is almost always advantageous, *so long as one doesn't just believe irresponsibly*.[317]

We can distinguish between a historical methodology that uses criteria of authenticity from a "minimal facts" approach that combines the "criteria of authenticity" with the requirement that "the vast majority of even critical scholars must recognize the occurrence's historical nature."[318] Furthermore, one can deploy a "minimal facts" approach with different degrees of strictness with respect to the required scholarly majority, and with or without appealing to well supported data beyond those admitted by that majority, as the rhetorical situation dictates.

Habermas lists some of the facts that are generally acknowledged by the relevant community of scholars, regardless of their personal worldview:

> The vast majority of critical scholars ... whatever their personal beliefs, espouse or at least concede that Jesus died by Roman crucifixion and that his disciples experienced grief and disillusionment at his death, usually allowing that Jesus' burial tomb was later found empty. Then, due to experiences that they believed were appearances of the risen Jesus, the disciples were transformed, even to the point of being willing to die for their faith. At a very early date they began to proclaim the death and resurrection of Jesus Christ, and the church was born shortly afterward, founded on this gospel message. Even a few former sceptics, such as James, the brother of Jesus, and

---

317. Stewart, "On Habermas's Minimal Facts Argument," 6, 7, and 9. For additional critiques of the "minimal facts" approach, see McGrew, "On the Minimal Facts Case for the Resurrection"; and *Eye of the Beholder*, ch. 8.

318. Habermas, "Minimal Facts on the Resurrection." For examples of a more criteria-centric approach, see Craig, *Did Jesus Rise from the Dead?*; *Reasonable Faith*, ch. 8; and *Son Rises*.

Paul, became believers after they, too, believed that they had seen the risen Jesus.[319]

Writing with New Testament historian Michael L. Licona, Habermas notes that:

> although the empty tomb lacks the nearly universal acceptance by critical scholars that these other events enjoy, the majority of scholars still clearly seem to think that it is probably also a historical fact.[320]

Licona categorizes the empty tomb as a "second order" historical fact[321] (a fact of the type Habermas says can and should be used as part of a supplementary argument, or as a tiebreaker between otherwise evenly matched hypotheses); yet chooses to argue for the resurrection without resting any weight on the historicity of the empty tomb.[322]

With respect to the testimony concerning purported resurrection appearances, as Licona comments:

> that subsequent to Jesus' execution, a number of his followers had experiences, in individual and group settings, that convinced them that Jesus had risen from the dead and had appeared to them in some manner . . . is granted by a nearly unanimous consensus of modern scholars. . . . Scholars differ, however, on the perceived nature of the experiences.[323]

Licona and Habermas address "the perceived nature of the experiences," and argue in favor of Jesus's physical resurrection, when they consider various theories which accept that a number of Jesus's followers "had experiences, in individual and group settings, that convinced them

---

319. Habermas, "Resurrection and Agnosticism," 281–82.

320. Habermas and Licona, *Case for the Resurrection of Jesus*, 74. See Williams, "Jesus' Tomb Was Empty" (YouTube playlist); Craig, "Historicity of the Empty Tomb"; "Disciples' Inspection of the Empty Tomb"; and "Reply to Evan Fales"; Habermas, "Empty Tomb of Jesus"; National Geographic Partners, "Unsealing of Christ's Reputed Tomb"; Williams, *Getting at Jesus*, 272–78.

321. Licona, *Resurrection of Jesus*, 469.

322. See Licona, *Resurrection of Jesus*, 461–63.

323. Licona, *Resurrection of Jesus*, 372–73. As Habermas writes: "The nearly unanimous consent of critical scholars is that, *in some sense*, the early followers of Jesus thought that they had seen the risen Jesus" ("Resurrection Research from 1975," 151), my italics.

that Jesus had risen from the dead and had appeared to them in some manner."[324]

In my own published work on the resurrection, I have used criteria of authenticity not only to argue for the "minimal" fact that a number of Jesus's followers "had experiences, in individual and group settings, that convinced them that Jesus had risen from the dead and had appeared to them in some manner,"[325] but to supplement the traditional historical case for a series of specific, multi-sensory experiences in which both disciples and non-disciples, in individual and group settings, not only *see* Jesus, but *hear* or *talk with* and even *touch* him as well.[326]

Figure 10 lists specific post-burial appearances of Jesus referenced by the NT in their apparent historical order and notes the sensory modes reportedly involved in these appearances.[327]

Fig. 10. Post-Burial Appearances of Jesus.

Resurrection Witnesses	Location	Senses Involved	Sources
Mary Magdalene	Empty tomb	Saw and talked with Jesus (perhaps touching him)	John 20:11–18
At least five other women, including Joanna & Mary the mother of James	Jerusalem	Saw, heard, and touched Jesus	Matt 28:1–10 (see Luke 24:8–11)
Cleopas & Mary	Emmaus Road	Saw and talked with Jesus (perhaps touching him)	Luke 24:13–32
Peter	Unspecified	Saw Jesus	1 Cor 15:5a; Mark 16:7; & Luke 24:34
Ten disciples (and others)	Unspecified room in Jerusalem	Saw and talked with Jesus	John 20:19–23 & Luke 24:36–43

324. Licona, *Resurrection of Jesus*, 372. See Habermas and Licona, *Case for the Resurrection of Jesus*, ch. 9; Licona, *Resurrection of Jesus*, ch. 5 and appendix.

325. Licona, *Resurrection of Jesus*, 372.

326. See Williams, *Getting at Jesus*, 278–82.

327. Based on Miller, *Did Jesus Really Rise?*, 106; and Wilkins, "Gospel of Matthew," 190–91.

Resurrection Witnesses	Location	Senses Involved	Sources
Eleven disciples including Thomas	Unspecified room	Saw and talked with Jesus (perhaps touching him)	John 20:24–29; see 1 Cor 15:5b
Seven disciples	Along the sea of Galilee (Tiberius)	Saw and talked with Jesus	John 21:1–23
500 individuals at once	Unspecified/Galilee	Saw Jesus	1 Cor 15:6; Mark 16:7
Eleven disciples	Galilee	Saw and heard Jesus	Matt 28:16–20
Eleven disciples	Jerusalem	Saw and heard Jesus	Luke 24:44–49 & Acts 1:4–5
Eleven disciples	Jerusalem & Mount of Olives	Saw and heard/talked with Jesus	Luke 24:50–53 & Acts 1:6–11
Saul	Road to Damascus	Saul saw a bright, physical manifestation of Jesus, with whom he talked in the presence of companions who saw the light and heard, but did not understand, the voice talking with him[328]	1 Cor 9:1 & 15:8; Acts 9:1–19, 22:1–21, & 26:1–32

From this data, it appears we should take notice of eleven or twelve distinct reports of post-mortem appearance events (depending on whether the appearance to the five hundred at once is the same event as the appearance to the eleven disciples in Galilee, as some commentators suggest). These reports feature post-mortem appearances of Jesus to two individuals and to nine or ten groups. These appearance reports all qualify as *early* reports[329] that pass the criterion of *memorability*.[330] In addition:

---

328. See Marshall, *Acts*, 178–79 and 375; Williams, *Getting at Jesus*, 282–87.

329. As classical historian Mark D. Smith avers: "In particular, there is a significant watershed between first-generation sources, written during the lifetime of at least some who knew the person or experienced the event in question, and sources from subsequent generations" (*Final Days of Jesus*, 29).

330. As J. Warner Wallace says: "When witnesses experience something that's unique, unrepeated, and personally important or powerful, they're much more likely to remember it" (Strobel, *Case for Miracles*, 197).

- We have *multiple early, independent sources*[331] for at least one individual and three group appearances.

- The (unfortunately detail-free) reported appearance to Peter is *multiply attested in different forms*[332] and additionally passes the criterion of *historical verisimilitude*[333] (see 1 Cor 15:5's use of the Aramaic *Cephus* instead of the Greek *Petros*[334]).

- The appearance to Mary Magdalene passes the criteria of *embarrassment*[335] and *historical verisimilitude* (note the popularity of the name *Mary* and the Aramaic *Rabboni* in John 20:16).

- The *group* appearance to the other women likewise passes the criteria of *embarrassment* and *historical verisimilitude* (the most common female name at the time was *Mary*).

- The appearance to the two disciples on the Road to Emmaus (husband and wife Cleopas and Mary[336]) passes the criteria of *embarrassment* (Luke 24:25) and *historical verisimilitude*.[337]

---

331. For a discussion of the nature of independence between sources, see Williams, *Getting at Jesus*, 243–45.

332. According to John P. Meier: "The criterion of multiple attestation focuses on those saying or deeds of Jesus that are attested in more than one independent literary source and/or in more than one literary form or genre. The force of this criterion is increased if a given motif or theme is found in both literary sources and different literary forms" (*Marginal Jew*, 175).

333. As James A. Beverley and Craig A. Evans explain: "One of the most important indications of an ancient document's veracity is something historians call verisimilitude. That is, do the contents of the document match with what we know of the place, people and period described in the document?" (*Getting Jesus Right*, 22). According to Thomas R. Yoder Neufeld, the criterion of verisimilitude includes "linguistic and cultural features that fit what we know of first-century Palestine" (*Recovering Jesus*, 44).

334. Both names mean "rock."

335. As Graham Stanton notes: "traditions which would have been an embarrassment to followers of Jesus in the post-Easter period are unlikely to have been invented" (*Gospels and Jesus*, 175). On why testimony from female witness passes the criterion of embarrassment, see Williams, *Getting at Jesus*, 273–74.

336. Boice, "Who Were the Disciples on the Road to Emmaus?"

337. Note the hospitality culture and the meal etiquette of prayer and bread breaking.

- The appearance to the *group* of ten male disciples[338] (plus others) is *multiply attested in different forms* and is reported by an *eyewitness* (John[339]).
- The *multiply attested* group appearance to the eleven including Thomas passes the criteria of *embarrassment* and is likewise reported by an *eyewitness* (John).
- The *group* appearance to seven disciples by the Sea of Galilee is reported by an *eyewitness* (John). Moreover, the specific count of fish (John 20:11) is an *unintentional sign of historicity*.[340]
- The group appearance to the eleven disciples (or more) in Galilee passes the criteria of *embarrassment* due to its mention that although "they worshiped [Jesus], some doubted" (Matt 28:17).
- The appearance to Saul is *multiply attested in different forms*, including a source containing the Aramaic of Saul's name ("Saoul, Saoul, why do you persecute me?" Acts 9:4; 22:7; 26:14), and the *eyewitness* testimony of the formerly hostile Saul himself.

As for the multi-sensory content of these eleven reports:

- Jesus was reportedly *seen* on at least eleven occasions.[341]
- At least nine reports concern appearances to *groups* of two, four, seven, ten, eleven, and even five hundred people.
- While Jesus purportedly appeared to Saul rather than to his travelling companions, they nevertheless both saw the bright light and *heard a voice without understanding it*. Perhaps they didn't speak Aramaic (see Acts 26:14); or perhaps they simply couldn't make out what the voice said.[342]

---

338. Luke employs a figurative synecdoche when he writes that "the eleven" were assembled with those with them: "because Judas was now gone from them, and dead; and this being their whole number, it is used, though every one might not be present, as particularly Thomas was not; see John 20:19" (*Gill's Exposition of the Entire Bible*, "Luke 24:33"). See also Jackson, "Does the Expression 'the Eleven.'"

339. On John as the eyewitness behind the Fourth Gospel, see chs. 2 and 3. See also, Blomberg, *Historical Reliability of John's Gospel*; McGrew, *Eye of the Beholder*.

340. This criterion "argues that particularly vivid details of an eyewitness can demonstrate accurate knowledge of the environment and the event. This contributes to the credibility of a text" (Beverley and Evans, *Getting Jesus Right*, 201).

341. See Davis, *Christian Philosophical Theology*, 136–37.

342. See Marshall, *Acts*, 178–79 and 375; Williams, *Getting at Jesus*, 282–87.

- On ten occasions, it is reported that people either *heard* Jesus or *talked with Jesus* (i.e., held a conversation involving both hearing and speaking to Jesus).
- Matthew reports an appearance in which the women *touch* Jesus.
- Luke and John narrate additional appearances in which various people might be taken to touch Jesus.

Fig. 11. Criteria of Authenticity That Nine Reported Resurrection Appearances Pass (*in addition* to being *early*, historically *coherent* reports of *memorable* events).

Appearance Witnesses	Report	Eyewitness Testimony	Multiple Literarily Independent Sources	Multiple Forms	Embarrassment	Verisimilitude	Unintentional Signs of History
Mary Magdalene	John 20:11–18				X	X	X
At least five other women (incl. Joanna, Salome, & Mary the mother of James)	Matt 28:1–10 (see Luke 24:8–11)				X	X	
Cleopas & Mary	Luke 24:13–32				X	X	
Peter	1 Cor 15:5, Luke 24:34		X	X		X	X
Ten disciples (and others)	John 20:19–23 & Luke 24:36–44	X	X				
Eleven disciples including Thomas	John 20:24–29; 1 Cor 15:5b	X	X	X	X		
Seven disciples	John 21:1–25	X					X
Eleven disciples (at least)	Matt 28:16–20				X		

Appearance Witnesses	Report	Eyewitness Testimony	Multiple Literarily Independent Sources	Multiple Forms	Embarrassment	Verisimilitude	Unintentional Signs of History
Saul (and others)	1 Cor 15:8 & Acts 9:1–19, 22:1–21, & 26:1–32	X	X	X		X	

Using positive criteria of authenticity to validate specific historical evidence that can underpin one's explanation of the Jesus of history is compatible with thinking that the sources containing that evidence are generally unreliable.[343] As Gary R. Habermas and Terry L. Miethe comment:

> Our arguments [for the resurrection are] based on a *limited number* of knowable historical facts and *verified by critical procedures*. Therefore, contemporary scholars should not spurn such evidence by referring to "discrepancies" in the New Testament texts or to its general "unreliability."[344]

However, *the greater application these criteria find in those sources, the more they indicate their general reliability*. As Lydia McGrew argues:

> If you sample a loaf of bread on both ends and at several points in the middle and find it good, it would be caviling to say that perhaps just the parts you haven't tasted happen to be the moldy ones.[345]

While there's much broader case for the historical reliability of the New Testament witness to the historical Jesus than is covered by the criteria

---

343. Note that a source being unreliable is not necessarily the same thing as its being deliberately misleading.
344. Miethe and Habermas, *Why Believe?*, 273–74.
345. McGrew, *Hidden in Plain View*, 225.

of tradition criticism,³⁴⁶ as Habermas affirms: "Both may be pursued together and can complement each other."³⁴⁷

Whether by using the "traditional," "criteria of authenticity" or "minimal facts" approaches, or by using a "criteria of authenticity" or "minimal facts" approach to lay the ground for a more maximal "traditional" approach, or by combining the "criteria of authenticity" approach with the "traditional" approach, one can use properly skeptical historical methods to *establish evidence* about Jesus that should be taken into account by any academically responsible historical *explanation* thereof.

Explaining the Historical Evidence Pertaining to Jesus

> Historians are seldom if ever interested in discrete facts entirely for their own sake; they have almost always been concerned with . . . the "interconnectedness" of those facts.
>
> —Richard J. Evans³⁴⁸

With the evidence in hand, one can turn to the task of assessing different competing theories of how best to explain that evidence. Was Jesus a liar or a madman? Were the disciples deceivers, deceived, or deluded? Did someone steal Jesus's body from the tomb? Were Jesus's reported postmortem appearances hallucinations? And so on. As philosopher Angus Menuge explains:

> Historians do not use *induction* (which applies to generalizations of repeatable effects) but *abduction*, an inference to the best explanation of a singular event. According to the logic of abduction, given the available data, we are to select the best of competing explanations.³⁴⁹

The evidence shows that Jesus repeatedly said and did things that, when taken together in their cultural context, communicated a Divine self-image. While anyone can make such claims, there is a solid abductive case for inferring that the best *explanation* of the relevant historical

---

346. See McGrew, *Testimonies to the Truth*; Williams, Peter J., *Can We Trust the Gospels?*; Williams, *Getting at Jesus*.
347. Habermas, *On the Resurrection*, 128.
348. Evans, *In Defence of History*, 76.
349. Menuge, "Justified Belief in the Resurrection," 131.

evidence pertaining to the historical Jesus is that he had an *accurate* self-image of being Divine with a capital D, a cumulative convergence of evidences "that lead forthrightly to the conclusion that he alone is the unique Son of God."[350]

The warrant of any historical explanation (including the Christian doctrine of the incarnation) depends on a combination of explanatory factors, including its *simplicity*, *explanatory scope* (covering the relevant facts), *explanatory power* (the degree to which it raises the probability of the facts to be explained), *explanatory plausibility* (the degree to which our background knowledge implies an explanatory hypothesis), degree of *explanatory disconfirmation* (avoiding conflict with our background knowledge), and degree of *explanatory ad hoc-ness* (the fewer contrived, un-evidenced hypotheses, the better).[351]

For example, the resurrection hypothesis offers a relatively simple[352] explanation of the historical evidence pertaining to Jesus's death, burial, empty tomb, reported appearances, and the origins of Christianity; an explanation that combines excellent explanatory scope (i.e., *if* the resurrection happened, it would explain "why the tomb was found empty, why the disciples saw post-mortem appearances of Jesus, and why the Christian faith came into being"[353]) and power (i.e., *if* God chose to resurrect Jesus, *then* his empty tomb, reported post-mortem appearances, and the early origin of belief in Jesus's resurrection all become highly probable) with a *fair* degree of plausibility and *low* degrees of *disconfirmation* and *ad-hoc-ness* (especially if one already accepts theism). Indeed, it seems to me that in a comparative analysis with alternative explanations, the relevant evidence is best explained by the hypothesis that *Jesus was physically resurrected* (indeed, trans-physically resurrected) *by God*.[354] As N. T.

---

350. Geisler, *Christian Apologetics* (2nd ed.), 393.
351. See Williams, *Getting at Jesus*, ch. 5.
352. See Richards, "Divine Simplicity."
353. Craig, "Resurrection of Jesus."

354. See Williams, *Getting at Jesus*, especially ch. 5. See also ch. 5 and appendix 1 in this volume. See also Williams, "Resurrection of Jesus" (YouTube playlist); and "Debating the Resurrection" (YouTube playlist); Craig, "Jesus' Resurrection"; "Bodily Resurrection of Jesus"; "Dale Allison on Jesus' Empty Tomb"; and "Dale Allison on the Resurrection of Jesus"; Habermas, "Dale Allison's Resurrection Skepticism"; Craig, *Did Jesus Rise?*; *Reasonable Faith*; and *Assessing the New Testament Evidence*; Davis, *Risen Indeed*; Dunn, *Why Believe in Jesus' Resurrection?*; Habermas, "Resurrection Appearances of Jesus," 262–75; *Risen Indeed*; and *On the Resurrection*; Habermas and Licona, *Case for the Resurrection of Jesus*; Hansen, "Tactile and True," 207–28; Licona, *Resurrection of Jesus*; Loke, *Studies on the Origin*; O'Connell, *Jesus' Resurrection and Apparitions*;

Wright argues, the resurrection hypothesis "possesses unrivalled power to explain the historical data at the heart of early Christianity."[355]

Moreover, although the resurrection hypothesis posits an explanation that's miraculous—and therefore unusual, and in this respect unlikely *a priori*—the hypothesis gains plausibility from our background knowledge about the (comparative and cumulative) case for theism,[356] about Jesus's fulfillment of prophecy,[357] about the miracles[358] and exorcisms[359] associated with his ministry, and about his claims in the context of his character.

Aut Deus Aut Malus Homo

> If Jesus was not who he claimed to be, then he was either a charlatan or a madman, neither of which is plausible.
>
> —William Lane Craig[360]

However one goes about establishing Jesus's claims about himself, those claims were astonishing enough to invite charges of insanity (if his claim was sincere) or blasphemy (if his claim was insincere). But the evidence appears to show that Jesus was both *sane and sincere*. This paradox, which is more to be expected on the hypothesis of the incarnation than on atheism, lies at the heart of an ancient argument for the divinity of Jesus summarized in Latin as "*aut deus aut malus homo*," that is "either God or a bad man."[361] As philosopher Peter Kreeft explains:

Swinburne, *Resurrection of God Incarnate*; Wright, *Resurrection of the Son of God*.

355. Wright, *Resurrection of the Son of God*, 718. See also Swinburne, *Resurrection of God Incarnate*; Williams, *Getting at Jesus*, ch. 5.

356. See Williams, *Getting at Jesus*, ch. 1. See also Williams, *Universe from Someone*.

357. See FOCLOnline, "Arguments for and from Fulfilled Biblical Prophecies"; Geisler, "Miraculous Bible Prophecy Fulfillments"; Scott, *Is Jesus of Nazareth the Predicted Messiah?*; Kaiser, *Messiah in the Old Testament*; Williams, *Understanding Jesus*, ch. 6; and *Getting at Jesus*, ch. 5.

358. See Williams, "Did Jesus Perform Miracles?" (YouTube playlist); Habermas, "Did Jesus Perform Miracles?"; Williams, *Getting at Jesus*, ch. 5.

359. See Williams, "Do Angels Really Exist?"; and "New Testament Criticism and Jesus the Exorcist"; Gallagher, *Demonic Foes*; Guthrie, *Gods of This World*; Williams, *Case for Angels*.

360. Craig, *Reasonable Faith*, 327.

361. See Williams, "'Lunatic, Liar or Lord' Argument" (YouTube playlist); Davis, "Mad/Bad/God Trilemma"; Kreeft, "Jesus"; Davis, "Was Jesus Mad, Bad or God?"; Horner, "Aut Deus Aut Malus Homo"; Kreeft, *Between Heaven and Hell*; Lewis, "What Are We to Make?"; Williams, Donald T., "Validity of Lewis's Trilemma"; Williams,

> The first premise is that Christ must be either God, as he claims to be, or a bad man, if he wasn't who he claims to be. The second premise is that he isn't a bad man. The conclusion is that he is God . . . he either believes his claim to be God, or he doesn't. If he does [and the claim is false], then he is intellectually bad . . . because that's a pretty large confusion! And if he does not believe his claim, then he is morally bad: a deceiver and a terrible blasphemer.[362]

Philosopher Stephen T. Davis comments:

> Virtually everyone who reads the Gospels . . . comes away with the conviction that Jesus was a wise and good man . . . Jesus shows none of the character traits usually associated with those who have delusions of grandeur or "divinity complexes." Such people are easily recognizable by their egotism, narcissism, inflexibility, predictable behaviour, and inability to relate understandingly and lovingly to others . . . We live in an age when scholars confidently make all sorts of bizarre claims about the historical Jesus. But few scripture scholars of any theological stripe seriously entertain the possibility that Jesus was either a lunatic or a liar.[363]

Davis formalizes these observations into what he calls the "Mad, Bad, or God" argument:

1. Jesus claimed, either explicitly or implicitly, to be divine

2. Jesus was either right or wrong in claiming to be divine

3. If Jesus was wrong in claiming to be divine, Jesus was either mad or bad

4. Jesus was not bad

5. Jesus was not mad

6. Therefore, Jesus was not wrong in claiming to be divine

7. Therefore, Jesus was right in claiming to be divine

8. Therefore, Jesus was divine.[364]

Getting at Jesus, ch. 2.
    362. Kreeft, *Between Heaven and Hell*, 38–39.
    363. Davis, *Christian Philosophical Theology*, 154.
    364. Davis, *Christian Philosophical Theology*, 152.

The main challenge to this argument comes from those who would deny the first premise. For example, while Richard Dawkins affirms that Jesus was "a great moral teacher,"[365] and concedes that "there's no evidence Jesus himself was barking mad," he reckons "the evidence that Jesus claimed any sort of divine status is minimal."[366] (Even Dawkins doesn't deny there is *some* evidence that Jesus claimed *some sort of* divine status!) Contra Dawkins, sufficient warrant for accepting that Jesus did indeed claim "either explicitly or implicitly, to be divine" (premise 1 of the "Mad, Bad, or God" argument) comes from a combination of direct evidence, concerning Jesus's explicit and implicit claims *about himself*, and indirect evidence, concerning the need to explain what other people believed *about Jesus*.

Dawkins's risible suggestion that the "Mad, Bad, or God" argument overlooks the possibility that Jesus was merely "honestly mistaken"[367] about his divinity constitutes a backhanded compliment to the strength of the argument. As Davis comments: "It is not easy to see how any sane religious first-century Jew could sincerely but mistakenly hold the belief: *I am divine*."[368]

At the very least, the "Mad, Bad, or God" argument provides *some* warrant for the conclusion that Jesus "was . . . who he claimed to be."[369] As I have emphasized elsewhere,[370] the arguments from Jesus's fulfilment of prophecy, from his miracles and exorcisms, from his resurrection from the dead, and from the paradox of his claims in the context of his character combine to form a *cumulative* historical case for the Christian doctrine of the incarnation.

The Context of Things to Come

Within the context set by the above discussion, one can see how the chapters and appendices to come contribute to the cumulative historical case for the doctrine "that God became flesh in the form of Jesus Christ, and

---

365. Dawkins, "Sorry Liberal Christians", §6.
366. Dawkins, *God Delusion*, 117.
367. Dawkins, *God Delusion*, 117.
368. Davis, *Christian Philosophical Theology*, .
369. Craig, *Reasonable Faith*, 327.
370. See Williams, *Understanding Jesus*.

that Christ acted in the world in such a way that we can get evidence of his existence, and of his divinity."[371]

Chapter 2 presents a slightly expanded version of my peer reviewed paper "The Epistle of St. James vs. Evolutionary Christology," which was originally published in *Theofilos* journal, 8:1 (2016) 49–65.[372] I argue that the Epistle of James provides evidence of a so-called "High Christology" (i.e., a view of Jesus as Divine) within a highly Jewish milieu prior to the AD 66–70 Jewish War with Rome, and plausibly within ten to fifteen years after Jesus's crucifixion. This chapter provides indirect historical evidence for the first premise of the "Mad, Bad, or God" argument, for in light of the Jewish beliefs of Jesus's earliest disciples "the claims being made would have seemed blasphemous had they not been given strong reason to believe them—and where better than from Jesus himself?"[373] This chapter also provides indirect historical evidence for thinking that *something unusual* must have happened to convince the first generation of Jesus's Jewish disciples that far from being the failure his crucifixion appeared to proclaim, he was in fact the Divine "Son of God" (i.e., Messiah).

Chapters 3 and 4 present a revised version of my two-part investigation offering "An Interdisciplinary Inquiry into Dating the Fourth Gospel." These papers revisit my discussion of the dating and provenance of the Fourth Gospel in my book *Getting at Jesus* (Wipf & Stock, 2019). The original version of part 1, which examines "John 5:2 and Papyrus 52," was published in the forum section of *Theofilos* journal, 13:1–2 (2021) 215–33. The original version of part 2, which examines "Other Evidence," was published in the forum section of *Theofilos* journal, 1/2 (2022) 151–61. Taken together, these chapters offer arguments for the *general* testimonial reliability of the Fourth Gospel and its claims about Jesus.

Chapter 5 presents a revised version of my paper "*Resurrection: Faith or Fact? Miracle Not Required?*," which was originally published in the forum section of *Theofilos* journal, 11:2 (2019) 209–31.[374] This chapter extends my interaction with American atheist Carl Stecher (1940–2019) over the case for the resurrection of Jesus.

Chapter 6 presents a revised (and substantially expanded) version of my peer reviewed paper offering "Scientific Rebuttals to 'Ancient Aliens' as Popular Alternatives to Biblical History," published in

---

371. Monton, *Seeking God in Science*, 71.
372. Williams, "Epistle of St. James."
373. O'Hear, *Jesus for Beginners*.
374. Williams, "*Resurrection: Faith or Fact?*"

Theofilos journal, 12:1 (2020) 85–111.[375] Claims about so-called "ancient aliens" offer people with a secular worldview historical counter-narratives to biblical history, including the New Testament testimonies about Jesus, that draw upon the scientific respectability of astrobiology and the search for extraterrestrial intelligence (SETI). Against these claims, I argue that "ancient alien" theories are intrinsically convoluted and highly *ad hoc*, and that multiple essential facets of such theories are disconfirmed by scientific evidence.

I present two shorter pieces as appendices. Appendix 1 is a revised version of my "Addendum to *Getting at Jesus*: The Deceptive Demon or Daemon Hypothesis," a contribution to the discussion about explaining the evidence for Jesus's resurrection, which was originally published on my website. Appendix 2, "Was Jesus's Claim to be God an Invention? Examining Ehrman's Arguments," returns us to the questions of Jesus's self-image and the general testimonial reliability of the canonical Gospels, in a revised version of an article commenting on a discussion between New Testament scholars Bart Ehrman and Peter J. Williams hosted by Justin Brierley's "The Big Conversation" video series, originally published online by Premier Christian Radio.[376]

Conclusion

In light of the foregoing discussion, I hope readers will be willing to read the following essays with a properly skeptical mindset and that they will consequently be convinced to take more seriously the opinion expressed by philosopher J. P. Moreland:

> I repeatedly return to the conviction that Jesus of Nazareth is simply peerless. He is the wisest, most virtuous, most influential person in history. . . . The power of his ideas, the quality of his character, the beauty of his personality, the uniqueness of his life, miracles, crucifixion, and resurrection are so far removed from any other person or ideology that, in my view, it is the greatest honor ever bestowed on me to be counted among his followers.[377]

---

375. Williams, "Scientific Rebuttals to 'Ancient Aliens.'"
376. Williams, "Was Jesus' Claim."
377. Moreland, "Why I Have Made Jesus Christ," 300.

Chapter Two

The Epistle of St. James vs. Evolutionary Christology[1]

SINCE IT IS UNLIKELY that those who lived alongside the historical Jesus would radically misunderstand his teachings and self-image, anyone who denies that he saw himself as more than merely human is forced to introduce a period of time in between Jesus and belief in his divinity (a so-called "High Christology"). This period of time must be sufficient for the evolution of a High Christology to plausibly take place in the absence of the sort of factors Christians believe shaped the Christology of the disciples (e.g., Jesus's exalted teaching about himself combined with his fulfilment of Old Testament prophecy; his miracles, exorcisms, and resurrection from the dead; as well as the ongoing religious experience of the early church[2]). To posit such an evolution is to embrace a so-called "evolutionary Christology." The time period postulated needs to move belief in the divinity of Jesus away from the Jewish roots of Christianity, because it is implausible to think that monotheistic Jews, like Peter, John, Saul, James, Mark, or Matthew, would divinize Jesus without extremely good reason. As theologian Michael Green explains:

---

1. My thanks to Dr. K. Martin Heide, professor of Semitic languages at the Centre for Near and Middle-East Studies, Philipps-Universität in Marburg, Germany, for his comments on an earlier draft of this paper. Thanks also for the anonymous comments of two reviewers for *Theofilos*. Listen to Williams's lecture on "High Christology in the Letter of James."

2. See Williams, *Understanding Jesus*.

> So jealously did they stick to the Second Commandment that the Jews fought to the death rather than allow the Roman military standards, with their imperial medallions, to enter the Holy City. So seriously did Jews take their monotheism that they would not take the sacred name of God (Yahweh) upon their lips. . . . In other words, if you had looked the whole world over for more stony and improbable soil in which to plan the idea of an incarnation you could not have done better than light upon Israel![3]

Dan Brown's best-selling novel *The Da Vinci Code* (2003) popularized the idea that High Christology was a late arrival on the theological scene, suggesting that divinity was foisted upon Jesus by a narrow vote of the church Council of Nicea in AD 325.[4] In response, the agnostic New Testament scholar Bart Ehrman observes that aspects of Brown's novel account—whether Brown himself believes them or not—are simply *fictional*:

> Constantine did call the Council of Nicea, and one of the issues involved Jesus' divinity. But this was not a council that met to decide whether or not Jesus was divine . . . everyone at the Council—and in fact, just about every Christian everywhere—already agreed that Jesus was divine. . . . The question being debated was how to *understand* Jesus' divinity in light of the circumstance that he was also human. Moreover, how could both Jesus and God be God if there is only one God? *Those* were the issues . . . not whether or not Jesus was divine. And there certainly was no vote to determine Jesus' divinity: this was already a matter of common knowledge among Christians, and had been from the early years of the religion.[5]

Indeed, there's more than sufficient evidence *from archaeological finds alone* to bury the suggestion that no one thought Jesus was divine until the fourth-century Council of Nicea.[6]

For example, archaeologist Yotam Tepper and epigraphist Leah Di Segni have dated a Christian "prayer hall," discovered in 2005 near Megiddo, to circa AD 230.[7] Writing in *National Geographic News* Mati Milstein comments that "dating to roughly the third century, it is popularly accepted

---

3. Green, "Jesus in the New Testament," 40.
4. See Brown, *Da Vinci Code*, 232–33.
5. Ehrman, "What Was the Council of Nicea?"
6. See Williams, "Archaeology, Jesus and the New Testament."
7. See Biblical Archaeological Staff, "Prison Makes Way"; Tepper, *Christian Prayer Hall*; Adams, "Ancient Church at Megiddo."

as the oldest church ever discovered."[8] The remains primarily consist of a series of mosaics grouped around a stone plinth that once supported a table used for the celebration of communion. One of these mosaics (see fig. 1) displays a Greek inscription about the donation of the table:

> The God-loving Akeptous has offered the table to God Jesus Christ as a memorial.

Fig. 1. Megiddo Mosaic.[9]

Vassilios Tzaferis, who argues that the Megiddo prayer hall dates to the second half of the third century, writes:

> What Tepper . . . exposed is probably the earliest church ever discovered in the Holy Land (the excavators date it to the first half of the third century, around 230 A.D.) and one of the very few churches from this early period anywhere in the world—from a time before Christianity became the religion of the Roman empire in the early fourth century during the reign of Constantine the Great.[10]

According to Charlie H. Campbell: "This discovery at Megiddo demonstrates that a belief in Jesus' deity was already in place long before the fourth century."[11] Even the latest dating of the Megiddo church predates the council of Nicea.

---

8. Milstein, "'Oldest Church' Discovery," §3.

9. Megiddo prayer hall mosaic, https://commons.wikimedia.org/wiki/File:Akeptous_Inscription_2.jpg. I have converted the Greek over-lining to underlining.

10. Tzaferis, "Inscribed to 'God Jesus Christ.'"

11. Campbell, *Archaeological Evidence for the Bible*, 119.

THE EPISTLE OF ST. JAMES VS. EVOLUTIONARY CHRISTOLOGY 91

Again, the "Alexamenos Graffito" is a stark piece of graffiti, discovered on a wall near the Palatine hill in Rome in 1857, which dates to "c. AD 200."[12] It depicts a man named Alexamenos, who stands with an up-stretched arm facing a donkey-headed figure on a cross. In rough-hewn scratches the picture is accompanied by the words: "Alexamenos worships his god." The only known crucifixion victim that Alexamenos might have worshiped is Jesus. Indeed, the late second-century Christian writer Tertullian tells of an arena worker in Carthage who had a picture ridiculing the Christian God by showing him with the head of a donkey.[13]

Historian Tom Holland provides some additional context:

> To Greek scholars, the question of what might be found within this "Holy of Holies" [in the Jewish temple] was a tantalising one. Posidonius, never knowingly without a theory, claimed that it contained a golden ass's head. Others believed it held "the stone image of a man with a long beard sitting on a donkey" [Diodorus Siculus 34:2].[14]

The donkey imagery in this ancient graffiti therefore suggests that the crucified man worshiped by Alexamenos—Jesus—*is supposed to be the Jewish God*.

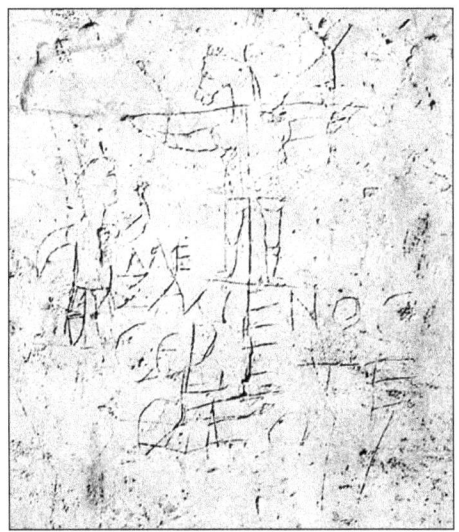

Fig. 2. Alexamenos Graffito.[15]

12. Bauckham, *Jesus*, 96. See Williams, *Digging for Evidence*.
13. See Roberts et al., *Translations of the Writings*, 31.
14. Holland, *Dominion*, ch. 2.
15. Credit: http://commons.wikimedia.org/wiki/File:Jesus_graffito.jpg.

While avoiding the extremes of *The Da Vinci Code*, atheist novelist Matthew Kneale asserts that "in the first decades after his death, Jesus still appears to have been regarded by his followers—including Paul—as thoroughly human and not a god,"[16] but that "by the early second century... Jesus had become fully supernatural."[17] Jesus Seminar co-founder Robert W. Funk suggests a four-stage development within which Jesus went from being seen as a mere human being who became "a son of God by virtue of his resurrection" to being thought of as "pre-existent from the beginning" by the time of the Gospel of John towards at the end of the first century.[18] Atheist John W. Loftus appeals to Funk's thesis to support his own claim that Christians gradually "developed a higher, more glorified view of Jesus"[19] in a process of deification "that took at least seventy years."[20] We can call the end of this supposed seventy year process (just into the second century AD) "the Loftus line."

Belief in a gradually evolving Christology is flatly contradicted by an overwhelming mass of literary evidence to the contrary, not least among the New Testament letters (and not least among these letters in this respect are the letters of Paul), the approximate dates of which are shown in figure 3.

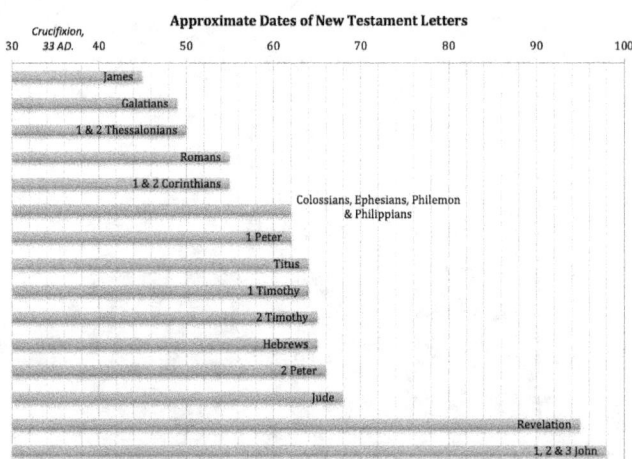

Fig. 3.[21]

16. Kneale, *Atheist's History of Belief*, 106.
17. Kneale, *Atheist's History of Belief*, 125.
18. Funk, *Honest to Jesus*, 279–96.
19. Loftus, *Why I Became an Atheist*, 329.
20. Loftus, *Why I Became an Atheist*, 330.
21. Chart draws upon data from various sources, including *NIV Thompson Student*

Luke Timothy Johnson observes that "Paul's letters (and probably other epistolary literature such as James and Hebrews) provide first-hand evidence for the Christian movement in its first three decades."[22] Reading these early Christian documents, it's hard to see how the first-century, Jewish followers of Jesus could have been any clearer in affirming belief in his divinity. For example: "the writer of Hebrews [ca. AD 65] addresses Christ thus: 'Thy throne, O God, is for ever and ever' (1:8)."[23] In Titus (ca. AD 64) Jesus is called "our great God and Savior" (2:13). Philippians 2:9–11 (ca. AD 62) applies God's words about himself in Isa 45:22–23 to Jesus: "at the name of Jesus every knee should bow, in heaven and on earth and under the earth, and every tongue confess that Jesus Christ is Lord." In 1 Cor 8:6 (ca. AD 55) Paul includes Jesus within the "shema," the sacred Jewish expression of allegiance to one God (found in Deut 6:4): "there is but one God, the Father, from whom all things came and for whom we live; and there is but one Lord, Jesus Christ, through whom all things came and through whom we live." In 1 Thess 3:11–13 (ca. AD 50) Paul *prays to* "our God and Father himself and our Lord Jesus."[24]

The first-century literary Letter or "Epistle" of James offers a particularly interesting case study in early High Christology. Halvor Moxnes, professor emeritus of New Testament studies at the University of Oslo, incorrectly states that the letter of James "has no references to Christ beyond the first verse."[25] However, James not only refers in exalted terms to "the Lord Jesus Christ" (Jas 1:1), but describes his readers as having faith in "our glorious Lord Jesus Christ" (Jas 2:1, see 1 Cor 2:8 and Eph 1:17)[26] and talks to them about "the ones who are *blaspheming* the noble [beautiful] name of him to whom you belong" (Jas 2:7, my italics).[27] Although the Greek βλασφημοῦσιν (*blaspheming*) can mean speech that "speaks evil of" or which "reviles" non-divine persons, the context clearly favors taking the term as a reference to "blaspheming" *in the strongest sense*[28] (and this is how the majority of English translations understand the reference[29]). In other words, Jas 2:7 is an indirect

---

Bible; Cabal, *Apologetics Study Bible*; and Geisler, *Popular Survey of the New Testament*.

22. Johnson, *Real Jesus*, 87.

23. Geisler, *Christian Apologetics*, 337–38. See Bruce, *Epistle to the Hebrews*, 59–60; Fudge, *Hebrews*, 52–53; Montefiore, *Commentary on Hebrews*, 47.

24. See Schmidt, "Contribution of 1 Thessalonians 3:11–13."

25. Moxnes, *Short History of the New Testament*, 34.

26. See Bible Hub, "James 2:1."

27. See Bible Hub, "James 2:7."

28. See Bible Hub, "987: βλασφημέω."

29. See Bible Hub, "James 2:7 Parallel"; and Bible Study Tools, "Compare

reference to Christ that exhibits a High Christology. Let us examine these references to Christ in more detail.

Jesus Is "Lord"

In light of the Jewish creed or *Shema*—"Hear, O Israel: The Lord our God, the Lord is one" (Deut 6:4), Paul Barnett argues that by calling Jesus *Lord*, early Christians like James were:

> identifying the risen and ascended Jesus with the Lord of the Old Testament. This is clear from Paul's word's, which echo but radically adapt the Jewish creed . . . "There is *one* God, the Father . . . and one Lord, Jesus Christ" (1 Corinthians 8:6). The *one* Lord of his Jewish faith Paul now redefined as the *one* Father and the *one* Lord.[30]

As Dean L. Overman explains:

> By the time of Jesus' birth, devout Jews avoided speaking the Hebrew name for God because the word was considered too sacred to be pronounced out loud. God's name was composed of four Hebrew letters: YHWH (*Yahweh*), known as the Hebrew Tetragrammaton. When Jewish believers referred to God, they used the Hebrew word *adonai* in speaking about or to God. Among Greek-speaking Jews, the Greek word *kyrios* was read out loud for the tetragrammaton (*Yahweh*).[31]

Linguistically, the Greek word *kyrios* could refer to *a* lord as well as to *the* Lord (i.e., *adonai* or *Yahweh*). However, Josephus reports that first-century Jews refused to address the Roman emperor as *kyrios* because they believed this term should only be applied to *Yahweh*.[32] Since the first disciples were Jewish, Overman argues that:

> When the early church proclaimed that "Jesus is Lord," it was using *kyrios* in its most exalted sense. For example, the author of the first letter of Peter, writing in the early 60's, ascribes to Jesus an Old Testament passage in which the term "Lord" refers to the Hebrew *Yahweh*. In First Peter 3:15, the author writes: ". . . but in your hearts sanctify Christ as Lord (*kyrios*)." (Careful Translations."

---

30. Barnett, *Messiah*, 40.
31. Overman, *Case for the Divinity of Jesus*, 21–22.
32. See Overman, *Case for the Divinity of Jesus*, 22.

study shows that "Christ" in the New Testament always refers to Jesus.) This passage refers to Isaiah 8:13: "*Yahweh Saboath*, him you shall sanctify."[33]

Moreover, James describes Jesus as not only "Lord," but as "the Lord of glory" (Jas 2:1). According to Douglas J. Moo:

> This translation, which takes *doxēs* as a descriptive genitive dependent on "Lord," is probably correct. Paul describes Jesus similarly in 1 Corinthians 2:8 and James is fond of this type of genitive construction.[34]

To refer to Jesus in this way "suggests particularly the heavenly sphere to which he has been exalted and from which he will come at the end of history to save and to judge (cf. Jas 5:9)."[35]

The application of "Lord" to Jesus in the Epistle of James thus evinces a High Christology amongst first-century Jewish Christians.

Blaspheming the Noble Name

James 2:6b–7 observes:

> Is it not the rich who are exploiting you? Are they not the ones who are dragging you into court? Are they not the ones who are blaspheming the noble name of him to whom you belong? (NIV)

In cultural context, this blasphemy may have happened through the use of "Christian" as an outsider term of abuse, since Christians originally described themselves as "followers of 'the Way'" (compare John 14:6; Acts 19:9, 19:23, 22:4, 24:14, 24:22; and perhaps Rom 3:17 and 9:31):

- Tacitus informs us in his *Annals* (15:44) that the Emperor Nero blamed the AD 64 Great Fire of Rome upon those "whom the crowd called Christians."

- The letter known as 1 Peter, written in Rome, shows (see 1 Pet 4:16) that the crowd's terminology had been appropriated by at least some in the Jesus-following community by ca. AD 62.[36]

---

33. Overman, *Case for the Divinity of Jesus*, 23.
34. Moo, *James*, 92.
35. Moo, *James*, 92–93.
36. On the dating of 1 Peter, see Clowney, *Message of 1 Peter*; Grudem, *1 Peter*; Marshall et al., *Exploring the New Testament*; Powers, *1 and 2 Peter, Jude*.

- Luke reports Herod Agrippa II teasing Paul the apostle ca. AD 61 by saying: "In a short time would you persuade me to be a Christian?" (Acts 26:28 ESV).

- Indeed, Luke notes that "the disciples were called Christians first in Antioch" (Acts 11:26). The context here suggests that the term "Christian" was already in use by critics of "the Way" ca. AD 46.

The Greek word Χριστιανός (*Christianos*) comes from Χριστός (*Christos*), meaning "anointed one," plus an adjectival ending borrowed from Latin to denote adhering or belonging to, as in slave ownership. The Septuagint translation of the Old Testament used Χριστός to translate the Hebrew word מָשִׁיחַ (*Mašíaḥ*, messiah), meaning "[one who is] anointed." So, a "Christian" is literally someone called upon by the name of, belonging to, and/or slaves of Jesus "the Christ." From the outsider perspective, "Christian" was thus a sarcastic reference to people who enslaved themselves to a crucified, would-be Jewish messiah.

According to Peter H. Davids: "'The good name called upon you' is certainly the name of Jesus," though he thinks it is "not necessarily the name Christ or Christian."[37] Davids notes that:

> The phrase "to call a name upon one" is a septuagintalism, indicating possession or relationship, particularly relationship to God. . . . For Christians the name of Jesus was substituted for that of Yahweh, or Yahweh translated as [*kyrios*] was simply transferred to Jesus. . . . And the "calling upon" became a fixed point; namely it was called over the believer at baptism (Acts 2:38; 8:16; 10:48; Hermas *Sim.* 9.16.3). . . . Thus the blasphemy referred to indicates the reviling of the name of Jesus.[38]

Several Bible translations contextually link James's description of Christians as belonging to the "noble name" with the practice of being baptized in and/or into the name of Jesus Christ, or as a "Christian":

- "Don't they blaspheme the noble name that was pronounced over you at your baptism?" (HCSB)

- "Is it not they who blaspheme the noble name that was invoked over you?" (NABRE)

---

37. Davids, *Epistle of James*, 113.
38. Davids, *Epistle of James*, 113.

- "Is it not they who blaspheme the excellent name that was invoked over you?" (NRSV)
- "Aren't they the ones who scorn the new name—'Christian'—used in your baptisms?" (The Message)

Hence, James's talk of blaspheming "the noble name of him to whom you belong" is either a reference to "Christian" (i.e., "One who is a slave of Christ") as a term of abuse for followers of "the Way," and thus an indirect blaspheming of Jesus Christ, or it is a reference to people directly blaspheming the name of Jesus Christ that was "called upon" Christians at their baptism. Either way, Jas 2:7 is a reference to people blaspheming Jesus Christ, as is made explicit in the NLT translation:

> Aren't they the ones who slander Jesus Christ, whose noble name you bear?

There are three reasons that jointly make a cumulative case for thinking that James understands this "slander" to be "blasphemy" in the fullest sense of the term. First of all, Jas 2:7 echoes several Old Testament passages that speak of humans being "called upon" *by God's name* (compare Deut 28:10; 2 Chr 7:14; Isa 4:1; and Amos 9:12). As Heinrich Meyer observes:

> The expression τὸ ὄνομα ἐπικαλεῖται ἐπί τινα is borrowed from the O.T., where it often occurs, and in the sense that one becomes the property of him whose name is called upon him; particularly it is said of Israel that the name of God was called upon them.[39]

Interestingly, in Luke's report of the Council at Jerusalem (ca. AD 48/49), James uses the Septuagint translation of the prophet Amos to the effect that "the rest of mankind may seek the Lord, even all the Gentiles who bear my name, says the Lord, who does these things" (Acts 15:17).[40] Thus Jas 2:7 probably intends to put Jesus Christ into the position of the Old Testament God.

Second, the Greek word that qualifies the "name" that is blasphemed in Jas 2:7 as being "noble" is *kalos*, a term that designates the attractive good.[41] This is plausibly a Greek translation of the Hebrew term used of

---

39. See StudyLight.org, "James 2:7."
40. See Hicks, "James Interprets Amos"; and Braun, "James' Use of Amos."
41. See Bible Hub, "2570. Kalos."

God's name in Pss 52:9 and 54:6, where God's name is *towb*—i.e., "is good" in the sense of being beautiful, attractive, and morally good.[42]

Finally, this conclusion is reinforced by James's elliptical Jewish style:

> the omission of all mention of the name, which would have come in very naturally, betrays Jewish usage; as Taylor truly remarks . . . "A feeling of reverence leads the Jews to avoid, as far as possible, all mention of the Names of God. This feeling is manifested . . . in their post-canonical literature, even with regard to less sacred, and not incommunicable Divine names. In the Talmud and Midrash, and (with the exception of the Prayer Books) in the Rabbinic writings generally, it is the custom to abstain from using the Biblical names of God, excepting in citations from the Bible; and even when Elohim is necessarily brought in, it is often intentionally misspelt."[43]

Indeed, The Voice translation opts to make this implicit reference explicit within the text (though obscuring thereby the implicit reference to Jesus): "Aren't they the ones mocking the noble name of our God, the One calling us?," while the International Standard Version of Jas 2:7 footnotes "the noble Name" with the comment "i.e., God."

The Authorship of James

A consideration of the authorship of the Epistle of James isn't a precondition for the fruitful discussion of either the publication date of the letter or the significance of its Christology, but it is helpful. So-called liberal scholarship attributes the Epistle to an admirer of James writing under a pseudonym[44] between AD 80 and 100. In favor of this view scholars from Erasmus to Joseph F. Kelly[45] have argued (with what appears to be a measure of condescension, if not outright prejudice) that the Greek of the letter is too good to be plausibly attributed to a Galilean Jew. It has also been suggested that the mention of "elders" in Jas 5:14 reflects a church leadership more advanced than existed prior to the fall of Jerusalem. Catholic theologian Scott Hahn responds to these arguments:

---

42. See Bible Hub, "2896. Towb."

43. *Expositor's Greek New Testament*, "James 2:7." See Butler, "Blasphemy"; Elwell, "Blasphemy."

44. See Moxnes, *Short History of the New Testament*, 34.

45. See Kelly, *Introduction to the New Testament*, 222.

> Scholarship continues to produce evidence that Galilee was thoroughly bilingual during the NT period (Aramaic and Greek), so the ability of a Palestinian Jew, especially one who was intellectually gifted, to write in excellent Greek is far from impossible (e.g., the Jewish historian Flavius Josephus was educated in first-century Jerusalem and acquired an impressive command of Hellenistic Greek, as well as classical Greek literature). Second, unless one disregards the Book of Acts as a witness to history, it is clear that a hierarchical system of leadership (with "elders" or "presbyters") had emerged well before the end of the first century (Acts 14:23; 20:17; cf. 1 Peter 5:1–2).[46]

Sophie Law confirms that:

> it is no longer possible to assert with complete confidence that James of Jerusalem could not have written the good Greek of the epistle, since the wide currency of language in Palestine is increasingly appreciated.[47]

Craig S. Keener points to "excavations showing that most of Galilee was not as backward as was once thought"[48] and to:

> the widespread use of amanuenses (scribes) who might, like Josephus's editorial scribes, help a writer's Greek. This last point would be especially appropriate for the leader of the mother church, in the one overwhelmingly Jewish city that also provided advanced education in Greek works (cf. the Greeks in Acts 15:23–29).[49]

That said, Douglas J. Moo suggests that while the involvement of amanuenses "cannot *a priori* be ruled out,"[50] it is an awkward hypothesis in light of the way in which "the exact wording is so often crucial to the flow of the letter."[51] Besides, as Alec Motyer points out: "Artistic skills and exceptional abilities owe nobody an explanation. Time and again they arise where least expected."[52]

---

46. Hahn and Mitch, *Letter of St. James*, 13.
47. Quoted in Motyer, *Message of James*, 19.
48. Keener, *IVP Bible Background Commentary*, 668.
49. Keener, *IVP Bible Background Commentary*, 668.
50. Moo, *James*, 30.
51. Moo, *James*, 30.
52. Motyer, *Message of James*, 17.

As for the more complex mediating theory of a later editor adapting materials by James,[53] Donald Guthrie comments that:

> why a [hypothetical] later editor should suddenly have conceived such a publication plan when the great majority of the intended readers must have known James was already dead is difficult to see, and it is even more difficult to see how the letter came to be received.[54]

Moo argues that the theory of a later editor is "unnecessary," and concludes: "It is more natural to take the reference to James as an indicator of the epistle's sole author."[55] In sum, as Motyer concludes: "the arguments proposed for later dates [and thus non-traditional authorship] lack impressiveness."[56]

Note that, even if it were correct, the liberal dating of the Epistle nevertheless permits it to stand in contradiction to the Council of Nicea thesis advanced within Dan Brown's *The Da Vinci Code*, and the lower end of the liberal date range is likewise incompatible with Loftus's theory of an evolving Christology that took at least seventy years to attribute divinity to Christ.

James the Just of Jerusalem, Son of Joseph, Brother of Jesus

There's a strong cumulative case for attributing the Epistle to James the Just of Jerusalem,[57] the brother of Jesus Christ:

- *Local Knowledge*

James of Jerusalem obviously fits the geographical situation of the Epistle:

> James lived in Jerusalem . . . and his readers are probably to be found in the regions just outside of Palestine along the coastline to the north, in Syria and perhaps southern Asia Minor. Several

---

53. See Guthrie, *New Testament Introduction*, 745–46; Moo, *James*, 29–31.
54. Guthrie, *New Testament Introduction*, 746.
55. Moo, *James*, 31.
56. Motyer, *Message of James*, 18.
57. According to Eusebius, Clement of Alexandria reported that "this James, whom the people of old called the Just because of his outstanding virtue, was the first, as the record tells us, to be elected to the episcopal throne of the Jerusalem church" (Wikipedia, "James," §4).

allusions in the letter, most notably the reference to the "earlier and latter rains" (5:7), seem to confirm this location; for only along the eastern coast of the Mediterranean Sea do the rains come in this sequence.[58]

- *Jewishness*

The highly Jewish nature of the Epistle, including its reverence for the Jewish law and the book of Proverbs, is consistent with the background of James the brother of Jesus. As Peter H. Davids writes: "Jewish culture forms the ideological background of the epistle."[59]

- *Linguistic Links*

There are some linguistic similarities between the Epistle and both the speech of James at the Council of Jerusalem reported by Luke in Acts 15 and the letter subsequently sent under the authority of James that is recorded in Acts 15:23–29.[60]

Fig. 4.

Epistle of James	James in Acts 15
Listen, my beloved brothers	Brothers, listen
the noble name of him to whom you belong	the Gentiles who bear my name
my beloved brethren	our beloved Barnabas and Paul

- *Unanimous Testimony*

On the one hand, early church fathers such as Athanasius, Cyril of Jerusalem, Eusebius, and Origen unanimously attributed the Epistle of James to James the brother of Jesus. No alternative author was ever suggested in ancient times.[61]

- *Argument by Elimination*

58. Moo, *James*, 36.
59. Davids, *Epistle of James*, 13.
60. On the translation of these phrases compare Bible Hub, "James 1:19," "James 2:7," and "James 2:5" with "Acts 15:13," "Acts 15:17," and "Acts 15:25."
61. See Holding, "Authorship of James," 221.

On the other hand, the other men by the name of James known from the NT are generally thought not to have been prominent enough to write an authoritative general Epistle:

> Two men of this name were among the apostles of Jesus: James son of Zebedee (Mk 1:19; 3:17) and James son of Alphaeus (Lk 6:15; Acts 1:13) . . . but most scholars think it improbable that either one wrote the Letter of James—the former was martyred in AD 44, probably too early to have been the author (Acts 12:2) and very little is known about the latter . . . Instead, scholars through the centuries have given preference to a third figure of the apostolic age: James of Jerusalem, also known as "the Lord's brother" (Gal 1:19).[62]

- *Authorial Prominence*

The lack of any qualifying designation specifying *which* James is writing the letter indicates that no further explanation was needed: "the opening self-description of James as a 'servant of the Lord Jesus' (Jas 1:1) . . . presupposes that he is already known to his readers and feels no need to assert his authority or credentials."[63] Unlike the other James known from the NT, James the brother of Jesus certainly would fit the requirement for a James who needs no introduction:

> A pseudonymous author, hoping to borrow the reputation of James for himself, would more likely have described him in exalted rather than humble terms. Or, at least, he would have given a sufficiently explicit description of James to help readers identify which of the ancient Jameses he was claiming to be.[64]

Peter H. Davids agrees that:

> In truth there was but one James in the early church who was well enough recognized to be able to use such a simple greeting and that was James the son of Joseph.[65]

In sum, "All the characteristics of the letter support the traditional attribution of it to James the brother of the Lord."[66] Thus Alister McGrath

---

62. Hahn and Mitch, *Letter of St. James*, 13. See Moo, *James*, 13.
63. Hahn and Mitch, *Letter of St. James*, 13.
64. Hahn and Mitch, *Letter of St. James*, 13.
65. Davids, "James," 1354.
66. Douglas and Tenny, *Zondervan Illustrated Bible Dictionary*, 691.

concludes that "the letter of James was probably [written by] James the brother of Jesus."[67] Many other New Testament scholars concur:[68]

- James B. Adamson affirmed the "probability that the Epistle is by James, the Lord's brother."[69]
- Walter A. Elwell and Robert W. Yarbrough write that the author of James "is most likely James the (half-) brother of Jesus."[70]
- Donald Guthrie argues at some length that "the authorship of James, the Lord's brother, must still be considered more probable than any rival."[71]
- Luke Timothy Johnson argues that "there are strong reasons for arguing that the extant letter was composed by James of Jerusalem, whom Paul designates as 'brother of the Lord.' . . . the preponderance of evidence makes that position one that can be held with a high degree of confidence."[72]
- While allowing for the involvement of an editor, Craig S. Keener rejects pseudonymity and states that "the material in the letter should be viewed as genuinely from James."[73]
- I. Howard Marshall, Stephen Travis, and Ian Paul agree that "there is . . . no strong reason to question the tradition of authorship by James of Jerusalem."[74]
- Douglas J. Moo argues for "James, the Lord's brother, as the most likely author of the epistle."[75]

---

67. McGrath, *NIV Bible Handbook*, 477.

68. See Holding, "Authorship of James," 221–24; Cook, "Introduction to the Letter of James:"; Howe, "Letter of James."

69. Adamson, *Epistle of James*, 22.

70. Elwell and Yarbrough, *Encountering the New Testament*, 345.

71. Guthrie, *New Testament Introduction*, 746.

72. Johnson, *Brother of Jesus*, 3.

73. Keener, *IVP Bible Background Commentary*, 668.

74. Marshall et al., *Exploring the New Testament*, 266.

75. Moo, *James*, 20.

Dating the Epistle of James according to Its Author

Hegesippus's account of James's death, as recorded by Eusebius, tells us that James was stoned for refusing to renounce his faith in Jesus. James's martyrdom is independently confirmed by the first-century Jewish historian Josephus (*Antiquities* XX.9.1) in a manner that enables us to date the event to AD 62.[76]

Archaeological corroboration of this date comes from the mid first-century chalk ossuary (or "bone box") recognized in 2002 as bearing the Aramaic inscription יעקוב בר יוסף אחוי דישוע ("Ya'akov bar Yosef akhui di Yeshua"): "Jacob, son of Joseph, brother of Jesus" (in English Jacob = James).

Fig. 5. The James Ossuary.[77]

New Testament scholar Ben Witherington comments that:

> If, as seems probable, the ossuary found in the vicinity of Jerusalem and dated to about AD 63 is indeed the burial box of James, the brother of Jesus, this inscription is the most important extrabiblical evidence of its kind.[78]

---

76. See Moo, *James*, 21.

77. Credit: http://commons.wikimedia.org/wiki/File:JamesOssuary-1-.jpg. The James ossuary was on display at the Royal Ontario Museum from Nov. 15, 2002 to Jan. 5, 2003.

78. Quoted in Meister, *Building Belief*, 146. See Witherington, "James Ossuary."

According to Hershel Shanks (1930–2021), editor in chief of the *Biblical Archaeological Review*:

> this box is [more] likely the ossuary of James, the brother of Jesus of Nazareth, than not. In my opinion . . . it is likely that this inscription *does* mention the James and Joseph and Jesus of the New Testament.[79]

Historian Paul L. Maier likewise concludes that:

> there is strong (though not absolutely conclusive) evidence that, yes, the ossuary and its inscription are not only authentic, but that the inscribed names are the New Testament personalities.[80]

Professor Camil Fuchs, a statistician from Tel Aviv University, has argued that "with a confidence level of 95 percent, we can expect there to be 1.71 individuals in the relevant population named James with a father named Joseph and a brother Jesus."[81] Moreover, as Joseph M. Holden and Norman L. Geisler explain:

> Of those ossuaries bearing an inscription, almost all speak of the deceased occupant's father, and occasionally of the person's brother, sister, or other close relative if that person is well known. The rare presence of the sibling's name (Jesus) would indicate that Jesus was a very prominent figure.[82]

They also report:

> Experts have confirmed the presence of microbial patina on the ossuary and on both parts of the inscription: "James, the son of Joseph" and "brother of Jesus," demonstrating the unity and antiquity of the inscription . . . this patina is generally deemed ancient . . . making a recent forgery impossible. The world's leading expert in biogeology and the patination process, Wolfgang Krumbein of Oldenburg University in Germany, affirmed that the patina on the ossuary and inscription most likely reflects a development process of thousands of years. He added that there is no known process of accelerating the development of patina . . . researchers from the Royal Ontario Museum in Toronto confirmed that the patina within the letter grooves is consistent with the patina on the surface of the ossuary; thus

---

79. Shanks and Witherington, *Brother of Jesus*, 64.
80. Maier, "James Ossuary."
81. Shanks, "James Ossuary Is Authentic."
82. Holden and Geisler, *Popular Handbook of Archaeology*, 314.

legitimizing the entire inscription's antiquity. According to expert paleographers Andre Lemaire and Ada Yardeni, who authenticated (and dated) the inscription based on the shape and stance of the letters, the Aramaic is fully consistent with first-century style and practice.[83]

In 2014, a peer-reviewed paper in the *Open Journal of Geology* validated the authenticity of the James ossuary inscription.[84] According to the paper's abstract:

> An archaeometric analysis of the James Ossuary inscription "James Son of Joseph Brother of Jesus" strengthens the contention that the ossuary and its engravings are authentic. The beige patina can be observed on the surface of the ossuary, continuing gradationally into the engraved inscription. Fine long striations made by the friction of falling roof rocks continuously crosscut the letters. Many dissolution pits are superimposed on several of the letters of the inscription. In addition to calcite and quartz, the patina contains the following minerals: apatite, whewellite and weddelite (calcium oxalate). These minerals result from the biogenic activity of microorganisms that require a long period of time to form a bio-patina. Moreover, the heterogeneous existence of wind-blown microfossils (nannofossils and foraminifers) and quartz within the patina of the ossuary, including the lettering zone, reinforces the authenticity of the inscription.

If James the brother of Jesus is indeed the author of James's letter, then it must have been written before his death. Moreover, because James writes to "the twelve tribes scattered among the nations" (Jas 1:1) the letter must date from long enough after Jesus's crucifixion for the Christian belief in his resurrection and divinity to have spread a fair way: "The Epistle must have been written, therefore, sometime between the late A.D. 30s and the early A.D. 60s."[85]

Dating the Epistle of James apart from Its Author

There are good reasons for dating the Epistle of James prior to the Jewish War (which began in AD 66) quite apart from consideration of the letter's authorship. Hahn observes that "evidence within the letter is generally

---

83. Holden and Geisler, *Popular Handbook of Archaeology*, 314.
84. See Rosenfeld et al., "Authenticity of the James Ossuary," 69–78.
85. Elwell and Yarbrough, *Encountering the New Testament*, 345.

THE EPISTLE OF ST. JAMES VS. EVOLUTIONARY CHRISTOLOGY

supportive of an early date."[86] John Drane concurs that "a number of facts suggest very strongly that it belongs to an early period of the church's life rather than a later one."[87] For example:

- There are signs of James in *The Shepherd of Hermas* (ca. AD 85–140)[88] and in the first letter of Clement (often dated to AD 96 but possibly as early as the 60s AD).[89]

- "In favour of the early date are the striking simplicity of church organization and discipline, the fact that Christians still met in the synagogue (Jas. 2:2), and the general Judaic tone."[90] Hahn concludes that the Letter of James comes from "a time . . . before Christianity and Judaism had irrevocably distinguished themselves from one another."[91]

- Drane notes that "much of the imagery of James is clearly Palestinian. The mention of 'autumn and spring rains' (5:7) would have meant nothing at all in other parts of the Roman empire, while the agricultural practices mentioned in the preceding verses are of a type that disappeared for good in Palestine after AD 70, but which were widespread in the days of Jesus."[92]

- Keener states that "the situation depicted in the letter best fits a period before A.D. 66."[93]

Given just the above data, we might agree with Peter H. Davids in dating the Epistle of James to the mid 60s AD.[94] Alister McGrath suggests the Epistle was written "at some point in the late 50's or early 60's."[95] I. Howard Marshall, Stephen Travis, and Ian Paul suggest a date "between AD 50 and 66."[96] However, there's more evidence to take into consideration.

---

86. Hahn and Mitch, *Letter of St. James*, 13.

87. Drane, *Introducing the New Testament*, 415.

88. For a defense of the earlier dating of *Shepherd of Hermas* see Robinson, *Redating the New Testament*.

89. See Holding, "Authorship of James," 221.

90. Douglas and Tenny, *Zondervan Illustrated Bible Dictionary*, 692.

91. Hahn and Mitch, *The Letter of St. James*, 13. See Moo, *James*, 13.

92. Drane, *Introducing the New Testament*, 415.

93. Keener, *IVP Bible Background Commentary*, 668.

94. See Davids, "James."

95. McGrath, *NIV Bible Handbook*, 477.

96. Marshall et al., *Exploring the New Testament*, 267.

For example, Douglas J. Moo points to "the absence of any reference to the controversy between Jew and Gentiles, particularly with respect to the 'ritual law.'"[97] James shows no awareness of the Acts 15 council (ca. AD 48/49), "which would have been relevant to his theme had it already occurred."[98]

Noting similarities between parts of James's letter and teachings of Jesus reported in Matthew's Gospel, Drane argues:

> The most likely explanation is that the writer of James knew these sayings of Jesus in a slightly different form than they now have in the New Testament gospels . . . and the fact that some of this teaching has a more primitive form in James than it does in Matthew might imply that James has access to it at an earlier stage than the writers of the gospels.[99]

According to Davids:

> No other letter of the NT has as many references to the teaching of Jesus per page as this one does. It is not that James quotes Jesus directly, although he sometimes does (see in 5:12), but he normally simply uses phrases and ideas which come from Jesus. His readers would have memorized much of the Lord's teaching, so they would recognize the source. Most of these phrases come from the teaching of Jesus now in Matthew's Sermon on the Mount (Mt. 5–7) or Luke's Sermon on the Plain (Lk. 6).[100]

Johnson likewise notes:

> James's speech is shaped by the sayings of Jesus. And when we realize that the form of some of the more certain allusions is simpler than the redacted form of the sayings found in the Synoptics, then we appreciate that James may be very close indeed to the formative stage of the Jesus traditions.[101]

Moreover:

> the use of an early form of the Jesus tradition suggests that the letter of James was written either before the composition of the

---

97. Moo, *James*, 35.
98. Geisler, *Popular Survey of the New Testament*, 243.
99. Drane, *Introducing the New Testament*, 414.
100. Davids, "James," 1354.
101. Johnson, *Brother of Jesus*, 38.

Synoptic Gospels, or at the very least before their version of Jesus' teachings became standard.[102]

At this juncture, the dates of the Synoptic Gospels become relevant to our thinking about the date of James's letter. Although I don't have room to examine the dating of the Synoptic Gospels here, I believe there are good arguments for dating Luke to circa AD 61 and Matthew to circa AD 61–63.[103] These arguments add to the case for dating James to within two to three decades after the crucifixion. Indeed, the parallel between Jas 1:6 and Mark 11:23–24 suggests James was written prior to the publication of Mark's Gospel, which I would place circa AD 49.[104] Even on a more "standard" dating of Mark (ca. AD 65–75[105]), this point alone would still place James early in the second half of the first century.

Moo observes that "the general social conditions in the Near East in the middle of the first century also correspond with the situation presupposed in James."[106] For example, "the merchants who ranged far and wide in search of profits (4:13–17) and the wealthy, often 'absentee' landlords who exploited an increasingly large and impoverished labour force (5:1–6) were familiar figures."[107] Another familiar feature of the times was the Zealots, who sought to win freedom for Israel by violent means: "some scholars, in fact, think that James 4:2—'you desire and do not have; so you kill'—may refer to zealot partisans who had brought their violent ideology into the church."[108]

Professor Barry D. Smith argues from the relationship between the Letter of James and the Letters of Paul:

> Paul must contend with Jewish believers who determined that gentiles should submit to the Law as a condition of final salvation; because of James' authority in the Jerusalem church, his opponents use portions of the Letter of James in support of their position. This forces Paul to correct their erroneous extrapolations from the letter, and, in so doing, sometimes to appear to be

---

102. Johnson, *Brother of Jesus*, 154.
103. See Williams, *Understanding Jesus*, 197–207.
104. On dating Mark's Gospel, see May, *Search for God*; Wallace, *Cold Case Christianity*; Williams, *Understanding Jesus*, 189–196.
105. See Cline, "Dating and Origins of Mark's Gospel"; Moxnes, *Short History of the New Testament*, 44.
106. Moo, *James*, 36.
107. Moo, *James*, 36.
108. Moo, *James*, 36–37.

in direct opposition to James, the leader of the Jerusalem church. (It is probable that the Letter of James quickly reached Antioch, where Paul resided, from Jerusalem.) . . . On the assumption that Paul had read the Letter of James before he wrote his Letter to the Galatians and Letter to the Romans . . . the *terminus a quo* [for the publication of James's epistle] is some time before 48, when Paul probably wrote the Letter to the Galatians.[109]

Finally, Smith argues that:

> If James wrote his letter before 48 A.D., then the persecution that he mentions in the present tense as still occurring (see Jas 1:2–12) could be the result of the persecution of the church instigated by Herod Agrippa I, who executed James the son of Zebedee (Acts 12) . . . In addition, it is possible that the references to helping the poor who are hungry and naked (see Jas 2:1–17) could be inspired by the fact that there were Jewish believers who were suffering deprivation during the famine that occurred c. 45–46.[110]

As Luke Timothy Johnson observes:

> Everything in the letter and everything lacking from the letter help confirm the impression that this social world was one shared by a leader of the Jerusalem church and Jewish messianists of the diaspora during the first decades of the Christian movement.[111]

Scott Hahn likewise argues that James comes from "the earliest decades of the Church, i.e., at a time when the mission field of the gospel was still concentrated in Israel and its environs."[112] According to Paige Patterson: "many scholars are convinced that James is the first book of the New Testament to be written, some dating it as early as A.D. 48."[113] Donald Guthrie concludes that "a date before A.D. 50 . . . has much to be said for it and is probably to be preferred."[114] Liberal theologian John A. T. Robinson thought James was written circa AD 47–48.[115] Henry Thiessen dated James from AD 45 to

---

109. Smith, "James."
110. Smith, "James."
111. Johnson, *Brother of Jesus*, 122.
112. Hahn and Mitch, *Letter of St. James*, 13. See Moo, *James*, 13.
113. Patterson, "James, the Letter," §8.
114. Guthrie, *New Testament Introduction*, 753.
115. See Fernandes and Larson, *Hijacking the Historical Jesus*, 144.

48.[116] It seems to me that the preponderance of evidence indicates Douglas J. Moo may well be correct when he concludes that James was written "around 45–47."[117] As Phil Fernandes and Kyle Larson conclude: "A date of 45 AD for James's epistle is not extreme."[118]

Conclusions

The author and audience of the letter known as the Epistle of James were first-century Jewish monotheists who nevertheless considered Jesus Christ to be divine. The evidence favors the traditional attribution of authorship to James the Just of Jerusalem, the (half-) brother of Jesus. This attribution both makes the High Christology of the letter all the more startling and suggests a publication date before AD 62 (when James was martyred). Even apart from the evidence for James of Jerusalem being the author, there's every reason to date the Epistle and its Christology to before the Jewish War of AD 66–70 (i.e., within about thirty-two years of the crucifixion). Indeed, there's good evidence for Donald Guthrie's conclusion that "a date before A.D. 50 . . . is probably to be preferred."[119] There is some reason to think that Douglas J. Moo may be correct when he concludes that James was written at "around 45–47."[120]

Of course, the author of James must have arrived at his opinion about Jesus at some time before he wrote. Likewise, the recipients of the Epistle obviously arrived at their belief in the divinity of Jesus at some time before the Epistle was sent to them. Since the intended audience were "scattered among the nations" (Jas 1:1), sufficient time must have passed for the gospel message—including the doctrine that Jesus was divine—to have gone out from Jerusalem, where Christianity originated, to the then current geographical spread of this Jewish-Christian diaspora. These factors plausibly push the High Christology reflected in James's letter back by several years. Indeed, since the balance of evidence suggests that the Epistle of James was published circa AD 45–47, and since belief in the divinity of Jesus must pre-date the Epistle, our data plausibly evinces a High Christology *within ten to fifteen years of the crucifixion*.

---

116. See Fernandes and Larson, *Hijacking the Historical Jesus*, 144.
117. Moo, *James*, 35.
118. Fernandes and Larson, *Hijacking the Historical Jesus*, 144.
119. Guthrie, *New Testament Introduction*, 753.
120. Moo, *James*, 35.

At the very least, the Epistle of James plausibly demonstrates the High Christology of Jewish Christians *before the Jewish War*. Either scenario excludes the sort of evolutionary Christology proposed by the likes of Brown, Funk, Kneale, and Loftus.

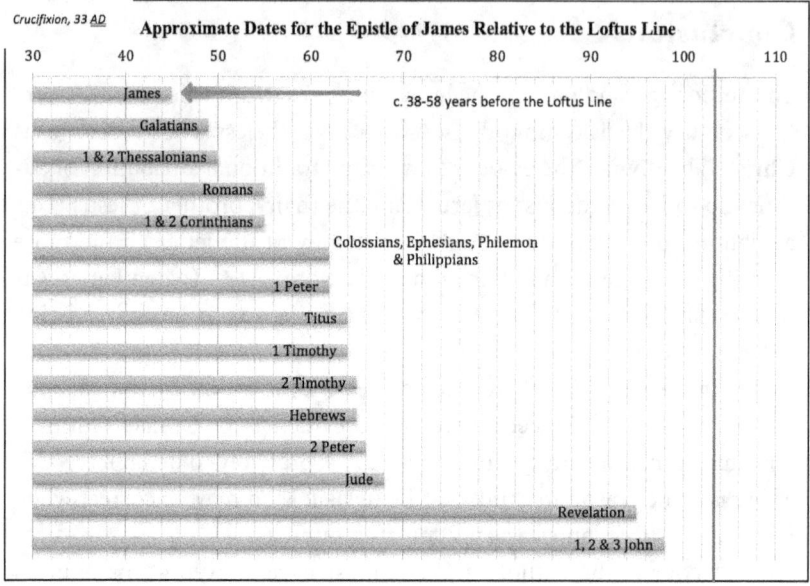

Fig. 6. The range of dates herein argued for the Epistle of James, ca. 12 to 32 years after the crucifixion, and thus ca. 38 to 58 years before the early second century "Loftus line" for the supposed evolution of a "high" Christology.

Chapter Three

An Interdisciplinary Inquiry into Dating the Fourth Gospel

Part I: John 5:2 and Papyrus 52

IN THE NINETEENTH CENTURY, German scholar F. C. Baur (1792–1860) dated the Fourth Gospel from AD 160–170 (partly due to the influence of Hegelian philosophy[1]). Similarly "late" datings of the Fourth Gospel continued to be offered by some scholars in the early twentieth century. As theologian Daniel B. Wallace reports: "In 1925 Delafosse saw 170–175 as the ceiling and in 1936 Loisy felt that 'the first publication can hardly have been effected before 135–40.'"[2] However, scholarship moved on, and by the middle of the twentieth century came to a consensus that the Fourth Gospel was issued no later than (though probably towards) the end of the first century.

Several things account for this shift in thinking, besides the waning of Hegelianism. One line of argument focuses upon the Fourth Gospel's depiction of Jerusalem before its fall in the Jewish War of AD 66–74.[3] Here one often sees discussion of John 5:2's accurate description of the Pool of Bethesda near the Sheep Gate. Another line of argument involves a key piece of external evidence known as "P52," a scrap of ancient papyrus which bears several verses of the Fourth Gospel, translated and

---

1. See Editors of Encylopaedia Britannica, "Ferdinand Christian Baur."
2. Wallace, "John 5,2 and the Date," 177–205.
3. See Sheppard, *Jewish Revolt AD 66–74*.

published in 1934 and dated by its translator, classical scholar Colin H. Roberts (1909–90), to AD 125 plus or minus *twenty-five years*. We will investigate both of these lines of evidence here in part 1 of this inquiry. Other arguments look at allusions to and quotations from the Fourth Gospel in other literature, or investigate the internal and external evidence about the origins of the Fourth Gospel. These arguments will be examined in part 2 of this inquiry.

The Perils of Interdisciplinary Studies

Now, as James K. Beilby and Paul Rhodes Eddy observe:

> It is no longer merely New Testament scholars and historians who are wading into the rushing waters of the quest [for the historical Jesus], but an entire cadre of interdisciplinary explorers, each bringing their own distinctive disciplinary methods, tools and insights to the historical study of Jesus and the Gospels.[4]

In particular, they note that "in recent times one can find a variety of philosophers and philosophical theologians weighing in on relevant matters."[5] I am one such a philosopher, who has been privileged to write or contribute to several books and papers dealing with the historical Jesus.[6]

One of the challenges of interdisciplinary study is that the need to integrate knowledge from different disciplines may require one to stray outside the bounds of one's professional expertise. In so doing, one must rely upon other scholars, doing one's best to digest and critically assess as many relevant, reputable resources as one can, and then referencing (at least some of) those sources as and when one draws upon them in publication. Given the possibility of making mistakes within one's own field of expertise, it's obviously even more likely that one may get things wrong when venturing outside that field. The only remedy (in either case) is to keep learning, and a particularly useful spur to continued learning can be interaction with those who disagree with you.

---

4. Beilby and Eddy, "Quest for the Historical Jesus," 41.
5. Beilby and Eddy, "Quest for the Historical Jesus," 41.
6. See Williams, "Epistle of St. James"; and "New Testament Criticism and Jesus"; Stecher et al., *Resurrection: Faith or Fact?*; Williams, *Getting at Jesus*; *Digging for Evidence*; *C. S. Lewis vs. the New Atheists*; and *Understanding Jesus*.

For example, in a June 2020 exchange of tweets debating the historical reliability of the Fourth Gospel, Edward T. Babinski convinced me that I needed to reconsider some arguments regarding the dating of the Fourth Gospel that are made from John 5:2 and P52. These were arguments that, in good faith, I had represented in several venues, including my book *Getting at Jesus: A Comprehensive Critique of Neo-Atheist Nonsense about the Jesus of History* (Wipf & Stock, 2019). I wrote this paper to revisit my thinking on the dating of the Fourth Gospel.

John 5:2 and the Pool of Bethesda

John 5:2 contains a reference to the so-called "Pool of Bethesda":

> Now there is in Jerusalem at the Sheep [Gate] a pool called in Hebrew Bethesda, with five porticoes. (NAB)

Now, as Calum Millar notes:

> In 1903 . . . scholar Alfred Loisy claimed that "The pool was a symbol of Judaism, and the five porticoes an allusion to the five books of the law." The name Bethesda, meaning "House of Mercy," was taken to be symbolic too.[7]

However:

> In 1956 archaeologists found the pool of Bethesda where 1st century Jewish-Roman historian Josephus described it, just north of the Temple Mount and near the Sheep Gate. And although most similar pools at the time would have had 4 porticoes (one for each wall), this pool actually turned out to be two pools with a dividing wall in the middle and hence would include a fifth portico—just as John says! And the Dead Sea Scrolls have shown that the pool was more fully known as "Bet 'Eshdatayin," meaning "place of twin outpourings," in reference to the pool having two basins. Archaeologists have suggested that water was only let into the southern pool at certain times, explaining the intermittent churning mentioned in John. And even more interestingly, pools dating to the next few centuries just next to the Pool of Bethesda appear to have been dedicated to Asclepius, the Greek god of medicine—which would fit Bethesda being known as a pool specifically for healing. So what archaeology

---

7. Millar, "Places in the Gospels and Archaeology."

shows matches up exactly with what John says, even on unusual details that he never could have guessed by chance.[8]

Moreover, archaeologist John McRay reports that:

> Evidence of the existence of a place with a pool called Bethesda has been found in the Copper Scroll from Qumran, which was written between A.D. 25 and 68. In a list of places in Jerusalem we find the desciption: "At Beth Eshdathayin, in the pool where you enter in the small[er] reservoir . . . near there at the west entryway of the porch of the triclinium [i.e., dining room]." The Hebrew name *Beth Eshdathayin* may mean "House of the Twin Pools."[9]

Fig. 1. The Pool of Bethesda Ruins (the walkway on the right hand side of the photo marks the division between the two pools).[10]

---

8. Millar, "Places in the Gospels and Archaeology."
9. McRay, *Archaeology and the New Testament*, 186.
10. Credit: https://commons.wikimedia.org/wiki/File:Ruins_of_Pool_of_Bethesda,_Jerusalem.jpg.

The discovery of *twin* pools explains John 5:2's reference to five porticoes without contradicting its reference to "a pool," since the Greek term translated here is κολυμβήθρα (*kolymbēthra*), which literally means "a diving or swimming place."[11] Thus Urban C. von Wahlde observes that, contra Loisy:

> The discovery of the pools proves beyond a doubt that the description of this pool was not the creation of the Evangelist but reflected accurate and detailed knowledge of Jerusalem, knowledge that is sufficiently detailed to now be an aid to archaeologists in understanding the site.[12]

Fig. 2. A Model of Herod's Temple at the Israel Museum, Jerusalem. The eastern wall is closest to the camera, so the northern wall and then the Pool of Bethesda with its five porticoes are to the right.[13]

So far, so good. However, many scholars press this data into an argument for assigning a first-century date to the Fourth Gospel. A typical example of this argument is philosopher and apologist Norman L. Geisler's statement that:

> John (5:2) mentions five colonnades at the pool of Bethesda. Excavations between 1914 and 1938 uncovered this pool and

11. See Bible Hub, "2861. Kolumbethra."
12. Wahlde, "Archaeology and John's Gospel," 566.
13. Credit: Berthold Werner, https://en.wikipedia.org/wiki/File:Jerusalem_Modell_BW_2.JPG.

found it to be just as John described it. Since that pool did not exist in the second century, it is unlikely any second-century fraud would have had access to such detail.[14]

Taking a slightly different line of approach, ancient historian Paul Barnett argues that "It is natural to infer from the present tense of the verb 'is' that both buildings [of the pool complex] were still standing at the time of writing."[15] Likewise, theologian Bruce Milne writes:

> In 5:2 John refers to the Pool of Bethesda by "there is," not "there was." While too much ought not to be placed on this, it equally should not be dismissed. If the Pool was still identifiable when John wrote we are looking at a date in the late 60's, certainly prior to AD 70.[16]

On the one hand, Milne's note of caution is well taken, for there is a scholarly dispute about whether to understand the Greek tense in John 5:2 as a "historical present."[17] On the other hand, while Geisler uses the data merely to argue for a first-century dating of the Fourth Gospel, Milne uses it to argue for a date in "the late 60's." Milne's "prior to AD 70" is inferred from the fact that the Romans laid waste to Jerusalem in AD 70. This is why Geisler states that the "pool did not exist in the second century."[18] Making the same argument as Milne, apologist J. Warner Wallace states that "the pool was destroyed in 70 AD when Jerusalem was sacked by the Romans."[19] Likewise, Catholic apologist Jimmy Akin argues that "John 5:2 . . . gives us reason to hold that the Gospel was written before the destruction in 70,"[20] and in support of this contention cites the Jewish historian Josephus's account of the fall of Jerusalem. And, indeed, Josephus wrote that, after the conquest of Jerusalem, the Roman soldiers received orders that:

> they should now demolish the entire city, and temple: but should leave as many of the towers standing as were of the greatest

---

14. Geisler, *Big Book of Christian Apologetics*, 279.
15. Barnett, *Is the New Testament History?*, loc. 65.
16. Milne, *Message of John*, 25.
17. See Wallace, "John 5:2 and the Date of the Fourth Gospel. . . Again"; Köstenberger, "John 5:2 and the Date of John's Gospel."
18. Geisler, *Big Book of Christian Apologetics*, 279.
19. Wallace, "John's Gospel May Have Been Last."
20. Akin, "When Was John Written?," §33.

eminency . . . there was left nothing to make those that came thither believe Jerusalem had ever been inhabited.[21]

However, as Babinski rightly pointed out to me, Josephus's statement must be interpreted as an example of hyperbole[22] in light of other sources which testify that *the Pool of Bethesda continued to be visible in Jerusalem until the fourth century.* As reported by archaeologist Shimon Gibson (a senior associate fellow at the W. F. Albright Institute of Archaeological Research and a visiting professor of archaeology at University of North Carolina Charlotte):

> The Bethesda Pool is referred to in third and fourth century sources but there is no mention of a church at this location until the fifth century. Judging by the testimony of Origen [*Commentary on John*, Catena fragment 61], the original four porticoes running around the edges of the twin pools with another across the middle, were still visible to visitors in his day ([ca. AD] 231). This information [about the arrangement of the porticoes] was repeated by Cyril of Jerusalem before 348 [*Homily on the Cripple at the Pool*], but the language of Eusebius suggests that in his day, before 331, the actual porticoes were already in ruins: "a bathing-pool in Jerusalem which is called the Probatike, and formerly had five porticoes." It is unclear from the description of the Bordeaux Pilgrim (333) whether the porticoes were still visible, but Jerome in the 380s repeats Eusebius' comment that the porticoes had "formerly" been around the pool. What is certain is that both pools were still in use and gathered water: according to Eucherius (441), the Northern Pool was filled with rainwater, and the Southern Pool with drained water stained with a reddish colour. A number of traditions continued to be associated with this site, notably that it was a place of healing.[23]

Gibson's sources are actually a mixed bag. Catena fragment 61—which may be written by either Origen (ca. AD 185–253) or Theodore of Heraclea (AD 328–355)[24]—contains a past tense commentary upon

21. Josephus, *Jewish War*, 7.1.
22. Just as Luke 19:44 is hyperbolic.
23. Gibson, "Excavations at the Bethesda Pool." The information about Catena fragment 61 in brackets is taken from Bruce, *Gospel of John*, 140n6. Bruce's commentary was originally published in 1983.
24. Heine notes: "Joseph Reuss has found four of the fragments (Frgs. 17, 51, 53, 120) attributed to Ammonius of Alexandria in other manuscripts of catenae; two attributed to Theodore of Heraclea (37, 61); and four attributed to Apollinaris of Laodicia (39, 59, 75, 121). Reuss is of the opinion that a few of these may belong to Origen" ("Can

what John 5:2 says about the pool.[25] The same goes for Cyril of Jerusalem's fourth century "Homily on the Cripple at the Pool," which says that "by the Sheep Market in Jerusalem there used to be a pool with five colonnades, four of which enclosed the pool, while the fifth spanned it midway."[26] Fragment 61 and Cyril's homily both go beyond John 5:2 by describing the unusual arrangement of the five porticoes, but this could be either the simplest way to imagine "a pool" with "five porticoes," or the result of a testimonial chain grounded in experience of the twin pool structure of the Pool of Bethesda, with or without its porticoes intact (since the arrangement of the five porticoes is obvious once one knows the architecture of the twin pools).

Eusebius of Caesarea's *Onomasticon*, "which was completed about 330 A.D. or shortly before"[27] has an entry (number 291) describing:

> Bēzatha (Bethsaida). Pool in Jerusalem which is (called probatike and interpreted by us) "sheep." Once it had five porticos. There are now pointed out twin pools, of which one is filled by the rain water (winter rains) and the other it appears that the water becomes miraculously red, as they say, bearing the traces of the sacrificial victims formerly washed in it. So it is called the sheep after the sacrifice. (Red like blood which in itself is seen as a sign of old. The sacrificial victims were brought unbound by the priests into the bath, whence it received its name.)[28]

According to the Bordeaux Pilgrim (AD 333):

> There are in Jerusalem two large pools (piscinae) at the side of the temple (ad latus templi), that is, one upon the right hand, and one upon the left, which were made by Solomon; and further in the city are twin pools (piscinae gemellares), with five porticoes, which are called Bethsaida (John 5:2–18). There persons who have been sick for many years are cured; the pools contain water which is red when it is disturbed.[29]

---

the Catena Fragments"). Thus, "fragment 61" *may* have been written by Theodore of Heraclea (AD 328–355).

25. Thanks to Lydia McGrew, Nathan Nadeau, and Donald Williams for their respective efforts in tracking down and translating Catena fragment 61 for me.

26. Cyril, "Homily on the Paralytic."

27. Wolf, "Introduction."

28. Eusebius, "Gospels: Bēzatha (Bethsaida)."

29. CenturyOne Bookstore, *Bordeaux Pilgrim*.

This appears to claim that the "five porticoes" are then extant, but the Pilgrim may simply be quoting "with five porticoes, which are called Bethsaida" from John 5:2, and "Jerome in the 380s repeats Eusebius' comment that the porticoes had 'formerly' been around the pool."[30] *The Epitome of S. Eucherius about Certain Holy Places* (ca. 440) doesn't have anything to add with respect to the porticoes, stating: "Bethesda is to be seen, remarkable for its twin pools, one of which is generally filled by the winter rain, while that water in the other is coloured red."[31] What all of this shows is that at least the twin pools of the "Pool of Bethesda" were *not* destroyed by the Romans in AD 70, and that they remained to be seen in Jerusalem at least until the middle of the fifth century. As for the "five porticos," they were lost at some time (or over some period of time) between Jesus's day and AD 330.

Clearly, Loisy missed the testimony of Eusebius, the Bordeaux Pilgrim, Jerome, and Eucherius when arguing against the historicity of John 5:2; but this omission was not corrected by later scholars who argued against Loisy from the archaeological discovery of the Pool of Bethesda. Consequently, the inference from the Fourth Gospel's accurate description of the Pool of Bethesda to the conclusion that it *must*, on that account, have been written by someone with either direct or indirect local knowledge of Jerusalem *in the first century* (or "prior to AD 70"[32]), is mistaken. Unfortunately, following the widespread use of this argument, I stated in *Getting at Jesus* that John 5:2 "displays a detailed local knowledge of Jerusalem before AD 70."[33] Thanks to Babinski, I now recognize my statement as (unintentionally) misleading, and I conclude that this argument for a first-century dating of the Fourth Gospel is unsound.

John 5:2 and the Sheep Gate

Astronomer Guillermo Gonzalez (writing outside of *his* professional expertise) argues for a pre-AD 70 date for the Fourth Gospel by noting that:

---

30. Gibson, "Excavations at the Bethesda Pool in Jerusalem."
31. Stewart, *Epitome of S. Eucherius*, 9–10.
32. Milne, *Message of John*, 25.
33. Williams, *Getting at Jesus*, 210.

> John 5:2 describes the sheep gate in the present tense, even though the sheep gate was wiped out when the Temple was destroyed in 70 AD.[34]

Of course, the word "gate" isn't actually in the Greek of John 5:2. Nor is the King James version's "market." As Jonathan Lipnick (dean of the faculty of Holy Land studies at Israel Institute of Biblical Studies) explains:

> The original text of John literally says "next to the *sheepish*" (ἐπὶ τῇ προβατικῇ)—not "sheepish" is the metaphorical sense of "bashful" but in the literal sense of "something pertaining to the sheep."[35]

Although "sheep *pool*" or "sheep *market*" are both possible referents here,[36] "sheep Gate" is perhaps the most plausible reading in context.[37] As Charles Ellicott (1819–1905) comments in his classic *Commentary for English Readers*:

> For "sheep-market," we should read with the margin, *sheep-gate* (Nehemiah 3:1; Nehemiah 3:32; Nehemiah 12:39). This gate was known well enough to fix the locality of the pool, but is itself now unknown. St. Stephen's Gate, which has been the traditional identification, did not exist until the time of Agrippa. There is something tempting in the interpretation of the Vulgate adopted by some modern travellers and commentators, which supplies the substantive from the immediate context, and reads "sheep-pool." But the fact that the Greek adjective for "sheep," is used here only in the New Testament, and in the Old Testament [i.e., in the Septuagint—or LXX—Greek translation thereof] only in the passages of Nehemiah referred to above, seems to fix the meaning beyond doubt.[38]

---

34. Gonzalez, "When Were the Gospels Written?," §14.
35. Lipnick, "Gates of the Sheep and Lion," §7.
36. According to the *Zondervan NIV Archaeology Study Bible*: "Even today the area is periodically used as a sheep market" (692, notes for Neh 3:1).
37. See Bible Hub, "John 5:2 Commentaries." See also Holstein, "Sheep Gate."
38. Ellicott, "John 5:2."

Josephus mentions a gate on the north side of the first century Temple Mount (*Jewish War* 1.537; 6.222),[39] and the tractate *Middot*[40] (i.e., "measurement") of the Mishnah refers to the north gate of the Temple Mount as "the Tadi Gate."[41]

Jack Finegan (emeritus professor of New Testament history and archaeology at Berkeley) argues that "perhaps . . . there was some correspondence between the Tadi Gate on the north side of the temple enclosure and [the] Sheep Gate"[42] mentioned by Nehemiah's account of rebuilding the walls of Jerusalem in the fifth century BC:

> That there was in fact a Sheep Gate which is mentioned by Nehemiah (3:1; 12:39) and that, according to his references, this was probably in the north city wall on the north side of the Temple area, between the "corner" on the northeast and the Tower of the Hundred and Tower of Hananel, the latter probably predecessors of the Antonia [fortress] on the northwest. The fact that this gate was built by Eliashib the high priest and his brethren the priests (Neh 3:1) confirms its close association with the Temple area, and it may have been the same as the Tadi Gate mentioned by Middoth . . . as the portal on the north side of the Temple area.[43]

Archaeological architect and Temple Mount specialist Leen Ritmeyer comments that:

---

39. See Finegan, *Archaeology of the New Testament*, 214. Kathleen and Leen Ritmeyer note that "Herod not only doubled the original area of the Temple podium, he also wrought a complete change in the topography of the area. The Tyropoeon Valley, which bordered the Temple Mount on the west, was filled in, as was a small valley to the north of the Old Temple Mount" ("Reconstructing Herod's Temple Mount," §12). Richley Crapo comments: "Herod more than doubled the size of the Temple Mount courtyards by extending the eastern wall again, both to the south and the north, and by adding similar retaining walls on the east and north ends of the rectangle . . . Hadrian may have made additions to the walls of the Temple Mount as part of his building program in AD 135+, but the specifics are difficult to document" ("Where Was the Temple of Herod?," §8)

40. Also called "Tractate Middoth," this Jewish work describes the Second Temple "and is based on the memory of sages who saw the Temple and gave an oral description of it to their disciples, after its destruction in 70 CE" (Wikipedia, "Middot," §21).

41. Quoted in Jack Finegan, *Archaeology of the New Testament*, 206. See also Bahat, *Atlas of Biblical Jerusalem*, 26.

42. Finegan, *Archaeology of the New Testament*, 214.

43. Finegan, *Archaeology of the New Testament*, 228. See also *ESV Archaeology Study Bible*, 676–79.

> It is tempting to speculate that the mishnaic Tadi Gate stood in the same place as the pre-exilic Sheep Gate. The meaning of *Tadi* remains unknown. It has been suggested that Tadi is a misreading of Tali or Taleh, which means lamb in Hebrew. In that case, it would not be difficult to see the connection between the Sheep and the "Lamb" Gate.[44]

The original Tadi Gate was apparently located in the northern retaining wall of the pre-Herodian Temple Mount,[45] with a tunnel leading up into the temple complex. As archaeologist Dan Bahat notes: "There is a theory that cistern No. 1 [one of the many cisterns and tunnels within the Temple Mount mapped in 1864–65 by Major-General Sir Charles Wilson] was the tunnel which led from the Temple compound, directly out of the Temple Mount."[46] According to Charles Warren's *Recovery of Jerusalem* (1871), "Cistern 1" (the floor of which is thirty feet below the surface of the platform):

> is a tunnel about 130 feet long and 24 feet wide, cut in rock for 18 feet from bottom to springing of arch, which is segmental. Signor Pierotti describes a passage connecting this tank with a chamber under the Sakhra; and I have to suggest that this Sakhra cave is the gate Nitsots, from whence there was a passage through the tunnel to the gate Tadi.[47]

Ritmeyer explains that "this structure, originally built as an underground passageway, as its shape suggests, was plastered over and turned into a cistern much later, probably during the Early Muslim or Crusader period."[48] Moreover, discussing "Cistern 3," Warren notes that:

> A channel cut in the rock, leading into this tank . . . runs north and south, and conducts into the tank surface water from small ducts which run east and west. There are three chambers in this tank, which are separated by piers, through which there are low-arched doorways. I have to suggest that this may have been the House of Baptism, communicating with the room of Beth

---

44. Ritmeyer, *Quest*, 205.

45. Archaeologist W. Harold Mare states: "It is to be noted that the Tadi Gate is now in the northern wall of the temple platform" (*Archaeology of the Jerusalem Area*, 155). See Ritmeyer and Ritmeyer, *Jerusalem*, 145.

46. Bahat, *Atlas of Biblical Jerusalem*, 32. See Rudd, "Jerusalem Temple Mount."

47. Quoted by Rudd, "Jerusalem Temple Mount." See also Ritmeyer and Ritmeyer, *Jerusalem*, 145.

48. Ritmeyer, *Quest*, 204.

Mokad and the gate Tadi. It is to be noticed that the tanks Nos. 1 and 3 would, if produced north, meet together at the northern edge of the platform, where there is a hollow-sounding piece of ground. Under this may still be the gate Tadi, opening out through the scarped rock, one portion of which was found somewhat to the east at Souterrain 29.[49]

This pre-Herodian Tadi Gate was subsumed by Herod's renovations to the north of the Temple Mount and replaced by the Fourth Gospel's "sheep Gate."[50] The question is, *What architectural form did the Herodian Sheep Gate take*? While it was presumably in between the Antonia Fortress and the Israel Pool (which were positioned at the western and eastern ends of the north wall respectively), Dan Bahat laments that its "exact location is not known."[51] Today: "Very little can be seen of the Northern Wall of the Temple Mount,"[52] although "the remains of the Herodian northern retaining wall are still preserved below ground."[53] Archaeological access to the Temple Mount is highly restricted: "The evidence is there. But the site has not even been surveyed—looked at—for more than a century and a [half], and excavations, even small ones, are forbidden."[54] Even "the cisterns under the Temple Mount are inaccessible today because of Muslim religious and political sensitivities."[55] This ignorance hampers our arrival at any firm conclusion about the Sheep Gate's fate in the first century, leaving us to weigh the plausibility of different historical conjectures.

Leen Ritmeyer explains the "strange notice in *Middot* 1:3 that 'the Tadi gate [on the north] has no purpose at all'" as being "probably because the Tadi Gate was the northern gate of the original square Temple Mount,"[56] theorizing that "when Herod buried this area [north

---

49. Quoted by Rudd, "Jerusalem Temple Mount." See also Reznick, "Secret Chambers of the Temple Mount"; Ritmeyer and Ritmeyer, *Secrets of Jerusalem's Temple Mount*, 68 and 71.

50. There also seem to have been a prison gate somewhere on the north side of Herod's Temple Mount (see Crapo, "Where Was the Temple of Herod?"). Dan Bahat says that Herod's temple had "an unknown number [of gates] in the north" (*Atlas of Biblical Jerusalem*, 26).

51. Bahat, *Atlas of Biblical Jerusalem*, 20. See also Israel MyChannel, "All the Gates to Herod's Temple," 10:44–11:00.

52. Ritmeyer and Ritmeyer, *Jerusalem*, 87.

53. Ritmeyer, *Quest*, 123.

54. Ritmeyer and Ritmeyer, *Secrets of Jerusalem's Temple Mount*, 7.

55. Ritmeyer and Ritmeyer, *Secrets of Jerusalem's Temple Mount*, 83.

56. Ritmeyer, "Locating the Original Temple Mount," 85.

of the original Temple Mount] with fill to create his northern court, the Tadi Gate was completely buried and thus rendered useless."[57] Leen and Kathleen Ritmeyer jointly postulate that the Herodian Sheep Gate was located in the wall of the portico on the northern summit of the Herodian Temple Mount. Note that there would, in this case, have been some sort of ramp (or possibly a staircase) leading up to the Sheep Gate.[58] Given this hypothesis, the Sheep Gate probably *was* obliterated by the Romans in AD 70.

However, when Herod extended the Temple Mount north, might not the builders have extended the passage from the (now defunct) Tadi Gate to the new retaining wall, where it ended at the Sheep Gate? As Michael Lustig observes:

> Herod extended existing Temple path and passageways, like those of the Huldah Gates, to pass through his extensions to the exterior. This was likely also required for those of the Tadi Gate.[59]

Wouldn't this arrangement equally account for Middot's statement about the Tadi Gate having "no purpose"? Creating such a tunnel extension would preserve the existing social function of the Tadi Gate as being for the use of the priests.[60] It would also save the space taken up by the tunnel from having to be filled in with rocky hard core.[61]

Moreover, the Temple Mount was most vulnerable to attack from the higher ground to the north—hence the Antonia fortress—and a gate leading straight onto the temple platform seems like more of a vulnerability than a gate in the retaining wall. Storming a small gate under fire and then fighting up a long, narrow, underground tunnel against determined opposition is a poor military prospect, so a gate in the northern retaining wall could have been ignored by the Romans as an easily defendable chokepoint. The Jews might even have filled in part of the tunnel in order to block access (after all, they built an additional defensive wall within the Antonia fortress, where the Romans did attack[62]). Indeed, Warren

---

57. Ritmeyer, "Locating the Original Temple Mount," 85.
58. As depicted in Ritmeyer and Ritmeyer, *Jerusalem*, 89–90.
59. Lustig, *Herod's Temple*, 34. See also Ritmeyer and Ritmeyer, *Jerusalem*, ch. 2.
60. See Lustig, *Herod's Temple*, 33.
61. On the methods used in the construction of the Herodian extensions to the Temple Mount, see Ritmeyer and Ritmeyer, *Secrets of Jerusalem's Temple Mount*, ch. 3.
62. See Sheppard, *Jewish Revolt AD 66–74*, 67.

reported that the northern end of Cistern 1 was "closed with a rough stone wall,"[63] and Leen Ritmeyer notes of both Cisterns 1 and 3 that "the northern parts of both these passages are blocked by similar-looking walls that made it impossible for Warren to investigate their relation to the northern wall of the raised platform."[64]

What we do know, as summarized by Charles W. Wilson in his *Ordinance Survey of Jerusalem* (1886), is that Josephus says:

> that the design of Titus was "to take the Temple at the tower of Antonia;" and that for this purpose he raised great banks; one of which was at the tower of Antonia, and the other at about 20 cubits from it; and that for the purpose of obtaining materials for filling up the immense fosse and ravine to the north of the Temple, he had to bring them from a great distance; and that the country all round for a distance of 19 or 12 miles was made perfectly bare in consequence.[65]

If there was a gate onto the temple platform near the Antonia, Titus would presumably have been tempted to raise a bank so that battering rams could be bought to bear against that gate, as he did against the massive stonework of the fortress.[66] Inferring a negative from the absence of such an attack is an argument from silence, but isn't necessarily unsound.

In sum, there is a cumulative case for thinking that the Sheep Gate was situated in the northern retaining wall of the Herodian Temple Mount.

Apologist Don Stewart asserts (without documentation) that "the sheep gate was destroyed in the year A.D. 70, along with the rest of the city of Jerusalem."[67] But this assumes that the Sheep Gate led onto the Temple Platform. Leen and Kathleen Ritmeyer offer a slightly more nuanced report of events after the Roman's conquest of Jerusalem in AD 70:

> the Romans ploughed the Temple Mount and built a temple to Jupiter on the site. Not a trace of Herod's Temple was left. The mighty retaining walls of the Temple Mount, however, were deliberately left lying in ruins throughout the Roman (70–324

---

63. Quoted in Ritmeyer, *Quest*, 204.
64. Ritmeyer, *Quest*, 205.
65. Quoted in Rudd, "Jerusalem Temple Mount."
66. See Sheppard, *Jewish Revolt AD 66–74*, 66–78.
67. Stewart, "When Were the Four Gospels Written?," §15.

A.D.) and Byzantine (324–640 A.D.) periods—testimony to the destruction of the Jewish state.[68]

Now, Gonzalez is aware of the discussion over the Greek tense in John 5:2, and appeals to Daniel Wallace's case against taking the present tense as a historical present.[69] However, even if John 5:2 is not using a historical present, the fact that the retaining walls of the Temple Mount were "deliberately left lying in ruins"[70] means that *if* the Sheep Gate was in the retaining wall, *then* a present tense reference to the Sheep Gate *might* have been accurate well after AD 70. Indeed, even if the door or doors of the gate had been destroyed, an ordinary language reference to "the Sheep Gate" as a persisting architectural feature wouldn't have been misleading.[71]

Mishna Middot 1:3 indicates that at least three temple gateways survived its destruction:

> The Western wall of the Holy Temple [likely starting at the Broad step, toward which runs the probable Kiphonus gate passageway under Herod's addition from Warren's Gate on Herod's new wall] will never be destroyed . . . and the Gate of the Kohen [i.e., "the Gate of the Priest"—which probably refers to the Tadi/Sheep Gate], and the Gate of Huldah [today's Triple Gate entrance and Double Gate exist], were not destroyed.[72]

Since there's no evidence that the Shushan Gate in the eastern wall survived, identifying "the Gate of the Kohen" with the Tadi/Sheep Gate gives us three gates situated respectively in the southern, western, and northern retaining walls of the Temple Mount, roughly centered upon the rock in the Dome of the Rock.[73] However, it's hard to say whether

---

68. Ritmeyer and Ritmeyer, "Reconstructing Herod's Temple Mount," §3. See also Ritmeyer and Ritmeyer, *Jerusalem*, 31. On Jesus's prophecy concerning the destruction of the temple, see Jackson, "Jesus' Prophecy and the Destruction."

69. See Wallace, "John 5:2 and the Date of the Fourth Gospel . . . Again." See also Köstenberger, "John 5:2 and the Date of John's Gospel."

70. Ritmeyer and Ritmeyer, "Reconstructing Herod's Temple Mount."

71. In the English city of Southampton (where I live) the gate house of the twelfth-century town walls still exists. The original gates are no longer part of this structure, but it is nevertheless known as "Bargate" (it is on Above Bar Street). See Wikipedia, "Bargate."

72. See Lustig, *Herod's Temple*, 48. It would seem that "the Gate of the Kohen" was how the priests referred to the gate, while "Sheep Gate" was the public descriptor.

73. See Lustig, *Herod's Temple*, 48.

"the Gate of the Kohen" refers to the pre-Herodian Tadi Gate or its Herodian replacement.

In any case, according to the multiple-stage composition theory discussed later in this paper, *John 5:2 may have been written before AD 70 but published within the Fourth Gospel decades later*. Hence I do not think that John 5:2 currently offers a sound basis for dating the Fourth Gospel.

John 5:2 and Testimonial Reliability

The Fourth Gospel claims to have been written by an eyewitness and/or by those who knew and drew upon the written testimony of that eyewitness (see, in particular, John 21:20–24), thereby placing its composition somewhere between AD 33 (i.e., the date of Jesus's crucifixion[74]) and the middle of the second century (that is, within two generations of the crucifixion). *If* one takes this claim to eyewitness testimony seriously,[75] *then* what the extra-biblical archaeological and written evidence does show is that *the author/s of the Fourth Gospel accurately described the Pool of Bethesda and its relation to the Sheep Gate*. And this is evidence that weighs (albeit slightly) in favor of the *testimonial reliability* of the Fourth Gospel, regardless of its precise dating.[76]

P52 and Dating the Fourth Gospel

The designation "*P52*" refers to a scrap of ancient papyrus, also known as P. Rylands 3.457, which "measures 2½ by 3½ inches and contains only a few verses of the fourth gospel, John 18:31–33 (recto, the front), 37, and 38 (verso, the back)."[77] Edward D. Andrews explains that "through painstaking comparison of hundreds of small features within an ancient manuscript, a paleographer can provide us with a date that is usually

---

74. See Köstenberger, "April 3, AD 33"; Köstenberger et al., *Final Days of Jesus*.

75. Craig Keener observes: "We would accept an eyewitness claim in most other ancient biographies or histories, so why should skeptics be biased against John?" (*John*, loc. 4). Israeli archaeologist Ravi Arav and John Rousseau (a research associate at the University of California, Berkley, and a fellow of the Jesus Seminar) acknowledge that "the primary author of the Gospel of John was probably an eyewitness to several events in the life of Jesus," since he is "well acquainted with Jerusalem and its surroundings" (*Jesus and His World*, 157). See also Barnett, *Is the New Testament History?*

76. For commentary on John 5:2, see Blomberg, *Historical Reliability of John's Gospel*, 108–12; Bruce, *Gospel of John*, 121–28.

77. Andrews, *P52 Project*, loc. 112.

correct to plus or minus 25 to 50 years."⁷⁸ P52 was dated by its original editor, Colin Roberts, to circa AD 125 plus or minus *twenty-five years*.

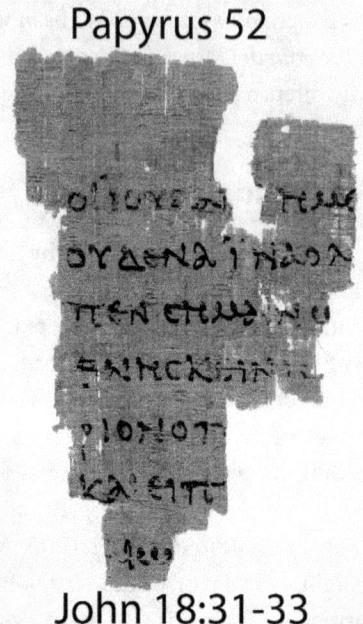

Fig. 3. P52 (RECTO).⁷⁹

Textual critics Philip Wesley Comfort and David P. Barrett report:

> Many scholars (Frederic G. Kenyon, H. I. Bell, Adolf Deissmann, and W.H.P. Hatch) have confirmed the dating of P52. Deissmann was convinced that it was written at least during the reign of Hadrian (A.D. 117–138) and perhaps even during the reign of Trajan (A.D. 98–117).⁸⁰

Papyrologist Eric Turner concluded that the Rylands papyrus could "be accepted as of the first half of the second century."⁸¹ Skeptical textual critic Bart Ehrman acknowledges that P52 "is usually dated to 125 CE, plus or minus 25 years."⁸² Arthur G. Patzia calls P52 "the oldest (ca. A.D.

---

78. Andrews, *P52 Project*, loc. 398.
79. Credit: https://commons.wikimedia.org/wiki/File:Jrlo20153tr.jpg.
80. Comfort and Barrett, *Text of the Earliest New Testament Manuscripts*, 1:337.
81. Turner, *Typology of the Early Codex*, 100.
82. Ehrman, "Why I'd Be Thrilled."

125–150) and one of the smallest . . . extant fragments of the New Testament known today."[83] Comfort says that the handwriting of P52 "clearly belongs to the early part of the second century, and could very well be as early as the late first century."[84] According to Andrews: "Many New Testament scholars would say that P52 was copied about 110 or about 125 C.E."[85] In a journal paper on the Fourth Gospel in the light of archaeology, Wilson Paroschi says of P52 that "most scholars argue for a date no later than A.D. 125."[86]

Now, as Andrews observes:

> for a long time before the discovery of P52, the Gospel of John was argued by liberal and moderate Bible scholars to have been written in about 170 C.E., and that came to a screeching halt the moment P52 was dated to 100–150 C.E.[87]

As Neil Godfrey comments:

> The main point of interest of this fragment is that it is generally dated to around 125 CE, and that since it was found in Egypt, this date accordingly is evidence that the Gospel of John, generally thought to have been composed in Asia Minor, must have been some time earlier than 125 CE.[88]

In light of this "standard" dating of P52, and the fact that it was discovered in Egypt, Patzia suggests "that the Gospel of John may have made its way from Ephesus to Egypt during the second century,"[89] *in line with a first-century date for the Fourth Gospel.* Craig S. Keener (author of a monumental commentary on the Fourth Gospel) observes that:

> Although some skeptical scholars once dated John . . . in the late second century, the discovery of a fragment of this Gospel from the first half of the second century laid that skepticism to rest. Allowing time for the work's circulation pushes the probable date of composition back into the first century.[90]

---

83. Patzia, *Making of the New Testament*, 195.
84. Comfort, *Text of the Earliest New Testament Manuscripts*, 2:313.
85. Andrews, *P52 Project*, loc. 1738.
86. Paroschi, "Archaeology and the Interpretation," 74.
87. Andrews, *P52 Project*, loc. 1738.
88. Godfrey, "'New' Date for That St John's Fragment," §4.
89. Patzia, *Making of the New Testament*, 195 (see also page 166).
90. Keener, *John*, loc. 4.

As Andreas J. Köstenberger, another specialist on the Fourth Gospel, writes:

> The latest date of writing is prior to c. AD 135, the date of ... the John Rylands papyrus ... On the back end, some time should be allowed for the manuscript to be written and copied and make its way to Egypt ... so that a date of writing in the 80s or early 90s seems most likely.[91]

Even if we push the date of P52 to the less likely outer edge of the standard dating (that is, ca. AD 150), leaving a similar window "for the manuscript to be written and copied [and] make its way to Egypt" would put the Fourth Gospel at the end of the first century. Hence, in the judgment of Philip Wesley Comfort and David P. Barrett, P52 "testifies to the fact that the autograph of John's Gospel must have been written before the close of the first century."[92] This may be an overstatement, but the standard dating of P52 certainly suggests that the Fourth Gospel was *probably* written before the turn of the first century.

Pushing the Envelope

In chapter 3 of *Getting at Jesus* I offered a discussion of the Fourth Gospel informed by the standard dating of P52, to the effect that since the fragment dated from circa AD 125–140 and was found in Egypt, "few scholars today would ... want to date John much later than about AD 100."[93] However, Babinski brought to my attention several scholars who have recently sought to push the dating envelope of P52 somewhat, in both directions. Neil Godfrey lists paleographers who date P52 anywhere from around AD 80 to 175.[94] Andrews notes that "Pasquale Orsini (Italian paleographer, librarian, and professor) and Willy Clarysse" believe that "P52 dates to [AD] 125–175."[95] Note that these dating envelopes still tell against the second century dates for the Fourth Gospel promulgated by nineteenth- and early-twentieth century scholars like Baur and Delafosse.

Wilson Paroschi reports that:

---

91. Köstenberger, "John," 501.
92. Comfort and Barrett, *Text of the Earliest New Testament Manuscripts*, 1:337.
93. Blomberg, *Historical Reliability of John's Gospel*, 42.
94. Godfrey, "'New' Date for That St John's Fragment."
95. Andrews, *P52 Project*, loc. 173.

A. Schmidt argues for a date around 170 AD, plus or minus twenty-five years ("Zwei Anmerkungen zu P. Ryl. III 457," *APF* 35 [1989]: 11–12), and Brent Nongbri criticizes all attempts to establish a paleographic date for papyri like P52 and contends that the date range for this papyrus fragment must be extended to late second and even early third century ("The Use and Abuse of P52: Papyrological Pitfalls in the Dating of the Fourth Gospel," *HTR* 98 [2005]: 23–48). Most New Testament scholars, however, continue to favor the earlier dating.[96]

Likewise, Comfort notes that:

> A. Schmidt has challenged the earlier dating of P52. He has placed it near the end of the second century ... This redating has appealed to some scholars, but most hold with the earlier dating and still affirm that P52 is probably the earliest New Testament manuscript.[97]

So, while the date for P52 used in *Getting at Jesus* accurately reflects the scholarly consensus, that consensus isn't monolithic, with several paleographers favoring a broader range of dates. And while some of these dates are *earlier* than the standard dating, many are *later*. Consequently, Stephen C. Carlson (senior research fellow in biblical and early Christian studies at Australian Catholic University) suggests that "P52 should be dated to the mid-second century, give or take a half-century."[98]

Responding to Dissent over P52

If we follow Carlson in simply averaging proposed dates for P52, then the most we can say about the Fourth Gospel *on the basis of P52* would be that it was written by the middle of the second century. This would still be within the two generation window between the crucifixion and the editorial voice that endorses the eye-witness status of the Fourth Gospel's primary witness to Jesus.

Indeed, it is worth noting that a date in the middle of the second century would still be sufficient to make the Fourth Gospel a relatively early historical source by the standards of ancient history. The following

---

96. Paroschi, "Archaeology and the Interpretation," 74n22. See Nongbri, "Use and Abuse of P52."

97. Comfort, *Text of the Earliest New Testament Manuscripts*, 2:316.

98. Nongbri, "Brent Nongbri on P52."

table (figure 4) shows a representative sample of ancient historical and biographical works, with dates for the reported events, the publication of the source reporting about those events, and calculations pertaining to the lapse between the events and the reports:

Fig. 4.

Author/Work	Reported Events	Report Published	Lapse between Events & Report	Average Lapse
Pliny, *Letters*	AD 97–112	AD 100–112	0–3 yrs	1.5 yrs
Thucydides, *History*	431–411 BC	410–400 BC	0–30 yrs	15 yrs
Xenophon, *Anabasis*	401–399 BC	385–375 BC	15–25 yrs	20 yrs
Polybius, *History*	200–120 BC	150 BC	20–70 yrs	45 yrs
Tacitus, *Annals*	AD 14–68	ca. AD 100–110	ca. 32–96 yrs	ca. 64 yrs
Heroditus, *History*	546–478 BC	430–425 BC	48–121 yrs	84.5 yrs
Suetonius, *Lives*	50 BC–AD 95	ca. AD 120	ca. 25–170 yrs	ca. 97.5 yrs
Josephus, *War*	200 BC–AD 70	ca. AD 80	ca. 10–280 yrs	ca. 145 yrs
Plutarch, *Lives*	500 BC–AD 70	ca. AD 100	ca. 30–600 yrs	ca. 315 yrs

If the Fourth Gospel were to date to the middle of the second century, then on this metric it would still be comparable to, or better than, ancient sources such as Suetonius, Josephus, and Plutarch (with a publication gap of ca. 120 years). In other words, it would still be the case that one could not doubt the testimony of the Fourth Gospel purely on grounds of its temporal distance from the life of Jesus without thereby severely curtailing the practice of ancient history.

That said, I do not think that simply averaging scholarly opinions about the date of P52 is the way to go here. As New Testament scholar Peter M. Head writes:

> As a general rule (the virtues of democracy notwithstanding) some opinions are worth a lot more than others. Of course the opinions of general NT scholars commenting on John (Moody Smith, Raymond Brown etc.) are pretty irrelevant to the dating of a particular manuscript. But the opinions of some scholars,

who handled and examined hundreds of manuscripts, remains important. In this connection Eric Turner's acquiescence to Roberts' dating (the only codex he admitted into the first half of the second century) and Roberts' own attention to P. Fayyum 110 as the closest datable text to P52 retain some force, especially since Nongbri has, in his own admission, not found a more recently published text from a later period that is closer to P52.[99]

Of course, on the one hand, it befits the non-specialist to err on the side of caution. This suggests the thought that it may be best simply to say that while *the majority of scholarly opinion* dates P52 to the early second century AD, there are some scholars with relevant expertise who offer a wider array of dates for the fragment that span between AD 80 at one extreme and the beginning of the third century at the opposite extreme. And while the fact that P52 comes from a codex copy of the Fourth Gospel[100] found in Egypt means that the autograph should probably be dated some time earlier than P52, we cannot conclude from this that John *must* have been written in the first century. Nevertheless, we can accurately observe that *the majority of scholars* give a date for P52 *that suggests a first-century date for the Fourth Gospel* (making the Gospel more comparable on this metric to Tacitus than Suetonius).

On the other hand, even the non-specialist is able to follow something of the scholarly debate over the dating of P52, and it seems to me that Peter M. Head's comments are on target. Daniel D. Wallace (New Testament scholar and executive director of the Center for the Study of New Testament Manuscripts[101]) observes that:

> Although Brent Nongbri recently argued that P52 is irrelevant for the dating of the Gospel of John, he is basing his views on what is possible, but not on what is probable. The likelihood that this fragment really belongs to the first half of the second century—and most likely to the first quarter of the second century—gives parameters as to when John's Gospel could have been written.[102]

---

99. Head, "Date of P52," §5.

100. As Edward D. Andrews notes: "The codex came into use by the Christians in the first century and was popularized by the Christians in the second century" (*P52 Project*, loc. 433).

101. See Center for the Study of New Testament Manuscripts.

102. Wallace, "John 5.2 One More Time."

Edward D. Andrews criticizes Nongbri for "attempting to find a couple of letterforms at later dates (maybe the fading, diminishing part of the timeline) that have similar features to letters in P52 so as to date P52 to a later date range, i.e., 75–225 C.E."[103] He notes that Nongbri is actually willing to accept the verdict of Roberts that "on the whole, we may accept with some confidence the first half of the second century as the period in which (P52) was most probably written."[104]

Papyrus Egerton 2 and P52

Andrews notes that "since P. Egerton Papyrus 2 fragments have so many parallel expressions found in John's Gospel, it strongly indicates that whoever wrote [them] . . . was using John's writing as a source."[105] As J. Warner Wallace explains:

> Papyrus Egerton 2 is a collection of three papyrus fragments, dated . . . to approximately 150 AD. These fragments describe events found in all four gospels, including a narrative resembling John 5:39–47. This would not be possible unless John's Gospel was written early enough to be available to the author(s) of this document.[106]

Now, Comfort observes that:

> Schmidt redates P52 to ca. 200 based on the fact that its hand parallels that of the Egerton Gospel, which is now thought by some to date closer to ca. 200 based on [the presence in that manuscript of the specific paleographic feature of a hooked apostrophe between two consonants] appearing in a newly published portion of the Egerton Gospel.[107]

However, as Andrews points out, this redating is based on a misunderstanding:

> The biggest piece of evidence for changing the dating of P52 to 200 C.E. or later was changing the dating of P. Egerton 2 from 150 C.E. to 200 C.E. The problem with changing P. Egerton 2

---

103. Andrews, *P52 Project*, loc. 1610–28.
104. Andrews, *P52 Project*, loc. 1051.
105. Andrews, *P52 Project*, loc. 966.
106. Wallace, "John's Gospel May Have Been Last."
107. Comfort, *Encountering the Manuscripts*, 108–9.

was a hooked apostrophe between two consonants. The scholars seeking a date change misunderstood [English papyrologist Eric] Turner's words [relating] to the hooked apostrophe. Turner said it became a practice in the third century, so the scholars re-dated P. Egerton 2, P52, and P66 based on a hooked apostrophe. The problem being that Turner did not say there were no cases in the second century. In fact, he cited two examples, and there are other examples. So, it was developing in the second century and became a common practice in the third century.[108]

Moreover, as Comfort argues:

> The previously assigned date of such manuscripts was given by many scholars according to their observations of several paleographic features. Thus, the presence of this particular feature (the hook or apostrophe between double consonants) determines an earlier date for its emergence [i.e., for the emergence of this handwriting feature], not the other way around. Thus, the Egerton Gospel, dated by many to ca. 150, should still stand, and so should the date for P52 (as early second century).[109]

Stanley Porter argues that both P52 and P. Egerton 2:

> fit comfortably within the second century. There are of course some letters that are similar to those in the third century (as there are some in the first century) but the letters that tend to be given the most individualization, such as alpha, mu and even sigma, appear to be second century.[110]

Other Manuscripts and P52

Comfort reports that he personally:

> examined the manuscript P. Oxyrhynchus 2533 at the Ashmolean Museum, and was immediately impressed by its likeness to P52.... The strong similarity between this manuscript (with a firm date) and P52 helps to establish a date of P52 as being at the latest early second century (or, A.D. 100–125.)[111]

---

108. Andrews, *P52 Project*, loc. 966.
109. Comfort, *Encountering the Manuscripts*, 108–9.
110. Porter, "Recent Efforts to Reconstruct," 82.
111. Comfort, *Text of the Earliest New Testament Manuscripts*, 2:314, 315.

He dates P52 via comparison with papyri such as P. Murabba'at 113 (ca. AD 132–135), P. Oxyrhynchus 2367, 4416 (second century), 5202 (second half of the first century), and 5178 (AD 132/133), stating that:

> this dated manuscript has handwriting that is remarkably like that of P52. . . . Thus, we have a manuscript (P. Oxyrhynchus 5178) that greatly helps us date P52 to the early second century, at least.[112]

He also notes that:

> Another two hundred Greek documentary papyri, dated AD 113–120, have come from the archive of Apollonios, a strategos of Hermopolis. A thorough study of these manuscripts prompted the papyrologist Ulrich Wilcken to date P52 to the same era, on the basis of comparable paleography.[113]

As Comfort explains elsewhere:

> The eminent papyrologist, Ulrich Wilcken, indicated that . . . P52 could be contemporary with manuscripts in the Apollonios Archives, dated A.D. 117–120 (the Bremer Papyri). This is quite a significant observation inasmuch as Wilken had just completed a publication of the Bremer papyri (which includes the Apollonios Archives) when he made this observation about P52. Therefore, he was drawing upon his keen observation of several manuscripts dated between A.D. 117–120.[114]

Comfort and Barrett jointly conclude that "P52 can safely be dated to A.D. 100–125. However, its comparability to manuscripts of an even earlier period (especially P. Fayum 110 and P. London 2078), pushes the date closer to A.D. 100, plus or minus a few years."[115] Hence Comfort affirms that "in the final analysis, P52 belongs to the beginning of the second century."[116] In light of P52, Paul Foster remarks: "Was John's Gospel written before the end of the first century? Yes, probably."[117]

---

112. Comfort, *Text of the Earliest New Testament Manuscripts*, 2:315.
113. Comfort, *Encountering the Manuscripts*, 107.
114. Comfort, *Text of the Earliest New Testament Manuscripts*, 2:313–14.
115. Comfort and Barrett, *Text of the Earliest New Testament Manuscripts*, 1:338.
116. Comfort, *Text of the Earliest New Testament Manuscripts*, 2:316.
117. Quoted in Andrews, *P52 Project*, loc. 1307.

In part 2 of this inquiry, we'll see how other lines of evidence can bring greater specificity to our thinking about the date of the Fourth Gospel.

Recommended Resources

Peter S. Williams, *Getting at Jesus: A Comprehensive Critique of Neo-Atheist Nonsense about the Jesus of History* (Wipf & Stock, 2019)

The Pool of Bethesda and John 5:2

Dan Bahat, *The Atlas of Biblical Jerusalem* (Carta, 1994)
Jack Finegan, *The Archaeology of the New Testament: The Life and Beginnings of the Early Church* (Princeton, 1992)
Eric Hatfield, "Archaeology and John's Gospel," Apr 3, 2020, www.is-there-a-god.info/belief/johnandarchaeology/
Michael S. Heiser, "Who Took John 5:4 out of My Bible?," https://www.crosswalk.com/church/pastors-or-leadership/who-took-verse-4-out-of-my-bible-11627917.html
Leen Ritmeyer and Kathleen Ritmeyer, *Jerusalem: The Temple Mount* (Carta, 2015)
Biblical Archaeological Society Staff, "The Bethesda Pool, Site of One of Jesus' Miracles," *Biblical Archaeological Society*, Aug 13, 2023, www.biblicalarchaeology.org/daily/biblical-sites-places/jerusalem/the-bethesda-pool-site-of-one-of-jesus-miracles/
Shimon Gibson, "The Excavations at the Bethesda Pool in Jerusalem: Preliminary Report on a Project of Stratigraphic and Structural Analysis," www.academia.edu/22894959/The_Excavations_at_the_Bethesda_Pool_in_Jerusalem_Preliminary_Report_on_a_Project_of_Stratigraphic_and_Structural_Analysis_Text
Peter S. Williams, *Digging for Evidence* (Christian Evidence Society, 2016), http://christianevidence.org/docs/booklets/digging_for_evidence.pdf

P52

Peter S. Williams, "Papyrus 52 and the Fourth Gospel," YouTube Playlist, https://youtube.com/playlist?list=PLQhh3qcwVEWjLmvbghjTtcb3of2vH3Oxg
Peter M. Head, "Date of P52 [Comment]," *Evangelical Textual Criticism*, Jan 19, 2006, https://evangelicaltextualcriticism.blogspot.com/2006/01/date-of-p52.html#comments
Philip Wesley Comfort, *The Text of the Earliest New Testament Manuscripts: Papyri 75–139 and Uncials*, vol. 2, 3rd ed. (Kregel Academic, 2019), 313–16
Edward D. Andrews, *The P52 Project: Is P52 Really the Earliest Greek New Testament Manuscript?* (Christian Publishing House, 2020)

Chapter Four

An Interdisciplinary Inquiry into Dating the Fourth Gospel

Part II: Other Evidence

IN PART 1 OF this inquiry (see chapter 3), we saw that although John 5:2's description of the Pool of Bethesda and the Sheep Gate does not provide grounds for thinking that the Fourth Gospel was published in the first century, evidence to this effect is provided by the papyrus known as P52.

Of course, when it comes to dating the Fourth Gospel, our evidence isn't limited to John 5:2 and P52. The Fourth Gospel mentions "the disciple whom Jesus loved . . . who had leaned back against Jesus at the supper" (John 21:20, see also 11:3, 11:36, 13:23, 19:26, 20:2, 21:7, and 21:20) and identifies him as "the disciple who testifies to these things and who wrote them down" (John 21:24). Whoever this disciple was, his status as a reliable source about life in Jerusalem before AD 70 is corroborated by a number of external points that have nothing to do with John 5:2:

> These include for example the apparent allusion to the practice of pouring living water over the altar at the Feast of Tabernacles [see John 7:37–38,] a practice discontinued after the destruction of Jerusalem, the peculiar inter-relationship between Jewish and Roman law and jurisdiction, the potentially shaky position of Pontius Pilate, exploited by the Jewish leaders in telling him that if he releases Jesus he is not Caesar's friend, etc.[1]

1. Lydia McGrew, personal correspondence, Jan 2024. On John 7:37–38, see

Even if we take into account the existence of an editorial group working with this disciple's testimony to produce the Fourth Gospel, the overlap between "the disciple whom Jesus loved" and his editors is a factor that on its own sets a *latest possible date* for the publication of the Fourth Gospel at about AD 180. Indeed, the existence of a Fourth Gospel is mentioned in the Muratorian Fragment, dated circa 180–200, which affirms: "The fourth book of the gospel is that of John, one of the disciples."[2] However, this data is consistent with F. C. Baur's nineteenth-century dating of the Fourth Gospel from AD 160–170. Is there any evidence, in addition to P52, for dating the Fourth Gospel earlier than Baur allowed?

Quotations from and Allusions to the Fourth Gospel

Jo-Ann A. Brant observes that "Justin Martyr, writing in about AD 155, knew the dialogue with Nicodemus in John 3:1–5 (1 *Apol.* 61)."[3] N. T. Wright and Michael F. Bird note that "Gnostic authors cited the [fourth] gospel, and alluded to it, perhaps as early as AD 135."[4] As F. F. Bruce writes:

> Hippolytus states that the gnostic Basilides (c. AD 130) quoted John 1:9 (about the true light coming into the world) as a gloss on the creative word "Let there be light" (Gen. 1:2); if he is right, then that is the earliest known explicit quotation from the gospel of John. *The Gospel of Truth* (c. AD 140), a gnostic work coming either from Valentinus or from one of his disciples, has several echoes of our Gospel if not direct quotations.[5]

Then again, Paul Barnett argues that "comparison with parallel passages in the early second century writer Ignatius, Bishop of Antioch, shows that John was not the very late author many believe him to be."[6] On the contrary: "since Ignatius wrote early in the second century, it follows that this gospel was written during the first century."[7] Likewise, Catholic theologians Scott Hahn and Curtis Mitch note that "Ignatius of Antioch

---

McGrew, *Testimonies to the Truth*, 35–36.

2. Barnett, *Is the New Testament History?*, loc. 58.
3. Brant, *John*, 4.
4. Wright and Bird, *New Testament in Its World*, 660.
5. Bruce, *Gospel of John*, 7.
6. Barnett, *Is the New Testament History?*, loc. 1120.
7. Barnett, *Is the New Testament History?*, loc. 1120.

seems to allude to the teaching of the Fourth Gospel in a collection of letters written about A.D. 107. This makes it probable that [the Fourth Gospel] was composed by at least A.D. 100."[8]

It might be objected that a disciple of Jesus would have been in his nineties at the end of the first century, and that this is implausible. However, Keener points out that "typical disciples were in their teens, however, making eighties likelier than nineties. Moreover, we know of other ancient thinkers in their eighties and nineties with sharp memories and wit."[9] If we suppose that the beloved disciple was eighteen when Jesus died in April of AD 33,[10] he'd have been eighty-three by April of AD 98, which was soon after the Roman Emperor Trajan began his reign.[11] Testimony from the beloved disciple in AD 98 about Jesus's crucifixion in AD 33 would be comparable to the contemporary testimony given by Mary Ellen Ford (1946–) about the day Dr. Martin Luther King Jr. was assassinated at the hotel where she worked as a cook in 1968.[12]

The Fourth Gospel according to Whom?

Craig S. Keener explains that:

> Classicists place heavy weight on external testimonies for authorship. External evidence (i.e., ancient writers starting in the generation immediately after this Gospel) attributes this Gospel to John the son of Zebedee. Indeed, early tradition is almost unanimous that the apostle "John" wrote the Fourth Gospel.[13]

The title "According to John" is attached to every manuscript of the Fourth Gospel that has a title attached, and these titled manuscripts date "at least from the end of the second century, if not earlier. It is found in manuscripts P66 and P75, which are usually dated around AD 200."[14] As Paul Barnett notes: "The Muratorian Fragment, dated c. 180–200 states: 'The fourth book of the gospel is that of John, one of the disciples.'"[15] Likewise,

---

8. Hahn and Mitch, *Gospel of John*, loc. 249, 262.
9. Keener, *John*, loc. 4.
10. See Köstenberger, "April 3, AD 33"; Köstenberger et al., *Final Days of Jesus*.
11. See Benario, "Trajan (A.D. 98–117)."
12. Gottlieb and Kim, "Eyewitness in Iconic Photo."
13. Keener, *John*, loc. 3.
14. Wright and Bird, *New Testament in Its World*, 653.
15. Barnett, *Is the New Testament History?*, loc. 58.

the early church fathers unanimously attribute the Fourth Gospel to the apostle John, one of the sons of Zebedee (see Mark 3:17 and 10:35; Luke 5:10; and John 21:2), and thus a cousin to Jesus on his mother's side.[16] As Francis Martin and William M. Wright IV comment, any alternative theory about the origins of the Fourth Gospel:

> requires an explanation as to why this Gospel would have been wrongly associated with John the Apostle at such an early date and by people who claim to have known him personally (e.g., Polycarp).[17]

Writing circa AD 180, Irenaeus (a protégé of John's disciple Polycarp, ca. AD 69–156[18]) stated that "John, the disciple of the Lord, who leaned back on his breast, published the Gospel while he was resident at Ephesus in Asia."[19] Irenaeus tracks this view back "to a group of Asian elders, probably including Papias of Hierapolis [ca. AD 60–130[20]] and Polycarp of Smyrna [ca. AD 69–156], who had conversed with John before his death after a long old age, probably during the reign of Trajan (AD 98–117)."[21] In the fourth century AD, Eusebius quoted Papias (via Irenaeus) as saying:

> If, then, any one came, who had been a follower of the elders, I questioned him in regard to the words of the elders . . . what was said by Philip, or by Thomas or by James, or by John, or by Matthew, or by any other of the disciples of the Lord, and what things Aristion and the presbyter [or "elder"] John, the disciples of the Lord, say. For I did not think that what was to be gotten from the books would profit me as much as what came from the living and abiding voice.[22]

Some scholars think that Papias (writing ca. AD 95–110[23]) distinguished between "John the disciple of the Lord" and "John the presbyter/elder," while others think these phrases have the same referent.[24] Several

---

16. See Wilkins, "Matthew," 134.
17. Martin and Wright, *Gospel of John*, 17.
18. *Christianity Today*, "Polycarp"; Bacchus, "St. Polycarp."
19. Irenaeus, *Against Heresies*, quoted in Köstenberger, "John," 500.
20. See Wikipedia, "Papias of Hierapolis."
21. Wright and Bird, *New Testament in Its World*, 654.
22. Eusebius, *Ecclesiastical History* 3.39.1–7.
23. Yarborough, "Date of Papias."
24. See Kruger, "Did Papias Know the Apostle John?"

scholars who distinguish between these referents attribute the Fourth Gospel to John "the elder" rather than John "the apostle."[25] Either way, the Gospel is rooted in the eyewitness testimony of a disciple. However, as Karen H. Jobes points out:

> Papias mentions John twice, once as a "disciple of the Lord" and again as an "elder." But Eusebius overlooked the fact that even when Papias refers to Peter and James, he doesn't at first call them "apostles" but "elders," suggesting that the two titles were not mutually exclusive in Papias.[26]

As Robert W. Yarborough elaborates:

> It seems that Eusebius exploits a linguistic ambiguity that had arisen between the respective apostolic and Nicene eras: Papias reflecting first-century usage could use "elder" to be inclusive of "apostle," as is occasionally the case in the NT (Acts 11:30; 21:18; 1 Pet. 5:1; possibly 2 John 1; 3 John 1). For Eusebius, however, it is feasible through selective quotation and tendentious exegesis to force on the word "elder" the connotation of a *follower* of an apostle or some other Christian leader.[27]

Moreover, Keener notes that "while tradition sometimes blended figures with two names, more often writers distinguished them more clearly than does the earliest second-century tradition about John, and sometimes they created two persons based on a single one."[28]

That the apostle John is in some sense the author of the Fourth Gospel would explain why it never mentions him by name although the Synoptic Gospels all present him as one of Jesus's inner circle. Milne draws attention to how "the notably close association in this gospel of the 'disciple whom Jesus loved' with Peter [echoes] the close association of John and Peter in Acts."[29] Moreover, while the Synoptic Gospels are careful to distinguish between John "the Baptist" and John "the Apostle," the Fourth Gospel simply refers to the Baptist as "John." As A. Rendle Short observes: "If there are two boys at school, J. Smith and T. Smith,

---

25. See Wright and Bird, *New Testament in Its World*, 656–59.
26. Jobes, "Who wrote 1, 2, and 3 John?"
27. Yarborough, *1–3 John*, 15.
28. Keener, *John*, loc. 3.
29. Milne, *Message of John*, 17.

other boys in writing will distinguish them by their initial, but when J. is writing, he will speak of the other simply as Smith."[30]

Finally, the association of the Fourth Gospel with John the brother of James and son of Zebedee is not contradicted by Jesus's response to the brother's request to sit at Jesus's right and left hand in his glory, as some have suggested. As Mark reports the incident:

> James and John, the sons of Zebedee, came up to [Jesus] and said to him, "Teacher, we want you to do for us whatever we ask of you." And he said to them, "What do you want me to do for you?" And they said to him, "Grant us to sit, one at your right hand and one at your left, in your glory." Jesus said to them, "You do not know what you are asking. Are you able to drink the cup that I drink, or to be baptized with the baptism with which I am baptized?" And they said to him, "We are able." And Jesus said to them, "The cup that I drink you will drink, and with the baptism with which I am baptized, you will be baptized, but to sit at my right hand or at my left is not mine to grant, but it is for those for whom it has been prepared." (Mark 10:35–40 ESV; see also Matt 20:20–27)

Theologian James A. Brooks observes that:

> vv. 38–39 does not necessarily refer to the disciples' martyrdom. Just as the disciples' death would not have the same significance as that of Jesus, so their "cup" and "baptism" would not necessarily take the same form as his.[31]

Commenting upon the parallel passage in Matt 20:20–27, Craig L. Blomberg says:

> Jesus asks if John and James are prepared to experience rejection and persecution for their faith. They may not literally die for their discipleship (James did—Acts 12:2; reasonably strong church tradition suggests that John did not) . . . but they can expect to encounter a variety of hostilities in response to their Christian testimony.[32]

Brooks notes that "the later epitomizer" (i.e., abridger or summarizer) of the mid fifth-century AD *Chronicle of Philip of Side*:

---

30. Short, *Why Believe?*, 37.
31. Brooks, *Mark*, 168–69.
32. Blomberg, *Matthew*, 307.

claimed that Papias (ca. A.D. 130) indicated that John and James were killed by the Jews. George the Sinner (ca. A.D. 840), who may have been dependent on Philip, said the same thing and claimed the deaths were a fulfillment of Mark 10:39.... Philip, however, so far as can be judged from the surviving fragments of his works and the comments of ancient historians about him, was unreliable.... Irenaeus (ca. A.D. 180) and Eusebius (ca. A.D. 325) had read Papias, and they mention no such statement. The much earlier and more widespread tradition is that John the apostle lived to a very old age and died a natural death in Ephesus in Asia Minor. His death, however, came after suffering exile and torture during the time of the emperor Domitian (ca. A.D. 95). The last item is also sufficient fulfillment of the prophecy.[33]

In sum, I agree with Scott Hahn and Curtis Mitch that "the combined weight of textual and traditional evidence suggests that [the disciple behind the fourth Gospel] is the Apostle John, one of the sons of Zebedee (Mt 4:21)."[34] In the words of Craig L. Blomberg:

> A good case can be made that the fourth Gospel was written by John, the "one Jesus loved" (as he referred to himself throughout his book), brother of James and son of Zebedee, just as early church tradition suggests. That same tradition places John in and around Ephesus, ministering to the churches of Asia Minor, until his death as an elderly man at roughly the end of the first century. The author would thus have been an eyewitness of much of the material he recounted and in a position to provide accurate information.[35]

The Fourth Gospel according to John, with Editorial Support from His Disciples

That said, John 21:20–24 appears to distinguish between the "beloved disciple" as the eyewitness author and/or source for the bulk of the Gospel's testimony (see John 13:23, 18:16, 19:26, 20:2–8, 21:7, and 21:20), and the commenting voice of the Gospel's editor/s:

> Peter turned and saw that the disciple whom Jesus loved was following them. (This was the one who had leaned back against

---

33. Brooks, *Mark*, 169.
34. Hahn and Mitch, *Gospel of John*.
35. Blomberg, "Introduction to John's Gospel," 1303.

Jesus at the supper and had said, "Lord, who is going to betray you?") When Peter saw him, he asked, "Lord, what about him?" Jesus answered, "If I want him to remain alive until I return, what is that to you? You must follow me." Because of this, the rumor spread among the believers that this disciple would not die. But Jesus did not say that he would not die; he only said, "If I want him to remain alive until I return, what is that to you?" *This is the disciple who testifies to these things and who wrote them down. We know that his testimony is true.* (John 21:2–24, my italics)

As Martin and Wright note:

> An intriguing possibility, proposed by C. K. Barrett and developed by John Painter, is that the Beloved Disciple is John the Apostle, the son of Zebedee, whose traditions and work were shaped into the Fourth Gospel by one of his disciples. This hypothesis accounts for the ancient traditions about authorship while also accounting for the evidence that the Gospel underwent some editing in its composition history.[36]

John Drane theorizes:

> It seems at least possible that the gospel was first written in Palestine, to demonstrate that "Jesus is the Christ" (20:31), perhaps over against the views of sectarian Jews influenced by ideas like those of the Qumran community, and then when the same teaching was seen to be relevant to people elsewhere in the Roman empire, it was revised, with Jewish customs and expressions being explained, and the prologue and epilogue added. The advice to church leaders in chapter 21 suggests that the final form of the gospel might have been directed to a Christian congregation comprised of both Jews and Gentiles somewhere in the Hellenistic world, perhaps at Ephesus.[37]

Blomberg argues that "the peculiar ending of chapter 21 is to be explained at least by John's advancing age if not his actual, recent death"[38] and comments that "there may have been something of a gap between the draft of the Gospel . . . (which itself could have circulated locally in and around Ephesus) and its final redaction."[39] Powell observes that:

---

36. Martin and Wright, *Gospel of John*, 17.
37. Drane, *Introducing the New Testament*, 217.
38. Blomberg, *Historical Reliability of John's Gospel*, 44.
39. Blomberg, *Historical Reliability of John's Gospel*, 44.

John is usually said to have been produced in the 90s, since that is when the final redaction is likely to have taken place, but the scholars who say this generally recognize that much of the material in John comes from an earlier time.[40]

According to historian John Dickson:

> Many scholars . . . detect an earlier source within the Gospel of John. They call it the Signs Source or SQ for short. . . . SQ appears to have been a collection of seven miracle stories or signs highlighting Jesus' status as Messiah.[41]

Bart Ehrman reports that:

> Scholars have long suspected that John had at his disposal an earlier written account of Jesus' miracles (the so-called Signs Source), at least two accounts of Jesus' long speeches (the Discourse Sources), and possibly another passion source as well.[42]

Geisler states that "John uses independent sources of his own that can be traced on linguistic grounds to between A.D. 30 and 66."[43]

In line with the multi-stage composition hypothesis, we might suppose that "the beloved disciple" built upon these sources in writing what we would now see as the literary ancestor of the Fourth Gospel, perhaps in the early 60s AD (or even earlier than that), but perhaps later in the first century. Indeed, it seems plausible to think that "the beloved disciple" was himself the source behind some or all of these "sources." The postulation of one source is, after all, simpler than the postulation of multiple sources. Then (whether before or after his death) associates of "the beloved disciple" produced a "second edition" of his Gospel, or of his draft of, or notes for a Gospel (this material may not have been circulated, at least not widely, if "the beloved disciple" didn't consider it to have been finished) in Ephesus some time after the Jewish War. J. Dongell speculates along these lines:

> Could these associates of the Beloved Disciple (perhaps younger believers discipled by him) have been responsible for collecting his writings, for merging them into a single, continuous narrative, and for identifying their mentor as "the disciple Jesus

---

40. Powell, *Introducing the New Testament*, 176.
41. Dickson, *Investigating Jesus*, 118.
42. Ehrman, *Did Jesus Exist?*, 82.
43. Geisler, *Christian Apologetics*, 313.

loved" wherever he appeared in the narrative? Such a theory makes sense of a variety of factors: the claim that the Beloved Disciple "wrote [these things] down" (21:24); the presence of the "we" of verse 24; the possibility that the disciple died shortly before the publication of the Fourth Gospel (see . . . 21:20–23); and the application of a title of such honor ("the disciple Jesus loved") to one identified as the writer (21:24).[44]

Of course, John's associates needn't have had so much to do as all that if they were working with a draft, or even a first edition, of the Fourth Gospel. Lydia McGrew argues that little editorial work seems to have been done on John's Gospel:

> given the very distinctive Greek style and the presence of things like unexplained allusions, which have a nicely "bumpy" testimonial texture that would understandably be edited out if one were trying to smooth the document.[45]

Moreover, the theory that the testimonial source behind the Fourth Gospel was already dead when it was published[46] is contradicted by Irenaeus's statement that "John, the disciple of the Lord, who leaned back on his breast, published the Gospel while he was resident at Ephesus in Asia."[47] Of course, it is *possible* that Irenaeus is mistakenly referring to material written by John that was later incorporated into the "Gospel according to John" after the disciple's death. However, in the absence of evidence to the contrary, the presumption of truth should be given to Irenaeus's information.[48]

---

44. Dongell, *John*, loc. 289.

45. Lydia McGrew, personal correspondence, Jan 2024.

46. I doubt that much significance can be attributed to the tense used when John 21:24 talks of "the disciple who *testifies* to these things," rather than the disciple who "testified" to these things.

47. Irenaeus, *Against Heresies*, quoted in Köstenberger, "John," 500.

48. J. Warner Wallace notes that "a set of early introductions to the Gospels, known as the Anti-Marcionite Prologues (penned as early as 150 AD), cites Papias as the source for the claim that 'the Gospel of John was revealed and given to the churches by John while *still in the body* (emphasis mine)'" ("John's Gospel May Have Been Last," §14). However, little weight should be put on this. As Robert M. Grant observes: "A so-called 'anti-Marcionite prologue' to the Gospel of John states that John dictated his gospel to Papias himself; but this highly garbled document is not likely to give us any trustworthy information about either Papias or John. Modern study of the prologue places it in the fourth century, or even later" (*Historical Introduction to the New Testament*, 106). Helmut Koester argues that "a date in the second half of the 4th century is likely for the *Prologues* for Mark and John" (*Ancient Christian Gospels*, 243).

Martin and Wright argue that:

> John 21:22–23 refutes a mistaken belief, circulating among some Christians, that the Beloved Disciple would survive to see the Parousia, and the need to refute such a belief may have been occasioned by the fact that the Beloved Disciple had died by the time of the Gospel's final editing.[49]

However, the need to refute the mistaken belief that the Beloved Disciple would survive to see the parousia may have simply been occasioned by the fact that John knew what Jesus had actually meant and wanted to set the record straight in light of a misinterpretation that took hold given his advanced age.[50] According to Irenaeus, John lived "up to the times of Trajan."[51]

John's Exile and Dating the Fourth Gospel within the Johannine Corpus

As D. Moody Smith observes:

> From the end of the second century onward, the Fourth Gospel, joined later by the letters and Revelation, gained wide, and ultimately universal, recognition as the work of John the Apostle, the disciple of the Lord.[52]

With respect to Revelation, Leon Morris notes that:

> The Gnostic *Apocryphon Johannis*, dated no later than c. A.D. 150, cites Revelation 1:19, in such a way as to indicate that the author was John the apostle. Support is found in Irenaeus, while the Muratorian Fragment twice speaks of the author as John, evidently meaning the apostle. Clement of Alexandrea appears

---

49. Martin and Wright, *Gospel of John*, 17.

50. As Albert Barnes comments: "This mistake arose very naturally: 1. From the words of Jesus, which might be easily misunderstood to mean that he should not die; and 2. It was probably confirmed when it was seen that John survived all the other apostles, had escaped all the dangers of persecution, and was leading a peaceful life at Ephesus. This mistake John deemed it proper to correct before he died, and has thus left on record what Jesus said and what he meant" ("Commentary on John 21"). Note that a) the Greek behind "I come" in John 21:22 is "erchomai," and may refer to the fall of Jerusalem in AD 70 (see Matthew 16:28), rather than the Parousia; b) John 21:22 is in the conditional.

51. Irenaeus, *Against Heresies* 2:22:5.

52. Smith, *First, Second, and Third John*, 16.

to support this view, as does Tertullian . . . . There does not appear to be evidence of an early or well-grounded tradition which regards anyone other than the apostle as the author.[53]

Martin and Wright note that:

> there are some curious similarities between the Gospel and Revelation. For instance, these are the only two New Testament writings to call Jesus "the Lamb" (John 1:29; Rev 5:6) and "the Word of God" (John 1:1; Rev 19:13). These are also the only two New Testament writings to cite clearly the oracle in Zech 12:10.[54]

According to Michael Wilcock, when it comes to dating the apocalypse: "some scholars . . . place the writing of the book at the end of Nero's reign (AD 54–68), or, less convincingly, in Vesputin's (AD 69–79). Most evidence, however, seems to favour a date in the latter part of the range of Domitian (AD 81–96)."[55] On this latter, majority dating, John would have written Revelation having been exiled to Patmos by the Domitian administration.[56] This circumstance would explain the much discussed linguistic differences and similarities between Revelation and the Fourth Gospel. As Morris comments: "Revelation was written in exile. The writer had no access to the tools of scholarship . . . it is possible that one and the same author had the help of an amanuensis in composing the Gospel, but not in Revelation."[57] According to Irenaeus, John's apocalyptic vision "was seen no very long time since, but almost in our day, towards the end of Domitian's reign."[58] Hence M. Eugene Boring affirms that Revelation "is best understood as a letter written in 96 by John."[59] Revelation was presumably copied and spread out from Ephesus upon John's return from exile. Indeed, in his third-century commentary on Revelation, Victorianus of Pettau claimed that the apocalypse had been written during Domitian's rule, but published under Nerva.[60] We might

---

53. Morris, *Revelation*, 27–28.
54. Martin and Wright, *Gospel of John*, 22.
55. Wilcock, *Message of Revelation*, 22.
56. Gordon Franz suggests "that John was exiled to Patmos because of its Artemis/Ephesus connections. The proconsul of Asia Minor wanted John out of Ephesus so he sent him to Patmos, also within his jurisdiction" ("King and I," §10). See also Rapske, "Exiles, Islands, and the Identity," 311–46.
57. Morris, *Revelation*, 31, 32.
58. Irenaeus, *Against Heresies*, 5:30:3.
59. Boring, *Revelation*, 10. See also Jackson, "When Was the Book of Revelation."
60. See Jańczuk, "Dating the Book of Revelation."

even conjecture that this circumstance encouraged the completion and publication of the Fourth Gospel.

According to *On the Apostles and Disciples*, which was originally attributed to the second- or third-century Christian theologian Hippolytus of Rome, but is today generally attributed to an anonymous author of the fourth century dubbed "Pseudo-Hippolytus":

> John, again, in Asia, was banished by Domitian the king to the isle of Patmos, in which also he wrote his Gospel and saw the apocalyptic vision; and in Trajan's time he fell asleep at Ephesus.[61]

We probably shouldn't rely upon a single, anonymous, and comparatively late source such as this for the claim that John wrote his Gospel as well as his apocalypse while in exile, but it *may* reflect a tradition about the two documents appearing around about the same time.

Domitian was succeeded by Nerva, who was in turn succeeded by Trajan. Donald L. Wasson recounts that after Nerva died a natural death in January AD 98:

> Trajan was quickly named emperor by the Roman Senate, the second of those who would become known as the Five Good Emperors . . . . As an emperor who was concerned with both good government and the public welfare, he instituted an excellent domestic policy—providing for the children of the poor, restoring the dilapidated road system, as well as building new bridges, aqueducts, public baths, and a modern port at Ostia. Lastly, *he continued his predecessor's policy of undoing much of the harm done by Domitian by freeing prisoners and recalling exiles.*[62]

Thus, at some time after the death of Domitian: "John was released from Patmos, whereupon he returned to Ephesus, where he had been ministering before his exile. Then, several years later, around A.D. 100, John died."[63] There is a clear window of opportunity, after his return from exile and before his death, for John to have "published the Gospel while he was resident at Ephesus in Asia"[64] as Irenaeus reported. We might even speculate that it was John's exile that accounts for the "gap between the draft of the Gospel . . . (which itself could have circulated locally in and around Ephesus) and its final redaction"[65] hypothesized by some

---

61. Roberts et al., "On the Disciples."
62. Wasson, "Trajan," §1–2, my italics.
63. Barton et al, *Revelation*, xiii.
64. Irenaeus, *Against Heresies*, quoted in Köstenberger, *Gospels and Acts*, 500.
65. Blomberg, *Historical Reliability of John's Gospel*, 44.

scholars (though it remains *possible* that the Gospel according to John was published before his exile).

With respect to the Johannine Epistles, Karen H. Jobes argues that "the relationship between the three letters and between them and the [fourth] gospel indicates that the same author likely wrote all three letters."[66] As Martin and Wright observe:

> The Gospel of John is closest in theology and literary style to the three Letters of John. Like the Gospel, 1 John does not name its author, but 2 and 3 John claim to be written by "the Presbyter," or Elder. The Gospel and Letters of John are stylistically similar in their special theological vocabulary and pairs of opposites. The Letters were likely written after the Gospel, and they elaborate on topics found in the Gospel (e.g., the love command in 1 John 5:1–5).[67]

Hence, as Yarborough concludes: "It is not unreasonable to adopt the interpretative assumption that the John of the Gospel also stands behind the Johannine Epistles."[68]

According to Marianne Meye Thompson, the Johannine Epistles are typically "assigned to the end of the first century, perhaps somewhere between the years A.D. 90 to 100. . . . If the Epistles were written after the [fourth] Gospel, as most scholars assume, then they must fall in the last decade of so of the last century."[69] Our reconstruction can certainly accommodate time after the publication of John's Gospel for him to issue his three brief Epistles towards the end of the first century and of his life.

In sum, it seems to me that the Fourth Gospel was most likely published *within John's lifetime, with his approval, either during the reign of Nerva* (AD 96–98) *or close to the start of Trajan's reign* (which commenced in AD 98, when John would have been in his early eighties). Indeed, we can plausibly date John's Apocalypse within the AD 90–96 time frame, John's Gospel within the AD 96–98 time frame, and John's Epistles circa AD 96–100.

Conclusion

The Fourth Gospel is notoriously difficult to date. J. Ramsey Michaels simply dates the Gospel to the second half of the first century (AD 50–100),

---

66. Jobes, "Who Wrote 1, 2, and 3 John?"
67. Martin and Wright, *Gospel of John*, 22.
68. Yarborough, *1–3 John*, 15.
69. Thompson, *1–3 John*, 20–21.

while leaning toward a date after AD 70.[70] In my book *Getting at Jesus* (Wipf & Stock, 2019) I pegged the production of the Fourth Gospel to "ca. AD 60–90,"[71] proposing that John had composed much of the Gospel in the early 60s, and quoting a selection of scholars who placed the final publication of the Gospel in the 80s or 90s. For example, Blomberg writes:

> While it is true that the external evidence focuses primarily on John's age and location of ministry rather than explicitly tying the authorship of his Gospel to the late date, the subsequent conviction of the church that became the "traditional" position should probably be accepted, dating the Fourth Gospel either to the 80s or to the 90s.[72]

In this two part inquiry—after considering (a) the evidence provided by P52, (b) the Fourth Gospel's internal testimony to have been completed by people who knew the eyewitness "beloved disciple" behind the bulk of its testimony, and (c) the external testimony and evidence from Papias, Ignatius, and Irenaeus—I retain the two-stage composition theory, allowing that the literary origins of the Gospel *may* stretch back to the 60s AD or even earlier, while tentatively concluding that the final form of John's Gospel was probably published with John's approval in Ephesus circa AD 96–98.

This dating of the Fourth Gospel is entirely mainstream. We've already seen that a wide variety of scholars see earlier sources behind or within the Fourth Gospel, and Porter reports that "virtually all scholars agree that John's Gospel was the last written and that this would have occurred, at the latest, around AD 90."[73] Keener reckons that "most scholars maintain a date in the mid-90s."[74] J. Dongell cautiously argues that:

> Supposing John the son of Zebedee to be the author of the Gospel, and his disciples to have been its editors and publishers shortly after his death, it seems reasonable to suggest from A.D. 80 to 100 as the span within which the Gospel was published. The time of John's own writing activity may have preceded his death by moments or decades. Such are the ambiguities involved in dating.[75]

---

70. Michaels, *Gospel of John*, 38.
71. Williams, *Getting at Jesus*, 207.
72. Blomberg, *Historical Reliability of John's Gospel*, 44.
73. Porter, *How We Got the New Testament*, 86.
74. Keener, *John*, loc. 4.
75. Dongell, *John*, loc. 215.

Indeed, Dongell thinks "it most probable that John, son of Zebedee, one of the twelve disciples, was the Beloved Disciple, that he wrote the bulk of the contents of the Fourth Gospel, and that his disciples edited and published his work sometime after his death."[76] However, it seems to me that the testimony of Irenaeus should be given the benefit of the doubt, with the result that the publication of the Fourth Gospel should be dated *before the end of the apostle's life*. Consequently, and allowing time for the Johannine Epistles to postdate the Fourth Gospel, I suggest that John's Gospel was probably published in its extant form under the Emperor Nerva (AD 96–98). This (necessarily tentative) conclusion is only slightly more definite than that of N. T. Wright and Michael F. Bird, who say: "There is no strong evidence against the traditional date near the end of the century, either towards the end of Domitian's reign (AD 81–96) or at the beginning of Trajan's (AD 98–117)."[77]

And while the Fourth Gospel's accurate description of the Pool of Bethesda and the Sheep Gate *doesn't* require a first-century date for the testimony contained within the Fourth Gospel, it is one piece of evidence among many[78] that indicate the *reliability* of the Fourth Gospel's eyewitness, first-century testimony to the life, death, and resurrection of Jesus.

Recommended Resources

Peter S. Williams, "John's Gospel," YouTube Playlist, www.youtube.com/playlist?list=PLQhh3qcwVEWjZ96UEngK_Iojs-_hX-H9O

Chad, "59 Confirmed or Historically Probable Facts in the Gospel of John," *Truthbomb* (blog), Nov 9, 2017, http://truthbomb.blogspot.com/2012/02/59-confirmed-or-historically-probable.html

David A. Croteau, "An Analysis of the Arguments for the Dating of the Fourth Gospel," *Faculty Publications and Presentations*, paper 118 (2003), https://core.ac.uk/download/pdf/58821862.pdf

Andreas J. Köstenberger and Stephen O. Stout, "'The Disciple Jesus Loved': Witness, Author, Apostle—A Response to Richard Bauckham's *Jesus and the Eyewitnesses*," *Bulletin for Biblical Research* 18:2 (2008) 209–31, https://s3.amazonaws.com/5mt.bf.org/2017/10/40-Disciple-Jesus-Loved.pdf

Craig L. Blomberg, *The Historical Reliability of John's Gospel: Issues and Commentary* (Apollos, 2001)

Andreas J. Köstenberger, "John," in *The Gospels and Acts*, edited by Jeremy Royal Howard, The Holman Apologetics Commentary on the Bible (Holman, 2013)

Lydia McGrew, *The Eye of the Beholder: The Gospel of John as Historical Reportage* (DeWard, 2021)

---

76. Dongell, *John*, loc. 303.
77. Wright and Bird, *New Testament in Its World*, 661.
78. See Blomberg, *Historical Reliability of John's Gospel*; McGrew, *Eye of the Beholder*.

Chapter Five

Resurrection: Faith or Fact? Miracle Not Required?[1]

I WAS PRIVILEGED TO have the opportunity to contribute two chapters to *Resurrection: Faith or Fact?* (Pitchstone, 2019). One of these chapters reviewed the written resurrection debate therein between atheist Carl Stecher (professor emeritus of English at Salem State University) and Christian Craig L. Blomberg (distinguished professor of the New Testament at Denver Seminary in Colorado).[2] While I had a couple of critical comments relating to Professor Blomberg's chapters, I focused my attention on Professor Stecher's contribution to the debate, grouping my observations under the headings listed in the title of my review chapter: "Evidence, Explanation and Expectation" ("EEE"). In his closing essay, "Miracle Not Required," Stecher responded to "EEE." Here, I respond in turn to "Miracle Not Required," using the same categories used in "EEE."

---

1. This is a revised version of my paper "*Resurrection: Faith or Fact? Miracle Not Required?*"

2. My other contribution was one of the four biographical chapters that opened the book. Atheist Richard Carrier likewise contributed a biographical chapter and a chapter reviewing the debate between Carl and Craig, to which Craig responds in his closing remarks. As far as I'm aware, this was and is the only volume debating the resurrection that's published by a secular printing press.

Evidence—Part One: Historical Methodology

Stecher opens his debate with Blomberg by asserting that "what is lacking is any method for differentiating the historical from the legendary and fictional,"[3] genres he believes are mixed together in the New Testament. In "EEE" I note that if Stecher lacks a method for differentiating between historical and non-historical material, he cannot justify his assertion that the Gospels contain both types of material (for example, Stecher holds that the crucifixion is historical but the empty tomb isn't). Contra Stecher, I maintain that, even on his assumption that the canonical Gospels "contradict each other" and that consequently "at least some of the information" in them "must be wrong,"[4] the historical criteria of authenticity[5] provide us with principled ways of "determining what if any of it [i.e., the resurrection narratives] is actually historical."[6]

In "Miracle Not Required," Stecher makes an apparent *mea culpa* that quickly turns into *a red herring*:

> Peter's challenge is justified; at the very least my point needs clarification. My statement reflects a position of skepticism and the rejection of Christian biblical literalism and infallibility . . . This is, after all, a pivotal issue in any consideration of the historicity of the New Testament accounts of Jesus' resurrection.[7]

However, my point was that Stecher's skepticism isn't methodologically principled, and this response simply avoids the issue at hand. Moreover, by using criteria of historicity, one can argue for *specific* points of historical veracity within the NT, and even for the *general* historical reliability of the NT, without appealing to any notion of biblical "infallibility" (or inerrancy).[8]

I wonder whether Stecher is at least *gesturing* towards an argument here, to the effect that there exists a warranted connection between belief in Jesus's resurrection and belief in the "infallibility" of the NT, such that evidence against the latter is thereby evidence against the former. This elaboration of Stecher's mention of infallibility would be of a piece with

---

3. Stecher, "Historical Evidence Is Insufficient," 61.
4. Stecher, "Historical Evidence Is Insufficient," 63.
5. See Stein, "Criteria for the Gospel's Authenticity"; Williams, *Getting at Jesus*, 242–48.
6. Stecher, "Historical Evidence Is Insufficient," 63.
7. Stecher, "Miracle Not Required," 265.
8. See Williams, "Inspiration, Authority and Activity."

his indirect arguments, which I will examine later, about the accessibility of salvation and the problem of evil. *If* Stecher has such an argument in mind, *then* he's relying upon several additional assumptions: that "infallibility" is inconsistent with a specific type of textual data, that there's warrant for believing that this specific type of data exists within the NT, and that this warrant is stronger than the warrant for belief in the resurrection. Since Stecher doesn't actually articulate an indirect argument along these lines, he doesn't explicitly defend any of these assumptions. That said, Stecher does pursue something in the ballpark of assumption 2, doubling down on his assertion "that the historicity of the resurrection accounts is undermined by passages in the Gospels and in Paul's epistles that . . . are clearly legends or fictionalizations."[9] Stecher lists several passages that he thinks are "clearly legends or fictionalizations":

> I place in these categories the birth legends in Matthew and Luke (which contradict each other and are in conflict with known facts about the period); the opening of John, with its portrayal of Jesus' role in the creation about six thousand years ago; those passages in which the voice of God comes out of the sky (Matthew 3: 16–17 and many others) . . . conversations recorded verbatim and at length for which there were no plausible witnesses (Judas and the Temple priests in Matthew 27:3–6; the guards and the temple priests plotting false testimony in Matthew 28:12–13); Pilate questioning Jesus in a private interview in John 18:28–38, despite our being told, "It was now early morning, and the Jews themselves stayed outside the headquarters to avoid defilement, so that they could eat the Passover Meal" (18:28).

However, even if Stecher had a principled method that allowed him to reliably detect "legends or fictionalizations" within a text, and even if that method supported his designation of all the passages he mentions as such, this still wouldn't negate the recognition of *specific* points of historical veracity gleaned from the NT via the historical criteria of authenticity. Nor would it undermine the inference from the enumeration of many *specific* examples of historical veracity in the NT to the *general* historical reliability thereof.[10]

Moreover, we must remember that NT scholarship recognizes a number of sources, written or otherwise, that stand behind the Gospels

---

9. Stecher, "Miracle Not Required," 267.

10. See McGrew, *Hidden in Plain View*; Williams, Peter J., *Can We Trust the Gospels?*; Williams, *Getting at Jesus*; and *Digging for Evidence*.

(for example, the "Q" source common to Matthew and Luke). Even if it were shown that one or other of these sources is historically inaccurate, this wouldn't demonstrate that all of these sources are unreliable. In short, Stecher's critique of the NT is *methodologically unsound on multiple grounds*.

As to Stecher's examples:

- I refute Stecher's unsupported assertions that the birth accounts in Matthew and Luke "contradict each other" and "are in conflict with known facts about the period."[11] (Even if these accounts did contradict each other *in every particular*, the possibility of one of the accounts being historically reliable would be left open. Again, even if both accounts were demonstrably "in conflict with known facts about the period" *to an extent that undermined belief in their general reliability*, this would be compatible with making sound arguments for *specific* points of historical veracity either within the birth narratives or within other testimonial sources woven into these Gospels. In particular, since Matthew and Luke drew upon various sources, proving the birth narratives to be unreliable wouldn't justify the conclusion that the passion narrative sources are unreliable. Finally, criticism of the birth narratives in Matthew and Luke has no application to the Gospels of Mark or John, to relevant information from the creed quoted in 1 Cor 15, etc.)

- The preface to John's Gospel offers a theological portrait of the divine *logos* having a role in creation before the incarnation, but it makes no claim about how long ago this occurred. It certainly doesn't say that creation took place "about six thousand years ago" (relative either to the composition of John or to our own time). Although Stecher should know from my biographical essay (in *Resurrection: Faith or Fact?*) that I think young-earth creationism requires an implausible interpretation of the relevant biblical texts, he reads a young-earth creationist perspective into John's preface, without offering any hermeneutical justification for doing so.[12]

11. Stecher, "Miracle Not Required," 267. See Williams, "Nativity" (YouTube playlist); Brindle, "Census and Quirinius"; McLatchie, "Nativity Defended"; Scott, "Matthew's Intention to Write History"; Crowe, *Was Jesus Really Born of a Virgin?*; Edwards, *Virgin Birth in History*; Machen, *Virgin Birth of Christ*; Nicholl, *Great Christ Comet*; Quarles, *Midrash Criticism*; Redford, *Born of a Virgin*; Williams, "Nativity."

12. See Williams, "Young Earth Creationism" (YouTube playlist); Barnes, "Why I'm No Longer"; Jones, "Origins of Young Earth Creationism"; Keathley, "Confessions of

- Stecher's assertion that "passages in which the voice of God comes out of the sky" are "clearly legends or fictionalizations" rests upon his rejection of the supernatural and is therefore question begging.
- Stecher's skepticism about the conversation between Judas and the temple priests in Matt 27:3–6 ignores relevant evidence that Blomberg drew to Stecher's attention during their debate:

> As for the exchange between Judas and the priests not involving Jesus at all (Matthew 27:3–10), here Acts 6:7 gives us an important clue. We read that "a large number of priests became obedient to the faith." If even just one of them had been among those who met with Judas, or had heard from their priestly friends about what transpired, they could easily have passed the word along to other Christians.[13]

- Turning to Pilate's questioning of Jesus in John 18:28–38, Stecher once again ignores evidence that Blomberg has already brought to his attention:

> First of all, it is highly unlikely that any Roman governor would ever be left alone with an accused criminal; other guards would have been present. We know that John had "friends in high places" sufficient to gain entry to the high priest's courtyard (John 18:16); who knows what other acquaintances he might have had among the Roman guard? Craig Keener sees evidence here for actual legal proceedings, in which case at least one Roman official would have been assigned to Jesus as counsel. Records of proceedings would have been kept and could have been consulted. Moreover, the plausibility of the disciples hearing about this kind of conversation may be bound up with the plausibility of the resurrection itself. If Jesus did spend considerable time with his disciples over a forty-day period after the resurrection teaching them (Acts 1:3), then he would have had plenty of time to tell them all the details.[14]

---

a Disappointed Young-Earther"; Marston, "Understanding the Biblical Creation Passages"; Ortlund, "Did Augustine Read Genesis 1 Literally?"; Charles, *Reading Genesis 1–2*; Collins, *Genesis 1–4*; Williams, "Mythology."

13. Blomberg, "Reply to Carl," 92–93.
14. Blomberg, "Reply to Carl," 92.

More or Less Evidence Required?

Stecher observes:

> Peter writes, "In general, the more criteria of authenticity a saying or event passes, the more seriously we should take it." This seems reasonable to me. But I would like to suggest a corollary: The fewer and weaker the evidence for any alleged "fact," the weaker the case for accepting it. In this regard another general rule might be the greater the importance of an event involving the eternal fate of billions of people, the more compelling should be the evidence that this event actually happened.[15]

However, wouldn't prudential rationality actually encourage us to act on the basis of *less* evidence in such cases?[16]

An Alarmingly Absent Ascension?

Stecher quotes neo-atheist physicist Victor J. Stenger back to me:

> "Absence of evidence is evidence of absence when the evidence should be there and is not." I agree. I've argued on this basis that the report of Jesus' final words and his physical and visible ascension into heaven clearly meet this criteria. Yet this event, alleged by the author of Acts, is nowhere confirmed or even hinted at by Paul or the authors of Mark, Matthew, or John, our only first-century sources for the stories of Jesus' resurrection. These documents have not a hint that their authors have ever heard the story told by Luke of Jesus' final words and ascension. Craig [Blomberg] suggests that all the other first-century accounts do not mention Jesus' last words and ascension because Luke has saved this for the "sequel" to his Gospel, the Acts of the Apostles. This, however, fails to account for the other Gospel accounts not completing the story with its natural climax. Peter also does not explain their silence.[17]

First of all, I should say I don't think Stecher meant to deny that Luke is a first-century source for narratives of the resurrection, although that's what he seems to imply here.

---

15. Stecher, "Miracle Not Required," 269.

16. Consider William James's famous pragmatic argument in "The will to believe." I discuss James's argument in the final chapter of Williams, *Case for God*.

17. Stecher, "Miracle Not Required," 270–71.

Second, Stecher's argument from silence holds that the failure of any NT author to meet his literary expectations means they must have all been making it all up. This argument makes the false assumption that an argument from silence automatically trumps any and all other historical arguments.[18]

In any case, not only does Luke report the ascension in both Luke 25:50–52 and Acts 1:1–11, but Jesus's ascension is in fact pre-figured or alluded to in several NT texts:

- Eph 4:8 (ca. AD 60–62): "Therefore it says, 'When he [Christ] *ascended on high* he led a host of captives, and he gave gifts to men.'" (ESV, my italics)
- 1 Tim 3:16 (ca. AD 62): "Great indeed, we confess, is the mystery of godliness: He was manifested in the flesh, vindicated by the Spirit, seen by angels, proclaimed among the nations, believed on in the world, *taken up in glory*." (ESV, my italics)
- Heb 4:14 (ca. AD 63–66): "Therefore, since we have a great high priest who has *ascended into heaven*, Jesus the Son of God, let us hold firmly to the faith we profess." (NIV, my italics)[19]
- John 20:17 (ca. AD 96–98): "Jesus said to her, 'Do not cling to me, for I have not yet *ascended to the Father*; but go to my brothers and say to them, "I am *ascending to my Father* and your Father, to my God and your God."'" (ESV, my italics.)

Note that the Fourth Gospel does far more than "hint" at Jesus's ascension. It explicitly references it. Twice in a row. The fact that this double reference features within the first of a sequence of resurrection appearances related in John 20 and 21 allows the Fourth Gospel to focus on the resurrected Jesus interacting with his disciples as its "natural climax."

Thus, we actually have *early testimony* (including some from within thirty years of the purported event) *from multiple sources* (four sources when we add Luke to the above list, if it is granted that Hebrews wasn't written by Paul[20]), presented in *multiple forms* (two Gospels and

---

18. See McGrew, Lydia, "Arguments from Silence"; McGrew, Timothy, "Argument from Silence."

19. On Heb 4:14, see Bruce, *Epistle to the Hebrews*, 115.

20. See Bruce, *Epistle to the Hebrews*; Zondervan Academic Blog, "Who Wrote the Book of Hebrews?"; Campbell, "Authorship of Hebrews."

three Epistles), and including John's *eyewitness* source,[21] that reference Jesus's ascension.

The fact that Mark's Gospel doesn't narrate the ascension is hardly surprising in light of the fact that he ends his Gospel before even narrating any resurrection appearances (though he does foreshadow at least one resurrection appearance in Mark 16:7). In light of the above, Mark's Gospel not foreshadowing the ascension and Matthew's Gospel ending with the resurrected Jesus, likewise without foreshadowing the ascension don't seem to offer a sufficient case for thinking that the ascension was invented by Luke.[22]

Contradictory Accounts?

Stecher often asserts that there are contradictions within the NT, and he responds to my observation that his "critique of the canonical gospels often stems from an uncharitable and historically uninformed hermeneutic"[23] by writing: "I'm sorry to be characterized as 'uncharitable' in my analysis of the Gospel accounts, but I'm unclear on what role charity should have in the understanding of these texts."[24] Given that Stecher is an emeritus professor of English, I'm surprised by his self-professed ignorance of the principle of hermeneutical charity. Allow me to clarify by quoting our atheist co-contributor Richard Carrier, who makes the following plea in his book *Sense and Goodness without God*:

> I ask that my work be approached with the same intellectual charity you would expect from anyone else . . . ordinary language is necessarily ambiguous and open to many different interpretations. If what I say anywhere in this book appears to contradict, directly or indirectly, something else I say here, the principle of interpretive charity should be applied: assume you are misreading the meaning of what I said in each or either case.

---

21. For a defense of John's role in the testimony of the Fourth Gospel, see Blomberg, *Historical Reliability of John's Gospel*; McGrew, *Eye of the Beholder*; Williams, *Getting at Jesus*.

22. See McGrew, Lydia, "Arguments from Silence"; McGrew, Timothy, "Argument from Silence."

23. Williams, "Evidence, Explanation, and Expectation," 228.

24. Stecher, "Miracle Not Required," 271.

Whatever interpretation would eliminate the contradiction and produce agreement is probably correct.[25]

As theologian Craig S. Keener observes:

> Although harmonization is sometimes implausible, at other times it rightly values what survives of our sources above what we think we know based on our lack of surviving information. Thus, for example, scholars at one point noted two "contradictory" oral accounts of an 1881 lynching: in one, the men hang "from a railroad crossing," in the other, they hang from a pine tree. Subsequently, however, historians found "old photographs that showed the bodies hanging *at different times from both places*"; after being lynched in one place, they were hanged again in another . . . it seems best methodologically to begin by seeking to explain our sources as they are.[26]

As philosopher Lydia McGrew writes, literary "harmonization is not a desperate, specially religious activity used for preserving an *a priori* notion of inerrancy but rather is just good historical practice, applicable to *any* putatively historical accounts, not just to Scripture."[27] Unfortunately, when Blomberg and myself offer what seem to us to be plausible harmonizations of the texts Stecher asserts are contradictory, he fails to respond to our arguments.

(Far worse than Stecher's lack of engagement, in an endorsement solicited by our publisher, Blomberg and I are accused by atheist Robert M. Price of "behaving like 'eel wrigglers' (the Buddha's term for wily and evasive opponents), retreating behind ingenious harmonizations. Naturally: they are spin doctors for the dogma of an institution they serve."[28] Talk about poisoning the well![29])

Stecher persists in highlighting what he takes to be contradictions between the Gospels despite my explanation that the criteria of historical authenticity allow us to side-step questions like "Was Jesus's first appearance to the male disciples in Jerusalem or Galilee?," establishing *specific* data that can be shown to be historically likely and that therefore needs to be explained, quite apart from debates about the

---

25. Carrier, *Sense and Goodness without God*, 5–6.
26. Keener, *Christobiography*, 315.
27. McGrew, "Licona Wrap-Up."
28. Robert M. Price, endorsement for *Resurrection: Faith or Fact?*
29. See Bennett, "Poisoning the Well."

general reliability of the NT. As Terry L. Miethe and Gary R. Habermas emphasize in a passage I quoted in "EEE":

> Our arguments [for the resurrection are] based on a *limited number* of knowable historical facts and *verified by critical procedures.* Therefore, contemporary scholars should not spurn such evidence by referring to "discrepancies" in the New Testament texts or to its general "unreliability" . . . Jesus' resurrection appearances can be historically demonstrated *based only on a limited amount of critically recognized historical facts.*[30]

Stecher ignores this key point and reiterates his objection:

> In the Matthew account, Jesus at the tomb instructs his female disciples to tell his male disciples to "Go and take word to my brothers that they are to leave for Galilee. They will see me there." In the parallel passage in Luke's Gospel, Jesus does not appear at the empty tomb.[31]

Stecher then explores Michael Licona's suggestion, based upon his study of ancient compositional devices in biographical works, that Matthew relocates Jesus's resurrection appearance from Jerusalem to Galilee.[32] While I included Licona's suggestion in a draft of "EEE" that Stecher saw, Stecher knew I was withdrawing this material from the final version. I did this not only to reduce my word length, but because I'd decided *I didn't agree with it.* I think Licona's hypothesis is unnecessarily complex in this instance.[33]

In point of fact, Matthew *doesn't* report that Jesus appeared to the women at the empty tomb. Rather, Matthew states that "an angel of the Lord" appeared at "the tomb" (see Matt 28:1–8) and said to the women:

> Do not be afraid, for I know that you seek Jesus who was crucified. He is not here, for he has risen, as he said. Come, see the place where he lay. Then go quickly and tell his disciples that he has risen from the dead, and behold [i.e., take heed], he is going

---

30. Miethe and Habermas, *Why Believe?*, 273–74.
31. Stecher, "Miracle Not Required," 272.
32. See Licona, *Why Are There Differences*, 178–80.
33. Licona has subsequently made clear that he endorses the alternate suggestion that he makes in the same pages—namely, that it is *Luke* who geographically moves that appearance (in order to "compress" the narrative). See Licona, "DEBATE: Are the Gospels Historically Reliable?," 1.46:00–1.48:40. I find this theory just as unnecessary as the former. See Blomberg, "How to Approach Apparent Contradictions."

before you to Galilee; there you will see him. See, I have told you. (Matt 28:5–7 ESV)

Theologian Ned B. Stonehouse comments that the present tense of the verb in Matt 28:7:

> may not be pressed . . . to mean that even at that moment Jesus was on the journey into Galilee, for this would bring Mt. 28:7 into conflict with 28:10 which locates Jesus still in the vicinity of Jerusalem. . . . Rather than being a progressive, therefore, the form in question must be understood as a vivid future, which is essentially the equivalent of the future in Mt. 26:32.[34]

Having referenced several works on Greek grammar "on the use of the present [tense] for the future [tense],"[35] Stonehouse continues:

> With regard to the words "there ye shall see him," it should be observed that they are so closely connected with the reference to Galilee that they serve to make explicit what has been constantly implied in the prophetic word of Jesus, namely, that Jesus would be waiting for them in Galilee and would welcome them there. They do not represent an independent disclosure by the angel as to when the disciples would first see the risen Christ but, taken in connection with the preceding clause, they serve to recall the substance of Jesus' promise. Now that Jesus has risen from the dead, they may be assured that his declaration, that after his resurrection he would be in Galilee before they reached there, was about to be fulfilled.[36]

According to Matthew, it was *after* "the women hurried away from the tomb" (Matt 28:8 ESV) that Jesus appeared to them, saying: "tell my brothers [i.e. brethren/followers] to go to Galilee, and there they will see me" (Matt 28:10 ESV). This message, given by the angel and by Jesus, seems to have been designed to remind the disciples who'd accompanied Jesus to the Mount of Olives from the last supper of his words to them there: "after I am raised up, I will go before you to Galilee" (Matt 26:32 ESV; see Matt 26:17–32 and Mark 14:12–28). Now, as Blomberg writes in his commentary on Matthew:

> This does not preclude other earlier resurrection appearances, as described in Luke 24 and John 20, but does prepare the way

---

34. Stonehouse, *Witness of the Synoptic Gospels*, 173–74.
35. Stonehouse, *Witness of the Synoptic Gospels*, 174.
36. Stonehouse, *Witness of the Synoptic Gospels*.

for his appearance "up north" following the end of the week-long festival of Unleavened Bread, when the Galilean pilgrims would return home. During this appearance, Jesus commissioned his disciples for their future ministry: herein lies Matthew's particular interest.[37]

That both messages about Galilee, from the angel and from Jesus, were intended for a group that extended beyond the core group of male disciples (known as "the Twelve," of which only eleven now remained), is indicated by the early creedal affirmation that after Jesus's appearances "to Cephas and then to the Twelve" he subsequently "appeared to more than five hundred brothers at one time, most of whom are still alive, though some have fallen asleep" (1 Cor 15:5–6 ESV; see also Matt 28:16; Luke 8:3, 10:1, and 24:33–35; and Acts 1:21–26). This is plausibly the same meeting described in Matt 28:16–20 as taking place in Galilee (though Matthew keeps his literary spotlight on the eleven disciples). As Stonehouse explains:

> By the term "brethren" as used in Mt. 28:10, it is by no means clear that only the eleven disciples are meant. . . . In only two instances besides Mt. 28:10 does Jesus use the expression "my brethren," and both clearly describe in the broadest possible way those who were attached to him. . . . Accordingly the command of 28:10 that his brethren should depart for Galilee would most naturally be understood as including all persons attached to his cause who were then in the vicinity of Jerusalem . . . a company of persons by no means restricted to the twelve.[38]

Joseph Benson argued in the same vein:

> *Go quickly, and tell his disciples* . . . and assure them further, that he is *going before them into Galilee*; and that *there they shall see him*—In his appearance to them all together. But their gracious Lord would not be absent so long from the eleven and several others [e.g., those gathered indoors with the eleven apostles (see John 20:19 and Luke 24:9)]; he appeared to them several times before then . . . . This message, as well as that from Jesus himself, Matthew 28:9–10, was sent to all the disciples [note the grouping called "the seventy-two" (Luke 10:1) and the group of "about 120" brethren (Acts 1:15)], and not to the apostles in particular. The reason may have been this: our Lord

---

37. Blomberg, *Matthew*, 428.
38. Stonehouse, *Witness of the Synoptic Gospels*, 175–76 and 178.

intending to visit his apostles that very evening, there was no occasion to order *them* into Galilee to see him. But as most of his disciples were now in Jerusalem, celebrating the Passover, it may easily be imagined, that on receiving the news of their Master's resurrection, many of them would resolve to tarry in expectation of meeting with him; a thing which must have been very inconvenient for them at that time of the year, when the harvest was about to begin . . . Wherefore, to prevent their being so long from home, the message mentioned was sent, directing them to return into Galilee, well assured that they should have the pleasure of seeing their Lord there.[39]

Thus, we may agree with Stonehouse that:

> Quite apart from the evidence of Luke and John, and judging Matthew's testimony in the light of the structure of his resurrection narrative as a whole, as well as of the character of his gospel, the conclusion that he definitely excludes the possibility of a prior reunion with the eleven in Jerusalem seems to us not to be well established.[40]

Now, Luke reports Jesus instructing the disciples in Jerusalem to "wait here in this city until you are armed with power from above"; and this is indeed, as Stecher observes, "a seeming reference to the day of Pentecost."[41] However, Stecher mistakenly states that Pentecost is then "forty days in the future."[42] To substantiate his point, he quotes Acts 1:3–4: "To these men [the eleven apostles] he showed himself after his death . . . over a period of forty days . . . he directed them not to leave Jerusalem. ([Acts] 1:3–4)."[43] However, note the temporal context provided by Acts 1:5, which Stecher doesn't quote:

> And while staying with them he ordered them not to depart from Jerusalem, but to wait for the promise of the Father, which, he said, "you heard from me; for John baptized with water, but you will be baptized with the Holy Spirit *not many days from now*." (ESV, my italics)

---

39. Benson, "Matthew 28:7."
40. Stonehouse, *Witness of the Synoptic Gospels*, 181–82.
41. Stecher, "Miracle Not Required," 272.
42. Stecher, "Miracle Not Required," 272.
43. Stecher, "Miracle Not Required," 272–73.

So, while Stecher places Jesus's instruction to stay in Jerusalem "forty days" before Pentecost, Luke places it "not many days" before Pentecost, and thus towards the end of the "span of forty days" during which the resurrected Jesus "appeared to them." Nothing in Luke's Gospel contradicts this (see Luke 24:46–51).

Stecher insists that the resurrection appearances in Luke's Gospel are presented as having all happened on Easter day in Jerusalem, a reading that not only uncharitably creates a contradiction with the other Gospels (since they indicate or narrate resurrection appearances in Galilee), but uncharitably creates a contradiction between Luke's Gospel and Luke's book of Acts, where we are given the time frame of Jesus "appearing to them during forty days" (Acts 1:3 ESV). As John Wenham observes, Luke "is not packing into one day or even into one day and one night all the events between resurrection and ascension, as his fuller account in Acts I shows."[44]

Something that would only be apparent to someone who looked at the Greek of Luke's Gospel is that the appearance narrative is stitched together using the Greek particle *"de,"* which connects events *without necessarily implying that they happened in immediate conjunction*. As Wenham comments, translating *de* as "then" gives "a much sharper suggestion of chronological continuity than the Greek justifies. The paragraphs are linked by a weak connective non-temporal particle (*de*) which would better be left untranslated."[45] If one chooses to translate *de*, it can be rendered in English as "moreover, on-top of this, then or next."[46] Hence it's entirely plausible to think that while the events of Luke 24:1–43 happened on Easter day, those of Luke 24:44 and following ("Then [*de*] he said to them . . ." ESV) happened days or weeks later. As Eric Lyons comments:

> The Greek conjunctive particle *de* [translated "and" (ASV), "then" (NKJV), and "now" (NASV)] [used] to begin verse 44, does not necessarily denote a close connection between the two verses, but only a general continuation of the account. . . . Even though many twenty-first-century readers assume that the events recorded in Luke 24:44–49 occurred on the very day Jesus rose from the grave, the text actually is silent on the matter.[47]

44. Wenham, *Easter Enigma*, 107.
45. Wenham, *Easter Enigma*, 107.
46. See Bible Hub, "1161. De."
47. Lyons, "To Galilee or Jerusalem?," §11.

Indeed, the process of Jesus teaching the disciples about himself through the Old Testament scriptures (Luke 24:45–49) presumably took some time. Jesus's instruction to "stay in the city [Jerusalem] until clothed with power from on high" (Luke 24:49) was given before he led them to the location of his ascension, on the Mount of Olives (about a thousand yards outside Jerusalem). Luke's Gospel is *entirely consistent* with the information Luke adds in Acts 1:4–5 about the events of Luke 24:49 happening "not many days" before Pentecost. In sum, Luke's accounts of the resurrection *complement* both each other and the other Gospels.

Evidence—Part Two: Data

Stecher acknowledges as "bedrock facts"[48] that "Jesus . . . was crucified by the Romans"[49] and that "after his death some of his disciples had experiences that convinced them that Jesus had been miraculously resurrected."[50] Indeed, Stecher recognizes not only that "Jesus' disciples came to believe that Jesus had been miraculously resurrected from the dead,"[51] but also that (according to his opening case) "some of Jesus' disciples thought they saw Jesus raised from the dead."[52]

In "Miracle Not Required" Stecher focuses on two points of evidential *disagreement*: the existence of Jesus's empty tomb and the purported appearance of the resurrected Jesus to Saul on the road to Damascus.

The Empty Tomb[53]

Stecher states that "as evidence for the empty tomb, Peter cites the Jewish Toledot Yeshu."[54] He reports that:

---

48. Stecher, "Historical Evidence Is Insufficient," 79.
49. Stecher, "Historical Evidence Is Insufficient," 52.
50. Stecher, "Historical Evidence Is Insufficient," 52.
51. Stecher, "Reply to Craig," 161.
52. Stecher, "Historical Evidence Is Insufficient," 79.
53. See Williams, "Jesus' Tomb Was Empty" (YouTube playlist); Craig, "Historicity of the Empty Tomb of Jesus"; "Disciples' Inspection of the Empty Tomb"; and "Reply to Evan Fales"; Habermas, "Empty Tomb of Jesus"; National Geographic Partners, "Unsealing of Christ's Reputed Tomb."
54. Stecher, "Miracle Not Required," 267.

> According to classical Judaism scholar Mika Ahuvia, "Toledot Yeshu is a decidedly non-rabbinic counter-narrative and satire of the foundational story of Christianity, which likely originated in the late antique or early medieval period ... in the genre of the folk story, no two manuscripts are identical and storytellers likely embellished it with every recounting." Peter's citing of this obscure and certainly unreliable document signals to me how thin and fraught with problems the actual evidence is.[55]

Gary R. Habermas notes that although *Toledot Yeshu* wasn't compiled until the fifth century AD, "it does reflect early Jewish tradition."[56] As Mika Ahuvia says, *in the article Stecher quotes*:

> *Toledot Yeshu* is a decidedly non-rabbinic counter-narrative and satire of the foundational story of Christianity, which likely originated in the late antique or early medieval period. It probably circulated orally for centuries before being transcribed in various places and times.[57]

That said, I quoted from one of the later, and thus probably less reliable, "Group II traditions" (traditions dominated by Queen Helene, Constantine the Great's mother, anachronistically placed in the first century).[58]

However, the thing is, I *didn't* quote *Toledot Yeshu* "as evidence for the empty tomb" as Stecher says I did. Rather, in the process of arguing that while "the Jews believed in a general bodily resurrection at the end of time [they] did not have an expectation of an earlier, immediate, special resurrection for anyone,"[59] I quoted it *to corroborate the plausibility within a Jewish worldview of Matthew's report concerning the Sanhedrin's motive for posting a guard at Jesus's tomb* (see Matt 27:62–66). This is clear if my remarks about *Toledot Yeshu* are read in context:

> If Jesus's contemporaries made anything of his elliptical predictions about the Son of Man (i.e. himself) "rising" ... they'd have thought in terms of a) the resurrection of the dead *at the last judgement* (see Mark 12:25 and John 11:24), b) *revivification* to earthly life, as with Lazarus (though they'd probably assume a dead man couldn't revive *himself*), or c) the story of Elijah. The

---

55. Stecher, "Miracle Not Required," 267. See Ahuvia, "Introduction to Toledot Yeshu."
56. Habermas, *Historical Jesus*, 205.
57. Ahuvia, "Introduction to Toledot Yeshu," §5.
58. See Vehlow, "Michael Meerson and Peter Schäfer."
59. Bock, *Acts*, 125.

dominance of these cultural assumptions is seen in the Sanhedrin's reason for having Jesus' tomb guarded: "lest his disciples go and steal him away and tell the people, 'He has risen from the dead'" (Matthew 27:64, ESV). The Greek translated as "risen from the dead" here isn't *anastēsetai* (resurrected), but *ēgerthē* (raised up).... The Jewish *Toledot Yeshu* places this interpretation of events on the disciple's own lips: "On the first day of the week his bold followers came to Queen Helene with the report that he who was slain was truly the Messiah and that he was not in his grave; *he had ascended to heaven as he prophesied*." The Sanhedrin's concern was probably "that the disciples would steal the body and claim it had ascended to heaven."[60]

In sum, Stecher has simply misunderstood my use of *Toledot Yeshu*. Stecher thinks I make an inadequate case for the empty tomb:

About the alleged empty tomb, which is not clearly referenced until Mark's Gospel written decades later, Peter writes that my questioning of the conclusions cited by a conservative Christian study group committed to a literalist interpretation of the Bible is an ad hominem argument, assuming that "scholars who believe in inerrancy can't distinguish between what they believe on the basis of inerrancy and what they can demonstrate on the basis of historical scholarship." But this suggests that such believers are not subject, as we all are, to confirmation bias. I certainly do not mean to question the character of these scholars, but given that membership in this group might well be viewed as an honor, and a negative finding about the evidence for the empty tomb might lead members to feel they have to resign from the organization, a finding confirming historicity is hardly surprising. None of us achieve complete objectivity.[61]

In reply, let me begin by mentioning two points in passing. First, while Stecher vaguely places Mark's Gospel "decades" after Easter Sunday, the scholarly consensus holds that "Mark was most likely written anywhere between ten to thirty years after Jesus' death,"[62] and that I think the evidence suggests Mark was published circa AD 49.[63] Second, it was Blom-

---

60. Williams, "Evidence, Explanation, and Expectation," 239–40. The quote at the end is from Holding, "Hallucinations and Expectations," 269.
61. Stecher, "Miracle Not Required," 274.
62. Huff, "Extant Literary Sources."
63. See Williams, *Getting at Jesus*, 189–96.

berg who appealed to the conclusions of "a conservative Christian study group" (The Gospels Research Project of Tyndale House, Cambridge).

More to the point, allow me to reiterate a point made in "EEE" with which Stecher fails to engage: The empty tomb is accepted by a good many NT scholars *who cannot be accused of harboring the sort of bias Stecher assumes*. As David Mishkin writes in his study of *Jewish Scholarship on the Resurrection of Jesus*:

> Many non-Jewish scholars already have a faith commitment to Jesus. This does not mean that their scholarship should summarily be discarded as biased. It should be evaluated on its own merit. Nevertheless, the reality is that presuppositions are influential. Jewish scholars begin with a different set of presuppositions. But, what is interesting to note is that the main historical events that make up this discussion are virtually the same for both groups: crucifixion, burial, disciples' belief, empty tomb, and Paul's dramatic turnaround.[64]

For example, noted Jewish NT scholar Geza Vermes argues that:

> The evidence furnished by female witnesses had no standing in a male-dominated Jewish society. . . . If the empty tomb story had been manufactured by the primitive Church to demonstrate the reality of the resurrection of Jesus, one would have expected a uniform and fool proof account attributed to patently reliable witnesses.[65]

The empty tomb is verified by multiple criteria of authenticity, and that explains why it is accepted by many NT scholars *irrespective of their worldview*. As atheist historian Michael Grant concludes: "The historian cannot justifiably deny the empty tomb . . . the evidence necessitates the conclusion the tomb was found empty."[66]

If the existence of confirmation bias justifies Stecher's rejection of expert opinion and argumentation, then, given that we are all subject to confirmation bias, such that "none of us achieve complete objectivity," all that remains is silence. I might as well replace this paper with the observation that Stecher undoubtedly suffers from confirmation bias, which means that his rejection of the resurrection "is hardly surprising," and leave matters there.

---

64. Mishkin, *Jewish Scholarship on the Resurrection*, 210.
65. Vermes, *Resurrection*, 142.
66. Grant, *Jesus*, 176.

Stecher reckons that the "most compelling argument against the empty tomb is the complete lack of evidence that Jesus' tomb ever became a holy shrine in the first century. Peter does not respond to this argument."[67] Space limitations meant that I didn't respond to this point, so I'm glad to be able to respond here by noting that, while the site of Jesus's tomb was apparently *remembered* by the early church, the fact that no *veneration* appears to have taken place there supports the contention that the tomb was empty (i.e., that there was no body in the tomb to venerate).[68] As J. P. Moreland writes:

> In Palestine during the days of Jesus, at least fifty tombs of prophets or other holy persons served as sites of religious worship and veneration. However, there is no good evidence that such a practice was ever associated with Jesus' tomb. Since this was customary, and since Jesus was a fitting object of veneration, why were such religious activities not conducted at his tomb? The most reasonable answer must be that Jesus' body was not in his tomb, and thus the tomb was not regarded as an appropriate site for such veneration.[69]

Saul on the Road to Damascus

Stecher responds to my defense of the resurrection appearance to Saul on the road to Damascus:

> that Paul's anonymous companions "knew something had happened" is hardly the equivalent of a shared group experience of Jesus. And do we really think that Paul's companions would have had a modern understanding of psychological experiences?[70]

However, the distinction between (a) an event that's experienced differently by various members of a group and (b) one member of a group claiming an experience that, for all the other members of the group can tell, is purely subjective, is hardly restricted to "a modern understanding of psychological experiences"! The road to Damascus event, as reported by Luke, falls into the former rather than the latter category. As Timothy Keller writes:

---

67. Stecher, "Miracle Not Required," 275.
68. See Craig, "Dale Allison on Jesus' Empty Tomb."
69. Moreland, *Scaling the Secular City*, 161.
70. Stecher, "Miracle Not Required," 266.

"Paul did not have simply a trance or a dream . . . since even the other men with Paul recognized the presence (Acts 9:7)."[71]

Stecher says that here I am "forgetting or ignoring the dispute between Saul and Peter recorded in Galatians,"[72] but this dispute is irrelevant because (a) it happened *after* Saul converted, and (b) it wasn't motivated by rivalry but by theology with which Peter was officially in agreement (see Acts 15:1–29 and especially 7–11).

Explanation

Stecher suggests that there are plausible natural explanations for the genesis of the disciples' belief in Jesus's resurrection: grief hallucinations, mistaken identity, dreams mistaken for reality, misheard or misinterpreted testimony, unconscious appropriation of another's experience, memory distortion, and disciple rivalry:

> No one of these would likely be sufficient for the sincere belief of some of the disciples that Jesus had been resurrected. But . . . [t]hese quite natural, understandable beginnings could have easily led to a belief that Jesus had been miraculously resurrected, and to all the Gospel stories, with their fundamental contradictions and fictional and legendary embellishments. No miraculous resurrection required.[73]

In "EEE" I argued on the one hand that the resurrection hypothesis offers a relatively simple and wholly adequate explanation of the relevant historical evidence, an explanation that combines excellent explanatory scope and power with a fair degree of plausibility and low degrees of disconfirmation and *ad hoc* ness (especially if one already accepts theism). On the other hand, I also argued that Stecher's explanatory factors not only "have limited explanatory power [but] suffer from problems of disconfirmation, *ad hoc*–ness, and insufficient explanatory scope."[74] While I noted that "the most interesting hypothesis advanced by Stecher is that a combination of psychological factors might explain the resurrection 'appearances,'"[75] I critiqued the explanatory adequacy of Stecher's appeal

---

71. Keller, *Galatians for You*, 26.
72. Stecher, "Miracle Not Required," 275.
73. Stecher, "Historical Evidence Is Insufficient," 71–72.
74. Williams, "Evidence, Explanation, and Expectation," 243.
75. Williams, "Evidence, Explanation, and Expectation," 252–53.

to co-opted memories (whether sparked by mistaken identity, dreams mistaken for reality, etc.) and demonstrated that "the appeal to co-opted memories can't eliminate the appeal to multiple hallucinations, including multiple group hallucinations."[76] Given that the appeal to multiple hallucinations suffers from multiple shortcomings, it seems to me that Stecher fails to provide a better explanation of the relevant evidence than is provided by the resurrection hypothesis.[77]

Explaining the Empty Tomb

According to Stecher:

> Peter places considerable emphasis on the alleged empty tomb. For Christian scholars, the discovery of Jesus' empty tomb, which can only be explained by his having risen from the dead, is a major piece of evidence.[78]

However, I neither claim nor think that the empty tomb "can *only* be explained by [Jesus] having risen from the dead." I do think that the need to explain the empty tomb puts additional strain on naturalistic alternatives to the resurrection hypothesis.

Stecher complains that he referenced "the many plausible arguments for natural explanations detailed in [Robert M.] Price and [Jeffery Jay] Lowder's [*The Empty Tomb:*] *Jesus beyond the Grave*; Peter does not respond to any of these possibilities."[79] Stecher has me here: In the interests of brevity, I focused upon arguing against Stecher's denial of the empty tomb, rather than upon the possible explanations he referenced for the empty tomb.[80]

---

76. Williams, "Evidence, Explanation, and Expectation," 254.
77. See Williams, "Evidence, Explanation, and Expectation"; and *Getting at Jesus*.
78. Stecher, "Miracle Not Required," 273.
79. Stecher, "Miracle Not Required," 273.
80. On explanations for the empty tomb, see Williams, *Getting at Jesus*, ch. 5 and Appendix I in this book. For responses to Price and Lowder, *Empty Tomb: Jesus beyond the Grave*, see CASE, "Book Review: Empty Assumptions"; Geisler, "Critical Review of *Empty Tomb* (2005)"; Hays et al., "Joyful Eastertide: Critical Review of *Empty Tomb*."

Explaining the Appearances

Responding to my review of evidence showing that false memories are co-opted by under half of subjects in studies of the phenomena, evidence that disconfirms the hypothesis that the disciple's claim about Jesus being resurrected was grounded in co-opted memories, Stecher objects:

> But I never made such a claim. I did argue that co-opted memories might be one of many plausible explanations for the disciples' belief—in fact, I listed eight such natural explanations. I certainly do not believe that co-opted memories alone could account for the resurrection belief. But Peter has confirmed that this does happen, even if only for a minority of the population.[81]

However, I critiqued each sub-hypothesis offered by Stecher before addressing the combined hypothesis, so I didn't ignore his argument. Besides, with a success rate of under half, any hypothesis that employs a more than *incidental* reliance upon co-opted memories in pursuit of explaining away the disciple's reports and beliefs about the resurrection is going to be disconfirmed by the relevant clinical evidence.[82]

Stecher concedes:

> I would have made a stronger case . . . if I had reversed Peter (the disciple) and Andrew in my speculation on how the resurrection belief might have begun—one of many ways—since so much more is known of Peter's life.[83]

Note that here Stecher rests his case on a single (*ad hoc*) natural explanation for the *origin* of belief in resurrection:

> imagine that Peter reports a dream experience of the risen Jesus to the disciples. Andrew, arriving late, doesn't realize that Peter is relating a dream, and claims a similar encounter with the risen Jesus. This would be only human—and the Gospels make clear there was disciple rivalry. Several years later Andrew remembers the occasion very imperfectly: in his recollection, he had an encounter with the risen Lord—and it wasn't a dream![84]

---

81. Stecher, "Miracle Not Required," 276.
82. See Williams, "Memory Implantation" (YouTube playlist); Brewin and Andrews, "Creating Memories."
83. Stecher, "Miracle Not Required," 276.
84. Stecher, "Miracle Not Required," 276.

Several years later? That's far too late! The disciples were preaching the resurrection in Jerusalem during Pentecost (see Acts 2:1—4:22) and the appearance traditions quoted by Paul in 1 Cor 15 were probably packaged in creedal form within months, or at most a few years, of the crucifixion.[85] So, Andrew lies, and then comes to believe his own lie, years later, but the other disciples, including Peter, believe Andrew at the time?! Without their own experiences? But what about Jesus's brother James? What about "doubting" Thomas? What about Saul the persecutor? Simply swapping Peter and Andrew around does Stecher's hypothesis no favors.

Expectation

Stecher raises a number of issues in the areas of theology and philosophy of religion that limit his expectations of what any historical argument for the Christian revelation claim can demonstrate.

An Unreliable Prophet?

Stecher protests:

> In his discussion of Jesus as a prophet, Peter writes, "There's every reason to think Jesus was an accurate prophet." But Peter has done nothing to refute the evidence to the contrary that I have already cited . . . For example, what of Jesus' failure to return as promised within the generation of those living then? Consider Jesus' words in Mark when challenged by the high priest: "'Are you the Messiah, the Son of the blessed One?' 'I am,' said Jesus, 'and you will see the Son of Man seated at the right hand of the Almighty and coming with the clouds of heaven'" (14:61–62). Clearly this is a claim by Jesus that his return will be witnessed by the priests interrogating him.[86]

In point of fact, I dealt with Stecher's assertions about Jesus being a failed prophet at some length in "EEE," but Stecher dismisses my exegetical arguments and references because he's content to rely upon his "literal" reading of the texts he "cited":

> I am unable to see the connection between these passages and the events of 70 C.E. Note the similarities of these passages with

---

85. See Williams, *Getting at Jesus*, 250–55.
86. Stecher, "Miracle Not Required," 267.

passages that Peter does not quote, passages that make clear Jesus' promise to return during the present generation. Jesus is responding to this question from his disciples: "Tell us, they said ... what will be the sign of your coming and the end of the age?" (Matthew 24:3).[87]

Stecher doesn't make any exegetical arguments for his interpretation of the texts he "cited." Nor does he engage with the exegetical arguments I made, or with the exegetes I quoted and referenced, such as Paul Copan's explanation that:

> Certain gospel passages speak of the "coming [*erchomenon*]" of the Son of Man to the Father ("the Ancient of Days")—a reference to Daniel 7—within his generation. Most New Testament scholars take passages such as Matthew 16:28 and Mark 14:62/ Matthew 26:64 and Luke 22:69 as references to AD 70—not some distant "second coming."[88]

That Jesus didn't believe his public vindication—his "coming" (*erchomenon*) to God for public enthronement—would coincide with the end of earthly history is indicated by his (hyperbolic) assertion that in those days "there will be great tribulation, such as has not been from the beginning of the world until now, no, and never will be" (Matt 24:21 ESV),[89] which implies that history would continue. That Jesus is predicting a passing historical event is clear from his comment that "if those days had not been cut short, no one would survive" (Matt 24:22 NIV), and his warnings not to believe anyone claiming "at that time" (Matt 24:23 NIV) that the messiah has appeared: "For as the lightning comes from the east and shines as far as the west, so will be the coming [*parousia*—presence] of the Son of Man" (Matt 24:27 ESV).

Here we see a distinction between Jesus's temple-related *erchomenon* within a generation, and his later but otherwise unspecified *parousia* or second coming: "A close look at Matthew 24 shows that Jesus was answering two questions [see verse 3]. Jesus knew the answer to the first [see Matt 24:34]. But he didn't know the answer to the second [see Matt 24:36 and 42–44]."[90]

---

87. Stecher, "Miracle Not Required," 273–74.
88. Copan, *When God Goes to Starbucks*, 173. See also France, *Matthew*.
89. See Bible Hub, "Matthew 24:21."
90. Copan, *When God Goes to Starbucks*, 168.

When Jesus predicts the destruction of the temple, signifying the *erchomenon* of the Son of Man to God the Father à la Dan 7, he says: "this generation will certainly not pass away until all these things have happened" (Matt 24:34 ESV). When he discusses his *parousia* (his "second coming") he says: "But about that day or hour no one knows, not even the angels in heaven, nor the Son, but only the Father . . . you do not know on what day your Lord will come . . . the Son of Man will come at an hour when you do not expect him" (Matt 24:36–44 ESV).[91] There's every reason to think Jesus was an accurate prophet.[92]

Accessible Salvation

As noted in "EEE": "According to Stecher, believing in the resurrection means believing God excludes billions from salvation. Blomberg disagrees, as do I."[93] In the written debate, Blomberg wrote:

> As for those who have never heard the gospel, it is sad that there are Christians who say that everyone who has never heard the gospel is damned or lost for all eternity. There are plenty of people in the Bible who never heard of Jesus who are called God's people—many of them are Old Testament Jews, but some are Gentiles also who come to hear about the God of the Jews. May we not extrapolate from these examples and leave it in God's hands to judge those who have never heard? Abraham asked God, "will not the Judge of all the earth do right?" (Genesis 18:25) and the context suggests the answer is that he indeed will.[94]

In "EEE" I observed:

> Peter affirms, "The Lord is not willing that any should perish but [desires] that all should reach repentance" (2 Peter 3:9, NIV). John states, "God did not send his Son into the world to condemn the world, but to save the world through him" (John 3:17, NIV). Paul writes that God "desires all men to be saved and to come to a knowledge of the truth" (1 Timothy 2:4, NIV). He also makes it clear that God doesn't condemn anyone for ignorance, but only for a culpable refusal to welcome "the truth that would

---

91. See Copan, *When God Goes to Starbucks*, 162–90.
92. See FOCLOnline, "Arguments for and from Fulfilled."
93. Williams, "Evidence, Explanation, and Expectation," 259. See Williams, "Particular and Exclusive Christ."
94. Blomberg, "Rejoinder to Carl", 190.

save them" (2 Thessalonians 2:9–10, ISV). Those who will "come under judgment" are people "who have refused to believe the truth and have taken pleasure in unrighteousness' (2 Thessalonians 2:12, Weymouth NT). If our understanding of the "good news" contradicts these apostolic affirmations, our understanding must be improved![95]

Furthermore, while affirming that "the fullest expression and experience of 'the truth that would save' is found 'in Christ' (see Acts 19:1–6; Romans 10:1–21; 2 Thessalonians 2:13),"[96] I noted with Rev. Nicky Gumbel that:

> Abraham and David . . . were justified by faith. Jesus tells us in the parable of the Pharisee and the tax collector that the tax collector who said "God, have mercy on me, a sinner," went home justified before God (Luke 18:9–14).[97]

I referenced scriptural warrant for my belief that "everyone saved by faith will ultimately receive salvation 'in Christ' (see John 8:56; Acts 10:1–48; Romans 11:23–24; Hebrews 11:39–40)."[98] I noted how "this jives with the venerable theory that salvation is possible postmortem."[99] Finally, I noted that "given divine middle-knowledge, we may reckon that people who refuse salvation are people who would make the same choice in any possible world wherein it's feasible for God to create them."[100]

Unfortunately, Stecher's "Miracle Not Required" pays no attention to these remarks. Indeed, Stecher ignores everything Blomberg and I say on this topic, failing to engage with either our positions or the arguments we give for them, even to the point of misrepresenting our beliefs:

---

95. Williams, "Evidence, Explanation, and Expectation." See Craig, *On Guard for Students*; Pinnock, *Grace of God*; Walls, *Heaven*; Walls and Dongell, *Why I Am Not a Calvinist*; Willard, *Knowing Christ Today*.

96. Williams, "Evidence, Explanation, and Expectation," 260.

97. Gumbel, *Searching Issues*, 36.

98. Williams, "Evidence, Explanation, and Expectation," 260.

99. Williams, "Evidence, Explanation, and Expectation," 260. Jewish belief in the possibility of post-mortem forgiveness is seen in 2 Maccabees (12:38–45). The "Harrowing of Hades" was taught by many theologians of the early church (including Ambrose, Athanasius, Clement of Alexandria, Origen, John of Damascus, and Tertullian). Belief in post-mortem evangelism has been supported by modern scholars such as G. R. Beasley-Murray, James Beilby, Donald Bloesch, C. E. B. Cranfield, Stephen T. Davis, Brian Hebblethwaite, Richard Swinburne, and Jerry L. Walls. See Beilby, *Post-mortem Opportunity*; Sanders, *No Other Name*; Walls, *Heaven*.

100. Williams, "Evidence, Explanation, and Expectation," 260–61. See Craig, *On Guard for Students*; and *Only Wise God*; Craig and Gorra, *Reasonable Response*.

> If Peter and Craig [Blomberg] are not mistaken, having the correct interpretation of this alleged event is determinative of whether upon dying one ascends to heaven to experience eternal joy with God, or whether one ceases to exist or descends to hell, there to spend all eternity because of a failure to believe in Jesus and his resurrection.[101]

Rather, with theologians Clark H. Pinnock and Robert C. Brow, I affirm that:

> Because God is love, we can be sure that no one will be excluded from knowing God by ignorance or lack of opportunity. Only those who deliberately reject God's love will be excluded, and they will really have excluded themselves. God has decided to exclude no one—exclusion can happen only as a result of the human decision to love darkness rather than light.[102]

Moreover, I lean towards the "annihilationist" view that "hell" and ceasing to exist are, at least in the long term, one and the same thing.[103]

According to Stecher:

> [The] inability of Christians through the centuries to agree upon the true faith undermines the claims of contemporary Christians that salvation or damnation is consequent on correct belief in Jesus' reported resurrection (or indeed anything Jesus taught).[104]

Stecher once again writes as if non-culpable failure to accept "correct belief" is determinative of one's eternal destiny.

While it's obvious that Christians have many in-house disagreements (as do atheists!), I'd have thought it equally obvious that Christians share many theological agreements, and that many of these agreements concern matters of central import. For all their diversity of theological interpretation and emphasis, different Christian communities and communions nevertheless find much common cause in the historic orthodoxy of creeds such as the Apostles' Creed and the Nicene Creed.[105]

---

101. Stecher, "Miracle Not Required," 269.
102. Pinnock and Brow, *Unbounded Love*, 32.
103. See Fudge, *Fire That Consumes*.
104. Stecher, "Miracle Not Required," 276.
105. See Church of England, "Apostles' Creed"; Anglicans Online, "Nicene Creed."

Concerning salvation, what matters is *faith in Jesus* (that is, an active trust in Jesus and allegiance to Jesus as Lord and Savior).[106] It may interest Stecher to know that, according to the 1999 "Joint Declaration on the Doctrine on Justification by the Lutheran World Federation and the Catholic Church" (and although it was initially a Catholic-Lutheran agreement, this declaration has since been affirmed by the Methodist, Anglican, and Reformed churches):

> Together we confess [that] as sinners our new life [in Christ] is solely due to the forgiving and renewing mercy that God imparts as a gift and we receive in faith, and never can merit in any way.... We confess together that sinners are justified by faith in the saving actions of God in Christ.... Such a faith is active in love and thus the Christian cannot and should not remain without good works.[107]

Discussing the Reformation in his article on "Justification by Faith," Catholic philosopher Peter Kreeft writes:

> Luther discovered the simple bombshell truth that God had forgiven his sins freely.... The watchword of the Reformation became Saint Paul's summary of the gospel: "The just (justified, saved) shall live [have eternal life] by faith [in Christ]" (Rom 1:17). Where then do good works come in? In *Christian Liberty*, Luther explains that after the great liberation about faith—that we are saved by faith in Christ's work, not by our works—comes a great liberation about works: they need not be done slavishly, to buy our way into heaven, to pile up merits or Brownie points with God, but can be done freely and spontaneously and naturally, out of gratitude to God—not to get to heaven but because heaven has already gotten to us. Thus they can be done for the sake of our neighbor, not for our own sake, to purchase salvation.[108]

On Miracles and Evil[109]

Stecher's expectations, which shape how he interacts with the historical argument for Jesus's resurrection, are dominated by a rejection of miracles, a rejection that's ultimately grounded in the problem of evil.

106. See Williams, "Nature of Faith" (YouTube playlist); and "Faith and Rationality."
107. Lutheran World Federation, "Joint Declaration on the Doctrine."
108. Kreeft, "Justification by Faith."
109. On miracles see Williams, "Miracles" (YouTube playlist); Beckwith, "Theism,

Stecher affirms that since neither he nor any family member or friend has ever "heard the voice of God" coming out of the sky, it would take confirmation "from a respected news source" of "a voice from the sky that could only be the voice of God" to get him to reconsider his worldview; although he would first "check the date to make sure it was not April 1st."[110]

On the one hand, Stecher's desire to avoid gullibility is both sensible and biblical (see 1 Thess 5:20–21 and 1 John 4:1). On the other hand, the avoidance of gullibility shouldn't drive us into the arms of cynicism. Why shouldn't a voice that was simply *more likely than not* the voice of God be adequate to prompt Stecher to reconsider his worldview? Again, secular news sources probably share Stecher's worldview and are therefore unlikely to report anything that would force Stecher to "check the date" (unless *they* had confirmation from an equally respected and skeptical source, and so on *ad infinitum*). Indeed, Stecher's discussion of evidential standards for belief in miracles has an air of artificiality about it that speaks of an underlying antipathy towards taking evidence for miracles seriously, for he contends that there is "indisputable evidence"[111] against the possibility of miracles:

> the greatest significance of this debate on Jesus' alleged resurrection is the place this event has in the closely related questions of God and his supposed plan for the world and for all who live in it. As conservative Christian scholars Gary Habermas and J.P. Moreland correctly note, "Often a particular belief is part of a larger system of beliefs, and it gains rational support from its role in that system." But I would suggest a corollary to this observation: "When a particular belief is part of a system which lacks coherence or is contradicted by indisputable evidence, that belief lacks credibility."[112]

Miracles, and the Modern Mind"; and *David Hume's Argument against Miracles*; Earman, *Hume's Abject Failure*; Geivett and Habermas, *In Defence of Miracles*; Houston, *Reported Miracles*; Larmer, *Legitimacy of Miracle*; McGrew, "Arguments from Providence and Miracles"; Williams, *Getting at Jesus*, ch. 1. On the problem of evil, see Williams, "Problem of Evil" (YouTube playlist); "Problems with the Problem of Evil"; and "Can Moral Objectivism Do without God?"; Craig, "Problem of Evil"; Baggett and Walls, *Good God*, ch. 8; Ganssle, "God and Evil"; Meister, *Evil*; Meister and Drew, *God and Evil*; Plantinga, *Warranted Christian Belief*; Rea, *Evil and the Hiddenness of God*; Williams, *Faithful Guide to Philosophy*, ch. 17.

110. Stecher, "Miracle Not Required," 268.
111. Stecher, "Miracle Not Required," 277.
112. Stecher, "Miracle Not Required," 277.

Stecher asserts (he doesn't argue the point) that the existence of natural evil constitutes "indisputable evidence" against an all-powerful and all-loving creator, before arguing (via his version of the corollary principle) that belief in Jesus's resurrection therefore "lacks credibility."

On the one hand, this argument pits Stecher's professed openness to evidence against his professed worldview. On the other hand, strictly speaking, this argument is a *non sequitur*, for it's *possible* for belief in the resurrection to fit within more than one "system" of thought. For example, the Orthodox Jewish rabbi and theologian Pinchas Lapide argues on historical grounds for the resurrection,[113] yet he resists the inference to the truth of the Christian understanding of Jesus. In the face of evil, Rabbi Harold S. Kushner abandons belief in the omnipotence of God, yet without abandoning belief in monotheism *per se*.[114] The combination of these two positions does an end run around Stecher's argument, showing that Stecher's corollary principle is unsound because it's too strict. The right way to formulate the corollary principle is surely something like this:

- When a particular belief is a part of a larger system of beliefs, the denial of the particular belief gains support from arguments against that system to a degree that depends upon (a) *the strength of the arguments against that system* and (b) *how tightly the particular belief is tied to that system*.

Now, I'd happily agree with Stecher that belief in the resurrection of Jesus is *most plausibly* associated with the Christian "system," and that evidence for or against either one therefore translates into evidence for or against the other; but this is a matter of an inference that needs to be weighed in the balance rather than a deductive *fait accompli*.

Stecher highlights Blomberg's suggestion that:

> my own conclusions are based on something other than the merits of the case at hand: ". . . at the end of Stecher's chapter he makes reference to the problem of evil. He did this briefly in the two live debates . . . He has done so in email exchanges with me more recently. I suspect that this is the real nub of the problem. There can't be an all-powerful and all-loving God because of the amount of evil in the universe. If there is no God, then there are no miracles. If there are no miracles, there is no resurrection. I suspect that for all of Stecher's more sophisticated arguments

---

113. Lapide, *Resurrection of Jesus*.
114. Kushner, *When Bad Things Happen to Good People*.

this is really the reasoning that has led him to his conclusions. If this is the case, then the real issue to be debated is not the resurrection but the problem of evil."[115]

In reply, Stecher writes:

> My response is we live in a world that is beset by lethal natural disasters . . . termed "Acts of God" by insurance companies. Given that we poor humans can do nothing to stop these forces of nature, but that an all-powerful God could do so without any effort, the label seems justified. . . . Millions of Christians believe in a God who is supposedly everywhere, all-powerful, all-knowing, loving of all his children, morally perfect. I cannot share this belief.[116]

Disappointingly, Stecher fails to interact with any of the responses to the problem of evil made by either Blomberg or myself.

Conclusion

Jesus's resurrection is a key piece of the Christian jigsaw. This key piece integrates with other pieces. The overall picture one thinks these pieces jointly form, one's assessment of that picture and of the many reasons for and against embracing it, will influence one's view of the matter at hand. That is, what one makes of the resurrection depends not only upon one's methodology in the gathering of the directly relevant historical evidence and upon how one assesses competing explanations for that evidence, but also upon an open and critical dialogue with one's philosophical expectations.

While Stecher's desire to avoid gullibility is both sensible and biblical, it seems to me that his skepticism has been submerged by a methodologically unsound cynicism. Indeed, Stecher's methodology is fundamentally flawed:

- He mistakenly prioritizes arguments from silence over and against the standard criteria of historicity.
- He mistakenly makes arguments that are both logically invalid and factually incorrect against the general reliability of the Gospels as

---

115. Stecher, "Miracle Not Required" (mainly quoting Blomberg), 277.
116. Stecher, "Miracle Not Required," 277–78.

if they could vitiate any and all arguments for specific points of NT historicity.

- Despite his protests to the contrary, Stecher's dismissal of work by scholars who believe in inerrancy is *ad hominem*.
- Ironically, given his remarks about literalism, Stecher consistently assumes a literalistic reading of the texts he cites rather than a literarily informed reading. Indeed, Stecher's reading of the NT is surprisingly naive, lacking in attention to literary genre, the meaning of key terms in the original language, etc. He rides roughshod over my exegesis of the biblical texts he cites, favoring historically un-contextualized and linguistically uninformed readings he apparently thinks so obvious that they can be defended without exegetical argumentation, simply by quoting an English translation.
- He repeatedly ignores evidence that has been brought to his attention in rebuttal of accusations he nevertheless persists in repeating.
- In the final analysis, Stecher begs the question against miracles in favor of his atheistic presuppositions.

As Blomberg concludes, the sticking point for Stecher isn't really the resurrection of Jesus, but "the problem of suffering and evil in the world, and secondarily the question of the unevangelized, those who have never had a chance to hear the gospel."[117] Indeed, Stecher openly admits that his willingness to reconsider his atheism on the basis of evidential arguments for Jesus's resurrection is constrained by his "impulse to assume that such events are either mistaken reports or they have a natural, non-miraculous explanation."[118] As Stecher rightly says: "This takes us back to . . . our differing senses of reality."[119]

Postscript

As *Resurrection: Faith or Fact?* was being edited, Carl Stecher told his co-authors that he'd already outlived the expectations of his oncologists: "so I've actually been very lucky; I just don't know how long this will

---

117. Blomberg, "Rejoinder to Carl", 190.
118. Stecher, "Miracle Not Required," 268.
119. Stecher, "Miracle Not Required," 268.

continue."[120] After the submission of the original version of this paper to *Theofilos* journal, I was saddened to see the announcement that "STECHER, Carl Age 78, passed away peacefully on November 24th [2019], in the care of family in his home in Georgetown, MA."[121] I wish to record my tribute to Carl as a generous friend and collaborator. As Carl's family wrote in his obituary:

> As a humanist and a skeptic, he often pondered the Big Questions, first and foremost what happens after we die. We love you Carl . . . and now that you have your answer, we hope that you are pleasantly surprised.[122]

---

120. Personal email correspondence, Jan 5, 2019.
121. "Carl Stecher, Obituary."
122. "Carl Stecher, Obituary."

Chapter Six

Scientific Rebuttals to "Ancient Aliens" as Popular Alternatives to Biblical History[1]

> Abstract: Just as Christian apologists need to rebut the "alternative" historical claims of *The Book of Mormon*, so they need to rebut claims about so-called ancient aliens. These claims offer people with a secular worldview historical counter-narratives to biblical history that draw upon the scientific respectability of astrobiology and the search for extra-terrestrial intelligence (SETI). Rather than interacting with the specifics of "ancient alien" narratives on a case-by-case basis, I argue that "ancient alien" theories are intrinsically *convoluted* and highly *ad hoc*, and that multiple essential facets of such theories are *disconfirmed by scientific evidence*. Not only do we lack convincing evidence that extra-terrestrial intelligences have visited Earth, but SETI has provided observational evidence that suggests technologically advanced aliens simply don't exist, at least in our cosmic neighborhood. In sum, it's those who believe in "ancient aliens," not Christians, who are swimming against the scientific evidence.

---

1. This chapter is a revised and expanded version of my peer reviewed paper "Scientific Rebuttals to 'Ancient Aliens' as Popular Alternatives to Biblical History." You can listen to the talk I gave proposing this paper topic at the 2018 Veritas Symposium: Williams, "Scientific Rebuttals to Ancient Alien Conspiracy Theories." I gave a talk at the 2020 European Leadership Forum based on the published paper: FOCLOnline, "Ancient Aliens" (video); Williams, "Ancient Aliens?" (audio).

Introduction

CHRISTIAN APOLOGETICS SHOULD DEVOTE some attention to rebutting "alternative" historical claims, whether those claims are contained in, for example, *The Book of Mormon*,[2] or in the many books and television "documentaries" that offer counter-narratives to the biblical understanding of various events and figures (including the origins of humanity, the biblical prophets, and the reality of the incarnation), by making claims about so-called ancient aliens. These controverted subjects all feature within the apologetic fields of "natural theology" or "ramified natural theology."[3]

Proponents of "ancient aliens" see the contradiction between their alien related beliefs and Christianity as a reason to doubt Christianity and thus Christian ramified natural theology. A legitimate but lengthy response to this doubt would be to offer a sufficiently robust positive apologetic for Christianity. This paper offers another legitimate, and more direct, response by critiquing the core tenets of "ancient alien" beliefs, *principally on the basis of scientific evidence*.

At a methodological level, this paper can be viewed as a case study in addressing anti-Christian claims in contemporary popular culture by drawing upon data from culturally esteemed sources of evidence that constitute common ground between Christians and non-Christians (indeed, to avoid any appearance of bias, I will quote principally from *secular* scientific sources). Rather than engaging with the specifics of the many different "ancient alien" beliefs in contemporary culture, this paper focuses upon using evidence from multiple scientific fields (including physics, psychology, origin of life studies, astrobiology, and the search for extra-terrestrial intelligence) to critique the key propositions that (a) intelligent extra-terrestrials exist, and that (b) they have visited planet Earth. I will also consider the hypothesis that aliens may have used advanced technology to fake the resurrection of Jesus.

---

2. See Williams, "Mormonism" (YouTube playlist); and "Mormonism"; Beverley, *Mormon Crisis*; Larson, *Quest for the Gold Plates*; Scott, *Mormon Mirage*; Williams, *Getting at Jesus*, 374–81.

3. See Williams, *Universe from Someone*; *Faithful Guide to Philosophy*; and *Getting at Jesus*.

Ancient Aliens in Contemporary Culture

Narratives about alien visitors to Earth, whether in ancient or modern times, are given credence by the intellectually superficial bent of contemporary popular culture. As John A. Keel comments:

> The E.T. [Extra-Terrestrial] premise has been promoted by the movies and by the UFO buffs so tenaciously the average person in the street now sort of accepts it, because they haven't given much thought to it. They don't realise how much of it is based upon wishful thinking and faulty logic. They have seen the movies or they have heard the UFO buffs on the radio or the TV and they say, "Well, that make sense, we're being visited by aliens."[4]

Such beliefs combine a superficial respect for science *per se* with ignorance of the relevant scientific data. Historical claims about "ancient aliens" get packaged into entertainment driven TV "documentaries" and shared as YouTube videos that spread through our social media environment like the common cold among H. G. Well's ill-prepared Martian invaders.[5]

Journalist Fiona Macdonald defines "fake news" as "news from dubious sources, advertising content, or stories that are just totally made up—but which still go viral on Facebook and Twitter."[6] As an example of "fake news," consider a July 2017 article from the website of well-known British national newspaper *The Sun*:

> LITTLE GREEN AMEN. Does this painting prove ALIENS were present at the Crucifixion of Jesus? Probably not . . . but that's what UFO watchers are claiming. The painting appears to show "crafts" . . . but they might just represent guardian angels.[7]

While stating that "art historians who have studied the 11th century piece say the weird dome-shaped 'crafts' represent guardian angels," the *Sun* article contrasts this expert opinion with that of the website TheAncientAliens.com *as if they were on a par*: "The unknown artist seems to be telling us that these flying saucers were present during the death of Jesus."[8]

---

4. Quoted in Clarke, *How UFOs Conquered the World*, 243.
5. See Wells, *War of the Worlds*.
6. Macdonald, "Bad News," §4.
7. Kamouni, "Little Green Amen." See also Martin, "Aliens Were Present at Crucifixion of Jesus"; Waugh, "Painting 'Proves Aliens Were Present.'"
8. Kamouni, "Little Green Amen," §3, 6.

Fig. 1. The Crucifixion of Christ Fresco, by Unknown Artist, Svetitskhoveli Cathedral in Georgia.[9]

According to the TheAncientAliens.com website, from which the *Sun* article is clearly cribbed:

> Art historians explain these to be representational of angels watching the event. However, angels were depicted with wings, and halos in Byzantine art of this time, as were all divine entities. We can see in this same painting that Jesus, Mary and John have halos. Others speculate these represent the sun and the moon. However, the sun and moon as personas was not accepted by christianity [sic]. The two objects were not given identities or deity status by the church as was the practice in Sumerian, Egypt and China.[10]

---

9. Credit: https://free-images.com/display/svetitskhoveli_fresco_crucifixion.html.
10. "ALIENS IN ART: Crucifixion of Christ."

These comments reveal a startling ignorance of Christian theology and art, neither of which would portray angels as "divine." As a matter of fact, I haven't been able to find *any* art historian who thinks the objects in the Svetitskhoveli Cathedral crucifixion fresco are angels, as the *Sun* reports the expert opinion to be. Moreover, that an artist personifies the sun and moon doesn't entail attributing literal "personas" to them, still less "deity status"! According to Nigel Watson, author of the *UFO Investigations Manual*:

> There are numerous examples of what to our modern eyes look like astronauts and spaceships in ancient and religious artworks. What we have to understand is that artists in the past did not adhere to literal representations of things and often used symbolism to tell a story to give greater meaning to the picture. In this crucifixion of Christ the UFOs are representations of light (life) and darkness (death). Many artists painted the Sun and Moon, faces or angels to present these symbolic elements. Basically, there are no aliens to see here.[11]

As Italian art historian Diego Cuoghi reports: "most of the crucifixions done in the Byzantine style show the same 'objects' on either side of the cross. They are the Sun and the Moon, often represented with a human face or figure."[12] Cuoghi points out that those who consider such symbolic elements as representations of alien spacecraft:

> assume that the artist, e.g. an Italian artist of the 15th century or an anonymous Byzantine painter, would actually be allowed to insert any non-canonical or un-codified element into a religious representation. On the contrary, in past times the commissioners (those who choose the subject and supervised the execution of the art work—in these cases the religious institutions) would have never allowed the author to insert into a work of art anything other than what [they] previously decided, especially in case of religious subjects.[13]

In short, this "ancient aliens" story is fake news disguised with the form, but not the substance, of journalistic balance. Indeed, the superficially balanced opinions presented by the article appear to have both been drawn from one and the same unreliable source!

11. Quoted in Waugh, "Painting 'Proves Aliens Were Present,'" §5–7.

12. Cuoghi, "ART and UFOs? No Thanks, Only Art . . . Part 2," §3. See Cuoghi, "Art of Imagining UFOs."

13. Cuoghi, "ART and UFOs? No Thanks, Only Art . . . Home," §5.

A Brief History of Ancient Aliens and Modern Religion

As theologian David Wilkinson observes: "The link between extraterrestrial intelligence and a religious quest has had a significant time in the last hundred years, with various new religious movements built on the mythology of aliens."[14] Science fiction author L. Ron Hubbard (1911–86) founded the Church of Scientology in 1952, blending the "ancient aliens" hypothesis with his "Dianetics" system of "auditing":

> Auditing purports to identify spiritual distress from a person's current life and from past lives. Scientologists believe each person is an immortal being, a force that believers call a thetan. "You move up the bridge to freedom by working toward being an 'Operating Thetan,' which at the highest level transcends material law," says David Bromley, a professor of religious studies at Virginia Commonwealth University. "You occasionally come across people in Scientology who say they can change the material world with their mind." Bromley and other scholars say the church promotes the idea of an ancient intergalactic civilization in which millions of beings were destroyed and became what are known as "body thetans," which continue to latch onto humans and cause more trauma . . . "It's part therapy, part religion, part UFO group," says Bromley.[15]

In the mid 1950s, George King claimed to have been contacted by an alien named Aetherius and founded The Aetherius Society to promote the belief that Jesus was an alien.[16] According to Mark Bennett, a contemporary member of The Aetherius Society:

> It makes much more sense [to many people] to say that Jesus was an interplanetary being who came to Earth to help mankind, than to say that God created a one and only son, who was also himself at a random point in history, who came to come to earth and forgive people their sins for some reason we don't really know.[17]

---

14. Wilkinson, *Science, Religion, and the Search*, 13.
15. Gilgoff and Escobedo, "Scientology," §10–12, 23.
16. See Mamer, "Toronto Aetherius Society: Jesus, Venusians" and "Toronto Aetherius Society: His Master's Voice."
17. Quoted in *Alltime Conspiracies*, "Was Jesus an Alien?"

Alternatively (and accommodating the existence of two independent historical birth accounts for Jesus[18]), it might be suggested that aliens "implanted" Jesus into Mary's womb.[19]

Swiss UFO religion leader "Billy" Eduard Albert Meier, who began publishing UFO photographs in the 1970s:

> claims to be the seventh incarnation of the "prophet" connecting Earth to the Plejaren [aliens]. The first incarnation was Henoch around 11,000 years ago followed by Elijah around 2,800 years ago, then Isiah [sic], Jeremiah, and [Jesus Christ] around 2,000 years ago, and then Mohammed around 1,400 years ago.[20]

The Raëlian religion, founded by Claude Vorilhon (a.k.a. Raël), claims humans were created 25,000 years ago by aliens using genetic engineering, and that genetic engineering holds the key to eternal life. Vorlihon claims aliens visited him in 1973 and commissioned him to prepare humans for the second coming of their extraterrestrial creators by teaching a message of sexual freedom and eternal life through science:

> According to Raël, all life on Earth was created by the Elohim, the same aliens who visited Vorilhon. The Elohim have been appearing to humans for millennia, usually in the guise of angels or gods, passing on their message to humanity through human figures like Buddha and Jesus.[21]

(Raëlianism illustrates the logical gap between Intelligent Design Theory within the biological realm and design-based argumentation within natural theology.[22])

In his 1970 book *Chariots of the Gods?*, Erich von Däniken[23] followed the Reverend John Miller[24] in misinterpreting a vision of the prophet Ezekiel as an encounter with alien machinery, an oft-debunked

---

18. See Ward, *Evidence for the Virgin Birth*; Barnett, *Messiah*; Crowe, *Was Jesus Really Born of a Virgin?*; Edwards, *Virgin Birth in History and Faith*; Machen, *Virgin Birth of Christ*; Nicholl, *Great Christ Comet*; Quarles, *Midrash Criticism*; Redford, *Born of a Virgin*.

19. See Millar, "Question: Was Jesus of Alien Parentage?"; Wilkinson, *Science, Religion, and the Search*, 122.

20. Bartholomaus, "Who Is Billy Meier?" See also Korff, *Spaceships of the Pleiades*; Sheaffer, *UFO Sightings*, 33–34.

21. Vago, "Greetings from the UFO Zealots," §2.

22. See Williams, "Raelians Successfully Clone Naturalism"; and *Informed Cosmos*.

23. See Feder, "Ancient Astronauts."

24. See Miller, "Whirling Wheels."

theory that nevertheless continues to circulate.[25] To someone lacking background knowledge of ancient Jewish literature, such an interpretation has a superficially "scientific" appeal, as Christian philosopher William Lane Craig testifies:

> When I was in high school as a non-Christian young man I was really quite into UFOs and read a lot of the literature... I remember seeing one article in a popular science magazine in which it claimed that Ezekiel's vision was of extraterrestrial beings in [a] sort of hovercraft and wearing helmets and things of this sort that he described in his primitive way as having the face of an ox and the face of an eagle and things of that sort. To me as a young high school teenager at the time it seemed very convincing... But as you become a little more sophisticated and understand Jewish apocalyptic literature and symbolism I think it makes it highly, highly unlikely that this was what Ezekiel was seeing; that this was in fact a typical sort of Jewish apocalyptic vision that he described.[26]

Recently, the popular TV series *Ancient Aliens*[27] "purports to be an actual, independent, serious documentary series exploring the ancient astronaut theory [and] pays lip service to being 'scientific.'"[28] In reality, *Ancient Aliens* offers up a mixture of "claims unsupported by evidence, leading questions [and] random facts marshalled with circular logic into self-referential 'theories.'"[29] *Ancient Aliens* connects the idea of aliens "to a whole range of myths, legends, structures and artefacts that already have perfectly adequate explanations in terms of the cultures they originated in."[30] As Vernon Macdonald observes: "Every Ancient Aliens episode, whether dealing with ancient civilizations, artifacts or legends is always made up of some noxious combination of willful deception, wild speculation, and at times just plain stupidity."[31]

---

25. See Gaia, "Aliens of the Old Testament"; White, "UFO in the Bible?"; Butt, "Ezekiel's Vision"; Callahan, "Spaceships of Ezekiel; Blumrich, *Spaceships of Ezekiel*.

26. Craig, "UFOs."

27. See Coumes, "Ancient Aliens Is Everything"; Colavito, "*Ancient Aliens*"; and *Critical Companion to Ancient Aliens*.

28. Colavito, *Critical Companion to Ancient Aliens*, 6.

29. Colavito, *Critical Companion to Ancient Aliens*, 33 and 54.

30. May, *Astrobiology*, 32. See White, *Past Is Human*.

31. Macdonald, *Ancient Aliens Exposed*, 91.

Popular Belief in Extra-Terrestrial Intelligences

The impulse to reinterpret religion by invoking extra-terrestrial intelligences (ETIs) gains a superficial legitimacy from the fact that speculation about alien life (including intelligent aliens) is a scientifically respectable pastime known as astrobiology. Since the early 1960s, astrobiology has included the empirical research of the search for extra-terrestrial intelligence (SETI).[32]

Many people agree with atheist Richard Dawkins that "there probably is intelligent life elsewhere in the Universe."[33] According to polling in 2015:

> More than one in two people in the UK, Germany and the US believe there is intelligent life out there in the universe. The next time the subject comes up at the dinner table and you hear sniggers when someone admits they believe in aliens, it is worth remembering that it is not a fringe belief to think there is intelligent life out there—it is the mainstream viewpoint across the western world.[34]

A 2017 survey conducted in 24 countries showed that 47 percent of 26,000 respondents believed:

> in the existence of intelligent alien civilizations in the universe. . . . Russians were the biggest believers—with whopping 68 percent saying they think intelligent alien life exists, trailed closely by Mexicans and Chinese respondents. The Netherlands ranked as the most skeptical of life beyond Earth, with only 28 percent of Dutch survey-takers entertaining in the possibility, according to the findings.[35]

Also in 2017, a study reported that 47 percent of surveyed Americans said they believe in aliens, while *39 percent said they believe aliens have visited Earth before* and 18 percent said they believed in alien

---

32. Oberhaus, "Brief History of Scientists."

33. Quoted in Stannard, *Science and Wonders*, 73. For a discussion of the existence of "intelligent life elsewhere in the universe" *per se* in relation to Christian theology, see Gonzalez, "Would Extraterrestrial Intelligent Life"; Williams, "Christianity, Space and Aliens"; Kelly and Regan, *God, Life, Intelligence*; Wilkinson, *Science, Religion, and the Search*.

34. Dahlgreen, "You Are Not Alone," §1.

35. Woods, "Half of Humans Believe," §2, 10–11.

abduction.[36] According to a 2018 Cambridge University study, 8 percent of UK adults believe their government has covered up contact with aliens.[37] In a 2019 Gallup poll:

> 68 percent of Americans believe the U.S. government knows more about UFOs than it is sharing with the public. Meanwhile, 33 percent of polled U.S. adults believed that some of the UFO sightings have, in fact, been extraterrestrial spacecraft visiting Earth.[38]

A 2020 study of 2,000 adults in the UK "found half believe in alien existence."[39] Furthermore: "Of those who indicated a belief in alien life, some 71% think this planet has already been visited at by aliens."[40] In a 2021 survey by the Pew Research Center: "about two-thirds of Americans (65%) say their best guess is that intelligent life exists on other planets."[41] Moreover, according to the same survey: "A smaller but still sizable share of the public (51%) says that UFOs reported by people in the military are likely evidence of intelligent life outside Earth."[42]

Given this cultural background, even if they don't believe the sort of "aliens explain away the supposedly supernatural elements of the Bible" theories advanced by the likes of von Däniken, many will think that alien conspiracy theories have at least one foot in "scientific reality," and are *at least no less plausible* than traditional, supernatural explanations of the same data. This viewpoint is expressed by journalist David Clarke:

> If someone visits a church or mosque to worship we tend to treat their faith with respect. But if they visit a hilltop to charge a prayer battery on the orders of Master Aetherius we write them off as "crackpot" or "UFO nut." I could not see why the beliefs of those who claim that flying saucers bring messages from the gods should be regarded as any less genuinely held, or unbelievable, than the tenets of any other religion.[43]

---

36. Rojas, "New Survey Shows."
37. Haridy, "From Aliens to Immigration."
38. Osborne, "Whistleblower Alleges U.S. Government," §4.
39. Hannan, "50% of UK Adults Believe Aliens Exist," §2.
40. Hannan, "50% of UK Adults Believe Aliens Exist," §11.
41. Kennedy and Lau, "Most Americans Believe in Intelligent Life," §1.
42. Kennedy and Lau, "Most Americans Believe in Intelligent Life," §2.
43. Clarke, *How UFOs Conquered the World*, 193.

Christian apologists shouldn't argue that the Aetherians' beliefs are less "genuinely held" than are Christian beliefs, but they should argue that they are more "unbelievable" than Christian beliefs.

An instructive example of the need for Christian apologetics to engage with this issue comes from a question posed by an audience member after a talk on the resurrection by William Lane Craig:

> I do find . . . the hypothesis that Jesus Christ was taken up into heaven by aliens to be as plausible as the resurrection. You know, I think one of them is absurd, but so's the other one, so what makes one more plausible than the other?[44]

As Craig replied, in contrast to the resurrection hypothesis,[45] the "ancient alien" hypothesis is:

> *ad hoc* and . . . implausible . . . . In fact . . . given the religio-historical context of Jesus' life and teachings, the hypothesis that the God of Israel raised Jesus from the dead fits like a hand in a glove, whereas the alien abduction hypothesis is . . . completely *ad hoc* and out of left field and doesn't do anything to illuminate the religio-historical context. And I think this is especially true if, as I say, you have independent reasons to believe in the existence of God . . . so that we've already got the existence of a supernatural being in place when we come to the evidence for the resurrection. [That] would be analogous [to,] if before we came to the evidence for the resurrection, you already had good evidence that there are these extra-terrestrial aliens who've come to earth. . . . That would make [the alien hypothesis] more plausible, if there were some evidence for that, but there just isn't; so I think the God hypothesis is much more plausible than that.[46]

The Drake Equation

Speaking scientifically, the existence of extra-terrestrial life *of any kind* remains an open question; let alone the existence of *intelligent* alien life with the *motive*, *means*, and *opportunity* to participate in a religious

---

44. Craig, "Is the Resurrection Hypothesis."

45. See Stecher et al., *Resurrection*; Williams, *Getting at Jesus*; and relevant sections of this book.

46. Craig, "Is the Resurrection Hypothesis"

conspiracy on planet Earth! And contrary to popular opinion, "of the search for *intelligent* life in particular, many scientists are skeptical."[47]

The so-called "Drake Equation," devised by American astronomer and astrophysicist Frank Drake, which is a "formula designed to provide a rough numerical estimate of an unknown quantity,"[48] suggests that the number of detectable alien civilizations (N) can be estimated by multiplying:

- the rate of formation of stars suitable for life (R^*)
- the fraction of those with planets (fp)
- the number of those planets that are suitable for life (ne)
- the fraction of these planets where life actually evolves (fl)
- the fraction of these on which intelligent life evolves (fi)
- the fraction of these that develop civilizations that produce detectable signs of their existence (fc)
- the length of time in which such civilizations will produce detectable signs of their existence (L)

That is:

- $N = R^* \times fp \times ne \times fl \times fi \times fc \times L$

According to science writer Andrew May: "The first factor in the Drake equation ... is the only one that's reasonably well established ... The other factors are subject to debate."[49] The value of N derived from this equation tends to owe more to the philosophical assumptions underlying the values assigned to its component parts than to scientific evidence. For naturalists, the value of N principally hinges upon whether or not the evolution of sentient life by purely natural processes is a likely occurrence (i.e., upon the value of fl x fi), for even many naturalists argue that (barring intelligent intervention of some kind) both the origin and subsequent macro-evolution of life (whether on Earth or elsewhere) are "non-trivial" contingencies that cannot be taken for granted.[50]

---

47. Watts, "Is There Life on Other Planets?," 203.
48. May, *Astrobiology*, 32.
49. May, *Astrobiology*, 34.
50. See Williams, "Origin of Life" (YouTube playlist); "Intelligent Design" (YouTube playlist); and "Introduction to *Informed Cosmos*"; Meyer, "DNA and the Origin of Life"; Tour, "Open Letter to My Colleagues"; Abel, *Primordial Prescription*; Behe, *Darwin*

The pre-conditions for eukaryotic plant and animal life aren't as simple as the "star plus rock plus water" formula popularized by media reports about the discovery of extra-solar planets![51] According to astrobiologist Lewis Dartnell:

> Complex animal life . . . may only be possible around Sun-like stars, on very Earth-like planets with plate tectonics, oceans of water, continental land, a thick oxygen-rich atmosphere and large moon.[52]

As of March 2024, despite the confirmed discovery of 5,595 exoplanets,[53] no such planet is known besides our own.

Of course, having the right kind of planet (or moon) hardly guarantees that abiogenesis will occur. In the words of Harvard biologist Itai Yanai: "It is fair to say that all origins of life models suffer from astoundingly low probabilities of actually occurring."[54]

Panspermia or Directed Panspermia?

To explain the existence of life on Earth, some scientists invoke the hypothesis of "panspermia," the idea that "life didn't begin on Earth, but elsewhere in the universe, and that it [or some ingredients thereof] was carried here on meteoroids and other space bodies."[55] However, the farther this organic material is supposed to travel, the less likely it is to make or survive the journey.[56] These problems are mitigated somewhat by the theory of "directed panspermia," first proposed by Nobel laureate Francis Crick and origin-of-life researcher Leslie Orgel in an article published in

---

Devolves; *Edge of Evolution*; and *Darwin's Black Box*; Klinghoffer, *Debating Darwin's Doubt*; and *Signature of Controversy*; Marks et al., *Introduction to Evolutionary Informatics*; Meyer, *Darwin's Doubt*; and *Signature in the Cell*; Tan and Stadler, *Stairway to Life*; Thaxton et al, *Mystery of Life's Origin*; Williams, *Informed Cosmos*; and *Outgrowing God?*

51. See Williams, "Rare Earth Hypothesis" (YouTube playlist); McIntyre et al., "Planetary Magnetism as a Parameter"; Berger, *How Unique Are We?*; Ward and Brownlee, *Rare Earth*; Waltham, *Lucky Planet*.

52. Dartnell, *Life in the Universe*, loc 2507.

53. See NASA, "Exoplanet Exploration."

54. Quoted in Koonin, "Cosmological Model."

55. Marshall, "Panspermia." See also Mcnichol and Gordon, "Are We from Outer Space?"; Steele et al., "Cause of Cambrian Explosion."

56. See Melosh, "Exchange of Meteorites"; Botkin-Kowacki, "Did Life on Earth." See also Marshall, "Panspermia."

Icarus (volume 19, 1973, 341–46).[57] Crick expanded upon the idea in his book *Life Itself* (Simon & Schuster, 1981), suggesting that an advanced alien species sent one or more spacecraft to Earth with the intent of peppering it with the necessary life forms (or components of life) to generate a zoo of diverse species. However, even leaving aside the difficulties associated with transporting organic material to Earth through interstellar space, the hypothesis of "directed panspermia" merely displaces the problem of abiogenesis without solving it.[58]

The Low Probability of Drake's fl & fi

Atheist philosopher Thomas Nagel takes Richard Dawkins to task over the origin of life:

> Dawkins . . . says that there are . . . a billion billion planets in the universe with life-friendly physical and chemical environments like ours. So all we have to suppose [to account for the origin of life on Earth] is that the probability of something like DNA forming . . . is not much less than one in a billion billion . . . [However] no one has a theory that would support anything remotely near such a high probability . . . at this point the origin of life remains, in light of what is known about the huge size, the extreme specificity, and the exquisite functional precision of the genetic material, a mystery.[59]

Eugene V. Koonin (senior investigator at the National Center for Biotechnology Information in Bethesda, Maryland, USA) calculates that "in a finite universe . . . the emergence of a coupled replication-translation system is unlikely to the extent of being, effectively, impossible."[60] (To avoid the implication of design, Koonin turns to the *ad hoc* and unparsimonious hypothesis of a multiverse.[61]) Likewise, cosmologist and astrobiologist Paul Davies concludes:

> we are probably the only intelligent beings in the observable universe, and I would not be very surprised if the solar system

57. See Crick and Orgel, "Directed Panspermia."
58. See Luskin, "With New Theory."
59. Nagel, "Dawkins and Atheism," 24–25.
60. Koonin, "Cosmological Model."

61. Craig critiques the cosmological model that Koonin uses in "Vilenkin's Cosmic Vision." For my own critique of the multiverse hypothesis, see Williams, *Outgrowing God?*

contains the only life in the observable universe. I arrive at this dismal conclusion because I see so many contingent features involved in the origin and evolution of life.[62]

According to a 2018 analysis by physicists Anders Sandberg, Eric Drexler, and Toby Ord, of the Future of Humanity Institute at Oxford University:

> existing calculations for the probability of extra-terrestrial intelligent life . . . rest on uncertainties and assumptions that lead to outcomes containing margins for error spanning "multiple orders of magnitude." Constraining these, as much as possible, by factoring in models of plausible chemical and genetic mechanisms, results, they conclude, in the finding "that there is a substantial probability that we are alone."[63]

The co-authors highlight:

> critical questions regarding the emergence of life from non-living material—a process known as abiogenesis—and the subsequent likelihoods of early RNA-like life evolving into more adaptive DNA-like life. Then there is the essential matter of that primitive DNA-like life undergoing the sort of evolutionary symbiotic development that occurred on Earth, when a relationship between two different types of simple organisms resulted in the complex "eukaryotic" cells that constitute every species on the planet more complicated than bacteria.[64]

They conclude:

> When we take account of realistic uncertainty, replacing point estimates [in the Drake Equation] by probability distributions that reflect current scientific understanding, we find no reason to be highly confident that the galaxy (or observable universe) contains other civilizations.[65]

---

62. Davies, *Eerie Silence*, 207.
63. Masterson, "Stop Looking for ET," §8–9.
64. Masterson, "Stop Looking for ET," §22–23.
65. Masterson, "Stop Looking for ET," §25.

An Accumulating Evidence of Absent Aliens

As far as we know, the only body in space to host life, or to have hosted life, is Earth. On the one hand, as Paul Davies notes, we can at the very least "be pretty sure that there are zero prospects for intelligent life arising on any other planet in the solar system."[66] On the other hand, as Andrew May observes: "despite the thousands of exoplanets we've discovered over the last couple of decades, we've yet to find conclusive evidence of life on any of them."[67] Indeed, NASA admits that "so far, we have no evidence of life beyond Earth."[68]

Is There Life on Mars?

In our own solar system, Mars may have been a habitable world with a global ocean for several billion years, up until around four billion years ago;[69] but even supposing it was discovered that (most plausibly, microbial) life once existed (or even currently exists) on Mars,[70] it may well have been transferred there on rocks from impact events on Earth, or vice versa, in which case it wouldn't be truly *alien* life.[71]

Life in the Atmosphere of Venus?

In 2020, a paper in *Nature Astronomy* reported the detection of phosphine gas in the atmosphere of Venus, a gas that *may* be a biosignature (i.e., an indicator of life). As Kate Howells, public education specialist at The Planetary Society, reports:

> In 2020 scientists announced they found phosphine gas . . . in Venus' clouds 50 kilometers . . . above the surface, where temperatures and pressures are much more Earth-like. Phosphine's presence has since been disputed, then later reclaimed but with an alternative explanation for its origins, disputed once again,

---

66. Davies, *Eerie Silence*, 17.
67. May, *Astrobiology*, 106.
68. NASA, "Are We Alone?," §2.
69. See Kohler, "Mars's Leaky Atmosphere and Habitability."
70. See NASA, "NASA Finds Ancient Organic Material"; Southwest Research Institute, "Scientists Have Modeled Mars Climate"; Zaske, "Study Finds Organic Molecules."
71. See May, *Astrobiology*, 77; Mortillaro, "Could Life Have Started"; Siegel, "5 Possibilities for Life on Mars."

and redetected lower in the atmosphere. The verdict on whether phosphine exists in the clouds of Venus, and whether its presence would mean there were life forms producing it, is still very much undecided.[72]

However, phosphine gas "is not a widely-accepted signature of life."[73] As Howells notes:

> even if there is phosphine in the Venusian atmosphere, it doesn't necessarily mean the planet hosts life. Abiotic processes, some of which we don't fully understand, could also be generating the stuff on Venus.[74]

In light of the fact that Venus has an average surface temperature of about 464 Celsius, and sulfuric acid rain, science journalist Jamie Carter likewise concludes that "these detections of phosphine are evidence not of life, but that we simply don't understand the phosphorus cycle on Venus."[75] As astronomer Hugh Ross and chemist Fazale Rana observe:

> prebiotic molecules that form at high temperatures or under highly acidic or highly alkaline conditions face a dramatically increased likelihood of rapid chemical destruction. The biochemical modifications needed to stabilize proteins and RNA structures in extreme environments exacerbate the already enormous problems of producing these information-rich molecules via natural mechanisms.[76]

Astronomer Jane Greaves (lead scientist in the original discovery) calls the existence of life in the atmosphere of Venus "a remote possibility"[77] and notes:

> There's a big school of thought that you can make phosphine by lobbing phosphorus-bearing rocks up into the high atmosphere and kind of eroding them with water and acid and stuff and getting phosphine gas.[78]

---

72. Lea, "Life on Venus?," §7.
73. Beall, "Scientists Found Signs," §3.
74. Howells, "Life on Venus."
75. Carter, "Phosphine Confirmed Deep within Venus' Atmosphere," §5.
76. Ross and Rana, *Origins of Life*, 175.
77. Quoted in Bello, "Phosphine Discovery Could Indicate," §7. See also Cooper, "No Alien Life Needed."
78. Jane Greaves, quoted in Lea, "Life on Venus?," §8.

In a June 2021 article for *Live Science*, science journalist Tereza Pultarova reported:

> The amount of water in the atmosphere of Venus is so low that even the most drought-tolerant of Earth's microbes wouldn't be able to survive there, a new study has found. The findings seem to wipe out the hope stirred by last year's discovery of molecules potentially created by living organisms in the scorched planet's atmosphere . . . "When we looked at the effective concentration of water molecules in those clouds, we found that it was a hundred times too low for even the most resilient Earth organisms to survive." John Hallsworth, a microbiologist at Queen's University in Belfast, U.K., and lead author of the paper, said in a news conference on Thursday (June 24). "That's an unbridgeable distance."[79]

Responding to the Hallsworth-led study, Greaves suggested that some cloud droplets might nevertheless have a sufficient water content: "It's also likely that conditions are not uniform . . . and so parts of the clouds could be much more favourable than others."[80] However, David L. Chandler reports that Nathalie Cabrol, who is the director of the Carl Sagan Center for the Study of Life in the Universe at the SETI Institute in California:

> says she can accept the idea of a habitable zone on Venus, but she finds it unlikely that it is actually inhabited. While there are living organisms in Earth's atmosphere, she points out, none of them truly reside there. They are simply being transported from one place to another. That they could survive and create an ecosystem that is entirely airborne seems unlikely, she says, because that environment would simply be far too unstable.[81]

In the words of Paul Byrne, associate professor of Planetary Science at North Carolina State University, the balance of evidence seems to suggest that "if phosphine is confirmed beyond doubt to be present at Venus, it's very unlikely to be biotic in origin."[82] Indeed, Cornell University astronomer Jonathan Lunine argues that the detection of phosphine in the Venusian atmosphere is "not telling us about the biology

---

79. Pultarova, "No Hope for Life," §1, 3.
80. Quoted in Crane, "Clouds of Venus Are Too Dry," §10.
81. Chandler, "Could the Clouds of Venus Support Life?," §26.
82. Quoted in Beall, "Scientists Found Signs," §19.

of Venus. It's telling us about the geology."[83] According to Ngoc Truon, a doctoral candidate in geology who co-authored a paper to this effect with Professor Lunine: "Volcanism could supply enough phosphide to produce phosphine. The chemistry implies that phosphine derives from explosive volcanoes on Venus, not biological sources."[84]

Even supposing that scientists confirm that there is phosphine in the atmosphere of Venus, and discover that it is produced by some form of microbial life, thereby suggesting that similar microbes could exist in similar exoplanetary environments, such life would hardly be in a promising position to evolve a space-faring civilization!

Enceladus

Perhaps the best prospect for extra-terrestrial life in the solar system is Enceladus,[85] the sixth largest moon of Saturn (with a diameter of about six hundred kilometers),[86] which harbors an about ten-kilometer deep ocean of salty, liquid water below its thirty-to-forty-kilometer deep icy crust,[87] an ocean that may well contain hydrothermal vents.[88] Data from the Cassini spacecraft has shown that this ocean contains "carbon, hydrogen, nitrogen, oxygen, phosphorus and sulfur,"[89] which are key ingredients for life. According to science writer Rebecca Sohn: "Enceladus' subsurface ocean likely contains most, if not all of the chemical ingredients necessary for life."[90] However, the fact that phosphorus was detected in "a concentration thousands of times greater than in Earth's big blue ocean [gives] rise to a glaring conundrum," since on Earth "any available phosphorus is rapidly scavenged by life."[91] As planetary scientist Yasuhito Sekine asks: "If life exists [on] Enceladus, why [does] such [an] abundance of chemical energy and nutrients remain?"[92] One possible explanation is that any life on Enceladus "may simply consume the

83. Quoted in Friedlander, "Trace Gas Phosphine," §3.
84. Quoted in Friedlander, "Trace Gas Phosphine," §6.
85. See Wall, "If We Find Life on Europa."
86. See Wikipedia, "Enceladus."
87. See Australian Academy of Science, "Is There Life on Saturn's Moons?"
88. See Wall, "Methane in Plume of Saturn's Moon."
89. See Lea, "Finding Life on Saturn's Moon Enceladus," §6.
90. Sohn, "Enceladus," §5.
91. Ogasa, "Last Vital Ingredient for Life," §8, 11.
92. Quoted in Ogasa, "Last Vital Ingredient for Life," §11.

nutrient at a sluggish pace."[93] Alternatively: "It's possible that the moon is simply barren of life."[94] In the absence of evidence for the existence of life on Enceladus, this remains the simplest explanation.

Cassini did detect a "surprisingly large amount of methane"[95] in the plumes of Enceladus, and mathematical models have been used to investigate the hypothesis that some of this methane has an organic source:

> The team determined that abiotic (without the aid of life) hydrothermal-vent chemistry as we know it on Earth does not explain the methane concentrations observed by Cassini very well. Adding the contributions of methanogenic microbes, however, fills the gap nicely.
>
> To be clear: The new study, which was published . . . in the journal Nature Astronomy, does not argue that life exists on Enceladus. For instance, it's possible that the icy moon features some types of abiotic methane-producing reactions that aren't prevalent here Earth—perhaps the decay of primordial organic matter left over from the moon's birth, the researchers said. Indeed, that latter hypothesis would fit nicely if Enceladus formed from organic-rich material delivered by comets, as some scientists believe.[96]

To quote Régis Ferrière, an associate professor in the University of Arizona's Department of Ecology and Evolutionary Biology, and the co-lead author of this study:

> It partly boils down to how probable we believe different hypotheses are to begin with. For example, if we deem the probability of life in Enceladus to be extremely low, then such alternative abiotic mechanisms become much more likely, even if they are very alien compared to what we know here on Earth.[97]

In the final analysis, even if we assume that Enceladus does host life, it doesn't offer an environment conducive to the development of space-faring civilization. Nor is there any evidence of intelligent life on Enceladus.

---

93. Ogasa, "Last Vital Ingredient for Life," §12.
94. Ogasa, "Last Vital Ingredient for Life," §12.
95. Wall, "Methane in Plume of Saturn's Moon," §6.
96. Wall, "Methane in Plume of Saturn's Moon," §9–10. See Anderson, "Methane on Enceladus"; Evolution News, "Methane Causes Space Aliens?"
97. Quoted by Wall, "Methane in Plume of Saturn's Moon," §11.

Signs of Life on K2-18 b?

Exoplanet K2-18b[98] has its (probably tidally locked) orbit around a small red dwarf star in the constellation of Leo, some 124 light years away from us. K2-18b orbits its star "at a distance of just 40% of Mercury's orbital distance from the Sun. However, because this exoplanet's host star is so much smaller and colder than the Sun, it's possible that K2-18b's surface temperature permits the existence of liquid water there."[99] With a radius 2.6 times that of Earth,[100] and a mass 8.92 times that of Earth,[101] K2-18b's surface gravity is "much larger than Earth's."[102] Moreover, given its close orbit around a red dwarf star, "its radiation environment may be hostile."[103] Red dwarf stars present multiple challenges to planetary habitability.[104]

In September 2023, media reports appeared asserting that "spectral data from the . . . James Webb space telescope showed evidence of methane, carbon dioxide and hints of dimethyl sulfide (DMS) on K2-18 b."[105] The possible presence of DMS on K2-18b caused excitement in popular media, because on Earth the molecule is made by living things (mainly marine phytoplankton). As Hugh Ross explains:

> a team of six astronomers led by Nikku Madhusudhan positively detected methane in K2-18b's atmosphere . . . at the 5-sigma level (five standard deviations, or about five times greater than the background noise). . . . Madhusudhan's team also detected carbon dioxide . . . but only at the 3-sigma level. Their search for water (H_2O), ammonia (NH_3), carbon monoxide (CO), and hydrogen cyanide (HCN) revealed no evidence for the presence of any of these molecules. However, they were able to establish upper limits for the abundance of water, ammonia, carbon monoxide, and hydrogen cyanide, and they were low. What generated all the excitement was the team's "potential" detection

---

98. See Dr. Becky, "Did JWST find a MARKER OF LIFE?"

99. Ross, "Have Astronomers Found Life?," §2. But see Shorttle et al., "Distinguishing Oceans of Water"; Wogan et al., "JWST Observations of K2-18b."

100. NASA Webb Telescope Team, "Webb Discovers Methane."

101. NASA, "K2-18 b."

102. NASA Hubble Mission Team, "NASA's Hubble Finds Water Vapor," §1.

103. NASA Hubble Mission Team, "NASA's Hubble Finds Water Vapor," §1.

104. Launch Pad Astronomy, "Could Life Exist"; SETI Institute, "Trouble with M Dwarf Stars"; Ross, "More Evidence That Planets."

105. Herath, "Science Sensationalism in the Media," §9.

of dimethyl sulfide (CH_3SCH_3) and chloromethane (CH_3Cl) . . . In reality, the detections were marginal, at best.[106]

While the detection of methane was fairly robust at the 5-sigma level,[107] and the detection of carbon dioxide was at a lower 3-sigma level, the detection of DMS was less statistically significant (at around 1 or 2 sigma, depending on the model used), and the detection of chloromethane was even less significant.[108] Oxford University astrophysicist Becky Smethurst comments that:

> while the claim for the detection of methane is really strong, the claim for the detection of dimethyl sulfide really isn't. It isn't even over the statistical thresholds that we usually use to actually claim a detection. So, from that alone, I don't think we can even claim we've detected dimethyl sulfide in the atmosphere of K2-18 b.[109]

Ross notes that "to their credit, Madhusudhan and his colleagues referred to their discovery as 'tentative' and recommended more sensitive spectral measurements of K2-18b's atmosphere."[110]

Science journalist Adam Mann observes that the DMS results:

> which have yet to be confirmed, highlight the trickiness of such methods. If dimethyl sulfide is truly present in the planet's atmosphere, then starlight should also break it down to form ethane, a molecule that has yet to be seen.[111]

As planetary scientist Ravi Kopparapu warns: "No single gas is a biosignature. You need to see a combination of them."[112]

The existence of methane and carbon dioxide on K2-18b would lend credence to the hypothesis that it is a "Hycean" (Hydrogen-Ocean) world with a thin hydrogen atmosphere and deep, dense "global water ocean."[113]

---

106. Ross, "Have Astronomers Found Life," §6–8.

107. Chandler, "Explained: Sigma."

108. See Dr. Becky, "Did JWST find a MARKER OF LIFE?"; Ross, "Have Astronomers Found Life ."

109. Dr. Becky, "Did JWST find a MARKER OF LIFE?"

110. Ross, "Have Astronomers Found Life," §9.

111. Mann, "Are We Alone in the Universe?," §15.

112. Quoted in Mann, "Are We Alone in the Universe?," §15. Indeed, recent research found DMS in abiotic cometary matter. See Hänni et al., "Is Dimethylsulfide a Good Biomarker?"

113. Anderson, "Did Webb Find Signs," §3. But see Shorttle et al., "Distinguishing

However, as NASA cautioned in a press release on K2-18b, while "Hycean worlds are predicted to have oceans of water . . . it is also possible that the ocean is too hot to be habitable or be liquid."[114]

According to Ross, the claim that life might originate on a Hycean ocean world faces a challenge "from research on ocean acidification. The team of Amit Levi and Dimitar Sasselov has demonstrated that the pH of such an ocean would range from 2 to 4."[115] While there are extremophile microbes on Earth that can survive in such an environment, "life cannot *originate* under such acidic conditions."[116]

Preconditions of Science

It's one thing for alien life to exist, quite another for it to be intelligent; and as Cambridge University paleobiologist Emily Mitchell observes: "there's a massive, massive difference between being able to find life elsewhere, and being able to find evidence of intelligent life."[117] Moreover, even if aliens intelligent enough to cross the stars were to exist, whether they actually develop the sophisticated science and technology that would allow them to visit Earth is a separate matter. As botanist William C. Burger observes: "Whether here on planet Earth or elsewhere in the universe, the assumption that since science happened once, science ought to happen often is wishful thinking."[118] Biologist Michael Denton argues that on Earth:

> the march of technological advance from the Stone Age . . . was only possible because of what would appear to be an outrageously fortuitous set of environmental conditions, without which, despite our genius . . . no advance beyond the most primitive stone tools would have been possible.[119]

Oceans of Water"; Wogan et al., "JWST Observations of K2-18b."

114. NASA Webb Telescope Team, "Webb Discovers Methane," §8.

115. Ross, "Have Astronomers Found Life," §17. On the ice mantle problem also mentioned by Ross in this article, see Cooper, "On Alien Worlds."

116. Ross, "Waterworld Planets Are Acidic," §6. See also Cleaves and Chalmers, "Extremophiles May Be Irrelevant."

117. Emily Mitchell, quoted in Achenbach, "What We Actually Know about Aliens," §43.

118. Berger, *How Unique Are We?*, 270.

119. Denton, *Fire Maker*, 614. See also Williams, "Physical Preconditions of Science" (YouTube playlist); Parker et al., "Pyrophilic Primate Hypothesis," 54–63; Berger, *How Unique Are We?*, 241–44.

According to Denton:

> There is . . . every justification for viewing our planetary home with its oxygen-containing atmosphere, large land masses covered in trees, with its readily available and well scattered metal-bearing rocks as an ideal and perhaps unique environment for the use of fire and the development of metallurgy and ultimately the emergence of a technologically advanced complex society.[120]

Second, consider the fact that on Earth "the scientific perspective flowered in Europe as an outworking of medieval biblical theology."[121] As Paul Davies comments:

> It was from the intellectual ferment brought about by the merging of Greek philosophy and Judeo-Islamic-Christian thought that modern science emerged, with its unidirectional linear time, its insistence on nature's rationality, and its emphasis on mathematical principles . . . [Today] even the most atheistic scientist accepts as an act of faith that the universe is not absurd, that there is a rational basis to physical existence manifested as a law-like order in nature that is at least in part comprehensible to us.[122]

Historian of science James Hannam confirms that:

> the metaphysical background to Christianity turned out to be uniquely conducive to successfully understanding the working of nature . . . Christianity was a necessary, if not sufficient, cause of the flowering of modern science.[123]

Indeed, it was Christian belief in the incarnation that elevated:

> the dignity of matter and of manual work . . . Modern science was possible only when investigators became willing to dirty their hands in workshops and laboratories, and only when they began to see all material things, which have been created by God, as good in themselves.[124]

---

120. Denton, *Nature's Destiny*, 394.

121. Mangalwadi, *Book That Made Your World*, 223. See also Williams, "Theological Roots of Science" (YouTube playlist); Hannam, "How Christianity Led to the Rise"; Berger, *How Unique Are We?*, 251–70; Chapman, *Slaying the Dragons*; Grant, *History of Natural Philosophy*; Hannam, *God's Philosophers*; Harrison, *Bible, Protestantism*.

122. Davies, "Physics and the Mind of God," §10–11.

123. Hannam, "How Christianity Led to the Rise," §19.

124. Koons, "Science and Theism," §22.

In other words, there's a chance that an alien civilization might never develop the scientific knowledge required to allow them to visit Earth and be mistaken for a divine incarnation unless they themselves happen to develop a belief in a divine incarnation! In sum:

> The origin of modern science and technology depend on a precise configuration of economic, cultural, philosophical, and theological precursors, and an unusually long-lasting and stable warm climate. Technology requires dexterity and a level of capacity to communicate that, of millions of known species of life, only humans possess. It also requires access to an oxygen-rich atmosphere, dry land, and concentrated ores. The laws of physics did not uniquely determine any of these. Until these factors came together, no civilization developed technology advanced enough to harness radio communication. And even on Earth, this has happened only once. What justification do we have for assuming that it's an inevitable result of life, even intelligent life, everywhere?[125]

Hence, as astrophysicist John Gribbin concludes: "the kind of intelligent, technological civilization that has emerged on Earth may be unique, at least in our Milky Way Galaxy."[126] It would certainly seem that the burden of proof is on the ancient alien theorist.

SETI

Since the early 1960s, scientists have been searching for intelligent extraterrestrials beyond our solar system by looking for signals that might emanate from a technologically advanced civilization. Over a half century of this "search for extra-terrestrial intelligence" (SETI)—"mainly in the radio, but occasionally in the infrared and increasingly in the visible"[127]—has thus far produced a null result, despite rapid technological improvements in the field.[128]

---

125. Gonzalez and Richards, *Privileged Planet*, 287–88. See also Berger, *How Unique Are We?*; Dartnell, *Life in the Universe*, ch. 8; Denton, *Fire Maker*; and *Nature's Destiny*; Gribbin, *Alone in the Universe*; Webb, *Where Is Everybody?*, 211–32.

126. Gribbin, *Alone in the Universe*, xiv.

127. Webb, *Where Is Everybody?*, 101.

128. See Webb, *Where Is Everybody?*, 88–105. See also O'Connell, "Alien Megastructure 'Discovery.'"

Historian of science George Basalla reports that "many SETI supporters expected extraterrestrial contact well before the coming of the millennium."[129] Consequently, as Stephen Webb observes: "the continuing silence, despite intensive searches, is beginning to worry even some of the most enthusiastic proponents of SETI."[130] Philosopher David Lamb argues that:

> Generous estimates of the number of planets with intelligent communicative life suffered a serious setback in 1992 following the completion of a radio search conducted by D.G. Blair... The search covered the neighbourhoods of 176 stars... within forty light years of the Earth. No signal was detected. The negative results weaken [the] assumption that technological intelligence will inevitably emerge through enough time on an Earth-sized planet near a Sun-like star.[131]

Likewise, writing in a 2006 *Skeptical Inquirer* article, Peter Schenkel observed:

> Since project OZMA I in 1959 by Frank Drake, about a hundred radio-magnetic and other searches were conducted in the U.S. and in other countries and a considerable part of our sky was scanned thoroughly and repeatedly, but it remained disappointingly silent... If a hundred searches were unsuccessful, it is fair to deduce that estimates of a million or many thousands ETI are unsustainable propositions.[132]

Of particular note: "Between 1995 and 2004, Project Phoenix used radio telescopes to look at hundreds of Sun-like stars within a couple of hundred light years of Earth without detecting any sign of alien civilization."[133] Schenkel concluded: "Earth may be more special, and intelligence much rarer, than previously thought."[134]

More recent SETI projects, especially since the launch of the Kepler space telescope, have sometimes been guided by hard data about extra-solar planets. For example, a 2013 targeted search of "86 Kepler Objects of Interest... hosting [164] planet candidates judged to be most

---

129. Basalla, *Civilized Life in the Universe*, 167.
130. Webb, *Where Is Everybody?*, 25.
131. Lamb, *Search for Extraterrestrial Intelligence*, 55.
132. Schenkel, "SETI Requires a Skeptical Reappraisal," 27.
133. Al-Khalili, *Aliens*, 3.
134. Schenkel, "SETI Requires a Skeptical Reappraisal," 26.

amenable to the presence of Earth-like life" looked for narrow band radio emissions but found "no signals of extraterrestrial origin . . . no evidence of advanced technology indicative of intelligent life," thus "placing limits on the presence of intelligent life in the galaxy."[135]

In 2016, philosopher David R. Koepsell wrote that there are about 500 [sun-like "G" class] stars within a one-hundred light-year radius of us: "and so far, listening to them, we have heard nothing, although we have observed nearly 100 planets in that vicinity."[136]

In 2018 a paper by Jean-Luc Margot et al. detailed the results of "A Search for Technosignatures from 14 Planetary Systems in the *Kepler* Field with the Green Bank Telescope at 1.15–1.73 GHz."[137] Focusing on 14 planetary systems, 858,748 candidate narrowband radio signals were analyzed, producing a short-list of 19 candidate signals of interest. However, "all of these candidates were observed in more than one direction on the sky, thereby ruling them out as extraterrestrial signals."[138]

In 2019, the Berkeley SETI Research Center "Breakthrough Listen" project "completed a comprehensive scan of 1,372 nearby stars, but no evidence of aliens was detected over the course of the three-year survey."[139] This search:

> involved an analysis of 1,372 stars out of a total sample pool of 1,702 stars, none of which are farther than 160 light-years away. The survey included a wider variety of star types than usual, including stars that aren't similar to our Sun.[140]

Study co-author Andrew Siemion commented that "these results will . . . lead us toward further analysis that will place yet more stringent limits on the distribution of technologically capable life in the universe."[141]

In 2020, a paper by Dr. Chenoa Tremblay and Professor Steven Tingay, of the International Centre for Radio Astronomy Research, published in the *Publications of the Astronomical Society of Australia*,

---

135. Siemion et al, "1.1 to 1.9 GHz SETI Survey."

136. Koepsell, "Drake vs. Fermi," §5. See Sol Company, "G Stars within 100 Light-Years." According to David Wilkinson, Project Phoenix surveyed "1,000 nearby stars similar to our Sun, out to a distance of 100 light-years" (*Science, Religion, and the Search*, 89).

137. Margot et al., "Search for Technosignatures."

138. Margot et al., "Search for Technosignatures."

139. Dvorsky, "Ambitious Search for Aliens," §4.

140. Dvorsky, "Ambitious Search for Aliens," §9.

141. Quoted in Dvorsky, "Ambitious Search for Aliens," §6.

detailed how they "used the Murchison Widefield Array (MWA) telescope to explore hundreds of times more broadly than any previous search for extraterrestrial life."[142] This "groundbreaking survey of over 10 million star systems"[143] observed the sky around the constellation of Vela ("a region of space known to contain at least six exoplanets"[144]), "looking more than 100 times broader and deeper than ever before."[145] The researchers reported that "with this dataset we found no technosignatures—no sign of intelligent life."[146]

Initially "promising" radio signals detected by Parkes Observatory's Murriyang radio telescope in 2019 appeared to come from Proxima Centauri, but "a study concluded that this signal likely came from malfunctioning human equipment."[147] Likewise, reports in June 2022 that Chinese astronomers had detected narrow-band radio signals from an alien civilization had to be walked back when it turned out to be a case of terrestrial radio interference.[148]

In January 2023 results were published from a project using artificial intelligence to reinvestigate "820 unique targets observed with the Robert C. Byrd Green Bank Telescope, totaling over 480 [hours] of on-sky data."[149] This data "had previously been searched through in 2017 by classical techniques but labeled as devoid of interesting signals."[150] Among the mass of information generated by these observations, "the algorithm found almost 3 million distinctive patterns, which further filtering reduced to just 20,515."[151] Among these, the team visually flagged "8 promising ETI signals of interest for re-observation."[152] However, "re-examinations of these new targets of interest have yet to result in re-detections of these signals."[153] Hence, "for the moment, the team come

---

142. Curtin University, "Australian Telescope Finds No Signs," §2.
143. Dvorsky, "Another Sweeping Search for Aliens," §1.
144. Dvorsky, "Another Sweeping Search for Aliens," §6.
145. Curtin University, "Australian Telescope Finds No Signs," §8.
146. Curtin University, "Australian Telescope Finds No Signs," §9.
147. Young, "China's FAST Telescope Did Detect," §10. See also Shepherd, "Alien False Alarm."
148. Young, "China's FAST Telescope Did Detect."
149. Ma et al., "Deep-Learning Search for Technosignatures," §1.
150. Peter Ma, quoted in SETI Institute, "Will Machine Learning Help Us?," §2.
151. Physics arXiv Blog, "AI Hunt for Extraterrestrial Intelligence," §9.
152. Ma et al., "Deep-Learning Search for Technosignatures," §1.
153. SETI Institute, "Will Machine Learning Help Us?," §9.

to no conclusion about the origin of the signals of interest."[154] Study participant Dr. Cherry Ng commented: "I would still say there's a good chance these signals we detected are still interference."[155] Astronomer Michael Garrett, of the Jodrell Bank Center for Astrophysics, agrees that "realistically, it's most likely that these eight new signals were generated by human technology."[156]

Also in early 2023, Xiao-Hang Luan et al. reported on their search for "narrowband drifting signals" in "33 exoplanet systems" using "the Five-hundred-meter Aperture Spherical radio Telescope (FAST)."[157] Using a new search methodology, the team achieved "unprecedented sensitivity"[158] and flagged two signals of interest, which they ultimately discounted as terrestrial in origin: "we eliminate the possibility of the special signals being ETI signals based on much evidence, such as the polarization, drift, frequency and beam coverage characteristics."[159]

Astronomers have searched at the galactic level for the energetic signatures of any civilizations using much of a galaxy's starlight to satisfy their power requirements (civilizations at "type III" or above on the Kardashev scale[160]):

- In 1999 the *Journal of the British Interplanetary Society* reported the results of one such search, noting: "For a sample of 137 galaxies, no such outliers are found."[161]
- In 2015 a Swedish study of 1,359 spiral galaxies detected no signs of galactic scale civilization.[162]
- Also in 2015, another research group published the results of their extensive search for "the thermodynamic consequences of galactic-scale colonization."[163] According to *Scientific American*: "After examining some 100,000 nearby large galaxies a team of researchers

154. Physics arXiv Blog, "AI Hunt for Extraterrestrial Intelligence," §13.
155. Event Horizon, "8 Candidate Alien Signals."
156. Quoted in Anderson, "AI Search for Aliens," §15.
157. Luan et al., "Multibeam Blind Search," §1.
158. Luan et al., "Multibeam Blind Search," §1.
159. Luan et al., "Multibeam Blind Search," §1.
160. Hughes, "Kardashev Scale."
161. Annis, "Placing a Limit," abstract.
162. See Zackrisson et al., "Extragalactic SETI."
163. Billings, "Alien Supercivilizations Absent," §5. See Griffith et al., "Ĝ Infrared Search for Extraterrestrial Civilizations."

lead [sic] by The Pennsylvania State University astronomer Jason Wright has concluded that none of them contain any obvious signs of highly advanced technological civilizations."[164]

In December 2023 the latest results of the "Breakthrough Listen" project were published, in a paper detailing "a radio technosignature search of the centers of 97 nearby galaxies"[165] looking for "high-powered" signals from civilizations at "type II" or above on the Kardashev scale.[166] The paper notes that this search:

> marks the one [sic] of the largest and broadest searches for radio evidence of extraterrestrial intelligence ever undertaken, surveying trillions of stars at four frequency bands. We cover the largest number of stars of any targeted radio technosignature search to date, and present the deepest search yet for high-power continuous beacons from nearby galaxies.[167]

The paper's conclusion reported that:

> After algorithmic processing, correlation of signal characteristics with known RFI [Radio Frequency Interference] populations, and extensive visual inspection, we found no compelling candidate signals that were not attributable to RFI among the 1,519 events that passed our filters.[168]

In recent decades, several extensive searches for alien *optical* emissions have been conducted:

- In a 2015 paper, University of California Berkeley astronomers Nathaniel K. Tellis and Geoffrey Marcy "present a search for laser emission coming from point sources in the vicinity of 2796 stars, including 1368 Kepler Objects of Interest (KOIs) that host one or more exoplanets" and note: "We did not find any such laser emission coming from any of the 2796 target stars."[169]

---

164. Billings, "Alien Supercivilizations Absent," §4. See also SciShow Space, "Fermi Paradox and Our Search."

165. Choza et al., "Breakthrough Listen Search for Intelligent Life," 1. See Dr. Becky, "Biggest EVER Scientific Search."

166. Hughes, "Kardashev Scale."

167. Choza et al., "Breakthrough Listen Search for Intelligent Life," 23.

168. Choza et al., "Breakthrough Listen Search for Intelligent Life," 23.

169. Tellis and Marcy, "Search for Optical Laser Emission," 127.

- In a 2017 paper, Tellis and Marcy report being unable to detect any optical signatures from advanced civilizations in over 67,000 individual spectra produced within the planetary regions of 5,600 stars in the Milky Way:

  > We searched high resolution spectra of 5600 nearby stars for emission lines that are both inconsistent with a natural origin and unresolved spatially, as would be expected from extraterrestrial optical lasers . . . . We found no such laser emission coming from the planetary region around any of the 5600 stars. Because they contain roughly 2000 lukewarm, Earth-size planets, we rule out models of the Milky Way in which over 0.1% of warm, Earth-size planets harbor technological civilizations that, intentionally or not, are beaming optical lasers toward us.[170]

- In December 2000, a Harvard-Smithsonian SETI project reported that almost 20,000 observations of nearly 5,000 sun-like stars had "found no evidence for pulsed optical beacons from extraterrestrial civilizations."[171]

This evidence doesn't do much to disconfirm the existence of technologically advanced alien life *per se* (the observable universe is a *very* big place to search); but it does disconfirm the hypothesis that technologically advanced alien civilizations abound in or around our slice of space and time.[172] As Peter D. Ward concludes: "The chances that there's one close enough to ever interact with is vanishingly small."[173] This is a conclusion that disconfirms theories involving historical (or present day) extraterrestrial visitors.

Space Is Very Big

Even if technologically sophisticated ETIs exist, they probably lack the means of visiting us. To quote Andrew May: "As far as we know, the

---

170. Tellis and Marcy, "Search for Laser Emission," abstract.
171. Horowitz et al., "Targeted and All-Sky Search," 3.2.
172. See Grimaldi, "Detection Probability of Non-Natural Signals"; Koberlein, "Alien Signals We Discover"; Grimaldi and Marcy, "Area Coverage of Expanding E.T. Signals"; Horvat, "Calculating the Probability."
173. Quoted in Achenbach, "What We Actually Know about Aliens," §50.

universe isn't literally 'infinite', but it's very big."[174] Richard Dawkins reckons that intelligent life "is probably extremely rare and isolated on far-flung islands of life, like a celestial Polynesia" and consequently concludes that "visitations to one island by another are hugely more likely to be in the form of radio waves than visitations by corporeal beings."[175] Indeed, our *closest* extra-solar star (Proxima Centauri[176]) is 4.22 light years away![177]

Dartnell comments that "the laws of physics . . . strongly constrain movement across the vast gulfs between stars."[178] Although atheist physicist Lawrence M. Krauss finds it "hard to believe that we are alone,"[179] he calculates that "energy expenditures beyond our current wildest dreams would be needed"[180] to facilitate interstellar travel and so concludes that "we probably don't have to worry too much about being abducted by aliens."[181]

What about interstellar travel using a so-called "warp" drive (which hypothetically circumvents the light-speed limit by "warping" space)? Krauss argues that the energetic requirements for such a drive are prohibitive:

> The gravitational field near the surface of the Sun is miniscule in terms of the kind of gravitational effects required to perturb space-time [in the way required by a warp drive] . . . One way to estimate how much energy would have to be generated is to imagine producing a black hole of the size of the [fictional *Star Trek* ship] *Enterprise*—since certainly a black hole of this size would produce a gravitational field that could significantly bend any light beam that travelled near it . . . it would take more than the total energy produced by the Sun during its entire lifetime to generate such a black hole.[182]

---

174. May, *Astrobiology*, 18.

175. Dawkins, *Science in the Soul*, 210.

176. Proxima Centauri is a red dwarf star that probably doesn't have any habitable planets. See Darling, "Earth-Like Atmosphere"; Mack, "'Goldilocks' Planets Might Not"; Davis, "Proxima b."

177. One light year is the distance light travels in one year, being "roughly 9.5 billion km or 5.9 billion miles" (Gribbin, *Alone in the Universe*, 1).

178. Dartnell, "Unwelcome Visitors," 31.

179. Krauss, *Physics of* Star Trek, 127.

180. Krauss, *Physics of* Star Trek, 128.

181. Krauss, *Physics of* Star Trek, 128.

182. Krauss, *Physics of* Star Trek, 60. See also White, *Science of the* X Files, 18–19.

What about interstellar travel via a so-called "wormhole"? In 2016 Ping Gao and Daniel Jafferis of Harvard University and Aron Wall of Stanford University described how "a new species of traversable wormhole"[183] could *theoretically* result from the quantum coupling of two black holes linked by Hawking radiation, such that "something tossed into one will shimmy along the wormhole and, following certain events in the outside universe, exit the second [albeit as Hawking radiation!]."[184] While the authors note that quantum coupling "allows information to be recovered from black holes," they also note it means that "the wormhole doesn't offer any superluminal boost."[185] Professor Robert Matthews comments:

> calculations based on the wormhole types studied so far suggest that using them would actually be slower than simply travelling directly through space . . . The laws of nature seem to insist that wormholes can either perform amazing feats but collapse in an instant, or be traversable but useless.[186]

Krauss cautions:

> My understanding of wormholes is that we have no idea how to make them stable and traversable without exotic unknown forms of energy, so any discussion of traversable wormholes as realistic travel devices is highly speculative at best.[187]

Nobel Prize winning theoretical physicist Kip Thorne muses that "if a wormhole can be held open, the precise details of *how* remain a mystery,"[188] and states: "I doubt the laws of physics permit traversable wormholes."[189] He concludes: "There are very strong indications that wormholes that a human could travel through are forbidden by the laws of physics."[190]

Wormholes remain purely "hypothetical constructs."[191] According to Dr. Eric Christian and Dr. Louis Barbier:

---

183. Wolchover, "Newfound Wormhole Allows Information," §3.
184. Wolchover, "Newfound Wormhole Allows Information," §4.
185. Wolchover, "Newfound Wormhole Allows Information," §15–16.
186. Matthews, "Through the Wormhole," 44.
187. Quoted in NBC News, "Interstellar Reality Check," §13.
188. Thorne, *Science of* Interstellar, 132.
189. Thorne, *Science of* Interstellar, 136.
190. Kip Thorne, quoted in Wall, "'Interstellar' Science," §4.
191. Al-Khalili, *Paradox*, 203.

> Wormholes are allowed to exist in the math of "General Relativity" . . . [So, if] general relativity is correct, there may be wormholes. But no one has any idea how they would be created, and there is no evidence for anything like a wormhole in the observed Universe.[192]

Krauss concludes: "Physics cannot give us what we need to roam the galaxy."[193] Once again, a substantial burden of proof falls upon anyone claiming aliens have visited Earth.

Space Is Very Dangerous

Colliding with even very small objects can be hazardous in space, and this problem gets worse the faster one goes. At 20 percent of light-speed "even individual atoms can damage the vehicle, and a collision with a bit of dust could be catastrophic."[194]

Exposure to cosmic radiation increases the risk of fatal health problems in humans, and would plausibly be detrimental to any space-faring organic lifeform:

> A recent study of the 24 astronauts who left Earth's low orbit on Nasa's [sic] Apollo missions in the 60s and 70s showed that they were five times more likely to die of heart disease than the astronauts who didn't enter deep space—a result scientists think may have been caused by excessive radiation exposure. Astronauts on missions at the [International Space Station] are shielded from too much radiation by Earth's atmosphere and magnetic field. But on a trip to Mars, humans would be exposed to radiation from the sun and from high-energy particles called galactic cosmic rays, which degrade DNA and drastically increase cancer risk.[195]

The farther one travels, the worse this problem becomes, as one's exposure increases; and while increasing one's speed may reduce the temporal *length* of one's exposure to these health risks, it creates its own set of catastrophic problems:

---

192. NASA, "Space Physics," §1.
193. Krauss, *Physics of* Star Trek, 61.
194. Timmer, "Just How Dangerous Is It to Travel?," §3.
195. Taylor, "Heart Disease, Depression," §16.

as spaceship velocities approach the speed of light, interstellar hydrogen H . . . turns into intense radiation that would quickly kill passengers and destroy electronic instrumentation. In addition, the energy loss of ionizing radiation passing through the ship's hull represents an increasing heat load that necessitates large expenditures of energy to cool the ship. Stopping or diverting this flux, either with material or electromagnetic shields, is a daunting problem. Going slow to avoid severe H irradiation sets an upper speed limit of $v \sim 0.5$ c. This velocity . . . would not substantially assist galaxy-scale voyages. Diffuse interstellar H atoms are the ultimate cosmic space mines and represent a formidable obstacle to interstellar travel.[196]

In short: "there's a natural speed limit imposed by safe levels of radiation due to hydrogen, which means [biological beings] couldn't travel faster than half the speed of light unless they were willing to die almost immediately."[197] Of course, aliens might avoid the physiological (and psychological) problems of space travel[198] by sending robots in their stead. However, that wouldn't negate the threat radiation poses for electronics, or the heat load it creates.

Aliens from a Parallel Universe?

One might attempt to avoid the problems of having ancient aliens or their proxies travel to Earth through space by positing that they came here—somehow—from a parallel universe, but this hypothesis is not only *ad hoc* and *implausible*,[199] but far more *complex* than positing visitors from the only universe we know.

---

196. Edelstein and Edelstein, "Speed Kills," §1.
197. Condliffe, "Super-Fast Space Travel," §5.
198. Regis, "Interstellar Travel as Delusional Fantasy." Philosopher David R. Koepsell writes that "as a radio-communicating species, our presence would so far only be known to other radio-listening species within a 100 light year radius of us. There are about 500 ['G' type] stars within that radius, and so far, listening to them, we have heard nothing, although we have observed nearly 100 planets in that vicinity" ("Drake vs. Fermi," §5).
199. To cut down on space travel, the extra-cosmic visitors must fortuitously just happen to be able to travel between universes on or near to Earth.

Close Encounters?

Although our evidence suggests that the existence of intelligent, technologically advanced extra-terrestrials with the motive, means, and opportunity to visit Earth is unlikely, do claimed sightings of alien space-craft, or reports of close encounters with, and/or abductions by aliens (ancient or modern) meet the burden of proof required to overturn this conclusion? They do not. As Stephen Hawking comments: "I discount suggestions that UFOs contain beings from outer space, as I think that any visits by aliens would be much more obvious—and probably also much more unpleasant."[200]

Such UFO claims as we have are generally susceptible to mundane explanations.[201] Upon investigation, the vast majority of Unidentified Flying Objects (UFOs) become Identified Flying Objects of a non-alien nature. That some UFOs remain *unidentified* is, like the existence of unsolved crimes, hardly supportive of the hypothesis that ETIs exist. In the words of science journalist Patrick Pester:

> What's the best scientific evidence we've found for the existence of alien life? The sobering reality is that there isn't any yet. There's no scientific evidence for aliens in the declassified UFO videos, in mutilated cows whose injuries are blamed on extraterrestrial activities or in purported alien bodies. Nor is there any such evidence in the formal academic research.[202]

There is nothing substantive in the outlandish hearsay evidence given by retired Air Force intelligence official David Grusch before a US congressional subcommittee in June 2023.[203] Nor is there anything (besides fakery) in the humanoid "alien mummies" displayed to Mexican

---

200. Hawking, *Brief Answers to the Big Questions*, 83.

201. See Williams, "Aliens and UFOs" (YouTube playlist); Akpan and Barajas, "7 Times That Science"; Blackmore, "Abduction by Aliens"; Blackmore and Cox, "Alien Abductions, Sleep Paralysis"; Feder, "Help! I'm Being Followed"; French, "Close Encounters"; French et al., "Psychological Aspects"; Goode, "What about Alien Abductions?"; Nickell, "Abductions or Hoaxes?"; and "Navy Pilot's 2004 UFO"; Omohundro, "Von Däniken's Chariots"; Perina, "Alien Abductions"; George and Strickland, "Interstellar Object"; Wright, "Avi Loeb and 'Oumuamua"; Clancy, *Abducted*; Clarke, *How UFOs Conquered the World*; Colavito, *Cult of Alien Gods*; French, "Alien Contact"; Sheaffer, *UFO Sightings*; Webb, *Where Is Everybody?*, 29–34; White, *Past Is Human*.

202. Pester, "What's the Best Evidence," §1–2.

203. West, "Some Thoughts on David Grusch"; Colavito, "Opinion: Congress Is Too Credulous."

Congress in September 2023 by journalist turned "ufologist" José Jaime Maussan Flota.[204]

Physicist Stephen Webb notes that "the percentage of 'inexplicable' UFOs does not vary much within the overall number of sightings . . . whether it is a busy year or a quiet year for UFO sightings, the IFO/UFO ratio is about the same," which, he argues, is "not at all what one would expect if the 'inexplicable' UFO sightings represent alien craft."[205] On the basis of this data, Robert Sheaffer concludes: "the apparently unexplainable residue is due to the essentially random nature of gross misperception and misreporting."[206]

Astronomer Seth Shostak notes:

> Our technology for documenting alien spacecraft . . . is substantially better than even a few decades ago . . . fabulous cameras are in the hands of nearly two billion smartphone users worldwide. And yet the UFO photos are as blurry and muddy as ever. You'd think at least a few people could make snaps that aren't ambiguous or hoaxed. And I haven't mentioned the surveillance provided by the 1,100 active satellites in orbit above our heads.[207]

In the judgment of psychologist Susan A. Clancy:

> Alien-abduction memories are best understood as resulting from a blend of fantasy-proneness, memory distortion, culturally available scripts, sleep hallucinations, and scientific illiteracy, aided and abetted by the suggestions and reinforcement of hypnotherapy.[208]

The hypothesis that alien abduction experiences are delusional is supported by several recorded cases in which people have reported "full-blown abduction experiences whilst other witnesses could see that the individual in question had not physically gone anywhere. Instead, they appear to have either lost consciousness or to be in a trance state."[209]

---

204. Dirmyg, "Nazca Alien Mummies Were Debunked"; History with Kayleigh, "Nazca Mummies Are"; Pequeño, "Aliens in Mexico?"; Romano, "True Story of the Fake Unboxed Aliens."
205. Webb, *Where Is Everybody?*, 31.
206. Sheaffer, "Examination of the Claims," 20–28.
207. Shostak, "Whatever Happened to UFO Sightings?," §7.
208. Clancy, *Abducted*, 138. See also French, "Alien Contact," 48–64.
209. French, "Alien Contact," 63.

Inquiries into Unidentified Anomalous Phenomena

The US government undertook several investigations into UFOs in 2023, although "in part to move beyond the stigma often attached to UFOs [they] are now characterized by the U.S. government as UAPs, or unidentified anomalous phenomena."[210]

As reported by distinguished professor of astronomy and astronomer at Steward Observatory, Chris Impey:

> NASA's independent study team released its highly anticipated report on [UAPs] on Sept. 14, 2023. . . . Bottom line: The study team found no evidence that reported UAP observations are extraterrestrial. . . . the chair of the study team, astronomer David Spergel stated that the team had seen "no evidence to suggest that UAPs are extraterrestrial in origin."[211]

Sean M. Kirkpatrick, the first director of the Pentagon's "All-Domain Anomaly Resolution Office" (AARO), gave testimony to the United States Senate Committee on Armed Services, on April 19, 2023:

> Kirkpatrick definitively stated that, out of the hundreds of UAP cases his office has reviewed, "AARO has found no credible evidence thus far of extraterrestrial activity, off-world technology or objects that defy the known laws of physics."[212]

An AARO report submitted to the United Sates Congress in March 2024 found "'no evidence' that the US government had interactions with aliens."[213] The report concluded that "to date, AARO has not discovered any empirical evidence that any sighting of a UAP represented off-world technology."[214] Moreover:

> AARO found no empirical evidence for claims that the [United States Government] and private companies have been reverse-engineering extraterrestrial technology. AARO determined, based on all information provided to date, that claims involving specific people, known locations, technological tests, and

---

210. Impey, "NASA Report Finds No Evidence," §2.
211. Impey, "NASA Report Finds No Evidence, "§1, 3, 8.
212. Tingley, "Pentagon Has 'No Credible Evidence,'" §3.
213. Clinton, "No Evidence of Alien Life," 22.
214. All-Domain Anomaly Resolution Office, "Report on the Historical Record."

documents allegedly involved in or related to the reverse-engineering of extraterrestrial technology, are inaccurate.[215]

In sum: "The field of UFOlogy has failed to produce one concrete example of an alien visitation . . . the burden of proof remains squarely on the UFOlogists."[216]

The Fermi Paradox

The non-existence of technologically advanced ETIs is the *simplest* answer to "the Fermi paradox—the contradiction between the apparent absence of aliens, and the common expectation that we should see evidence of their existence."[217] William Borucki, principal investigator of NASA's planet-hunting Kepler mission, comments: "We have . . . no visits, no communications we've picked up . . . the evidence says, no one's out there."[218] Observing that "we've seen no convincing evidence of other civilizations among the stars in our skies," astrobiologist Lewis Dartnell concludes that technologically sophisticated intelligent life "may well be vanishingly rare in the Galaxy."[219] Andrew Norton, professor of astrophysics at the Open University, concurs that "intelligent, communicating life may well be extremely rare."[220] David Wilkinson concludes:

> The Fermi paradox seems to indicate that the Galaxy is not teeming with alien civilizations . . . we are either currently alone as an intelligent civilization in our Galaxy or . . . civilizations are relatively few and quite late developers in the history of the Milky Way. This would receive support from those biologists who stress the [unlikeliness of] evolution of intelligent life on other worlds.[221]

---

215. All-Domain Anomaly Resolution Office, "Report on the Historical Record," 7.

216. Ridpath, "Flying Saucers Thirty Years On," 79. See also Scharping, "70-year-old astronomy photos."

217. Webb, *Where Is Everybody?*, ix.

218. Quoted in Westcott, "'No One's Out There,'" §§4–5.

219. Dartnell, "(Un)welcome Visitors," 25.

220. Norton, "Ross 128 Mystery Signals Aren't from Aliens," §10.

221. Wilkinson, *Science, Religion, and the Search*, 115.

Ad Hoc Aliens with Complex Schemes Using Unlikely Hypothetical Technology?

Even if technologically sophisticated aliens existed in our cosmic neighborhood, and had the means to visit Earth, it's far from certain that they would do so. As Dartnell observes: "humanity has only been detectably civilised [that is, broadcasting radio waves] for about a century."[222] Andrew May notes that if aliens were simply looking for natural resources, they would:

> probably find it more cost-effective to pillage other parts of the Solar System instead. Rare elements would be far easier to extract from small asteroids than from the Earth, while water—if that's what they're after—is far more plentiful, in the form of ice, in the outer Solar System than it is on our own planet.[223]

But suppose, for the sake of argument, that ETIs (whether from this universe or a from a hypothetical parallel universe) visited first-century Earth, and happened to visit Israel in the first century. Might they have used hypothetical technology to fake Jesus's "resurrection" and other miracles (and if so, why)?[224] Might a "matter transporter" à la *Star Trek* have been used to remove Jesus's corpse from the tomb so he could be brought back to life somehow (using "science") before being "beamed" into the upper room to surprise the disciples? This hypothesis is not only *complex, ad hoc* and *implausible*, but, given the scientific problems facing such hypothetical technology, highly *unlikely*. Krauss explains:

> Building a transporter would require us to heat up matter to a temperature a million times the temperature at the centre of the Sun, expend more energy in a single machine than all of humanity presently uses, build telescopes larger than the size of the Earth . . . and avoid the laws of quantum mechanics.[225]

Hence, as Davies warns: "speculation about alien super-civilizations doing super-science and deploying super-technology is certainly great fun, but it needs to be tempered with a healthy skepticism."[226]

---

222. Dartnell, "(Un)welcome Visitors," 33.
223. May, *Astrobiology*, 44.
224. See Manning, "5 Reasons Why Jesus."
225. Krauss, *Physics of Star Trek*, 83.
226. Davies, *Eerie Silence*, 151.

Conclusion

The scientific evidence strongly suggests that, at least on a naturalistic worldview, the odds are against the existence of extra-terrestrial life. Even if extra-terrestrial life does exist, it seems unlikely (again, at least on a naturalistic worldview) that it would develop into anything complex, let alone intelligent. And even if extra-terrestrial intelligences (ETIs) exist, it seems unlikely (again, at least on a naturalistic worldview) that they'd be blessed with the ecological and cultural preconditions for the development of science and advanced technology.

Moreover, the scientific search for extra-terrestrial intelligence has provided observational evidence that suggests there are few if any technologically advanced ETIs in our cosmic neighborhood; and the non-existence of technologically advanced ETIs remains the *simplest* answer to the Fermi paradox.

That said, even if some technologically advanced ETIs did exist in our cosmic neighborhood, there are significant psychological and physical barriers to interstellar travel, and even technologically advanced ETIs both willing and able to engage in interstellar travel wouldn't necessarily possess the motive, means, and opportunity to visit Earth, let alone Jerusalem (especially in its pre-radio-signaling past). And even if they did visit first-century Jerusalem, it seems unlikely that, for example, they'd both have and use the hypothetical technology required to convince a bunch of first-century Jews that Jesus of Nazareth was the crucified-but-risen, miracle-working Son of Man. The compound improbability of any such sequence of events is enormous.

Theories about "ancient aliens" being behind events of perceived religious significance are intrinsically *convoluted* (i.e., complex) and *ad hoc*, have *low* a priori *plausibility*, and have multiple essential facets that are strongly *disconfirmed* by scientific evidence available from secular sources. In sum, when it comes to "ancient aliens," it's the conspiracy theorists and adherents of UFO religions, not Christians, who are swimming against the scientific evidence.

Appendix I

Addendum to *Getting at Jesus*

The Deceptive Demon or Daemon Hypothesis[1]

THE LAST CHAPTER OF *Getting at Jesus: A Comprehensive Critique of Neo-Atheist Nonsense about the Jesus of History* (Wipf & Stock, 2019) critically assessed alternative explanations for the historical evidence relevant to the question of Jesus's purported resurrection from the dead, ranging from the mundane to the paranormal and the frankly supernatural. After publication, I realized that despite my best efforts, there was an alternative class of explanations on the supernatural end of the spectrum that I'd overlooked . . .

The Deceptive Demon or Daemon Hypotheses

One might hope to avoid the theistic resurrection hypothesis by suggesting that some supernatural being or other besides God either (a) caused it to appear to the disciples that Jesus had risen from the dead, or (b) caused Jesus to be raised from the dead. Technically, this wouldn't be a *resurrection* with a "spiritual body" in tune with the Spirit of God (as described in 1 Cor 15:35–49), but a return from the dead sufficient to cause the disciples (and Jesus himself) to conclude that Jesus had been resurrected by God. Such deception hypotheses gain what explanatory

---

1. I'm grateful to Peter Harris for comments that led me to revise the original version of this addendum posted on my website.

advantages they have over attempts to explain the relevant data (Jesus's death, burial, empty tomb, etc.[2]) in mundane or paranormal terms[3] by frankly embracing the supernatural, and this means they will provide cold comfort to metaphysical naturalists. Indeed, if the supernatural is admitted into our pool of live explanatory options, the theistic resurrection hypothesis looks like the best interpretation of the relevant historical data according to the standard criteria of explanation.[4] Moreover, the existence of finite, unembodied supernatural agents—whether we call them demons or daemons—is arguably something that would be best explained by a theistic worldview.[5]

The Deceptive Demon Hypothesis: Did Satan Have a Cunning Plan?

The Jewish Pharisees accepted that Jesus exorcised demons, but they attributed these good deeds to his being empowered by the "prince of demons," rather than by "the finger of God" (see Exod 8:19; Mark 3:22; Matt 12:24; and Luke 11:15–20). The Pharisees' accusation appears to have made the *ad hoc* assumption that Satan's formerly united "kingdom" had become perilously divided against itself (see Mark 3:23–26; Matt 12:25–26; and Luke 11:17–18), inasmuch as Satan was now empowering Jesus to fight against the demonic possession and oppression over which he had formerly ruled. As theologian G. B. Caird observes:

> Jesus is accused of being in league with the devil [but] the devil is not such a fool as to allow civil war among his servants; mental and physical disease are part of the control which he holds over human life, and he cannot be expected to provide the means of relaxing it.[6]

In his 1857 *Commentary of the Old and New Testaments*, nineteenth-century theologian Joseph Benson quoted a rhetorical paraphrasing of Jesus' opening rebuttal in Matt 12:25–26:

---

2. See Williams, *Getting at Jesus*, ch. 4.
3. See Williams, *Getting at Jesus*, ch. 5.
4. See Williams, *Getting at Jesus*, ch. 5.
5. See Williams, *Case for Angels*, appendix 3.
6. Caird, *Saint Luke*, 154. For a psycho-physical account of the phenomena involved here, see Guthrie, *Gods of This World*.

> As if he had said, "If evil spirits assist me in working miracles for the confirmation of my doctrine, they do what they can to promote the spiritual worship and ardent love of the true God, and, as effectually as possible, excite men to the practice of universal justice, benevolence, temperance [i.e., wise self-restraint], and self-government; all these virtues being powerfully recommended by my doctrine. But thus to make the evil spirits fight against themselves, is evidently to make them ruin their own interest; unless it can be thought that the strength and welfare of a society is advanced by jarring discord and destructive civil wars. Your judgment, therefore, of my conduct, is palpably malicious and absurd."[7]

The Pharisees' accusation also committed the fallacy of self-exception, given the existence of the Pharisee's own exorcists (see Matt 12:27 and Luke 11:19).

Jesus's rebuttals are not knock-down rejoinders to the Pharisees' accusation, but *prima facie*, opening moves in a potential debate about how Jesus's exorcisms are most plausibly to be interpreted in the context of his ministry and first century Judaism. Hence theologian Joel B. Green frames Jesus's first rebuttal as a rhetorical question:

> To imagine that Jesus was one of Satan's deputies and that he was casting other satanic agents from people, then, would be to pit Satan against himself. Why would Satan himself endorse a civil war in his own domain?[8]

The synoptic reports of this controversy do not record whether or not the Pharisees attempted to continue the debate, but it was surely open to them to conjecture that Satan either forced demons to leave people or collaborated with demons in order to make it appear that he forced them to leave people, in order to make it *seem* that Jesus exorcised demons "by the finger of God," with a view to deceiving Israel into accepting Jesus was the messiah when he was, in fact, no such thing. That's quite the conspiracy theory! And it's one that requires us to view Jesus as either deluded or as a lying co-conspirator (a hypothesis ill at ease with the data we have about Jesus).

---

7. Benson, "Matthew 12," vv. 25–26, §2. Benson attributes the quoted paragraph to "Macknight," whom I hazard from context to be Scottish theologian Dr. James MacKnight (1721–1800). See Wikipedia, "James MacKnight."

8. Green, *Gospel of Luke*, 455.

Extending the "Satan did it" hypothesis, one might propose that the devil subsequently made it *appear* that Jesus was resurrected by "the finger of God," either by causing the witnesses to hallucinate the relevant events (e.g., the empty tomb, multiple multi-sensory appearances of an apparently resurrected Jesus meeting with various individuals and groups of people), or else by "raising" Jesus from the dead himself.[9]

Either way, why would Satan (or any other demon) be interested in providing Jesus with such apparent miraculous validation? One might suppose Satan wanted to deceive people into adulterating Judaism with Christocentric additions. However, this requires us to believe that Satan either didn't mind or didn't foresee (and couldn't prevent) his cunning plan giving birth to a Christocentric variant of Jewish monotheism that would draw gentiles away from pagan worship (see 1 Cor 10:20) and spread both monotheism and the moral virtues of Jesus's "doctrine," as mentioned by Benson, all around the world.

Not only does the suggestion that Satan (or some other demon) caused the multiple and sometimes mass hallucinations required by this conspiracy theory somewhat lacking in *plausibility*, it is more *complex* than the resurrection hypothesis, and it is *ad hoc*. The "demonic deception hypothesis" becomes even more *implausible* and *ad hoc* (albeit somewhat less *complex*) if it attributes to its satanic culprit the power to actually perform a tomb-emptying "resurrection" on Jesus's corpse. Whether we infer from an acceptance of biblical or contemporary reports of demonic activity, such activity doesn't seem to offer a causally adequate account for Jesus actually rising from the dead. Even hypothesizing that Satan made all those involved hallucinate the emptiness of the tomb, the angelic visitors, and the string of resurrection appearances they report might be considered an unprecedented stretch.[10]

Neither does the "Deceptive Demon" hypothesis seem to provide a causally adequate account for the long string of deceptive "miracles" (or the hallucinatory appearance thereof) that would be needed to explain away all the other relevant evidence (see Exod 8:16–19; Deut 32:39; 1 Sam 2:6; Isa 41:22–23; and John 10:21). Indeed, within the biblical tradition, God keeps Satan on a short leash. Hence the "Deceptive Demon" hypothesis lacks *explanatory power*.

---

9. For an argument against the hypothesis that Satan or other demons can directly manipulate the physical world, see Guthrie, *Gods of This World*.

10. See Williams, "Do Angels Really Exist?"; Gallagher, *Demonic Foes*; Guthrie, *Gods of This World*.

The "Deceptive Demon" hypothesis either involves Jesus in a deliberate conspiracy to deceive, or paints him as having been deluded into accepting that he was the *resurrected, divine (and thus sinless)* "Son of Man." Not only are both scenarios *ad hoc*, but both are *disconfirmed* by the available evidence pertaining to Jesus's character. They are also *disconfirmed* by several other lines of evidence (e.g., Jesus's record of miraculous deeds,[11] his fulfilment of messianic prophecy[12]) that support a specifically *Christian* theism, unless one makes the deceptive demon hypothesis *even more complex* by extending it to explain away this disconfirming evidence as well.

In short, the "Deceptive Demon" hypothesis lacks *plausibility* and *explanatory power* and, in addition to also being *complex* and *ad hoc*, is either *disconfirmed* or else even more *complex* than it first appears.

The Deceptive Daemon Hypotheses

Whether one takes inspiration from biblical demonology, polytheistic religious notions of trickster gods, or from some sort of "finite godism" (à la Plato's *Demiurge*), one might seek to avoid the theistic resurrection hypothesis by positing the existence of some non-biblical "finite" supernatural being (or beings) conveniently endowed with the motive, means, and opportunity to either deceive people into believing that Jesus was resurrected or to actually raise (and thereby appear to *resurrect*) Jesus from the dead. Let us stretch the ancient Greek term for a lesser deity or spirit guide somewhat by calling this "The Deceptive Daemon Hypothesis."

In the absence of an adequate apologetic for the existence of a deceptive "daemon," such a *complex* hypothesis is of course *entirely ad hoc*. Indeed, one might well conclude, in light of the internal problems with polytheism and finite godism,[13] and the positive case for Christian monotheism,[14] that the "Deceptive Daemon" hypothesis is not only *complex* and *ad hoc*, but is also *disconfirmed*.

---

11. See Habermas, "Did Jesus Perform Miracles?"; Williams, *Getting at Jesus*, ch. 5.

12. See FOCLOnline, "Arguments for and from Fulfilled Biblical Prophecies"; Geisler, "Miraculous Bible Prophecy Fulfillments"; Scott, *Is Jesus of Nazareth the Predicted Messiah?*; Kaiser, *Messiah in the Old Testament*; Williams, *Understanding Jesus*; Williams, *Getting at Jesus*, ch. 5.

13. See Geisler, *Christian Apologetics* (2nd ed.), chs. 12 and 13.

14. See Williams, *Universe from Someone*; *Getting at Jesus*.

Like the "Deceptive Demon" hypothesis, any "Deceptive Daemon" hypothesis either involves Jesus himself in a deliberate conspiracy to deceive or paints him as having been deluded. Both scenarios are *ad hoc*. Both scenarios are *disconfirmed* by the available evidence pertaining to Jesus's character. And both scenarios are disconfirmed by several other lines of evidence (Jesus's record of miraculous deeds, fulfilled prophecy, etc.) that support a specifically *Christian* theism, unless one makes the "Deceptive Daemon" hypothesis even more *complex* by extending it to explain away this disconfirming evidence as well.

In sum, neither the "Deceptive Demon" hypothesis nor the "Deceptive Daemon" hypothesis outperforms the "Theistic Resurrection" hypothesis.

Recommended Resources

Eitan Bar, "Did Jesus Use Magic And Sorcery?," www.oneforisrael.org/bible-based-teaching-from-israel/did-jesus-use-magic-and-sorcery/

Erik Manning, "No, Jesus Could Not Have Been Raised Supernaturally by Any Other Being But God," https://isjesusalive.com/no-jesus-could-not-have-been-raised-supernaturally-by-any-other-being-but-god/

Peter S. Williams, "Do Angels and Demons Exist?," www.bethinking.org/christian-beliefs/do-angels-really-exist

Kirsten R. Birkett, *Spells, Sorcerers and Spirits: Magic and the Occult in the Bible* (Latimer, 2015)

Richard Gallagher, *Demonic Foes: My Twenty-Five Years as a Psychiatrist Investigating Possessions, Diabolic Attacks, and the Paranormal* (HarperOne, 2022)

Norman L. Geisler, *Christian Apologetics*, 2nd ed. (Baker, 2013), chapters 12 and 13

Shandon L. Guthrie, *Gods of This World: A Philosophical Discussion and Defense of Christian Demonology* (Pickwick, 2019)

Peter S. Williams, *Getting at Jesus: A Comprehensive Critique of Neo-Atheist Nonsense about the Jesus of History* (Wipf & Stock, 2019)

Peter S. Williams, *Understanding Jesus: Five Ways to Spiritual Enlightenment* (Paternoster, 2011)

Peter S. Williams, *The Case for Angels* (Paternoster, 2002)

Appendix II

How Far Can We Trust the Gospels?

Philosopher Peter S. Williams reviews The Big Conversation between New Testament scholars Bart Ehrman and Peter J. Williams[1]

BART EHRMAN AND PETER J. Williams were notionally discussing the question "Can we trust the story of Jesus?" In other words, can we trust the story of Jesus presented by the four, canonical, New Testament Gospels? As in his recent book *Can We Trust the Gospels?* (Crossway, 2018), Peter J. Williams argued that the many instances wherein the Gospels are demonstrably reliable sources of information about early first-century Israel build a cumulative case for the presumption of reliability when it comes to their reports about Jesus. "I know there are problems," said Williams, but the evidence suggests "we have a lot of the traditions of Jesus coming through." In light of the evidence, the simplest hypothesis is one of overall or general historical accuracy, and the burden of proof rests with the sceptic.

---

1. This is a revised version of Williams, "Was Jesus' Claim to Be God an Invention?" For the conversation between Ehrman and Williams, see Premier Unbelievable, "Peter J Williams vs Bart Ehrman."

Surprising Agreement

As a self-professed sceptic, Ehrman was happy to shoulder that burden of proof. That said, what may have surprised some listeners was the extent to which Ehrman was actually *in agreement with* Williams. Ehrman said: "I'm not arguing the Gospels are completely unreliable. The Gospels have historical information in them." Ehrman affirmed: "There's a lot of material in the Gospels that absolutely go back to the historical Jesus." Crucially, towards the end of the show, Ehrman stated:

> I'm arguing against a fundamentalist view of the Bible, that it has no mistakes of any kind. I'm not arguing against Christianity. I'm not arguing against believers. I'm not arguing against people who think the Bible has a lot of historical information in it.

In other words, Ehrman doesn't doubt that the story of Jesus presented in the Gospels contains "a lot of historical information." Rather, he doubts it contains *nothing but* historical information. Indeed, he doubts the Gospels contain so much historical information that they qualify as historically trustworthy *in general*. The former doubt points us towards a theological debate about the revelatory status and nature of the Gospels. The latter doubt is open to historical debate.

The Irreconcilable Deaths of Judas?

Ehrman focused on two arguments against the *general* reliability of the Gospels. First, he asserted that the presentation of the death of Judas in Matthew's Gospel "can't be reconciled" with Luke's presentation of Judas's death at the beginning of Acts. As Williams observed, Ehrman also said that "You can reconcile anything," but the charitable way to interpret Ehrman's argument is to take him as claiming that any and all harmonizations between Matthew and Luke's accounts, while *possible*, are also *implausible*. Williams argues otherwise (applying the same charity to the New Testament writers as he applies to Ehrman), and in this historical judgment call, my sympathies are with Williams.[2]

---

2. See Premier Unbelievable?, "Is the Death of Judas Iscariot a Bible Contradiction?"; Inspiring Philosophy, "Death of Judas"; Wallace, "How (and Where) Did Judas Really Die?"; Cabal, *Apologetics Study Bible*, 1455; Köstenberger, "John."

Ehrman's Argument from Silence

Ehrman's second argument was that the end of century Gospel according to John reports Jesus making several astonishing claims about himself that the earlier Synoptic Gospels would surely have reported had their authors known about them. Ehrman concludes from the silence of the Synoptic Gospels with respect to these sayings that they must have been invented. Ehrman combines this argument from silence[3] with his relatively late dating of all the Gospels to infer that other material about Jesus therein was probably invented. Against this, I don't think the testimonial chains between Jesus and the Gospels (or their sources) are either as long or as tenuous as Ehrman suggests,[4] and arguments from silence are notoriously unreliable.[5]

John's Gospel presents several famous "I Am" sayings, the most famous of which is probably: "Before Abraham was, I Am" (John 8:58 ESV). Mark doesn't report this saying. However, as Robert M. Bowman Jr. points out:

> When Jesus walked on the Sea of Galilee up to the fishing boat of some of his disciples, he responded to their fear at seeing him by saying, "I am [he]; fear not" (John 6:20). . . . In context, Jesus' response to the disciples echoes the words of God in Isaiah 43 [v. 5]. . . . In both Matthew and Mark, the same event is reported, with Jesus walking on the sea and saying to the disciples, "I am [he]; fear not" (Matt. 14:27; Mark 6:50). The Greek words here are identical in all three Gospels . . .[6]

Moreover, as Williams points out, Mark presents Jesus as a divine figure from the opening verses of his Gospel. Ehrman concedes that (in some sense): "Mark does see Jesus as divine . . . Mark understands Jesus as a divine being." Ehrman dates Mark later than I do, but one finds the same high Christology in the Epistle of James (see chapter 2). This is significant because James is one of the oldest piece of literature in the New Testament, perhaps the oldest. It predates the Jewish war, and plausibly takes us back to the mid-late 40s AD.[7] It's highly implausible

---

3. See BiteSizePhilosophy, "Logical Fallacies."

4. For a critical review of these testimonial chains and a defense of earlier dating's for the Synoptic Gospels, see Williams, *Getting at Jesus*, ch. 3.

5. See McGrew, "Argument from Silence."

6. Bowman, "Top 10 Reasons."

7. See ch. 2; FOCLOnline, "Defending Early High Christology."

to think that Jesus's original, Jewish followers would have arrived at a high Christology if Jesus himself hadn't encouraged this. As philosopher Anthony O'Hear comments:

> We should remember that his first followers were pious Jews, to whom the claims being made would have seemed blasphemous had they not been given strong reason to believe them—and where better than from Jesus himself?[8]

Ehrman's example of President Trump getting many details right about his inauguration but the number of attendees wrong shows that it's *possible* to display local knowledge and yet report false information. It doesn't show that the Gospel writers *probably* reported false information. The independently verified local knowledge displayed by the Gospel writers suggests that they have an accurate handle on events in Israel in the early first century, establishing a presumption of reliability for their reports about Jesus. To borrow an analogy from philosopher Lydia McGrew:

> If you sample a loaf of bread on both ends and at several points in the middle and find it good, it would be caviling to say that perhaps just the parts you haven't tasted happen to be the moldy ones.[9]

And as Catholic blogger K. Albert Little comments:

> Skeptics of President Trump analyzed pictures of the inauguration and used these to demonstrate that he was exaggerating precisely because *he was known to exaggerate*. Because experience and outside sources indicated that, in the past, President Trump was known to employ hyperbole. As a result, his claims were under particular scrutiny. But no such precedent exists for the Gospels.[10]

Based on the Evidence

In his opening remarks Ehrman asserted that Jesus was "the most important figure in the history of our civilization" and that in getting to grips with Jesus he didn't believe "in toeing a party line one way or the other: If

8. O'Hear, *Jesus for Beginners*, 84.
9. McGrew, *Hidden in Plain View*, 225.
10. Little, "Fake News?"

you're an atheist you have to believe that, if you're an historian you have to believe that." Rather, Ehrman said: "You have to decide what appears to be right, based on the evidence." I can say a hearty "Amen" to that.

Recommended Resources

Peter S. Williams

Website: www.peterswilliams.com
YouTube playlist, "Peter S. Williams Video." https://www.youtube.com/playlist?list=PLQhh3qcwVEWgmFh_mVgG9rrQl-jXyJk-z
Peter S. Williams Podcast: http://peterswilliams.podbean.com/?source=pb
YouTube Playlists: https://www.youtube.com/user/peterswilliamsvid/playlists
Academia.edu profile with links to published papers:
https://mediehogskolen.academia.edu/PeterSWilliams

Websites

BeliefMap: www.beliefmap.org
BeThinking: www.bethinking.org
Justin Brierley: https://justinbrierley.com/
Paul Copan: www.paulcopan.com/
William Lane Craig: Reasonable Faith, www.reasonablefaith.org
John Dickson: www.johndickson.org
Gary R. Habermas: www.garyhabermas.com/
Lydia McGrew: https://lydiamcgrew.com/
Theofilos: https://theofilos.no/

Online Papers

Beck, W. David. "God's Existence." https://digitalcommons.liberty.edu/cgi/viewcontent.cgi?article=1086&context=sor_fac_pubs.
Blomberg, Craig L. "How to Approach Apparent Contradictions in the Gospels: A Response to Michael Licona." https://www.equip.org/articles/how-to-approach-apparent-contradictions-in-the-gospels-a-response-to-michael-licona/.

———. "Jesus of Nazareth: How Historians Can Know Him and Why It Matters." http://tgc-documents.s3.amazonaws.com/cci/Blomberg.pdf.
Buchak, Lara. "Reason and Faith." https://philarchive.org/archive/BUCRAF.
Copan, Paul. "God, Naturalism, and the Foundations of Morality." http://www.paulcopan.com/articles/pdf/God-naturalism-morality.pdf.
———. "Hume and the Moral Argument." http://www.paulcopan.com/articles/pdf/Paul_Copan-Hume_and_Moral_Argument-In_Defense_Natural_Theology.pdf.
———. "Jesus' Followers Fabricated the Stories and Sayings of Jesus." http://www.paulcopan.com/articles/pdf/Jesus-followers-fabricated-stories-and-sayings-of-Jesus.pdf.
———. "Review: *The Impossibility of God*." https://www.equip.org/articles/the-impossibility-of-god/.
Craig, William Lane. "The Bodily Resurrection of Jesus." www.reasonablefaith.org/writings/scholarly-writings/historical-jesus/the-bodily-resurrection-of-jesus.
———. "The Concept of God in Islam and Christianity." http://www.reasonablefaith.org/concept-of-god-in-islam-and-christianity.
———. "The Evidence for Jesus." https://www.reasonablefaith.org/writings/popular-writings/jesus-of-nazareth/the-evidence-for-jesus.
———. *Five Arguments for God*. https://christianevidence.org/booklet/five_arguments_for_god/.
———. "The Historicity of the Empty Tomb of Jesus." www.reasonablefaith.org/writings/scholarly-writings/historical-jesus/the-historicity-of-the-empty-tomb-of-jesus.
———. "Jesus' Resurrection." www.reasonablefaith.org/writings/scholarly-writings/historical-jesus/jesus-resurrection.
———. "The Problem of Evil." https://www.reasonablefaith.org/writings/popular-writings/existence-nature-of-god/the-problem-of-evil.
———. "Rediscovering the Historical Jesus: The Evidence for Jesus." https://www.reasonablefaith.org/writings/scholarly-writings/historical-jesus/rediscovering-the-historical-jesus-the-evidence-for-jesus.
———. "Rediscovering the Historical Jesus: Presuppositions and Pretensions of the Jesus Seminar." https://www.reasonablefaith.org/writings/scholarly-writings/historical-jesus/rediscovering-the-historical-jesus-presuppositions-and-pretensions-of-the-j.
———. "Visions of Jesus: A Critical Assessment of Gerd Lüdemann's Hallucination Hypothesis." www.reasonablefaith.org/writings/scholarly-writings/historical-jesus/visions-of-jesus-a-critical-assessment-of-gerd-ludemanns-hallucination-hypo.
Davis, Stephen T. "The Mad/Bad/God Trilemma: A Reply to Daniel Howard Snyder." https://place.asburyseminary.edu/faithandphilosophy/vol21/iss4/4/.
Evans, C. Stephen. "The Mystery of Persons and Belief in God." https://www.leaderu.com/truth/3truth07.html.
Geisler, Norman L. "Miraculous Bible Prophecy Fulfillments." https://philosophical11.wordpress.com/2012/09/12/miraculous-bible-prophecy-fulfillments/#more-151.
Habermas, Gary R. "Recent Perspectives on the Reliability of the Gospels." www.equip.org/articles/recent-perspectives-on-the-reliability-of-the-gospels/.
———. "Why I Believe the New Testament Is Historically Reliable." www.monergism.com/thethreshold/sdg/Why%20I%20Believe%20the%20New%20Testament%20is%20Historically%20Reliable%281%29.pdf.

Howard-Snyder, Daniel. "Does Faith Entail Belief?" www.academia.edu/11819008/Does_Faith_Entail_Belief_2016_.

Howard-Snyder, Daniel, and Daniel McKaughan. "Faith." https://www.academia.edu/35582270/Faith_2020_.

Humphreys, Colin. "The Star of Bethlehem." https://www.asa3.org/ASA/topics/Astronomy-Cosmology/S&CB%2010-93Humphreys.html.

Koons, Robert C. "The Incompatibility of Naturalism and Scientific Realism." www.leaderu.com/offices/koons/docs/natreal.html.

Köstenberger, Andreas J. "April 3, AD 33." www.firstthings.com/web-exclusives/2014/04/april-3-ad-33.

Kreeft, Peter. "Jesus: Considering the Options." www.bethinking.org/jesus/jesus-considering-the-options.

Lewis, C. S. "The Cardinal Difficulty of Naturalism." http://thecslewis-studygroup.org/wp-content/uploads/2014/07/The-Cardinal-Difficulty-of-Naturalism.pdf.

———. "The Poison of Subjectivism." http://www.williamwoodall.weebly.com/uploads/1/0/2/2/10226906/the_poison_of_subjectivism.pdf.

———. "What Are We to Make of Jesus Christ?" http://xtianity.com/tfc/NTE103/C%20S%20Lewis%20What%20are%20we%20to%20make%20of%20Jesus%20Christ.pdf.

Maier, Paul L. "The Date of the Nativity and the Chronology of Jesus' Life." https://inchristus.com/wp-content/uploads/2010/12/maier-date-of-the-nativity.pdf.

Mavrodes, George. "Religion and the Queerness of Morality." https://afterall.net/wp-content/uploads/2021/08/religion-and-the-queerness-of-morality.pdf.

McGrew, Tim. "The Argument from Silence." https://timothymcgrew.com/wp-content/uploads/2024/01/The-Argument-from-Silence-Acta-Analytica-Tim-2013.pdf.

McGrew, Tim, and Lydia McGrew, "The Argument from Miracles: A Cumulative Case for the Resurrection of Jesus of Nazareth." https://lydiamcgrew.com/wp-content/uploads/2023/11/Resurrectionarticlesinglefile.pdf.

McLatchie, Jonathan. "The Nativity Defended." http://crossexamined.org/the-nativity-defended/.

Menuge, Angus J. "Dennett Denied: A Critique of Dennett's Evolutionary Account of Intentionality." static1.1.sqspcdn.com/static/f/38692/239704/1263390969587/A+Critique+of+Dennetts+Evolutionary+Account+of+Intentionality.pdf

Moreland, J. P. "The Historicity of the New Testament." www.bethinking.org/is-the-bible-reliable/the-historicity-of-the-new-testament.

Plantinga, Alvin. "Against Materialism." https://andrewmbailey.com/ap/Against_Materialism.pdf.

———. "Content and Natural Selection." https://andrewmbailey.com/ap/Content_Natural_Selection.pdf.

———. "An Evolutionary Argument against Naturalism." https://www.researchgate.net/publication/227992849_An_Evolutionary_Argument_Against_Naturalism

———. "Two Dozen (Or So) Arguments for God." https://appearedtoblogly.files.wordpress.com/2011/05/plantinga-alvin-22two-dozen-or-so-theistic-arguments221.pdf.

Pojman, Louis. "Faith without Belief?" https://place.asburyseminary.edu/faithandphilosophy/vol3/iss2/3.

Pruss, Alexander R. "Christian Faith and Belief." https://place.asburyseminary.edu/faithandphilosophy/vol19/iss3/2.

Reppert, Victor. "The Argument from Reason." https://appearedtoblogly.wordpress.com/wp-content/uploads/2011/05/the-argument-from-reason.pdf

Shanks, Hershel. "The James Ossuary Is Authentic." http://members.bib-arch.org/publication.asp?PubID=BSBA&Volume=38&Issue=4&ArticleID=2.

Simek, Slater. "A Bayesian Exploration of C. S. Lewis's 'Argument from Desire.'" https://link.springer.com/article/10.1007/s11841-021-00887-9.

Swinburne, Richard. *Evidence For God*. http://christianevidence.org/docs/booklets/evidence_for_god.pdf.

Ward, Keith. *Evidence for the Virgin Birth*. http://christianevidence.org/docs/booklets/evidence_for_the_virgin_birth.pdf.

Willard, Dallas. "Knowledge and Naturalism." https://dwillard.org/resources/articles/knowledge-and-naturalism.

―――. "Language, Being, God, and the Three Stages of Theistic Evidence." https://dwillard.org/articles/language-being-god-and-the-three-stages-of-theistic-evidence.

Williams, Peter S. *Digging for Evidence*. https://christianevidence.org/booklet/digging_for_evidence/.

―――. "Understanding the Trinity." https://www.bethinking.org/god/understanding-the-trinity.

Books

Alston, William P. *A Realist Conception of Truth*. Ithaca, NY: Cornell University Press, 1996.

Audi, Robert. *Epistemology: A Contemporary Introduction to the Theory of Knowledge*. 3rd ed. London: Routledge, 2010.

Baggett, David, ed. *Did the Resurrection Happen? A Conversation with Gary Habermas and Antony Flew*. Downers Grove, IL: InterVarsity, 2009.

Baggett, David, and Jerry L. Walls. *Good God: The Theistic Foundations of Morality*. Oxford: Oxford University Press, 2011.

Bauckham, Richard. *Jesus and the Eyewitnesses: The Gospels as Eyewitness Testimony*. 2nd ed. Grand Rapids, MI: Eerdmans, 2017.

―――. *Jesus: A Very Short Introduction*. Oxford: Oxford University Press, 2011.

Barnett, Paul. *The Birth of Christianity: The First Twenty Years*. Grand Rapids, MI: Eerdmans, 2005.

―――. *Finding the Historical Christ*. Grand Rapids, MI: Eerdmans, 2009.

―――. *Messiah: Jesus—The Evidence of History*. Nottingham: InterVarsity, 2009.

―――. *Paul: Missionary of Jesus*. Grand Rapids, MI: Eerdmans, 2008.

Beck, W. David. *Does God Exist? A History of Answers to the Question*. Downers Grove, IL: IVP Academic, 2021.

Beckwith, Francis J., ed. *To Everyone an Answer: A Case for the Christian Worldview*. Downers Grove, IL: InterVarsity, 2004.

Beilby, James. *Postmortem Opportunity: A Biblical and Theological Assessment of Salvation after Death*. Downers Grove, IL: IVP Academic, 2021.

Beverley, James A., and Craig A. Evans. *Getting Jesus Right: How Muslims Get Jesus and Islam Wrong*. Lagoon City, Ontario: Castle Quay, 2015.

Bignon, Guillame. *Confessions of a French Atheist: How God Hijacked My Quest to Disprove the Christian Faith*. Carol Stream, IL: Tyndale, 2022.
Bird, Michael F., et al. *How God Became Jesus: The Real Origins of Belief in Jesus' Divine Nature—A Response to Bart D. Ehrman*. Grand Rapids, MI: Zondervan, 2014.
Blomberg, Craig L. *The Historical Reliability of the Gospels*. 2nd ed. Downers Grove, IL: InterVarsity, 2008.
———. *Who Is Jesus of Nazareth?* Bellingham, WA: Lexham, 2021.
Boa, Kenneth D., and Robert M. Bowman Jr. *Faith Has Its Reasons: An Integrative Approach to Defending Christianity*. 2nd ed. Milton Keynes: Paternoster, 2000.
Bock, Darrell L. *Studying the Historical Jesus: A Guide to Sources and Methods*. Leicester: Apollos, 2007.
———. *Who Is Jesus? Linking the Historical Jesus with the Christ of Faith*. New York: Howard, 2012.
Bock, Darrell L., and Daniel B. Wallace. *Dethroning Jesus: Exposing Popular Culture's Quest to Unseat the Biblical Christ*. Nashville: Thomas Nelson, 2007.
Bock, Darrell L., and Robert L. Webb, eds. *Key Events in the Life of the Historical Jesus: A Collaborative Exploration of Context and Coherence*. Grand Rapids, MI: Eerdmans, 2010.
Bombaro, John J., and Adam S. Francisco. *The Resurrection Fact: Responding to Modern Critics*. Irvine, CA: NRP, 2016.
Bowman, Robert, and Ed Komoszewski. *Putting Jesus in His Place: The Case for the Deity of Christ*. Grand Rapids, MI: Kregel, 2007.
Brierley, Justin. *The Surprising Rebirth of Belief in God: Why New Atheism Grew Old and Secular Thinkers Are Considering Christianity Again*. Carol Stream, IL: Tyndale Elevate, 2023.
Burridge, Richard A. *What Are the Gospels? A Comparison with Graeco-Roman Biography*. 2nd ed. Cambridge: Cambridge University Press, 2004.
Casey, Maurice. *Jesus: Evidence and Argument or Mythicist Myths?* London: Bloomsbury, 2014.
Charlesworth, James H., ed. *Jesus Research: New Methodologies and Perceptions*. Grand Rapids, MI: Eerdmans, 2014.
Comfort, Philip W. *Encountering the Manuscripts: An Introduction to New Testament Paleography and Textual Criticism*. Nashville: B&H, 2005.
Comfort, Philip W., and Jason Driesbach. *The Many Gospels of Jesus: Sorting Out the Story of the Life of Jesus*. Carol Stream, IL: Tyndale, 2008.
Copan, Paul, ed. *Will the Real Jesus Please Stand Up? A Debate between William Lane Craig and John Dominic Crossan*. Grand Rapids, MI: Baker, 1998.
Copan, Paul, and William Lane Craig, eds. *Come Let Us Reason: New Essays in Christian Apologetics*. Nashville: B&H, 2012.
Copan, Paul, and Paul K. Moser, eds. *The Rationality of Theism*. London: Routledge, 2003.
Copan, Paul, and Ronald K. Tacelli, eds. *Jesus' Resurrection: Fact or Figment? A Debate between William Lane Craig and Gerd Lüdemann*. Downers Grove, IL: IVP Academic, 2000.
Copan, Paul, and Charles Taliaferro, eds. *The Naturalness of Belief: New Essays on Theism's Rationality*. Lanham, MD: Lexington, 2019.
Cottingham, John. *How Can I Believe?* London: SPCK, 2018.
Cowan, Steven B., ed. *Five Views on Apologetics*. Grand Rapids, MI: Zondervan, 2000.

Craig, William Lane. *Assessing the New Testament Evidence for the Resurrection of Jesus*. New York: Edwin Mellen, 2002.
———. *Did Jesus Rise from the Dead?* Pine Mountain, GA: Impact 360 Institute, 2014.
———. *Does God Exist?* Pine Mountain, GA: Impact 360 Institute, 2019.
———. *On Guard for Students: Defending Your Faith with Reason and Precision*. Colorado Springs: David C. Cook, 2015.
———. *The Only Wise God: The Compatibility of Divine Foreknowledge and Human Freedom*. Eugene, OR: Wipf & Stock, 2000.
———, ed. *Philosophy of Religion: A Reader and Guide*. Edinburgh: Edinburgh University Press, 2002.
———. *The Son Rises: Historical Evidence for the Resurrection of Jesus*. Eugene, OR: Wipf & Stock, 2001.
Craig, William Lane, and Joseph E. Gorra. *A Reasonable Response: Answers to Tough Questions*. Chicago: Moody, 2013.
Craig, William Lane, and J. P. Moreland, eds. *The Blackwell Companion to Natural Theology*. Oxford: Wiley-Blackwell, 2009.
———. *Naturalism: A Critical Analysis*. London: Routledge, 2001.
Crowe, Brandon D. *Was Jesus Really Born of a Virgin?* Philadelphia: Westminster Seminary, 2013.
Davis, Stephen T. *Christian Philosophical Theology*. Oxford: Oxford University Press, 2016.
———. *Risen Indeed: Making Sense of the Resurrection*. London: SPCK, 1993.
Dembski, William A., and Michael L. Licona. *Evidence for God: 50 Arguments for Faith from the Bible, History, Philosophy, and Science*. Grand Rapids, MI: Baker, 2010.
Dickson, John. *Bullies and Saints: An Honest Look at the Good and Evil of Christian History*. Grand Rapids, MI: Zondervan, 2021.
———. *Is Jesus History?* Epsom: Good Book, 2019.
Dunn, James. *Why Believe in Jesus' Resurrection?* London: SPCK, 2016.
Eddy, Paul Rhodes, and Gregory A. Boyd. *The Jesus Legend: A Case for the Reliability of the Synoptic Jesus Tradition*. Grand Rapids, MI: Baker Academic, 2007.
Edwards, Douglas. *The Virgin Birth in History and Faith*. London: Faber & Faber, 1943.
Evans, Craig A. *Fabricating Jesus: How Modern Scholars Distort the Gospels*. Downers Grove, IL: InterVarsity, 2007.
———. *Jesus and His World: The Archaeological Evidence*. London: SPCK, 2012.
———. *Jesus and the Remains of History: Studies in Jesus and the Evidence of Material Culture*. Peabody, MA: Hendrickson, 2015.
Evans, C. Stephen. *Despair: A Moment or a Way of Life?* Downers Grove, IL: InterVarsity, 1973.
———. *The Historical Christ and the Jesus of Faith: The Incarnational Narrative as History*. Oxford: Clarendon, 2004.
———. *Natural Signs and Knowledge of God: A New Look at Theistic Arguments*. Oxford: Oxford University Press, 2010.
———. *Why Believe? Reason and Mystery as Pointers to God*. Grand Rapids, MI: Eerdmans, 1996.
———. *Why Christian Faith Still Makes Sense: A Response to Contemporary Challenges*. Grand Rapids, MI: Baker Academic, 2015.
Evans, Richard J. *In Defence of History*. London: Granta, 2018.

Fudge, Edward William. *The Fire That Consumes: A Biblical and Historical Study of the Doctrine of Final Punishment.* 3rd rev. ed. London: James Clarke, 2012.

Gallagher, Richard. *Demonic Foes: My Twenty-Five Years as a Psychiatrist Investigating Possessions, Diabolic Attacks, and the Paranormal.* New York: HarperOne, 2022.

Ganssle, Gregory E. *Our Deepest Desires: How The Christian Story Fulfills Human Aspirations.* Downers Grove, IL: IVP Academic, 2017.

———. *A Reasonable God: Engaging the New Face of Atheism.* Waco, TX: Baylor University Press, 2009.

Geisler, Norman L. *Christian Apologetics.* 2nd ed. Grand Rapids, MI: Baker Academic, 2013.

Geisler, Norman L., and Paul D. Feinberg. *Introduction to Philosophy: A Christian Perspective.* Grand Rapids, MI: Baker, 1997.

Geivett, R. Douglas, and Gary R. Habermas, eds. *In Defence of Miracles: A Comprehensive Case for God's Action in History.* Leicester: Apollos, 1997.

Gilson, Tom, and Carson Weitnauer, eds. *True Reason: Confronting the Irrationality of the New Atheism.* Grand Rapids, MI: Kregel, 2013.

Glass, David H. *Atheism's New Clothes: Exploring and Exposing the Claims of the New Atheists.* Leicester: Apollos, 2012.

Goetz, Stewart, and Charles Taliaferro. *Naturalism.* Grand Rapids, MI: Eerdmans, 2008.

Gresham, Machen, J. *The Virgin Birth of Christ.* James Clarke, 1958.

Grindheim, Sigurd. *Christology in the Synoptic Gospels: God or God's Servant?* London: Continuum, 2012.

Groothuis, Douglas. *Truth Decay: Defending Christianity against the Challenges of Postmodernism.* Downers Grove, IL: InterVarsity, 2000.

Guthrie, Shandon L. *Gods of This World: A Philosophical Discussion and Defense of Christian Demonology.* Eugene, OR: Pickwick, 2018.

Habermas, Gary R. *The Historical Jesus: Ancient Evidence for the Life of Christ.* Joplin, MO: College Press, 1996.

———. *On the Resurrection.* Vol. 1, *Evidences.* Nashville: B&H Academic, 2024.

———. *Risen Indeed: A Historical Investigation Into the Resurrection of Jesus.* Bellingham, WA: Lexham, 2021.

———. *The Risen Jesus and Future Hope.* Lanham, MD: Rowman & Littlefield, 2003.

Habermas, Gary R., and Michael L. Licona. *The Case for the Resurrection of Jesus.* Grand Rapids, MI: Kregel, 2004.

Habermas, Gary R., Antony Flew, and Terry L. Miethe, eds. *Did Jesus Rise from the Dead?* Eugene, OR: Wipf & Stock, 2003.

Hackett, Stuart C. *The Reconstruction of the Christian Revelation Claim: A Philosophical and Critical Apologetic.* Eugene, OR: Wipf & Stock, 2009.

Hannam, James. *God's Philosophers: How the Medieval World Laid the Foundations of Modern Science.* London: Icon, 2010.

Hill, Charles E. *Who Chose the Books of the New Testament?* Bellingham, WA: Lexham, 2022.

———. *Who Chose the Gospels? Probing the Great Gospel Conspiracy.* Oxford: Oxford University Press, 2010.

Holder, Rodney D. *Big Bang, Big God: A Universe Designed for Life?* Oxford: Lion, 2013.

———. *God, the Multiverse, and Everything.* London: Routledge, 2016.

Holland, Tom. *Dominion: The Making of the Western Mind.* London: Abacus, 2020.

Howard, Jeremy Royal, ed. *The Gospels and Acts*. The Holman Apologetics Commentary on the Bible. Nashville: Holman, 2013.

Hunter, James Davison, and Paul Nedelisky. *Science and the Good: The Tragic Quest for the Foundations of Morality*. New Haven, CT: Yale University Press, 2018.

Hutchinson, Robert J. *Searching for Jesus: New Discoveries in the Quest for Jesus of Nazareth—And How They Confirm the Gospel Accounts*. Nashville: Nelson, 2015.

Jones, Timothy Paul. *Misquoting Truth: A Guide to the Fallacies of Bart Ehrman's Misquoting Jesus*. Downers Grove, IL: InterVarsity, 2007.

Kaiser, Jr. Walter C. *The Messiah in the Old Testament*. Grand Rapids, MI: Zondervan, 1995.

Keener, Craig S., and Edward T. Wright, eds. *Biographies and Jesus: What Does It Mean for the Gospels to Be Biographies?* Lexington, KY: Emeth, 2016.

Kitchen, K. A. *On the Reliability of the Old Testament*. Grand Rapids, MI: Eerdmans, 2006.

Köstenberger, Andreas, ed. *Whatever Happened To Truth?* Wheaton, IL: Crossway, 2005.

Köstenberger, Andreas J., and Alexander Stewart. *The First Days of Jesus: The Story of the Incarnation*. Wheaton, IL: Crossway, 2015.

Köstenberger, Andreas J., Darrell L. Bock, and John Chatraw. *Truth Matters: Confident Faith in a Confusing World*. Nashville: B&H Academic, 2014.

Köstenberger, Andreas J., Justin Taylor, and Alexander Stewart. *The Final Days of Jesus: The Most Important Week of the Most Important Person Who Ever Lived*. Wheaton, IL: Crossway, 2014.

Kreeft, Peter. *Between Heaven and Hell: A Dialog Somewhere beyond Death with John F. Kennedy, C. S. Lewis and Aldous Huxley*. 2nd ed. Downers Grove, IL: InterVarsity, 2008.

Larmer, Robert A. *The Legitimacy of Miracle*. Lanham, MD: Lexington, 2014.

Lennox, John C. *God's Undertaker: Has Science Buried God?* 2nd ed. Oxford: Lion, 2009.

Levering, Matthew. *Did Jesus Rise from the Dead? Historical and Theological Reflections*. Oxford: Oxford University Press, 2019.

Lewis, C. S. *Miracles*. 2nd ed. London: Fount, 1998.

Licona, Michael R. *Paul Meets Muhammad: A Christian-Muslim Debate on the Resurrection*. Grand Rapids, MI: Baker, 2006.

———. *The Resurrection of Jesus: A New Historiographical Approach*. Downers Grove, IL: InterVarsity, 2010.

Loke, Andrew Ter Ern. *The Origin of Divine Christology*. Cambridge: Cambridge University Press, 2017.

Marston, Paul, and Roger Forster. *God's Strategy in Human History*. Eugene, OR: Wipf & Stock, 2000.

May, Peter. *The Search for God and the Path to Persuasion*. Glasgow: Malcolm Down, 2016.

McGrath, Alister. *Making Sense of the Cross*. Leicester: InterVarsity, 1992.

———. *Mere Discipleship: On Growing in Wisdom and Hope*. London: SPCK, 2018.

———. *The Passionate Intellect: Christian Faith and the Discipleship of the Mind*. Downers Grove, IL: InterVarsity, 2010.

McGrew, Lydia. *The Eye of the Beholder: The Gospel of John as Historical Reportage*. Tampa, FL: DeWard, 2021.

———. *Hidden in Plain View: Undesigned Coincidences in the Gospels and Acts*. Tampa, FL: DeWard, 2017.
———. *Testimonies to the Truth: Why You Can Trust the Gospels*. Tampa, FL: DeWard, 2023.
Meister, Chad V. *Building Belief: Constructing Faith from the Ground Up*. Eugene, OR: Wipf & Stock, 2009.
———. *Evil: A Guide for the Perplexed*. 2nd ed. New York: Bloomsbury, 2018.
Meister, Chad, and James K. Drew Jr., eds. *God and Evil: The Case for God in a World Filled with Pain*. Downers Grove, IL: InterVarsity, 2013.
Meyer, Stephen C. *The Return of the God Hypothesis*. New York: HarperCollins, 2021.
Miller, Corey, and Paul Gould, eds. *Is Faith in God Reasonable?* London: Routledge, 2014.
Miller, Troy A. ed. *Jesus: The Final Days*. London: SPCK, 2008.
Moreland, J. P. *Consciousness and the Existence of God: A Theistic Argument*. London: Routledge, 2009.
———. *Love the Lord with All Your Mind: The Role of Reason in the Life of the Soul*. Colorado Springs: NavPress, 1997.
———. *The Recalcitrant Imago Dei: Human Persons and the Failure of Naturalism*. London: SCM, 2009.
———. *Scaling the Secular City: A Defence of Christianity*. Grand Rapids, MI: Baker, 1987.
———. *Scientism and Secularism: Learning to Respond to a Dangerous Ideology*. Wheaton, IL: Crossway, 2018.
Moreland, J. P., and William Lane Craig. *Philosophical Foundations for a Christian Worldview*. 2nd ed. Downers Grove, IL: IVP Academic, 2017.
Moreland, J. P., and Kai Nielsen. *Does God Exist? The Debate between Theists and Atheists*. Amherst, NY: Prometheus, 1993.
Moreland, J. P., and Brandon Rickabaugh. *The Substance of Consciousness*. Oxford: Wiley Blackwell, 2023.
Morley, Brian K. *Mapping Apologetics: Comparing Contemporary Approaches*. Downers Grove, IL: IVP Academic, 2015.
Morris, Thomas V. *Making Sense of It All: Pascal and the Meaning of Life*. Grand Rapids, MI: Eerdmans, 1998.
———. *Our Idea of God: An Introduction to Philosophical Theology*. Downers Grove, IL: InterVarsity, 1991.
Morrow, Jonathan. *Questioning the Bible: 11 Major Challenges to the Bible's Authority*. Chicago: Moody, 2014.
Murray, Michael J., ed. *Reason for the Hope Within*. Grand Rapids, MI: Eerdmans, 1999.
Nagel, Thomas. *Mind and Cosmos: Why the Materialist Neo-Darwinian Conception of Nature Is Almost Certainly False*. Oxford: Oxford University Press, 2012.
Neufeld, Thomas R. Yoder. *Recovering Jesus: The Witness of the New Testament*. Grand Rapids, MI: SPCK, 2007.
Nicholl, Colin R. *The Great Christ Comet: Revealing the True Star of Bethlehem*. Wheaton, IL: Crossway, 2015.
Nicholi, Armand, Jr. *The Question of God: C. S. Lewis and Sigmund Freud Debate God, Love, Sex, and the Meaning of Life*. New York: Free Press, 2002.
Overman, Dean L. *A Case for the Divinity of Jesus: Examining the Earliest Evidence*. Plymouth: Rowman & Littlefield, 2009.

Owen, H. P. *Christian Theism: A Study in its Basic Principles*. Edinburgh: T&T Clark, 1984.

Pinnock, Clark H., ed. *The Grace of God and the Will of Man*. Bloomington, MN: Bethany, 1989.

Pitre, Brant. *The Case for Jesus: The Biblical and Historical Evidence for Christ*. New York: Image, 2016.

Plantinga, Alvin. *Warranted Christian Belief*. Oxford: Oxford University Press, 2000.

Polkinghorne, John. *Science and Christian Belief: Theological Reflections of a Bottom-Up Thinker*. London: SPCK, 1994.

Porter, Stanley E. *How We Got the New Testament: Text, Transmission, Translation*. Grand Rapids, MI: Baker Academic, 2013.

Quarles, Charles. *Midrash Criticism: Introduction and Appraisal*. Lanham, MD: University Press of America, 1998.

Qureshi, Nabeel. *No God but One: Allah or Jesus?* Grand Rapids, MI: Zondervan 2016.

Rasmussen, Joshua, and Kevin Vallier, eds. *A New Theist Response to the New Atheism*. London: Routledge, 2020.

Redford, John. *Born of a Virgin: Proving the Miracle from the Gospels*. London: St Pauls, 2007.

Reppert, Victor. *C. S. Lewis's Dangerous Idea: In Defense of the Argument from Reason*. Downers Grove, IL: IVP Academic, 2009.

Roberts, Mark D. *Can We Trust the Gospels?* Wheaton, IL: Crossway, 2007.

Rosenberg, Alex. *An Atheists' Guide to Reality*. New York: Norton, 2013.

Ruloff, Colin, and Peter Horban, eds. *Contemporary Arguments in Natural Theology: God and Rational Belief*. London: Bloomsbury Academic, 2021.

Sanders, John. *No Other Name: Can Only Christians Be Saved?* London: SPCK, 1994.

Scott, Douglas D. *Is Jesus of Nazareth the Predicted Messiah? A Historical-Evidential Approach to Specific Old Testament Messianic Prophecies and Their New Testament Fulfillments*. Eugene, OR: Wipf & Stock, 2019.

Sennett, James F., and Douglas R. Groothuis, eds. *In Defence of Natural Theology: A Post-Humean Assessment*. Downers Grove, IL: IVP Academic, 2005.

Sinnott-Armstrong, Walter. *Think Again: How to Reason and Argue*. London: Pelican, 2018.

Sire, James W. *The Universe Next Door—A Basic Worldview Catalog*. 6th ed. Downers Grove, IL: IVP Academic, 2020.

Smart, J. J. C., and J. J. Haldane. *Atheism and Theism*. 2nd ed. Oxford: Blackwell, 2003.

Smith, Christian. *Atheist Overreach: What Atheism Can't Deliver*. Oxford: Oxford University Press, 2019.

Smith, Mark D. *The Final Days of Jesus: The Thrill of Defeat, The Agony of Victory: A Classical Historian Explores Jesus's Arrest, Trial, and Execution*. Cambridge: Lutterworth, 2018.

Stecher, Carl and Craig Blomberg, with contributions by Richard Carrier and Peter S. Williams. *Resurrection: Faith or Fact? A Scholars' Debate between a Skeptic and a Christian*. Durham, NC: Pitchstone, 2019.

Stewart, Robert B., and Gary R. Habermas, eds. *Memories of Jesus: A Critical Appraisal of James D. G. Dunn's Jesus Remembered*. Nashville: B&H Academic, 2010.

Stokes, Mitch. *A Shot of Faith (to the Head): Be a Confident Believer in an Age of Cranky Atheists*. Nashville: Thomas Nelson, 2012.

Strobel, Lee. *The Case for Christ*. 2nd ed. Grand Rapids, MI: Zondervan, 2016.

———. *In Defence of Jesus.* Grand Rapids, MI: Zondervan, 2016.
Swinburne, Richard. *The Resurrection of God Incarnate.* Oxford: Clarendon, 2003.
———. *Was Jesus God?* Oxford: Oxford University Press, 2008.
Taliaferro, Charles. *Consciousness and the Mind of God.* Cambridge: Cambridge University Press, 1994.
Taylor, James E. *Introducing Apologetics: Cultivating Christian Commitment.* Grand Rapids, MI: Baker Academic, 2013.
Vermes, Geza. *The Resurrection.* London: Penguin, 2008.
Wallace, J. Warner. *Cold Case Christianity: A Homicide Detective Investigates the Claims of the Gospels.* Updated and exp. ed. Colorado Springs: David C. Cook, 2023.
Walls, Jerry L. *Heaven: The Logic of Eternal Joy.* Oxford: Oxford University Press, 2002.
Walls, Jerry L., and Joseph R. Dongell. *Why I Am Not a Calvinist.* Downers Grove: InterVarsity, 2004.
Walls, Jerry L., and Trent Dougherty eds. *Two Dozen (or so) Arguments for God: The Plantinga Project.* Oxford: Oxford University Press, 2018.
Ward, Keith. *God, Chance and Necessity.* Oxford: OneWorld, 1996.
Wenham, John. *Easter Enigma: Are the Resurrection Accounts in Conflict?* 2nd ed. London: Paternoster, 1992.
Wilkins, Michael J., and J. P. Moreland, eds. *Jesus Under Fire: Modern Scholarship Reinvents the Historical Jesus.* Grand Rapids, MI: Zondervan, 1995.
Willard, Dallas. *Knowing Christ Today: How We Can Trust Spiritual Knowledge.* New York: HarperOne, 2009.
Williams, Peter J. *Can We Trust the Gospels?* Wheaton, IL: Crossway, 2018.
Williams, Peter S. *Apologetics in 3D: Essays on Apologetics and Spirituality.* Eugene, OR: Wipf & Stock, 2021.
———. *The Case for Angels.* Carlisle, Cumbria: Paternoster, 2002.
———. *The Case for God.* Tunbridge Wells: Monarch, 1999.
———. *C. S. Lewis vs. the New Atheists.* Milton Keynes: Paternoster, 2013.
———. *A Faithful Guide to Philosophy: A Christian Introduction to the Love of Wisdom.* Eugene, OR: Wipf & Stock, 2019.
———. *Getting at Jesus: A Comprehensive Critique of Neo-Atheist Nonsense about the Jesus of History.* Eugene, OR: Wipf & Stock, 2019.
———. *An Informed Cosmos: Essays on Intelligent Design Theory.* Eugene, OR: Wipf & Stock, 2023.
———. *I Wish I Could Believe in Meaning: A Response to Nihilism.* Southampton: Damaris, 2005.
———. *Outgrowing God? A Beginner's Guide to Richard Dawkins and the God Debate.* Eugene, OR: Cascade, 2020.
———. *A Sceptic's Guide to Atheism.* Milton Keynes: Paternoster, 2009.
———. *Understanding Jesus: Five Ways to Spiritual Enlightenment.* Milton Keynes: Paternoster, 2011.
———. *A Universe from Someone: Essays on Natural Theology.* Eugene, OR: Wipf & Stock, 2022.
Wright, N. T. *The Resurrection of the Son of God.* London: SPCK, 2003.
———. *Surprised by Hope: Rethinking Heaven, the Resurrection, and the Mission of the Church.* New York: HarperOne, 2018.

Bibliography

Abel, David L. *Primordial Prescription: The Most Plaguing Problem of Life Origin Science.* New York: LongView, 2015.
Achenbach, Joel. "What We Actually Know about Aliens, According to Science." *Washington Post*, Nov 25, 2023. https://www.washingtonpost.com/science/2023/11/25/aliens-uaps-scientific-evidence/.
Adams, Edward. "The Ancient Church at Megiddo: The Discovery and an Assessment of Its Significance." *The Expository Times* 120:2 (2008) 62–69. http://earlychristianwritings.com/info/Megiddo-TheExpositoryTimes-2008.pdf.
Adamson, James B. *The Epistle of James.* Grand Rapids, MI: Eerdmans, 1977.
Adler, Mortimer J. *Adler's Philosophical Dictionary.* New York: Scribner, 1995.
———. *Six Great Ideas.* New York: Collier, 1981.
Ahuvia, Mika. "An Introduction to Toledot Yeshu." *Ancient Jew Review*, Dec 25, 2014. https://www.ancientjewreview.com/read/2014/12/25/a-quick-introduction-to-toledot-yeshu.
Akin, Jimmy. "When Was John Written?" Dec 1, 2018. http://jimmyakin.com/2018/12/when-was-john-written.html.
Akker, Robin van der, and Timotheus Vermeulen. "Periodising the 2000s, or, the Emergence of Metamodernism." In *Metamodernism: Historicity, Affect and Depth after Postmodernism*, edited by Robin van der Akker et al., 1–19. London: Rowman & Littlefield, 2017.
Akpan, Nsikan, and Joshua Barajas. "7 Times That Science Explained Aliens." *PBS News Hour*, Oct 28, 2015. www.pbs.org/newshour/updates/7-times-aliens-explained-science/.
"ALIENS IN ART: Crucifixion of Christ." www.theancientaliens.com/alien-art---crucifixion-of-christ. URL no longer available.
Al-Khalili, Jim. *Aliens—Science Asks: Is There Anyone Out There?* London: Profile, 2016.
———. *Paradox: The Nine Greatest Enigmas in Physics.* London: Black Swan, 2013.
All-Domain Anomaly Resolution Office. "Report on the Historical Record of U.S. Government Involvement with Unidentified Anomalous Phenomena (UAP) Volume I." February 2024. https://www.aaro.mil/Portals/136/PDFs/AARO_Historical_Record_Report_Volume_1_2024.pdf.
Alltime Conspiracies. "Was Jesus an Alien?" YouTube video. https://youtu.be/Ey4eA0dAAN8.

Alston, William P. *A Realist Conception of Truth*. Ithaca, NY: Cornell University Press, 1996.

Andersen, Lene Rachel. *Bildung: Keep Growing*. Copenhagen: Nordic Bildung, 2020.

———. *Metamodernity: Meaning and Hope in a Complex World*. Copenhagen: Nordic Bildung, 2019.

Anderson, Paul Scott. "AI Search for Aliens Yields 8 Potential Signals." *EarthSky*, Feb 5, 2023. https://earthsky.org/space/ai-search-for-aliens-breakthrough-listen-seti-8-potential-signals/.

———. "Did Webb Find Signs of Life on Exoplanet K2-18 b?" *EarthSky*, Sep 13, 2023. https://earthsky.org/space/webb-k2-18-b-exoplanet-hycean-biosignature/.

———. "Methane on Enceladus: A Possible Sign of Life?" *EarthSky*, Jun 18, 2021. https://earthsky.org/space/methane-on-enceladus-methanogens/.

Anderson, Tawa J., et al. *An Introduction to Christian Worldview: Pursuing God's Perspective in a Pluralistic World*. Leicester: Apollos, 2017.

Andrews, Edward D. *The P52 Project: Is P52 Really the Earliest Greek New Testament Manuscript?* Cambridge, OH: Christian Publishing House, 2020. Kindle ed.

Anglicans Online. "The Nicene Creed." Last updated May 23, 2017. http://anglicansonline.org/basics/nicene.html.

Annis, J. "Placing a Limit on Star-Fed Kardashev Type III Civilisations." *Journal of the British Interplanetary Society* 52:1 (1999) 33–36. www.jbis.org.uk/paper.php?p=1999.52.33.

Arav, Rami, and John J. Rousseau. *Jesus and His World: An Archaeological and Cultural Dictionary*. Minneapolis: Augsburg Fortress, 1995.

Archive of Recorded Church Music. "BBC TV Coronation of Queen Elizabeth II: Westminster Abbey 1953 (William McKie)." YouTube video, Jun 2, 2018. https://www.youtube.com/watch?v=52NTjasbmgw.

Audi, Robert. *Epistemology: A Contemporary Introduction to the Theory of Knowledge*. 3rd ed. London: Routledge, 2010.

Australian Academy of Science. "Is There Life on Saturn's Moons?" https://www.science.org.au/curious/space-time/there-life-saturns-moons.

Bacchus, Francis Joseph. "St. Polycarp." *Catholic Encyclopedia*. www.newadvent.org/cathen/12219b.htm.

Baggett, David, and Jerry L. Walls. *Good God: The Theistic Foundations of Morality*. Oxford: Oxford University Press, 2011.

Baggini, Julian. *Atheism: A Very Short Introduction*. Oxford: Oxford University Press, 2003.

Bahat, Dan. *The Atlas of Biblical Jerusalem*. Jerusalem: Carta, 1994.

Baird, Iain. "The Beginning of the End of Black and White Television." Science and Media Museum, Jan 6, 2014. https://blog.scienceandmediamuseum.org.uk/the-decline-of-black-and-white-tv/.

Barnes, Albert. "Commentary on John 21." *Barnes' Notes on the Whole Bible*. www.studylight.org/commentaries/eng/bnb/john-21.html#verse-23.

Barnes, Luke. "Why I'm No Longer a Young Earth Creationist." *Premier Christianity*, Jul 29, 2021. www.premierchristianity.com/features/why-im-no-longer-a-young-earth-creationist/5288.article.

Barnett, Paul. *The Birth of Christianity: The First Twenty Years*. Grand Rapids, MI: Eerdmans, 2005.

———. *Is the New Testament History?* Rev. ed. Sydney: Aquila, 2018. Kindle ed.

———. *Messiah: Jesus—The Evidence of History*. Nottingham: InterVarsity, 2009.
Barthes, Roland. "The Death of the Author." https://archive.org/details/TheDeathOfTheAuthor/page/n1/mode/2up.
Bartholomaus, Derek. "Who Is Billy Meier?" *Billy Meier UFO Case*. www.billymeierufocase.com/index-6.html.
Barton, Bruce B., et al. *Revelation*. Life Application Bible Commentary. Wheaton, IL: Tyndale, 2000.
Basalla, George. *Civilized Life in the Universe*. Oxford: Oxford University Press, 2006.
Bassham, Gregory, ed. *C. S. Lewis's Christian Apologetics: For and Against*. Leiden: Rodopi-Brill, 2015.
Bauckham, Richard. *Jesus: A Very Short Introduction*. Oxford: Oxford University Press, 2011.
Beall, Abigail. "Scientists Found Signs of Life on Venus. Now They're Not So Sure." *Wired*, Oct 29, 2020. www.wired.co.uk/article/venus-phosphine-life-questions.
Beck, W. David. *Does God Exist? A History of Answers to the Question*. Downers Grove, IL: IVP Academic, 2021.
———. "God's Existence." In *In Defence of Miracles: A Comprehensive Case for God's Action in History*, edited by R. Douglas Geivett and Gary R. Habermas, 149–62. Leicester: Apollos, 1997. https://digitalcommons.liberty.edu/cgi/viewcontent.cgi?article=1086&context=sor_fac_pubs.
Beckwith, Francis J. *David Hume's Argument against Miracles: A Critical Analysis*. Lanham, MD: University Press of America, 1989.
———. "Theism, Miracles, and the Modern Mind." In *The Rationality of Theism*, edited by Paul Copan and Paul K. Moser, 221–36. London: Routledge, 2003.
———. "Why I Am Not a Moral Relativist." In *Why I Am a Christian: Leading Thinkers Explain Why They Believe*, edited by Norman L. Geisler and Paul K. Hoffman, 17–32. Rev. and exp. ed. Grand Rapids, MI: Baker, 2006.
Beckwith, Francis J., and Gregory Koukl. *Relativism: Feet Firmly Planted in Mid-Air*. Grand Rapids, MI: Baker, 1998.
Behe, Michael J. *Darwin Devolves: The New Science about DNA That Challenges Evolution*. New York: HarperOne, 2019.
———. *Darwin's Black Box: The Biochemical Challenge to Evolution*. 10th anniversary ed. New York: Free Press, 2006.
———. *The Edge of Evolution: The Search for the Limits of Darwinism*. New York: Free Press, 2007.
Beilby, James. *Postmortem Opportunity: A Biblical and Theological Assessment of Salvation after Death*. Downers Grove, IL: IVP Academic, 2021.
Beilby, James K., and Paul Rhodes Eddy. "The Quest for the Historical Jesus: An Introduction." In *The Historical Jesus: Five Views*, edited by James K. Beilby and Paul Rhodes Eddy, 9–54. London: SPCK, 2010.
Bello, Abdul-Rahman Oladimeji. "Phosphine Discovery Could Indicate Signs of Life on Venus." Interesting Engineering, Jul 9, 2023. https://interestingengineering.com/science/phosphine-discovery-could-indicate-signs-of-life-on-venus.
Benario, Herbert W. "Trajan (A.D. 98-117)." *De Imperatoribus Romanus*. http://roman-emperors.sites.luc.edu/trajan.htm.
Bennett, Bo. "Poisoning the Well." www.logicallyfallacious.com/tools/lp/Bo/LogicalFallacies/140/Poisoning-the-Well.

Benson, Joseph. "Matthew 12: Benson Commentary." Bible Hub. https://biblehub.com/commentaries/benson/matthew/12.htm.

———. "Matthew 28:7: Commentaries [*Benson Commentary*]." Bible Hub. https://biblehub.com/commentaries/matthew/28-7.htm.

Berger, William C. *How Unique Are We? Perfect Planet, Clever Species.* Amherst, NY: Prometheus, 2003.

Beverley, James A. *Mormon Crisis: Anatomy of a Failing Religion.* Lagoon City, Ont.: Castle Quay, 2013.

Beverley, James A., and Craig A. Evans. *Getting Jesus Right: How Muslims Get Jesus and Islam Wrong.* Lagoon City, Ont.: Castle Quay, 2015.

Bible Hub. "987: βλασφημέω. Strong's Greek." http://biblehub.com/greek/987.htm.

"1161. De: Strong's Greek." http://biblehub.com/greek/1161.htm.

———. "2570. Kalos: Strong's Greek." https://biblehub.com/greek/2570.htm.

———. "2861. Kolumbethra: Strong's Greek." https://biblehub.com/greek/2861.htm.

———. "2896. Towb: Strong's Hebrew." https://biblehub.com/hebrew/2896.htm.

———. "Acts 15:13." http://biblehub.com/acts/15-13.htm.

———. "Acts 15:17." http://biblehub.com/acts/15-17.htm.

———. "Acts 15:25." http://biblehub.com/acts/15-25.htm.

———. "James 1:19." http://biblehub.com/james/1-19.htm.

———. "James 2:1." http://biblehub.com/james/2-1.htm.

———. "James 2:5." http://biblehub.com/james/2-5.htm.

———. "James 2:7." http://biblehub.com/text/james/2-7.htm.

———. "James 2:7 Parallel." http://biblehub.com/parallel/james/2-7.htm.

———. "John 5:2 Commentaries." https://biblehub.com/commentaries/john/5-2.htm.

———. "Matthew 24:21: Greek Text Analysis." http://biblehub.com/text/matthew/24-21.htm.

Bible Study Tools. "Compare Translations for James 2:7." www.biblestudytools.com/james/2-7-compare.html.

Biblical Archaeological Staff. "Prison Makes Way for the Holy Land's Oldest Church." *Biblical Archaeological Society*, Apr 23, 2012. www.biblicalarchaeology.org/daily/biblical-sites-places/biblical-archaeology-places/prison-makes-way-for-the-holy-lands-oldest-church/.

Billings, Lee. "Alien Supercivilizations Absent from 100,000 Nearby Galaxies." *Scientific American*, Apr 17, 2015. www.scientificamerican.com/article/alien-supercivilizations-absent-from-100-000-nearby-galaxies/.

Bird, Michael F. "Did Jesus Think He Was God?" In *How God Became Jesus: The Real Origins of Belief in Jesus' Divine Nature—A Response to Bart D. Ehrman*, by Michael F. Bird et al., 45–70. Grand Rapids, MI: Zondervan, 2014.

Bird, Michael F., et al. *How God Became Jesus: The Real Origins of Belief in Jesus' Divine Nature—A Response to Bart D. Ehrman.* Grand Rapids, MI: Zondervan, 2014.

Bishop, James. "Historical Problems with Islam's View of Jesus' Crucifixion." Reasons for Jesus, Sep 28, 2019. https://reasonsforjesus.com/historical-problems-with-islams-view-of-jesus-crucifixion/.

BiteSize Philosophy. "Logical Fallacies: The Argument from Silence." YouTube video. https://youtu.be/qzKu44S8lag.

Blackmore, Susan. "Abduction by Aliens or Sleep Paralysis?" *Skeptical Inquirer* 22:3 (May/June 1998). www.csicop.org/si/show/abduction_by_aliens_or_sleep_paralysis.

Blackmore, Susan, and Marcus Cox. "Alien Abductions, Sleep Paralysis and the Temporal Lobe." *European Journal of UFO and Abduction Studies* 1 (2000) 113–18. www.susanblackmore.co.uk/articles/alien-abductions-sleep-paralysis-and-the-temporal-lobe/.

Blomberg, Craig L. *The Historical Reliability of the Gospels*. 2nd ed. Leicester: Apollos, 2007.

———. *The Historical Reliability of John's Gospel: Issues and Commentary*. Leicester: Apollos, 2001.

———. "How to Approach Apparent Contradictions in the Gospels: A Response to Michael Licona." Christian Research Institute, Mar 23, 2023. https://www.equip.org/articles/how-to-approach-apparent-contradictions-in-the-gospels-a-response-to-michael-licona/.

———. "Introduction to John's Gospel." In *CSB Apologetics Study Bible*, 1303. Nashville: Holman, 2017.

———. *Matthew*. New American Commentary 22. Nashville: B&H, 1992.

———. "A Reply to Carl." In *Resurrection: Faith or Fact? A Scholars' Debate between a Skeptic and a Christian*, by Carl Stecher et al., 80–107. Durham, NC: Pitchstone, 2019.

———. "A Rejoinder to Carl." In *Resurrection: Faith or Fact? A Scholars' Debate between a Skeptic and a Christian*, by Carl Stecher et al., 180–91. Durham, NC: Pitchstone, 2019.

Blumrich, J. F. *The Spaceships of Ezekiel*. London: Corgi, 1974.

Boa, Kenneth D., and Robert M. Bowman Jr. *Faith Has Its Reasons: An Integrative Approach to Defending Christianity*. 2nd ed. Milton Keynes: Paternoster, 2000.

Bock, Darrell L. *Acts*. Grand Rapids, MI: Baker Academic, 2007.

———. *Studying the Historical Jesus*. Leicester: Apollos, 2002.

———. *Who Is Jesus? Linking the Historical Jesus with the Christ of Faith*. New York: Howard, 2012.

Boethius. *The Consolation of Philosophy*. Book 3. https://www.gutenberg.org/files/14328/14328-h/14328-h.htm..

Boice, James. "Who Were the Disciples on the Road to Emmaus?" *Christianity.com*, Aug 5, 2019. https://www.christianity.com/jesus/death-and-resurrection/resurrection/who-were-the-disciples-on-the-road-to-emmaus.html.

Bond, Helen K. *The Historical Jesus: A Guide for the Perplexed*. Edinburgh: T&T Clark, 2012.

Boring, M. Eugene. *Revelation*. Interpretation: A Bible Commentary for Teaching and Preaching. Louisville: John Knox, 1989.

Botkin-Kowacki, Eva. "Did Life on Earth Come from Space? Chummy Microbes Offer Clues." *Christian Science Monitor*, Aug 26, 2020. www.csmonitor.com/Science/2020/0826/Did-life-on-Earth-come-from-space-Chummy-microbes-offer-clues.

Bowman, Robert M. "Top 10 Reasons for Accepting Jesus' 'I Am' Sayings in John as Historically Reliable." *Robert M. Bowman Jr.* (blog), Oct 4, 2017. https://robertbowman.net/2017/10/04/top-10-reasons-for-accepting-jesus-i-am-sayings-in-john-as-historically-reliable/.

Bowman, Robert M., and J. Ed Komoszewski. *Putting Jesus in His Place: The Case for the Deity of Christ*. Grand Rapids, MI: Kregel, 2007.

Brant, Jo-Ann A. *John*. Paideia Commentaries on the New Testament. Grand Rapids, MI: Baker Academic, 2011.

Braun, Michael A. "James' Use of Amos at the Jerusalem Council: Steps toward a Possible Solution of the Textual and Theological Problems." *Journal of the Evangelical Theological Society* 20:2 (Jun 1977) 113–21. https://etsjets.org/wp-content/uploads/2010/09/files_JETS-PDFs_20_20-2_20-2-pp113-121_JETS.pdf.

Breedlovecraft, W. R. "The Absurd Philosophy of Everything, Everywhere All at Once." YouTube video, Feb 26, 2023. https://www.youtube.com/watch?v=qrrzhhTW07k.

Brewin, Chris R., and Bernice Andrews. "Creating Memories for False Autobiographical Events in Childhood: A Systematic Review." *Applied Cognitive Psychology* 31:1 (Apr 8, 2016). http://onlinelibrary.wiley.com/doi/10.1002/acp.3220/full.

Brierley, Justin. *The Surprising Rebirth of Belief in God: Why New Atheism Grew Old and Secular Thinkers Are Considering Christianity Again*. Carol Stream, IL: Tyndale Elevate, 2023.

Brindle, Wayne. "The Census and Quirinius: Luke 2:2." *Journal of the Evangelical Theological Society* (1984). https://digitalcommons.liberty.edu/cgi/viewcontent.cgi?article=1072&context=sor_fac_pubs.

Brooks, James A. *Mark*. New American Commentary. Nashville: Broadman, 1991.

Brown, Dan. *The Da Vinci Code*. New York: Doubleday, 2003.

Bruce, F. F. *The Epistle to the Hebrews*. Grand Rapids, MI: Eerdmans, 1990.

———. *The Epistle to the Hebrews*. Rev. ed. Grand Rapids, MI: Eerdmans, 2012.

———. *The Gospel of John: Introduction, Exposition, and Notes*. Grand Rapids, MI: Eerdmans, 1994.

Buras, Todd, and Michael Cantrell. "C. S. Lewis's Argument from Nostalgia: A New Argument from Desire." *Two Dozen (Or So) Arguments for God*, edited by Jerry L. Walls and Trent Dougherty, 356–71. Oxford: Oxford University Press, 2018.

Burnett, David. *Clash of Worlds: What Christians Can Do in a World of Cultures in Conflict*. London: Monarch, 2002.

Butler, Christopher. *Postmodernism: A Very Short Introduction*. Oxford: Oxford University Press, 2002.

Butler, Trent C., ed. "Blasphemy." *Holman Bible Dictionary*. https://www.studylight.org/dictionaries/eng/hbd/b/blasphemy.html.

Butt, Kyle. "Ezekiel's Vision: An Alien UFO?" Apologetics Press, Oct 19, 2004. www.apologeticspress.org/apcontent.aspx?category=11&article=1061.

Cabal, Ted, ed. *The Apologetics Study Bible*. Nashville: Holman 2007.

Caird, G. B. *Saint Luke*. Pelican New Testament Commentaries. New York: Pelican, 1987.

Callahan, Tim. "The Spaceships of Ezekiel." eSkeptic. www.skeptic.com/eskeptic/05-07-28/.

Campbell, Charlie H. *Archaeological Evidence for the Bible*. Carlsbad, CA: Always BeReady, 2012.

Campbell, Kyle. "The Authorship of Hebrews." *Truth Magazine*, June 20, 1996. www.truthmagazine.com/archives/volume40/GOT040175.html.

Camus, Albert. *The Myth of Sisyphus*. Translated by Justin O'Brien. London: Penguin, 1975.

"Carl Stecher, Obituary." *Boston Globe*, Nov 27, 2019. www.legacy.com/obituaries/bostonglobe/obituary.aspx?n=carl-stecher&pid=194555412&fhid=15385.

Carrier, Richard. *Sense and Goodness without God: A Defense of Metaphysical Naturalism*. Bloomington, IN: AuthorHouse, 2005.
Carson, D. A. *The Gagging of God*. Grand Rapids, MI: Zondervan Academic, 2009.
———. *The Intolerance of Tolerance*. Grand Rapids, MI: Eerdmans, 2013.
Carter, Jamie. "Phosphine Confirmed Deep within Venus' Atmosphere, a Possible Sign of Life." *Forbes*, Jul 6, 2023. https://www.forbes.com/sites/jamiecartereurope/2023/07/06/phosphine-confirmed-deep-within-venus-atmosphere-a-possible-sign-of-life/.
CASE. "Book Review: Empty Assumptions amidst Genuine Debate." Mar 1, 2007. https://www.case.edu.au/blogs/case-subscription-library/book-review-empty-assumptions-amidst-genuine-debate-greg-clarke.
Casey, Maurice. *Jesus: Evidence and Argument or Mythicist Myths?* London: Bloomsbury, 2014.
Cavanaugh, William T. *The Myth of Religious Violence: Secular Ideology and the Roots of Modern Conflict*. Oxford: Oxford University Press, 2009.
Center for the Study of New Testament Manuscripts. "Preserving Ancient Manuscripts for a Modern World." https://www.csntm.org/.
CenturyOne Bookstore. *The Bordeaux Pilgrim*. Translated by Aubrey Stewart. http://www.centuryone.com/bordeaux.html.
Chamberlain, Theodore J., and Christopher Hall. *Realized Religion: Research on the Relationship between Religion and Health*. Radnor, PA: Templeton Foundation, 2000.
Chandler, David L. "Could the Clouds of Venus Support Life?" Astronomy, Sep 1, 2023. https://www.astronomy.com/science/could-the-clouds-of-venus-support-life/.
———. "Explained: Sigma." *MIT News*, Feb 9, 2012. https://news.mit.edu/2012/explained-sigma-0209.
Chapman, Allan. *Slaying the Dragons: Destroying Myths in the History of Science and Faith*. Oxford: Lion, 2013.
Charles, J. Daryl, ed. *Reading Genesis 1–2: An Evangelical Conversation*. Hendrickson, 2013.
Cheney, Liz. *Oath and Honor: The Explosive Inside Story from the Most Senior Republican to Stand Up to Donald Trump*. New York: Little, Brown, 2024.
Choza, Carmen, et al. "The Breakthrough Listen Search for Intelligent Life: Technosignature Search of 97 Nearby Galaxies." Dec 6, 2023. https://arxiv.org/pdf/2312.03943.pdf.
Christianity Today. "Polycarp: Aged Bishop of Smyrna." www.christianitytoday.com/history/people/martyrs/polycarp.html.
The Church of England. "The Apostles' Creed." www.churchofengland.org/our-faith/what-we-believe/apostles-creed.
Clancy, Susan A. *Abducted: How People Come to Believe They Were Kidnapped by Aliens*. Cambridge, MA: Harvard University Press, 2005.
Clarke, David. *How UFOs Conquered the World: A History of a Modern Myth*. London: Aurum, 2015.
Cleaves, H. James, and John H. Chalmers. "Extremophiles May Be Irrelevant to the Origin of Life." *Astrobiology* 4 (Mar 2004) 1–9. DOI: 10.1089/153110704773600195.
Cline, Austin. "Dating and Origins of Mark's Gospel." Learn Religions, Jun 25, 2019. http://atheism.about.com/od/biblegospelofmark/a/dating.htm.

Clinton, Jane. "No Evidence of Alien Life in UFO Sightings, Pentagon Finds." *The i Weekend* (Mar 9–10, 2024) 22.

Cloud, David. "The Illiad vs the New Testament." Way of Life Literature, Nov 10, 2016. https://www.wayoflife.org/reports/the-illiad-vs-the-new-testament.php.

Clowney, Edmund. *The Message of 1 Peter*. Nottingham: InterVarsity, 2010.

Colavito, Jason. "*Ancient Aliens*: Unauthorized Reviews." www.jasoncolavito.com/ancient-aliens-reviews.html.

———. *A Critical Companion to Ancient Aliens Series 3 and 4*. Morrisville, NC: Lulu, 2012.

———. *The Cult of Alien Gods: H. P. Lovecraft and Extraterrestrial Pop Culture*. New York: Prometheus, 2005.

———. "Opinion: Congress Is Too Credulous on UFOs." *Forbes*, Jul 28, 2023. https://edition.cnn.com/2023/07/28/opinions/ufo-testimony-aliens-congress-credulous-colavito/index.html.

Collicutt, Joanna. *The Psychology of Christian Character Formation*. London: SCM, 2015.

Collins, C. John. *Genesis 1–4: A Linguistic, Literary, and Theological Commentary*. Phillipsburg, NJ: Presbyterian and Reformed, 2012.

Collins, Robin. "Eastern Religions." In *Reason for the Hope Within*, edited by Michael J. Murray, 182–216. Grand Rapids, MI: Eerdmans, 1999.

Collins, Steven. *The Defendable Faith: Lessons in Christian Apologetics*. Albuquerque: Trowel, 2012.

Comfort, Philip Wesley. *Encountering the Manuscripts: An Introduction to New Testament Paleography and Textual Criticism*. Nashville: B&H, 2005.

———. *The Text of the Earliest New Testament Manuscripts*. Vol. 2, *Papyri 75–139 and Uncials*. 3rd ed. Grand Rapids, MI: Kregel Academic, 2019.

Comfort, Philip Wesley, and David P. Barrett. *The Text of the Earliest New Testament Manuscripts*. Vol. 1. 3rd ed. Grand Rapids, MI: Kregel Academic, 2019.

Comfort, Philip Wesley, and Jason Driesbach. *The Many Gospels of Jesus: Sorting Out the Story of the Life of Jesus*. Carol Stream, IL: Tyndale, 2008.

Condliffe, Jamie. "Super-Fast Space Travel Would Kill You in Minutes." *Gizmodo*, Nov 5, 2012. https://gizmodo.com/5957697/super-fast-space-travel-would-kill-you-in-minutes.

Cook, Steven R. "Introduction to the Letter of James." YouTube video, May 2, 2015. https://youtu.be/hYc9cdUgQfQ.

Cooper, Keith. "No Alien Life Needed: Dark Streaks in Venus' Atmosphere Can Be Explained by Iron Minerals." Space.com, Jan 15, 2024. https://www.space.com/dark-streaks-venus-atmosphere-iron-minerals-not-microbes.

———. "On Alien Worlds, Exotic Form of Ice May Transport Nutrients to Hidden Oceans." Space.com, Jun 22, 2022. https://www.space.com/alien-ocean-worlds-exotic-ice-transfer-nutrients.

Copan, Paul. "God, Naturalism, and the Foundations of Morality." http://www.paulcopan.com/articles/pdf/God-naturalism-morality.pdf.

———. "Hume and the Moral Argument." http://www.paulcopan.com/articles/pdf/Paul_Copan-Hume_and_Moral_Argument-In_Defense_Natural_Theology.pdf.

———. *True for You but Not for Me*. Rev. ed. Bloomington, MN: Bethany, 2009.

———. *When God Goes to Starbucks*. Grand Rapids, MI: Baker, 2009.

Copan, Paul, and Charles Taliaferro, eds. *The Naturalness of Belief*. Lanham, MD: Lexington, 2019.
Copan, Paul, and Paul K. Moser, eds. *The Rationality of Theism*. New York: Routledge, 2003.
Copan, Paul, and William Lane Craig, eds. *The Kalam Cosmological Argument*. Vol. 1, *Philosophical Arguments for the Finitude of the Past*. Bloomsbury Studies in Philosophy of Religion. New York: Bloomsbury Academic, 2019.
———. *The Kalam Cosmological Argument*. Vol. 2, *Scientific Evidence for the Beginning of the Universe*. Bloomsbury Studies in Philosophy of Religion. New York: Bloomsbury Academic, 2019.
Coumes, Jon. "Ancient Aliens Is Everything That's Wrong with America." *The AWL*, Sep 19, 2017. www.theawl.com/2017/09/ancient-aliens-is-everything-thats-wrong-with-america/.
Couto, Marcelle. "Reflecting on the Philosophy of 'Everything Everywhere All at Once.'" *The Observer*, Feb 16, 2023. https://www.ndsmcobserver.com/article/2023/02/philosophy-everything-everywhere-all-at-once.
Cowan, Steven B., ed. *Five Views on Apologetics*. Grand Rapids, MI: Zondervan, 2000.
Cowan, Steven B., and James S. Spiegel. *The Love of Wisdom: A Christian Introduction to Philosophy*. Nashville: B&H, 2009.
Craig, William Lane. *Assessing the New Testament Evidence for the Resurrection of Jesus*. New York: Edwin Mellen, 2002.
———. "The Bodily Resurrection of Jesus." *Reasonable Faith with William Lane Craig*. https://www.reasonablefaith.org/writings/scholarly-writings/historical-jesus/the-bodily-resurrection-of-jesus.
———. "Christ and Miracles: Introduction." In *To Everyone an Answer: A Case for the Christian Worldview*, edited by Francis J. Beckwith, 139–44. Downers Grove, IL: InterVarsity, 2004.
———. "Creation Ex Nihilo." *Reasonable Faith with William Lane Craig*. https://www.reasonablefaith.org/writings/popular-writings/existence-nature-of-god/creation-ex-nihilo-theology-and-science.
———. "The Concept of God in Islam and Christianity." *Reasonable Faith with William Lane Craig*. http://www.reasonablefaith.org/concept-of-god-in-islam-and-christianity.
———. "Dale Allison on Jesus' Empty Tomb, His Post-Mortem Appearances, and the Origin of the Disciples' Belief in His Resurrection." *Reasonable Faith with William Lane Craig*. www.reasonablefaith.org/writings/scholarly-writings/historical-jesus/dale-allison-on-jesus-empty-tomb-his-post-mortem-appearances-and-the-origin/.
———. "Dale Allison on the Resurrection of Jesus." *Reasonable Faith with William Lane Craig*. https://www.reasonablefaith.org/writings/question-answer/dale-allison-on-the-resurrection-of-jesus.
———. "Dawkins' Delusion." *Reasonable Faith with William Lane Craig*. https://www.reasonablefaith.org/writings/popular-writings/existence-nature-of-god/dawkins-delusion.
———. *Did Jesus Rise from the Dead?* Pine Mountain, GA: Impact 360 Institute, 2014.
———. "The Disciples' Inspection of the Empty Tomb." *Reasonable Faith with William Lane Craig*. www.reasonablefaith.org/the-disciples-inspection-of-the-empty-tomb.
———. *Does God Exist?* Pine Mountain, GA: Impact 360 Institute, 2014.

———. *Five Arguments for God*. Christian Evidence Society, 2016. https://christianevidence.org/booklet/five_arguments_for_god/.

———. "The Historicity of the Empty Tomb of Jesus." *Reasonable Faith with William Lane Craig*. https://www.reasonablefaith.org/writings/scholarly-writings/historical-jesus/the-historicity-of-the-empty-tomb-of-jesus.

———. "Is the Resurrection Hypothesis Really as Absurd as the Alien Hypothesis?" YouTube video, Dec 7, 2015. https://youtu.be/QW97epVeN7Y.

———. "Jesus' Resurrection." *Reasonable Faith with William Lane Craig*. https://www.reasonablefaith.org/writings/scholarly-writings/historical-jesus/jesus-resurrection.

———. *On Guard: Defending Your Faith with Reason and Precision*. Colorado Springs: David C. Cook, 2010.

———. *On Guard for Students*. Colorado Springs: David C. Cook, 2015.

———. *The Only Wise God: The Compatibility of Divine Foreknowledge and Human Freedom*. Eugene, OR: Wipf & Stock, 2000.

———. "The Problem of Evil." *Reasonable Faith with William Lane Craig*. https://www.reasonablefaith.org/writings/popular-writings/existence-nature-of-god/the-problem-of-evil.

———. *Reasonable Faith*. 3rd ed. Wheaton, IL: Crossway, 2008.

———. "Reply to Evan Fales: On the Empty Tomb of Jesus." *Reasonable Faith with William Lane Craig*. https://www.reasonablefaith.org/writings/scholarly-writings/historical-jesus/reply-to-evan-fales-on-the-empty-tomb-of-jesus.

———. "The Resurrection of Jesus." *Reasonable Faith with William Lane Craig*. https://www.reasonablefaith.org/writings/popular-writings/jesus-of-nazareth/the-resurrection-of-jesus.

———. "The Resurrection of Theism." *Reasonable Faith with William Lane Craig*. https://www.reasonablefaith.org/writings/popular-writings/existence-nature-of-god/the-resurrection-of-theism.

———. *The Son Rises: Historical Evidence for the Resurrection of Jesus*. Eugene, OR: Wipf & Stock, 2001.

———. "Theistic Critiques of Atheism." *Reasonable Faith with William Lane Craig*. https://www.reasonablefaith.org/writings/scholarly-writings/the-existence-of-god/theistic-critiques-of-atheism.

———. "UFOs." *Reasonable Faith with William Lane Craig*. Podcast, Aug 17, 2008. www.reasonablefaith.org/media/reasonable-faith-podcast/ufos/.

———. "Vilenkin's Cosmic Vision: A Review Essay of *Many Worlds in One: The Search for Other Universes*, by Alex Vilenkin." *Reasonable Faith with William Lane Craig*. https://www.reasonablefaith.org/writings/scholarly-writings/the-existence-of-god/vilenkins-cosmic-vision-a-review-essay-of-many-worlds-in-one-the-search-for.

———. "Who Was Jesus of Nazareth?" Be Thinking, 2007. www.bethinking.org/jesus/who-was-jesus-of-nazareth.

Craig, William Lane, and Chad Meister, eds. *God Is Great, God Is Good: Why Believing in God Is Reasonable and Responsible*. Downers Grove, IL: InterVarsity, 2009.

Craig, William Lane, and Joseph E. Gorra. *A Reasonable Response: Answers to Tough Questions*. Chicago: Moody, 2013.

Craig, William Lane, and J. P. Moreland, eds. *Naturalism: A Critical Analysis*. London: Routledge, 2001.

———. *The Blackwell Companion to Natural Theology*. Oxford: Wiley-Blackwell, 2009.

Crane, Leah. "The Clouds of Venus Are Too Dry to Support Life as We Know It." *New Scientist*, Jun 28, 2021. https://www.newscientist.com/article/2282212-the-clouds-of-venus-are-too-dry-to-support-life-as-we-know-it/.

Crapo, Richley. "Where Was the Temple of Herod?" *The Bible and Interpretation*, 2000. https://bibleinterp.arizona.edu/articles/2000/cra248001.

Crick, F. H. C., and L. E. Orgel. "Directed Panspermia." *Icarus* 19:3 (Jul 1973) 341–46. www.sciencedirect.com/science/article/pii/0019103573901103.

Crossley, James. "Against the Historical Plausibility of the Empty Tomb Story and the Bodily Resurrection of Jesus." *Journal for the Study of the Historical Jesus* (Jan 1, 2005) 171–86.

———. *The Date of Mark's Gospel: Insight from the Law in Earliest Christianity*. Journal for the Study of the New Testament Supplement S. 266. Edinburgh: T&T Clark, 2004.

Crowe, Brandon D. *Was Jesus Really Born of a Virgin?* Philadelphia: Westminster Seminary, 2013.

Cuoghi, Diego. "ART and UFOs? No Thanks, Only Art . . . Home." 2002. http://sprezzatura.it/Arte/Arte_UFO_eng.htm.

———. "ART and UFOs? No Thanks, Only Art . . . Part 2." http://sprezzatura.it/Arte/Arte_UFO_2_eng.htm.

———. "The Art of Imagining UFOs." *Skeptic Magazine*, Jul 2004. www.diegocuoghi.com/arte-ufo/SKEPTIC_CUOGHI_ARTUFO_complete.pdf.

Curtin University. "Australian Telescope Finds No Signs of Alien Technology in 10 Million Star Systems." Media release, Sep 8, 2020. https://news.curtin.edu.au/media-releases/australian-telescope-finds-no-signs-of-alien-technology-in-10-million-star-systems/.

Cyril of Jerusalem. "Homily on the Paralytic at the Pool (St. Cyril of Jerusalem)." https://www.johnsanidopoulos.com/2017/05/homily-on-paralytic-at-pool-st-cyril-of.html.

Dahlgreen, Will. "You Are Not Alone: Most People Believe That Aliens Exist." YouGov UK, Sep 24, 2015. https://yougov.co.uk/news/2015/09/24/you-are-not-alone-most-people-believe-aliens-exist/.

Damaris Norge. "Peter S. Williams—Discipleship in 3D: Change for Head, Heart and Hands." YouTube video, Apr 29, 2020. https://youtu.be/QTyEooJgIBI?si=sa-PotDjrTJ1jE5U.

Darling, Susannah. "An Earth-Like Atmosphere May Not Survive Proxima b's Orbit." NASA, Jul 31, 2017. www.nasa.gov/feature/goddard/2017/an-earth-like-atmosphere-may-not-survive-proxima-b-s-orbit/.

Dartnell, Lewis. *Life in the Universe: A Beginner's Guide*, Astrobiology. Oxford: OneWorld, 2007.

———. "(Un)welcome Visitors: Why Aliens Might Visit Us." In *Aliens*, edited by Jim Al-Khalili, 25–34. London: Profile, 2016.

Davids, Peter H. *The Epistle of James: A Commentary on the Greek Text*. Milton Keynes: Paternoster, 1982.

———. "James." In *New Bible Commentary*, edited by D. A. Carson et al. 21st century ed. Leicester: InterVarsity, 1994.

Davies, Paul. *The Eerie Silence: Searching for Ourselves in the Universe*. London: Penguin, 2011.

———. "Physics and the Mind of God." *First Things*, Aug 1995. www.firstthings.com/article/1995/08/003-physics-and-the-mind-of-god-the-templeton-prize-address-24.

Davis, Nicola. "Proxima b: Could We Live on This Newly Found Planet—Or Could Something Else?" *The Guardian*, Aug 27, 2016. www.theguardian.com/science/2016/aug/27/proxima-b-could-we-live-on-this-newly-found-planet-or-could-something-else.

Davis, Stephen T. *Christian Philosophical Theology*. Oxford: Oxford University Press, 2016.

———. "The Mad/Bad/God Trilemma: A Reply to Daniel Howard Snyder." *Faith and Philosophy* (Oct 1, 2004) 480–92. https://place.asburyseminary.edu/faithandphilosophy/vol21/iss4/4/.

———. *Risen Indeed*. London: SPCK, 1994.

———. "Was Jesus Mad, Bad or God?" In *Christian Philosophical Theology*, 149–71. Oxford: Oxford University Press, 2016.

Dawkins, Richard. *The God Delusion*. London: Black Swan, 2007.

———. *River out of Eden: A Darwinian View of Life*. New York: Basic, 1995.

———. *Science in the Soul: Selected Writings of a Passionate Rationalist*. London: Bantam, 2017.

———. "Sorry Liberal Christians, But Jesus Is Dead to Me." Richard Dawkins Foundation, Feb 24, 2014. https://richarddawkins.net/2014/02/sorry-liberal-christians-but-jesus-is-dead-to-me-2/.

Dember, Greg. "After Postmodernism: Eleven Metamodern Methods in the Arts." Apr 17, 2018. https://medium.com/what-is-metamodern/after-postmodernism-eleven-metamodern-methods-inthe-arts-767f7b646cae.

———. "Everything Metamodern All at Once." What Is Metamodern?, Jun 27, 2022. https://whatismetamodern.com/film/everything-everywhere-all-at-once-metamodern/.

Dempsey, Brendan Graham. *Metamodernism: Or, The Cultural Logic of Cultural Logics*. ARC, 2023.

Dennett, Daniel. *Breaking the Spell: Religion as a Natural Phenomenon*. London: Penguin, 2007.

Dennett, Daniel, and Alvin Plantinga. *Science and Religion: Are They Compatible?* Oxford: Oxford University Press, 2011.

Dennett, Daniel, and Nick Spencer. "Mounting Disbelief." Jun 2013. https://highprofiles.info/interview/daniel-dennett/.

Dennett, Daniel, and J. P. O'Malley. "Q&A with philosopher Daniel Dennett." *New Humanist*, Jun 8, 2017. https://newhumanist.org.uk/articles/5197/saying-something-is-a-miracle-is-a-failure-of-imagination.

Denton, Michael. *Fire Maker: How Humans Were Designed to Harness Fire and Transform Our Planet*. Seattle: Discovery Institute, 2016.

———. *Nature's Destiny*. London: Simon & Schuster, 1998.

Dickson, John. *Bullies and Saints: An Honest Look at the Good and Evil of Christian History*. Grand Rapids, MI: Zondervan, 2021.

———. *Investigating Jesus: An Historian's Quest*. Oxford: Lion Hudson, 2010.

Dirmyg. "Nazca Alien Mummies Were Debunked Way Back in 2021." YouTube video, Sep 14, 2023. https://www.youtube.com/watch?v=srqr6y19ZOE&list=PLQhh3qcwVEWiixwhvDhbqSoO3qcIK7zu5&index=58.

Dongell, Joseph. *John: A Commentary for Bible Students*. Indianapolis: Wesleyan, 1997. Kindle ed.

Douglas, J. D., and Merrill C. Tenny. *Zondervan Illustrated Bible Dictionary*. Revised by Moises Silva. Grand Rapids, MI: Zondervan, 2011.

Drane, John. *Introducing the New Testament*. Oxford: Lion, 1999.

Dr. Becky. "The Biggest EVER Scientific Search for ALIENS outside Our Galaxy." YouTube video, Dec 14, 2023. https://www.youtube.com/watch?v=2RQWiJox_R4.

———. "Did JWST Find a MARKER OF LIFE in an Exoplanet Atmosphere?" YouTube video, Sep 21, 2023. https://www.youtube.com/watch?v=F36oSGAlI8Y.

Dumitrescu, Alexandra. "Interconnections in Blakean and Metamodern Space." *Double Dialogues* 7 (Winter 2007). https://doubledialogues.com/article/interconnections-in-blakean-and-metamodern-space/.

———. "Metamodernism: A Few Characteristics." *Exploring Metamodernism*, Dec 26, 2013. https://metamodernism.wordpress.com/2013/12/26/metamodernism-a-few-characteristics/.

Dunn, James. *Why Believe in Jesus' Resurrection?* London: SPCK, 2016.

Dvorsky, George. "An Ambitious Search for Aliens Came Up Short—So Astrobiologists Are Thinking Bigger." *Gizmodo*, Jun 19, 2019. https://gizmodo.com/an-ambitious-search-for-aliens-came-up-short-so-astrob-1835658888.

———. "Another Sweeping Search for Aliens Comes Up Short." *Gizmodo*, Sep 8, 2020. https://gizmodo.com/another-sweeping-search-for-aliens-comes-up-short-1844983788.

Eagleton, Terry. *Culture and the Death of God*. New Haven, CT: Yale University Press, 2015.

———. *The Illusions of Postmodernism*. Oxford: Blackwell, 1996.

———. *Reason, Faith, and Revolution*: *Reflections on the God Debate*. New Haven, CT: Yale University Press, 2010.

Earey, Mark. *Liturgical Worship*. London: Church House, 2009.

Earman, John. *Hume's Abject Failure*. Oxford: Oxford University Press, 2000.

Edelstein, William A., and Arthur D. Edelstein. "Speed Kills: Highly Relativistic Spaceflight Would Be Fatal for Passengers and Instruments." *Natural Science* 4:10 (Oct 2012). www.scirp.org/journal/PaperInformation.aspx?paperID=23913.

Editors of Encylopaedia Britannica. "Ferdinand Christian Baur." *Britannica*. Last updated Feb 15, 2024. www.britannica.com/biography/Ferdinand-Christian-Baur.

Edwards, Douglas. *The Virgin Birth in History and Faith*. London: Faber & Faber, 1943.

Ehrman, Bart D. *Did Jesus Exist? The Historical Argument for Jesus of Nazareth*. New York: HarperOne, 2013.

———. "What Was the Council of Nicea?" BeliefNet. www.beliefnet.com/Faiths/Christianity/2005/06/What-Was-The-Council-Of-Nicea.aspx.

———. "Why I'd Be Thrilled If A First Century Manuscript Appeared." The Bart Ehrman Blog (Jan 29, 2015), https://ehrmanblog.org/why-id-be-thrilled-if-a-first-century-manuscript-appeared/.

Ellicott, Charles. "John 5:2." *Commentary for English Readers*. https://biblehub.com/commentaries/john/5-2.htm.

Elwell, Walter A., ed. "Blasphemy." *Baker's Evangelical Dictionary of Biblical Theology Online*. www.biblestudytools.com/dictionaries/bakers-evangelical-dictionary/blasphemy.html.

Elwell, Walter A., and Robert W. Yarbrough. *Encountering the New Testament*. Grand Rapids, MI: Baker, 1998.

ESV Archaeology Study Bible. Wheaton IL: Crossway, 2017.

Eusebius of Caesarea [Eusebius of Pamphilia]. "The Gospels: Bēzatha (Bethsaida)." Entry 291 in *Concerning the Place Names in Sacred Scripture*. Translated by C. Umhau Wolf. 1971. www.tertullian.org/fathers/eusebius_onomasticon_02_trans.htm.

Eusebius, *Ecclesiastical History* 3.39.1–7. Translated by Arthur Cushman McGiffert. In *Nicene and Post-Nicene Fathers*, 2nd series, vol. 1. Edited by Philip Schaff and Henry Wace. Buffalo, NY: Christian Literature Publishing, 1890. Revised and edited for New Advent by Kevin Knight. https://www.newadvent.org/fathers/250103.htm.

Evans, Craig A. *Jesus and His World: The Archaeological Evidence*. London: SPCK, 2012.

———. *Jesus and the Remains of History: Studies in Jesus and the Evidence of Material Culture*. Peabody, MA: Hendrickson, 2015.

———. "The Resurrection of Jesus in the Light of Jewish Burial Practices." Houston Christian University, 2016. https://hc.edu/news-and-events/2016/05/04/craig-evans-resurrection-jesus-light-jewish-burial-p-ractices/.

Evans, C. Stephen. *Despair: A Moment or a Way of Life?* Downers Grove, IL: InterVarsity, 1973.

———. *The Historical Christ and the Jesus of Faith: The Incarnational Narrative as History*. Oxford: Clarendon, 2004.

Evans, C. Stephen. "The Mystery of Persons and Belief in God." 1986. https://www.leaderu.com/truth/3truth07.html.

———. *Natural Signs and Knowledge of God: A New Look at Theistic Arguments*. Oxford: Oxford University Press, 2012.

Evans, Jules. "The New World of Metamodernism." *The Institute of Art and Ideas, iai news*, Oct 1, 2021. https://iai.tv/articles/the-new-world-of-metamodernism-auid-1923.

Evans, Richard L. *In Defence of History*. London: Granta, 1997.

Event Horizon. "8 Candidate Alien Signals from 5 Stars Found by AI Algorithm with Dr. Cherry Ng and Peter Ma." YouTube video, Feb 9, 2023. https://www.youtube.com/watch?v=2dIfaDuDejs&t=2412s.

Evolution News. "Methane Causes Space Aliens?" Jul 23, 2021. https://evolutionnews.org/2021/07/methane-causes-space-aliens/.

The Expositor's Greek New Testament. "James 2:7: Commentaries." Bible Hub. http://biblehub.com/commentaries/james/2-7.htm.

Feder, Kenneth L. "Ancient Astronauts." In *The Skeptic: Encyclopedia of Pseudoscience*, edited by Michael Shermer, 1:17–22. ABC-Clio, 2002. https://camidrcs.files.wordpress.com/2018/02/skepticencyclopedia1.pdf.

———. "Help! I'm Being Followed by Ancient Aliens!" *Skeptical Inquirer* 37:2 (Mar/Apr 2013). www.csicop.org/si/show/help_im_being_followed_by_ancient_aliens.

Fernandes, Phil, and Kyle Larson. *Hijacking the Historical Jesus: Answering Recent Attacks on the Jesus of the Bible*. Bremerton, WA: IBD, 2012.

Films Prophet. "Everything Everywhere All at Once: Nihilism v. Absurdism." YouTube video, Mar 25, 2023. https://www.youtube.com/watch?v=EKZbUofWurg.

Finegan, Jack. *The Archaeology of the New Testament: The Life and Beginnings of the Early Church*. New Jersey: Princeton University Press, 1992.

Flood, Gavin Denis. "Introduction." *Hindu Monotheism*. Cambridge: Cambridge University Press, 2020. https://books.google.co.uk/books?id=S732DwAAQBAJ&pg=PT4&source=gbs_selected_pages&cad=1#v=onepage&q&f=false.

FOCLOnline. "Ancient Aliens: Rebutting Alien Conspiracy Theories—Peter S. Williams." YouTube video, Jan 11, 2021. https://www.youtube.com/watch?v=d7OUXOfIo-g&list=PLQhh3qcwVEWiixwhvDhbqSoO3qcIK7zu5&index=1&t=1s.

———. "Archaeological Evidence for Jesus—Peter S. Williams." YouTube video, Nov 28, 2020. https://youtu.be/klsfgJdga5I?si=9xylLZY03grreSFv.

———. "Arguments for and from Fulfilled Biblical Prophecies—Peter S. Williams." YouTube video, Sep 19, 2020. https://youtu.be/QMwBlRL7w_Y?si=0DRpvcxUpqCbpJ3n.

———. "Defending Early High Christology with Archaeology and New Testament Letters—Peter S. Williams." YouTube video, Aug 1, 2019. https://youtu.be/vUha7-4Puy8.

France, R. T. "The Gospels as Historical Sources for Jesus, the Founder of Christianity." *Truth* 1 (1985).

———. *Matthew*. Tyndale New Testament Commentary. Nottingham: IVP Academic, 2008.

Franz, Gordon. "The King and I: Exiled to Patmos, Part 2." *Bible and Spade* (Fall 1999). https://biblearchaeology.org/research/new-testament-era/3099-the-king-and-i-exiled-to-patmos-part-2.

Freinacht, Hanzi. *The Listening Society: A Metamodern Guide to Politics, Book One*. Metamodern Guides 1. Metamoderna ApS, 2017. Kindle ed.

French, Christopher C. "Alien Contact and Abduction Claims." In *Parapsychology: The Science of Unusual Experience*, edited by David Groome and Ron Roberts, 48–64. 2nd ed. London: Routledge, 2017.

———. "Close Encounters of the Psychological Kind." The British Psychological Society, Sep 15, 2015. https://thepsychologist.bps.org.uk/volume-28/october-2015/close-encounters-psychological-kind.

French, Christopher C., et al. "Psychological Aspects of the Alien Contact Experience." https://www.sciencedirect.com/science/article/abs/pii/S0010945208001408?via%3Dihub.

Friedlander, Blaine. "Trace Gas Phosphine Points to Volcanic Activity on Venus." *Cornell Chronicle*, Jul 12, 2021. https://news.cornell.edu/stories/2021/07/trace-gas-phosphine-points-volcanic-activity-venus.

Fudge, Edward William. *The Fire That Consumes: A Biblical and Historical Study of the Doctrine of Final Punishment*. 3rd rev. ed. London: James Clarke, 2012.

———. *Hebrews: Ancient Encouragement for Believers Today*. Abilene, TX: Leafwood, 2009.

Funk, Robert W. *Honest to Jesus*. New York: HarperSanFrancisco, 1996.

Gage, Paul Logan. "Is the God Hypothesis Improbable? A Response to Dawkins." In *A New Theist Response to the New Atheism*, edited by Joshua Rasmussen and Kevin Vallier, 59–76. New York: Routledge, 2020.

Gaia. "Aliens of the Old Testament—Erich von Däniken: Beyond the Legend." YouTube video, Aug 31, 2017. https://youtu.be/Vg5R2mFDkZk.

Gallagher, Richard. *Demonic Foes: My Twenty-Five Years as a Psychiatrist Investigating Possessions, Diabolic Attacks, and the Paranormal*. New York: HarperOne, 2022.

Ganssle, Gregory E. "God and Evil." In *The Rationality of Theism*, edited by Paul Copan and Paul K. Moser, 259–77. London: Routledge, 2003.

———. *A Reasonable God: Engaging the New Face of Atheism*. Waco, TX: Baylor University Press, 2009.

Geisler, Norman L. *Baker Encyclopedia of Christian Apologetics*. Grand Rapids, MI: Baker, 1999.

———. *The Big Book of Christian Apologetics: An A to Z Guide*. A to Z Guides. Grand Rapids, MI: Baker, 2012.

———. *Christian Apologetics*. Grand Rapids, MI: Baker Academic, 1988.

———. *Christian Apologetics*. 2nd ed. Grand Rapids, MI: Baker, 2013.

———. "A Critical Review of *The Empty Tomb: Jesus beyond the Grave* (2005)." https://normangeisler.com/a-critical-review-of-the-empty-tomb/.

———. "Miraculous Bible Prophecy Fulfillments." *Philosophical11* (blog), Sep 12, 2012. https://philosophical11.wordpress.com/2012/09/12/miraculous-bible-prophecy-fulfillments/#more-151.

———. *A Popular Survey of the New Testament*. Grand Rapids, MI: Baker, 2014.

———. "Updating the Manuscript Evidence for the New Testament." 2013. URL no longer available.

Geisler, Norman L., and Frank Turek. *I Don't Have Enough Faith to Be an Atheist*. Wheaton, IL: Crossway, 2004.

Geisler, Norman L., and Paul D. Feinberg. *Introduction to Philosophy: A Christian Perspective*. Grand Rapids, MI: Baker, 1997.

Geisler, Norman L., and Peter Bocchino. *Unshakable Foundations: Contemporary Answers to Crucial Questions about the Christian Faith*. Bloomington, MN: Bethany, 2000.

Geisler, Norman L., and William D. Watkins. *Worlds Apart*. 2nd ed. Grand Rapids, MI: Baker, 1989.

Geivett, R. Douglas, and Gary R. Habermas, eds. *In Defence of Miracles: A Comprehensive Case for God's Action in History*. Leicester: Apollos, 1997.

George, Steve, and Ashley Strickland. "Interstellar Object May Have Been Alien Probe, Harvard Paper Argues, but Experts Are Skeptical." CNN, Nov 6, 2018. https://edition.cnn.com/2018/11/06/health/oumuamua-alien-probe-harvard-intl/index.html?utm_term=image&utm_content=2018-11-06T11%3A26%3A04&utm_medium=social&utm_source=twCNN.

Gibson, Shimon. "The Excavations at the Bethesda Pool in Jerusalem: Preliminary Report on a Project of Stratigraphic and Structural Analysis: Illustrations." https://www.academia.edu/22895235/The_Excavations_at_the_Bethesda_Pool_in_Jerusalem_Preliminary_Report_on_a_Project_of_Stratigraphic_and_Structural_Analysis_Illustrations.

Gilgoff, Dan, and Tricia Escobedo. "Scientology: What Exactly Is It?" CNN, Apr 19, 2017. https://edition.cnn.com/2017/03/22/us/believer-what-is-scientology/index.html.

Gill's Exposition of the Entire Bible. "Luke 24:33." Bible Hub. https://biblehub.com/commentaries/luke/24-33.htm.

Gilson, Tom, and Carson Weitnauer, eds. *True Reason: Confronting the Irrationality of the New Atheism*. Grand Rapids, MI: Kregel, 2013.

Glass, David H. *Atheism's New Clothes: Exploring and Exposing the Claims of the New Atheists*. Leicester: Apollos, 2012.

Godfrey, Neil. "'New' Date for That St John's Fragment, Rylands Library Papyrus P52." *Vridar* (blog), Mar 8, 2013. https://vridar.org/2013/03/08/new-date-for-that-st-johns-fragment-rylands-library-papyrus-p52/.
Goetz, Stewart, and Charles Taliaferro. *Naturalism*. Grand Rapids, MI: Eerdmans, 2008.
Gonzalez, Guillermo. "When Were the Gospels Written? The Challenge of Dating the Gospel of John." *The Stream*, Apr 1, 2021. https://stream.org/when-were-the-gospels-written-the-challenge-of-dating-the-gospel-of-john/.
———. "Would Extraterrestrial Intelligent Life Spell Doom for Christianity?" Christian Research Institute, Apr 16, 2018. www.equip.org/article/would-extraterrestrial-intelligent-life-spell-doom-for-christianity/.
Gonzalez, Guillermo, and Jay W. Richards. *The Privileged Planet: How Our Place in the Cosmos Is Designed for Discovery*. Washington, DC: Regnery, 2004.
Goode, Erich. "What about Alien Abductions?" *Psychology Today*, May 1, 2012. www.psychologytoday.com/blog/the-paranormal/201205/what-about-alien-abductions.
The Gospel Coalition Australia. "Love: A Surprisingly Underutilised Apologetic." Dec 15, 2016. https://au.thegospelcoalition.org/article/love-a-surprisingly-underutilised-apologetic/.
Gottlieb, Caroline, and Eun Kyung Kim. "Eyewitness in Iconic Photo Opens Up about Martin Luther King Jr. Assassination 50 Years Later." *Today*, Apr 3, 2018. www.today.com/news/eyewitness-martin-luther-king-jr-assassination-lorraine-motel-talks-50-t126354.
Grant, Edward. *A History of Natural Philosophy*. Cambridge: Cambridge University Press, 2007.
Grant, Michael. *Jesus: An Historian's Review of the Gospels*. New York: Charles Scribner, 1977.
Grant, Robert M. *A Historical Introduction to the New Testament*. London: Collins, 1963.
Gray, John. *Straw Gods: Thoughts on Humans and Other Animals*. London: Granta, 2002.
GreekNewTestament.net. https://greeknewtestament.net/.
Green, Joel B. *The Gospel of Luke*. New International Commentary on the New Testament. Grand Rapids, MI: Eerdmans, 1997.
Green, Michael. "Jesus in the New Testament." In *The Truth of God Incarnate*, edited by Michael Green, 17–57. London: Hodder & Stoughton, 1977.
Gribbin, John. *Alone in the Universe: Why Our Planet Is Unique*. Oxford: Wiley, 2011.
Griffith, Roger L., et al. "The Ĝ Infrared Search for Extraterrestrial Civilizations with Large Energy Supplies." *The Astrophysical Journal Supplement Series* 217:25 (Apr 2015). http://iopscience.iop.org/article/10.1088/0067-0049/217/2/25/pdf.
Grimaldi, Claudio. "Detection Probability of Non-Natural Signals in the Galaxy." Search for Extraterrestrial Intelligence. www.claudiogrimaldi.com/seti.html.
Grimaldi, Claudio, and G. W. Marcy. "Area Coverage of Expanding E.T. Signals in the Galaxy: SETI and Drake's N." *Astronomical Society of the Pacific* (Feb 2018). www.researchgate.net/publication/323410411_Area_coverage_of_expanding_ET_signals_in_the_galaxy_SETI_and_Drake%27s_N.
Grindheim, Sigurd. *Christology in the Synoptic Gospels: God or God's Servant?* London: Continuum, 2012.

Groothuis, Douglas. *Truth Decay: Defending Christianity against the Challenges of Postmodernism*. Downers Grove, IL: InterVarsity, 2000.
Grudem, Wayne A. *1 Peter*. Tyndale New Testament Commentaries. Nottingham: IVP Academic, 2009.
Gruneler, Royce Gordon. *New Approaches to Jesus and the Gospels: A Phenomenological Study of Synoptic Christology*. Grand Rapids, MI: Baker, 1982.
Gumbel, Nicky. *Searching Issues*. Eastbourne: Kingsway, 1995.
Guthrie, Donald. *New Testament Introduction*. 4th ed. Downers Grove, IL: IVP Academic, 1990.
Guthrie, Shandon L. *Gods of This World: A Philosophical Discussion and Defense of Christian Demonology*. Eugene, OR: Pickwick, 2018.
Habermas, Gary R. "Dale Allison's Resurrection Skepticism: A Critique." 2008. www.garyhabermas.com/articles/phil_christi/habermas_phil_christi_dale_allisons_res_skept.htm.
———. "Did Jesus Perform Miracles?" In *Jesus under Fire: Modern Scholarship Reinvents the Historical Jesus*, edited by Michael J. Wilkins and J. P. Moreland, 117–40. Grand Rapids, MI: Zondervan, 1995.
———. "The Empty Tomb of Jesus." North American Mission Board, Mar 30, 2016. https://www.namb.net/apologetics/resource/the-empty-tomb-of-jesus/.
———. *The Historical Jesus: Ancient Evidence for the Life of Christ*. Joplin, MO: College Press, 1996.
———. "Minimal Facts on the Resurrection That Even Skeptics Accept." Southern Evangelical Seminary and Bible College, Sep 28, 2016. https://ses.edu/minimal-facts-on-the-resurrection-that-even-skeptics-accept/.
———. *On the Resurrection*. Vol. 1, *Evidences*. Nashville: B&H Academic, 2024.
———. "Recent Perspectives on the Reliability of the Gospels." Christian Research Institute, Jun 11, 2009. https://www.equip.org/articles/recent-perspectives-on-the-reliability-of-the-gospels/.
———. "The Resurrection and Agnosticism." In *Reasons for Faith*, edited by Norman L. Geisler and Chad V. Meister, 281–82. Wheaton, IL: Crossway, 2007.
———. "The Resurrection Appearances of Jesus." In *In Defence of Miracles: A Comprehensive Case for God's Action in History*, edited by R. Douglas Geivett and Gary R. Habermas, 262–75. Leicester: Apollos, 1997.
———. "Resurrection Research from 1975 to the Present: What Are Critical Scholars Saying?" *Journal for the Study of the Historical Jesus* 3:2 (2005) 117–35. https://works.bepress.com/gary_habermas/16/.
———. *Risen Indeed: A Historical Investigation into the Resurrection of Jesus*. Bellingham, WA: Lexham, 2021.
———. *The Risen Jesus and Future Hope*. Lanham, MD: Rowman & Littlefield, 2003.
———. "Tracing Jesus' Resurrection to Its Earliest Eyewitness Accounts." In *God Is Good; God Is Great*, edited by William Lane Craig and Chad Meister, 202–16. Downers Grove, IL: InterVarsity, 2009.
———. *The Historical Jesus: Ancient Evidence for the Life of Christ*. Joplin, MO: College Press, 1996.
———. "My Magnum Opus on the Minimal Facts Argument for the Resurrection of Jesus." www.researchgate.net/project/My-Magnum-Opus-on-the-Minimal-Facts-Argument-for-the-Resurrection-of-Jesus. URL no longer available.

Habermas, Gary R., and Michael L. Licona. *The Case for the Resurrection of Jesus.* Grand Rapids, MI: Kregel, 2004.

Habermas, Gary R., et al., eds. *Did Jesus Rise From the Dead? The Resurrection Debate.* Eugene, OR: Wipf & Stock, 2003.

Habermas, Jürgen. "A Conversation about God and the World." In *Time of Transitions,* 149–69. Cambridge: Polity, 2006.

Haldane, John. "Philosophy, the Restless Heart and the Meaning of Theism." In *The Meaning of Theism,* edited by John Cottingham, 39–58. Oxford: Blackwell, 2007.

Hahn, Scott, and Curtis Mitch. *The Gospel of John. Ignatius Catholic Study Bible.* San Francisco: Ignatius, 2012.

———. *The Letter of St. James, the First and Second Letters of St. Peter and the Letter of St. Jude: Commentary, Notes and Study Questions. Ignatius Catholic Study Bible.* 2nd Catholic ed. San Francisco: Ignatius, 2008.

Hannam, James. *God's Philosophers: How the Medieval World Laid the Foundations of Modern Science.* London: Icon, 2010.

———. "How Christianity Led to the Rise of Modern Science." Christian Research Institute, Jan 17, 2017. www.equip.org/article/christianity-led-rise-modern-science/.

Hannan, Martin. "50% of UK Adults Believe Aliens Exist, Poll Finds." *The National,* Mar 16, 2020. https://www.thenational.scot/news/18306944.50-uk-adults-believe-aliens-exist-poll-finds/.

Hänni, Nora, et al. "Is Dimethylsulfide a Good Biomarker?" EGU General Assembly 2024, Vienna, Austria, April 14–19, 2024. https://meetingorganizer.copernicus.org/EGU24/EGU24-16695.html.

Hansen, Carolyn. "Tactile and True: The Physicality of the Resurrection." In *The Resurrection Fact: Responding to Modern Critics,* edited by John J. Bombaro and Adam S. Francisco, 207–28. Irvine, CA: NRP, 2016.

Haridy, Rich. "From Aliens to Immigration, International Study Finds Most Believe a Conspiracy Theory." *New Atlas,* Nov 30, 2018. https://newatlas.com/conspiracy-theory-belief-study-cambridge/57456/.

Harrison, Peter. *The Bible, Protestantism and the Rise of Natural Science.* Cambridge: Cambridge University Press, 2008.

Harris, Sam. *The End of Faith: Religion, Terror, and the Future of Reason.* New York: Norton, 2004.

Hart, David Bentley. *Atheist Delusions: The Christian Revolution and Its Fashionable Enemies.* New Haven, CT: Yale University Press, 2009.

Hassan, Ihab. "Beyond Postmodernism: Toward an Aesthetic of Trust (2003)." in *Supplanting the Postmodern: An Anthology of Writings on the Arts and Culture of the Early 21st Century,* edited by David Rudrum and Nicholas Stavris, 13–30. London: Bloomsbury Academic, 2015.

Hawking, Stephen. *Brief Answers to the Big Questions.* London: John Murray, 2018.

Hays, Steve, et al. "This Joyful Eastertide: A Critical Review of *The Empty Tomb.*" 2006. https://www.ntslibrary.com/PDF%20Books/A%20Critical%20Review%20of%20the%20EmptyTomb%20-%20Hays.pdf.

Head, Peter M. "Date of P52 [Comment]." *Evangelical Textual Criticism,* Jan 19, 2006. https://evangelicaltextualcriticism.blogspot.com/2006/01/date-of-p52.html#comments.

Hedin, Eric. "Information and Life's Origin—A Retrospective View." *Evolution News*, Jun 21, 2023. https://evolutionnews.org/2023/06/information-and-lifes-origin-a-retrospective-view/.

Heine, Ronald E. "Can the Catena Fragments of Origen's Commentary on John Be Trusted?" *Vigiliae Christianae* 40:2 (1986). https://brill.com/view/journals/vc/40/2/article-p118_2.xml?language=en&ebody=previewpdf-96220.

Henriques, Gregg, et al. "What Is Metamodern Spirituality? A New Vision for Science, Subjectivity, and Religion Is Emerging." *Psychology Today*, Oct 17, 2022. https://www.psychologytoday.com/us/blog/theory-knowledge/202210/what-is-metamodern-spirituality.

Herath, Mahesh. "Science Sensationalism in the Media Damages Trust." *McGill Daily*, Nov 20, 2023. https://www.pressreader.com/canada/the-mcgill-daily/20231120/281560885532268.

Hicks, John Mark. "James Interprets Amos 9:11–12 (Acts 15:13–18)." May 10, 2013. http://johnmarkhicks.com/2013/05/10/james-interprets-amos-911-12-acts-1513-18/

Hill, Charles E. *Who Chose the Books of the New Testament?* Bellingham, WA: Lexham, 2022.

———. *Who Chose the Gospels? Probing the Great Gospel Conspiracy*. Oxford: Oxford University Press, 2010.

Hill, Jonathan. *What Has Christianity Ever Done for Us?* Downers Grove, IL: InterVarsity, 2005.

History with Kayleigh. "Nazca Mummies Are a New ALIEN Species?!" YouTube video, Oct 15, 2023. https://www.youtube.com/watch?v=2YYaq5yrNWY.

Hoffmeier, James K. "Hoffmeier Rejoinder." In *The Exodus: Historicity, Chronology, and Theological Implications*, edited by Mark D. Janzen and Stanley N. Gundry, 129–33. Grand Rapids, MI: Zondervan Academic, 2021.

Hoffmeier, James K., et al., eds. *"Did I Not Bring Israel Out of Egypt?" Biblical, Archaeological, and Egyptological Perspectives on the Exodus Narratives*. Bulletin for Biblical Research Supplement 13. Winona Lake, IN: Eisenbrauns, 2016.

Holden, Joseph M., and Don Stewart. "Were the New Testament Manuscripts Copied Accurately?" Defending Inerrancy, Aug 5, 2019. https://defendinginerrancy.com/were-nt-mss-copied-accurately/.

Holden, Joseph M., and Norman L. Geisler. *The Popular Handbook of Archaeology and the Bible*. Eugene, OR: Harvest, 2013.

Holder, Rodney D. *Big Bang, Big God: A Universe Designed for Life?* Oxford: Lion, 2013.

———. *God, the Multiverse, and Everything*. London: Routledge, 2016.

Holding, James Patrick, ed. "The Authorship of James." In *Trusting the New Testament*. Maitland, FL: Xulon, 2009.

———, ed. "Hallucinations and Expectations." In *Defending the Resurrection*. Maitland, FL: Xulon, 2010.

———. *Shattering the Christ Myth: Did Jesus Not Exist?* Maitland, FL: Xulon, 2008.

Holland, Tom. *Dominion: The Making of the Western Mind*. London: Abacus, 2020.

Holmes, Arthur F. *Contours of a Worldview*. Grand Rapids, MI: Eerdmans, 1983.

Holstein, Joanne. "Sheep Gate." *Becker Bible Studies Library*, May 17, 2015. https://guidedbiblestudies.com/?p=2857.

Horner, David A. "Aut Deus Aut Malus Homo: A Defense of C. S. Lewis' 'Shocking Alternative.'" In *C. S. Lewis as Philosopher: Truth, Goodness and Beauty*, edited by David Baggett et al., 61–76. Downers Grove, IL: IVP Academic, 2008.

Horowitz, Paul, et al. "Targeted and All-Sky Search for Nanosecond Optical Pulses at Harvard-Smithsonian." http://seti.harvard.edu/oseti/oseti.pdf.

Horvat, Marko. "Calculating the Probability of Detecting Radio Signals from Alien Civilizations." https://arxiv.org/pdf/0707.0011.pdf.

Houston, J. *Reported Miracles*. Cambridge: Cambridge University Press, 2007.

Howard, Jeremy Royal, ed. *The Gospels and Acts*. The Holman Apologetics Commentary on the Bible. Nashville: Holman, 2013.

Howard-Snyder, Daniel, and Daniel McKaughan. "Faith." In *The Encyclopedia of Philosophy of Religion*, edited by Stewart Goetz and Charles Taliaferro. Oxford: Wiley-Blackwell, 2020. https://www.academia.edu/35582270/Faith_2020_.

Howells, Kate. "Life on Venus: Your Questions Answered." The Planetary Society, Jul 28, 2023. https://www.planetary.org/articles/life-on-venus-your-questions-answered.

Howe, Timothy. "The Letter of James." YouTube video, Feb 10, 2013. https://youtu.be/nT3FNt4i7w4.

Hoyler, Robert. "The Argument from Desire." *Faith and Philosophy* 5:1 (1988) 61–67. https://www.academia.edu/114806494/The_Argument_from_Desire.

Huff, Wesley. "The Extant Literary Sources for the Life of Jesus Compared with Emperor Tiberius, One of the Best Attested Characters in Antiquity." https://static1.squarespace.com/static/5a21fbb649fc2b2179ec1ac4/t/61f49b2f15d77850c75995d7/1643420465098/Jesus+and+Tiberius.png.

Hughes, Alex. "Kardashev Scale: What Is It and Where Is Earth Listed?" BBC *Science Focus*, May 18, 2022. https://www.sciencefocus.com/future-technology/kardashevs-scale.

Humphreys, Colin. "The Star of Bethlehem." *Science and Christian Belief* 5 (Oct 1995) 83–101. https://www.asa3.org/ASA/topics/Astronomy-Cosmology/S&CB%2010-93Humphreys.html.

Hup. "Everything Everywhere All at Once—The Bagel." YouTube video, Oct 6, 2022. https://www.youtube.com/watch?v=d6ie3PEmAr4.

Impey, Chris. "NASA Report Finds No Evidence That Ufos Are Extraterrestrial." *The Conversation*, Sep 15, 2023. https://theconversation.com/nasa-report-finds-no-evidence-that-ufos-are-extraterrestrial-213528.

Inspiring Philosophy. "The Death of Judas." YouTube video, Sep 27, 2019. https://www.youtube.com/watch?v=2_01suXK8lg.

Irenaeus. *Against Heresies*. Translated by Alexander Roberts and William Rambaut. From *Ante-Nicene Fathers* 1. Edited by Alexander Roberts et al. Buffalo, NY: Christian Literature Publishing, 1885. Revised and edited for New Advent by Kevin Knight. https://www.newadvent.org/fathers/0103.htm.

Israel MyChannel. "All the Gates to Herod's Temple Explained!" YouTube video, Aug 19, 2021. www.youtube.com/watch?v=8JwzqU4UD0Y.

Jackson, Wayne. "Does the Expression 'the Eleven' (Luke 24:33) Constitute an Error?" *Christian Courier*. https://christiancourier.com/articles/does-the-expression-the-eleven-luke-24-33-constitute-an-error.

———. "Jesus' Prophecy and the Destruction of the Temple." *Christian Courier*. https://christiancourier.com/articles/jesus-prophecy-and-the-destruction-of-the-temple.

———. "When Was the Book of Revelation Written?" *Christian Courier*. https://christiancourier.com/articles/when-was-the-book-of-revelation-written.

Jańczuk, Leszek. "Dating the Book of Revelation in Light of Tradition." *Ruch Biblijny i Liturgiczny* 71:1 (2018) 37–52. https://rbl.ptt.net.pl/index.php/RBL/article/download/296/3714/7488.

Joad, C. E. M. *Joad's Opinions*. London: Westhouse, 1945.

Jobes, Karen H. "Who Wrote 1, 2, and 3 John?" *Zondervan Academic Blog*, Oct 2019. https://zondervanacademic.com/blog/who-wrote-1-2-3-john.

Elwell, Luke Timothy. *Brother of Jesus Friend of God: Studies in the Letter of James*. Cambridge: Eerdmans, 2004.

———. *The Real Jesus*. New York: HarperOne, 1997.

Jones, Clay. "The Bibliographical Test Updated." Christian Research Institute, Oct 1 2013. https://www.equip.org/articles/the-bibliographical-test-updated/.

Jones, Michael. "The Origins of Young Earth Creationism." Peaceful Science, Apr 11, 2022. https://peacefulscience.org/prints/origns-yec/.

Jones, Timothy Paul. *Misquoting Truth: A Guide to the Fallacies of Bart Ehrman's Misquoting Jesus*. Downers Grove, IL: InterVarsity, 2007.

Josephus. *Jewish War*. In *The Works of Flavius Josephus*. Translated by William Whiston. Auburn and Buffalo: John E. Beardsley, 1895. https://www.perseus.tufts.edu/hopper/text?doc=J.+BJ+7.1.

Kaiser, Walter C. Jr. *The Messiah in the Old Testament*. Grand Rapids, MI: Zondervan, 1995.

Kamouni, Sara. "Little Green Amen: Does This Painting Prove Aliens Were Present at the Crucifixion of Jesus? Probably Not . . . But That's What UFO Watchers Are Claiming." *The Sun*, Jul 13, 2017. www.thesun.co.uk/news/4014174/does-this-painting-prove-aliens-were-present-at-the-crucifixion-of-jesus-probably-not-but-thats-what-ufo-watchers-are-claiming/.

Karl, Jonathan. *Tired of Winning: Donald Trump and the End of the Grand Old Party*. New York: Dutton, 2023.

Keathley, Kenneth D. "The Confessions of a Disappointed Young-Earther." Peaceful Science, Mar 7, 2013. https://peacefulscience.org/prints/confessions-disappointed-young-earther/.

Keener, Craig S. *Christobiography: Memory, History, and the Reliability of the Gospels*. Grand Rapids, MI: Eerdmans, 2019.

———. *John*. Zondervan Illustrated Bible Backgrounds Commentary. Grand Rapids, MI: Zondervan, 2019. Kindle ed.

———. *The IVP Bible Background Commentary: New Testament*. 2nd ed. Downers Grove, IL: InterVarsity, 2014.

Keller, Timothy. *Galatians for You*. Epsom: Good Book, 2017.

Kelly, Joseph F. *An Introduction to the New Testament for Catholics*. Collegeville, MN: Liturgical, 2006.

Kelly, Terrence J., and Hilary D Regan, eds. *God, Life, Intelligence and the Universe*. Australia: ATF, 2002.

Kennedy, Courtney, and Arnold Lau. "Most Americans Believe in Intelligent Life beyond Earth; Few See UFOs as a Major National Security Threat." Pew Research Center, Jun 30, 2021. https://www.pewresearch.org/short-reads/2021/06/30/most-americans-believe-in-intelligent-life-beyond-earth-few-see-ufos-as-a-major-national-security-threat/.

Kessler, Glenn, et al. *Donald Trump and His Assault on Truth: The President's Falsehoods, Misleading Claims and Flat-Out Lies.* New York: Scribner, 2020.

Kirby, Alex. "The Death of Postmodernism and Beyond (2006)." In *Supplanting the Postmodern: An Anthology of Writings on the Arts and Culture of the Early 21st Century*, edited by David Rudrum and Nicholas Stavris, 49–60. London: Bloomsbury Academic, 2015.

Kitchen, K. A. *On the Reliability of the Old Testament.* Grand Rapids, MI: Eerdmans, 2006.

Klinghoffer, David A., ed. *Debating Darwin's Doubt.* Seattle: Discovery Institute, 2015.

———. *Signature of Controversy: Responses to Critics of Signature in the Cell.* Seattle: Discovery Institute, 2010.

Kneale, Matthew. *An Atheist's History of Belief.* London: Vintage, 2014.

Koberlein, Brian. "Alien Signals We Discover Could Be the Echoes of Dead Worlds." *Forbes*, Apr 12, 2018. www.forbes.com/sites/briankoberlein/2018/04/12/alien-signals-we-discover-could-be-the-echoes-of-dead-worlds/#2e543ed0f3a5.

Koch, Monty. "How Many Monotheists Are There?" *Times Mojo*, Jul 7, 2022. https://www.timesmojo.com/how-many-monotheists-are-there/.

Koepsell, David R. "Drake vs. Fermi: Skepticism and SETI." Center for Inquiry, Apr 12, 2016. https://centerforinquiry.org/blog/drake_vs_fermi_skepticism_and_seti/.

Koester, Helmut. *Ancient Christian Gospels.* Atlanta: Trinity, 1990.

Kohler, Susanna. "Mars's Leaky Atmosphere and Habitability." *Nova*, May 30, 2018. https://aasnova.org/2018/05/30/marss-leaky-atmosphere-and-habitability/.

Komoszewski, J., et al. *Reinventing Jesus: How Contemporary Skeptics Miss the Real Jesus and Mislead Popular Culture.* Grand Rapids, MI: Kregel, 2006.

Koonin, Eugene V. "The Cosmological Model of Eternal Inflation and the Transition from Chance to Biological Evolution in the History of Life." *Biology Direct* 2:15 (2007). https://www.researchgate.net/publication/6296332_The_cosmological_model_of_eternal_inflation_and_the_transition_from_chance_to_biological_evolution_in_the_history_of_life.

Koons, Robert C. "The Incompatibility of Naturalism and Scientific Realism." Dec 22, 1998. www.leaderu.com/offices/koons/docs/natreal.html.

———. "Science and Theism: Concord, not Conflict." https://robkoons.net/uploads/1/3/5/2/135276253/science_and_theism.pdf.

Korff, Karl K. *Spaceships of the Pleiades.* New York: Prometheus, 1996.

Köstenberger, Andreas J. "April 3, AD 33." *First Things*, Apr 3, 2014. www.firstthings.com/web-exclusives/2014/04/april-3-ad-33.

———. "John." In *The Gospels and Acts.* The Holman Apologetics Commentary on the Bible, edited by Jeremy Royal Howard, 499–634. Nashville: Broadman & Holman, 2013.

———. "John 5:2 and the Date of John's Gospel: A Response to Dan Wallace." Biblical Foundations. https://www.biblicalfoundations.org/john-52-and-the-date-of-johns-gospel-a-response-to-dan-wallace/.

———, ed. *Whatever Happened to Truth?* Wheaton, IL: Crossway, 2005.

Köstenberger, Andreas J., et al. *The Final Days of Jesus: The Most Important Week of the Most Important Person Who Ever Lived.* Wheaton, IL: Crossway, 2014.

Köstenberger, Andreas J., et al. *Truth Matters: Confident Faith in a Confusing World.* Nashville: B&H Academic, 2014.

Kramer, Mark, ed. *The Black Book of Communism: Crimes, Terror, Repression*. Cambridge: Harvard University Press, 1999.
Krauss, Lawrence M. *The Physics of Star Trek*. London: Flamingo, 1996.
Kreeft, Peter. "The Argument from Desire." www.peterkreeft.com/topics/desire.htm.
———. *Between Heaven and Hell: A Dialog Somewhere beyond Death with John F. Kennedy, C. S. Lewis and Aldous Huxley*. Downers Grove, IL: InterVarsity, 1982.
———. "Jesus: Considering the Options." Be Thinking, 1988. www.bethinking.org/jesus/jesus-considering-the-options.
———. "Justification by Faith." Catholic Education Resource Center, 2014. www.catholiceducation.org/en/religion-and-philosophy/apologetics/justification-by-faith.html.
Kruger, Michael J. "Did Papias Know the Apostle John?" *Canon Fodder* (blog), Apr 4, 2016. https://www.michaeljkruger.com/did-papias-know-the-apostle-john/.
Kushner, Harold S. *When Bad Things Happen to Good People*. London: Pan, 2002.
Lamb, David. *The Search for Extraterrestrial Intelligence: A Philosophical Investigation*. London: Routledge, 2001.
Lapide, Pinchas. *The Resurrection of Jesus: A Jewish Perspective*. Eugene, OR: Wipf & Stock, 2002.
Larmer, Robert A. *The Legitimacy of Miracle*. Lanham, MD: Lexington, 2014.
Larson, Stan. *Quest for the Gold Plates: Thomas Stuart Ferguson's Archaeological Search for The Book of Mormon*. Salt Lake City: Freethinker, 2004.
Launch Pad Astronomy. "Could Life Exist around Red Dwarf Stars?" YouTube video, Apr 1, 2019. https://www.youtube.com/watch?v=28YZEmkTvew.
Lea, Robert. "Finding Life on Saturn's Moon Enceladus Might Be Easier Than We Thought." Space.com, Dec 20, 2023. https://www.space.com/life-saturn-moon-enceladus-easier-than-expected-ice-plumes.
———. "Life on Venus? Intriguing Molecule Phosphine Spotted in Planet's Clouds Again." Space.com, Jul 7, 2023. https://www.space.com/venus-clouds-phosphine-evidence-debate.
Leirman, Walter. *Cultures of Learning and Education: Complementary Synthesis*. Michigan Ethnic Heritage Center, 2009.
Lewis, C. S. *The Abolition of Man*. London: Fount, 1978.
———. "The Cardinal Difficulty of Naturalism." http://thecslewis-studygroup.org/wp-content/uploads/2014/07/The-Cardinal-Difficulty-of-Naturalism.pdf.
———. *Mere Christianity*. New York: Macmillan, 1943.
———. *Miracles*. 2nd ed. London: Fount, 1998.
———. "On Living in an Atomic Age." In *Present Concerns*, edited by Walter Hooper, 73–80. New York: Harcourt Brace, 1986.
———. *Surprised by Joy*. London: HarperCollins, 1955.
———. "What Are We to Make of Jesus Christ?" In *God in the Dock*. London: Fount, 1979. http://xtianity.com/tfc/NTE103/C%20S%20Lewis%20What%20are%20we%20to%20make%20of%20Jesus%20Christ.pdf.
Licona, Michael R. "DEBATE: Bart Ehrman vs Mike Licona. Are the Gospels Historically Reliable?" YouTube video, Mar 1, 2018. https://www.youtube.com/watch?v=qP7RrCfDkO4.
———. *Paul Meets Muhammad: A Christian-Muslim Debate on the Resurrection*. Grand Rapids, MI: Baker, 2006.

———. *The Resurrection of Jesus: A New Historiographical Approach.* Downers Grove, IL: InterVarsity, 2010.

———. *Why Are There Differences in the Gospels? What We Can Learn from Ancient Biography.* Oxford: Oxford University Press, 2017.

Lipnick, Jonathan. "The Gates of the Sheep and Lion." Israel Institute of Biblical Studies, May 21, 2016. https://blog.israelbiblicalstudies.com/holy-land-studies/where-is-the-gate-of-the-sheep/.

Little, K. Albert. "Fake News? Did the Gospel Writers Get the Facts Right but Their Stories Wrong?" Premier Unbelievable, Oct 30, 2019. https://www.premierunbelievable.com/topics/fake-news-did-the-gospel-writers-get-the-facts-right-but-their-stories-wrong/11654.article.

Loftus, John W. *Why I Became an Atheist: A Former Preacher Rejects Christianity.* New York: Prometheus, 2008.

Loke, Andrew Ter Ern. *The Origin of Divine Christology.* Cambridge: Cambridge University Press, 2017.

———. *Studies on the Origin of Divine and Resurrection Christology.* Eugene, OR: Cascade, 2023.

Luan, Xiao-Hang, et al. "Multibeam Blind Search of Targeted SETI Observations toward 33 Exoplanet Systems with FAST." *arXiv* (2023). DOI: 10.48550/arxiv.2301.10890.

Luskin, Casey. "With New Theory of the Cambrian Explosion, Scientists Reach (Literally) for the Stars." *Evolution News*, May 25, 2018. https://evolutionnews.org/2018/05/with-new-theory-of-the-cambrian-explosion-scientists-reach-literally-for-the-stars/.

Lustig, Michael. *Herod's Temple.* CreateSpace, 2017.

Lutheran World Federation. "Joint Declaration on the Doctrine on Justification." https://www.lutheranworld.org/jddj.

Lyons, Eric. "To Galilee or Jerusalem?" Apologetics Press, May 26, 2004. http://apologeticspress.org/apcontent.aspx?category=6&article=730.

Macdonald, Fiona. "Bad News: 80% of Students Can't Tell the Difference between Real and Fake News." Science Alert, Dec 7, 2016. www.sciencealert.com/bad-news-study-finds-80-of-students-can-t-tell-the-difference-between-real-and-fake-news.

Macdonald, Vernon. *Ancient Aliens Exposed: Debunking UFOS, Ancient Astronauts and Other Unexplained Mysteries.* CreateSpace, 2014. Kindle ed.

Machen, J. Gresham. *The Virgin Birth of Christ.* London: James Clarke, 1958.

Mackie, J. L. *Ethics: Inventing Right and Wrong.* London: Penguin, 1990.

Mack, Katie. "'Goldilocks' Planets Might Not Be So Nice." *Cosmos*, Jan 6, 2017. https://cosmosmagazine.com/space/goldilocks-planets-might-not-be-so-nice.

Maier, Paul L. "The Date of the Nativity and the Chronology of Jesus' Life." In *Chronos, Karios, Christos: Nativity and Chronological Studies Presented to Jack Finegan*, edited by J. Vardaman and E. M. Yamauchi, 113–30. Winona Lake, IN: Eisenbrauns, 1989. https://inchristus.com/wp-content/uploads/2010/12/maier-date-of-the-nativity.pdf.

———. *The Genuine Jesus: Fresh Evidence from History And Archaeology.* 3rd ed. Grand Rapids, MI: Kregel, 2021.

———. "The James Ossuary." *Lutheran Witness*, Jan 2003. https://www.issuesetcarchive.org/articles/bissar95.htm.

Mamer, Karl. "Toronto Aetherius Society: Jesus, Venusians, and Some Bad Astronomy (Part 1)." www.skepticnorth.com/2012/01/toronto-aetherius-society-jesus-venusians-and-some-bad-astronomy-part-1/. URL no longer available.

———. "Toronto Aetherius Society: His Master's Voice, Stuff That Goes Boom, and a Lack of Proof (Part 2)." www.skepticnorth.com/2012/01/toronto-aetherius-society-his-masters-voice-stuff-that-goes-boom-and-a-lack-of-proof-part-2/. URL no longer available.

Mangalwadi, Vishal. *The Book That Made Your World*. Nashville: Thomas Nelson, 2011.

Mann, Adam. "Are We Alone in the Universe?" *MIT Technology Review*, Nov 13, 2023. https://www.technologyreview.com/2023/11/13/1082873/the-biggest-questions-are-we-alone-in-the-universe/.

Manning, Eric. "5 Reasons Why Jesus Wasn't Resurrected by Aliens." Is Jesus Alive?, Jan 19, 2019. https://isjesusalive.com/5-reasons-why-jesus-wasnt-resurrected-by-aliens/.

Ma, Peter Xiangyuan, et al. "A Deep-Learning Search for Technosignatures of 820 Nearby Stars." *arXiv*, Jan 30, 2023. https://arxiv.org/abs/2301.12670.

Mare, W. Harold. *The Archaeology of the Jerusalem Area*. Grand Rapids, MI: Baker, 1988.

Margot, Jean-Luc, et al. "A Search for Technosignatures from 14 Planetary Systems in the Kepler Field with the Green Bank Telescope at 1.15–1.73 GHz." *Astronomical Journal* 155:5 (Apr 25, 2018). http://iopscience.iop.org/article/10.3847/1538-3881/aabb03.

Marks, Robert J. II, et al. *Introduction to Evolutionary Informatics*. World Scientific, 2017.

Marshall, I. Howard. *Acts*. Tyndale New Testament Commentary. Nottingham: IVP Academic, 2008.

Marshall, I. Howard, et al. *Exploring the New Testament: A Guide to the Letters and Revelation*. 2nd ed. Downers Grove, IL: IVP Academic, 2011.

Marshall, Michael. "Panspermia." NewScientist. www.newscientist.com/term/panspermia/#ixzz6dZZRx7g6.

Marston, Paul. "Understanding the Biblical Creation Passages." Lifesway, 2007. www.asa3.org/ASA/topics/Bible-Science/understanding_the_biblical_creation_passages.pdf.

Martin, Francis, and William M. Wright IV. *The Gospel of John*. Catholic Commentary on Sacred Scripture. Grand Rapids, MI: Baker Academic, 2015. Kindle ed.

Martin, Sean. "Aliens Were Present at Crucifixion of Jesus—And Here's the 'Proof.'" *Express*, Jul 14, 2017. www.express.co.uk/news/weird/828178/alien-jesus-christ-crucifixion-ufo.

Masterson, Andrew. "Stop Looking for ET: Modelling Suggests We're Alone in the Universe." *Cosmos*, Jun 20, 2018. https://cosmosmagazine.com/space/stop-looking-for-et-modelling-suggests-we-re-alone-in-the-universe.

Matthews, Robert. "Through the Wormhole." *Focus Magazine*, June 2018.

Mavrodes, George. "Religion and the Queerness of Morality." https://afterall.net/wp-content/uploads/2021/08/religion-and-the-queerness-of-morality.pdf.

May, Andrew. *Astrobiology (Hot Science)*. London: Icon, 2019.

May, Peter. *The Search for God and the Path to Persuasion*. Glasgow: Malcolm Down, 2016.

McDowell, Josh, and Sean McDowell. *Evidence That Demands a Verdict*. Nashville: Thomas Nelson, 2017.
McGowan, John. "They Might Have Been Giants (2007)." In *Supplanting the Postmodern: An Anthology of Writings on the Arts and Culture of the Early 21st Century*, edited by David Rudrum and Nicholas Stavris, 61–74. London: Bloomsbury Academic, 2015.
McGrath, Alister E. *Jesus: Who He Is and Why He Matters*. Leicester: InterVarsity, 1994.
———. *Mere Discipleship: On Growing in Wisdom and Hope*. London: SPCK, 2018.
———. *NIV Bible Handbook*. London: Hodder & Stoughton, 2014.
———. *The Passionate Intellect: Christian Faith and the Discipleship of the Mind*. Downers Grove, IL: InterVarsity, 2010.
———. *The Twilight of Atheism: The Rise and Fall of Disbelief in the Modern World*. London: Rider, 2004.
McGrew, Lydia. "Arguments from Silence: The Good, the Bad, and the Ugly." YouTube video, Apr 3, 2022. https://www.youtube.com/watch?v=W0VWCdw4epk.
———. *The Eye of the Beholder: The Gospel of John as Historical Reportage*. Tampa, FL: DeWard, 2021.
———. *Hidden in Plain View: Undesigned Coincidences in the Gospels and Acts*. Tampa, FL: DeWard, 2017.
———. "Licona Wrap-Up." *What's Wrong with the World*, Dec 15, 2017. http://whatswrongwiththeworld.net/2017/12/licona_wrapup.html.
———. "On the Minimal Facts Case for the Resurrection." *Extra Thoughts* (blog), Nov 22, 2021. https://lydiaswebpage.blogspot.com/2021/11/on-minimal-facts-case-for-resurrection.html.
———. *Testimonies to the Truth: Why You Can Trust the Gospels*. Tampa, FL: DeWard, 2023.
McGrew, Timothy. "The Argument from Silence." https://timothymcgrew.com/wp-content/uploads/2024/01/The-Argument-from-Silence-Acta-Analytica-Tim-2013.pdf.
———. "Arguments from Providence and Miracles: The State of the Art and the Uses of History." In *Two Dozen (Or So) Arguments for God: The Plantinga Project*, edited by Jerry L. Walls and Trent Dougherty, 341–55. Oxford: Oxford University Press, 2018.
McIntyre, Sarah R. N., et al. "Planetary Magnetism as a Parameter in Exoplanet Habitability." *Monthly Notices of the Royal Astronomical Society* 485:3 (May 2019) 3999–4012. https://doi.org/10.1093/mnras/stz667.
McKnight, Scot. "Jesus of Nazareth." In *The Face of New Testament Studies: A Survey of Recent Research*, edited by Scot McKnight and Grant R. Osborne, 161. Grand Rapids, MI: Baker Academic, 2004.
McLatchie, Jonathan. "The Nativity Defended." CrossExamined.org, Jun 21, 2012. http://crossexamined.org/the-nativity-defended/.
Mcnichol, Jesse C., and Richard Gordon. "Are We from Outer Space? A Critical Review of the Panspermia Hypothesis." *Genesis: In the Beginning* 22 (2012) 591–619. www.ncbi.nlm.nih.gov/pmc/articles/PMC7121572/.
McRay, John. *Archaeology and the New Testament*. Grand Rapids, MI: Revel, 1991.
Meier, John P. *A Marginal Jew: Rethinking the Historical Jesus*. New York: Doubleday, 1991.

Meister, Chad V. *Building Belief: Constructing Faith from the Ground Up*. Eugene, OR: Wipf & Stock, 2009.

———. *Evil: A Guide for the Perplexed*. 2nd ed. New York: Bloomsbury, 2018.

Meister, Chad, and James K. Drew Jr., eds. *God and Evil: The Case for God in a World Filled with Pain*. Downers Grove, IL: InterVarsity, 2013.

Melosh, H. J. "Exchange of Meteorites (and Life?) between Stellar Systems." *Astrobiology* 3:1 (Spring 2003) 207–15. https://pubmed.ncbi.nlm.nih.gov/12804373/.

Menuge, Angus. *Agents under Fire: Materialism and the Rationality of Science*. Lanham, MD: Rowman & Littlefield, 2004.

———. "Dennett Denied: A Critique of Dennett's Evolutionary Account of Intentionality." Oct 2003. static1.1.sqspcdn.com/static/f/38692/239704/1263390969587/A+Critique+of+Dennetts+Evolutionary+Account+of+Intentionality.pdf.

———. "Justified Belief in the Resurrection." In *The Resurrection Fact: Responding to Modern Critics*, edited by John J. Bombaro and Adam S. Francisco, 117–46. Irvine, CA: NRP, 2016.

———. "Libertarian Free Will and the Argument from Reason." www.reasonsforgod.org/wp-content/uploads/2012/09/Libertarian-Free-Will-and-The-Argument-From-Reason1.pdf.

———. "The Role of Agency in Science." Discovery Institute, Feb 3, 2008. https://www.discovery.org/a/10771/.

Meyer, Stephen C. *Darwin's Doubt: The Explosive Origin of Animal Life and the Case for Intelligent Design*. Boulder, CO: Bravo, 2014.

———. "DNA and the Origin of Life: Information, Specification, and Explanation." Discovery Institute, Jun 30, 2007. www.discovery.org/a/2184.

———. *The Return of the God Hypothesis*. New York: HarperCollins, 2021.

———. *Signature in the Cell: DNA and the Evidence for Intelligent Design*. New York: HarperOne, 2010.

Michaels, J. Ramsey. *The Gospel of John*. Grand Rapids, MI: Eerdmans, 2010.

Midgley, Mary. *Are You an Illusion?* Durham, NC: Acumen, 2014.

Miethe, Terry L., and Gary R. Habermas. *Why Believe? God Exists!* Joplin, MO: College Press, 1998.

Millar, Callum. "Places in the Gospels and Archaeology." https://calumsblog.com/apologetics/arguments-for-christianity/places-in-the-gospels-and-archaeology/. URL no longer available.

Millar, Glenn. "Question: Was Jesus of Alien Parentage?" Dec 2005. http://christianthinktank.com/alien2.html.

Miller, John. "Whirling Wheels: A Correlation of Flying Saucers and Visitors from Other Planets in the Bible." www.jasoncolavito.com/whirling-wheels.html.

Miller, Thomas A. *Did Jesus Really Rise from the Dead? A Surgeon-Scientist Examines the Evidence*. Eugene, OR: Wipf & Stock, 2022.

Milne, Bruce. *The Message of John*. Leicester: InterVarsity, 1993.

Milstein, Mati. "'Oldest Church' Discovery 'Ridiculous,' Critics Say." *National Geographic News*, Jun 14, 2008. https://web.archive.org/web/20080614140736/http://news.nationalgeographic.com/news/2008/06/080613-old-church.html.

Mishkin, David. *Jewish Scholarship on the Resurrection of Jesus*. Eugene, OR: Pickwick, 2017.

Montefiore, Hugh. *A Commentary on the Epistle to the Hebrews*. London: Adam & Charles Black, 1977.

———. *The Womb and the Tomb*. London: Fount, 1992.
Monton, Bradley. *Seeking God in Science: An Atheist Defends Intelligent Design*. Toronto, Ont.: Broadview, 2009.
Moo, Douglas J. *James*. Tyndale New Testament Commentaries. Nottingham: IVP Academic, 2009.
Moreland, J. P. *Consciousness and the Existence of God: A Theistic Argument*. London: Routledge, 2009.
———. "Four Degrees of Postmodernism." In *Come Let Us Reason: New Essays in Christian Apologetics*, edited by Paul Copan and William Lane Craig, 17–34. Nashville: B&H, 2012.
———. *The God Question: An Invitation to a Life of Meaning*. Eugene, OR: Harvest, 2009.
———. *Love the Lord with All Your Mind: The Role of Reason in the Life of the Soul*. Colorado Springs: NavPress, 1997.
———. "Postmodernism and Truth." In *Reasons for Faith: Making a Case for the Christian Faith*, edited by Norman L. Geisler and Chad V. Meister, 113–26. Wheaton, IL: Crossway, 2007.
———. *The Recalcitrant Imago Dei*. London: SCM, 2009.
———. *Scaling the Secular City*. Grand Rapids, MI: Baker, 1987.
———. *Scientism and Secularism: Learning to Respond to a Dangerous Ideology*. Wheaton, IL: Crossway, 2018.
———. "Why I Have Made Jesus Christ Lord of My Life." In *Why I Am a Christian: Leading Thinkers Explain Why They Believe*, edited by Norman L. Geisler and Paul K. Hoffman, 290–301. 2nd ed. Grand Rapids, MI: Baker, 2006.
Moreland, J. P., and Brandon Rickabaugh. *The Substance of Consciousness*. London: Wiley Blackwell, 2023.
Moreland, J. P., and William Lane Craig. *Philosophical Foundations for a Christian Worldview*. 2nd ed. Downers Grove, IL: IVP Academic, 2017.
Morley, Brian K. *Mapping Apologetics: Comparing Contemporary Approaches*. Downers Grove, IL: IVP Academic, 2015.
Morris, Leon. *Revelation*. Tyndale New Testament Commentaries. Rev. ed. Leicester: InterVarsity, 1992.
Morris, Thomas V. *Our Idea of God: An Introduction to Philosophical Theology*. Downers Grove, IL: InterVarsity, 1991.
Morrow, Jonathan. *Questioning the Bible: 11 Major Challenges to the Bible's Authority*. Chicago: Moody, 2014.
Mortillaro, Nicole. "Could Life Have Started on Mars before Coming to Earth? Possibly, New Study Suggests." CBC, Aug 26, 2020. www.cbc.ca/news/technology/mars-panspermia-1.5699671.
Motyer, Alec. *The Message of James*. Leicester: InterVarsity, 2003.
Mounce, William D. *Why I Trust the Bible: Answers to Real Questions and Doubts People Have about the Bible*. Grand Rapids, MI: Zondervan Reflective, 2021.
Moxnes, Halvor. *A Short History of the New Testament*. London: I.B. Tauris, 2014.
Nagel, Thomas. "Dawkins and Atheism." In *Secular Philosophy and the Religious Temperament*, 19–26. Oxford: Oxford University Press, 2010.
———. *Mind and Cosmos*. Oxford: Oxford University Press, 2012.
NASA. "Are We Alone?" https://exoplanets.nasa.gov/search-for-life/are-we-alone/.

———. "Exoplanet Exploration: Planets beyond Our Solar System." https://exoplanets.nasa.gov/.

———. "K2–18 b." https://exoplanets.nasa.gov/exoplanet-catalog/4847/k2-18-b/.

———. "NASA Finds Ancient Organic Material, Mysterious Methane on Mars." Jun 7, 2018. www.nasa.gov/press-release/nasa-finds-ancient-organic-material-mysterious-methane-on-mars.

———. "Space Physics: Wormholes, Time Travel, and Faster-Than-Speed-of-Light Theories." https://cosmicopia.gsfc.nasa.gov/qa_sp_sl.html.

NASA Hubble Mission Team. "NASA's Hubble Finds Water Vapor on Habitable-Zone Exoplanet for 1st Time." NASA, Sep 11, 2019. https://science.nasa.gov/missions/hubble/nasas-hubble-finds-water-vapor-on-habitable-zone-exoplanet-for-1st-time/.

NASA Webb Telescope Team. "Webb Discovers Methane, Carbon Dioxide in Atmosphere of K2-18 b." NASA, Sep 11, 2023. https://www.nasa.gov/universe/exoplanets/webb-discovers-methane-carbon-dioxide-in-atmosphere-of-k2-18-b/.

National Geographic Partners. "Unsealing of Christ's Reputed Tomb Turns Up New Revelations." *Orthodox Christianity*, Oct 31, 2016. https://orthochristian.com/98227.html.

NBC News. "Interstellar Reality Check: Could Our Galaxy Host a Wormhole?" Jan 21, 2015. https://www.nbcnews.com/science/weird-science/interstellar-reality-check-could-our-galaxy-host-wormhole-n290861.

Neufeld, Thomas R. Yoder. *Recovering Jesus*. London: SPCK, 2007.

Newman, Robert C. "Miracles and the Historicity of the Easter Week Narratives." In *Evidence for Faith: Deciding the God Question*, edited by John Warwick Montgomery, 409–452. 2nd ed. Irvine, CA: NRP Books, 2015.

Nicholl, Colin R. *The Great Christ Comet: Revealing the True Star of Bethlehem*. Wheaton, IL: Crossway, 2015.

Nickell, Joe. "Abductions or Hoaxes? The Man Who Attracts Aliens." *Skeptical Inquirer* 34:2 (May/Jun 2010) 19–20. https://skepticalinquirer.org/2010/05/abductions-or-hoaxes-the-man-who-attracts-aliens/.

———. "Navy Pilot's 2004 UFO: A Comedy of Errors." *Skeptical Inquirer* 42:3 (May/Jun 2018) 16–18. http://skepdigest.awardspace.us/Navy_Pilots_2004_UFO.pdf.

Nietzsche, Friedrich. "The Parable of the Madman." *The Gay Science*, 1882. http://nietzsche.holtof.com/reader/friedrich-nietzsche/the-gay-science/aphorism-125-quote_e4828eb63.html.

NIV Thompson Student Bible. Indianapolis: Kirkbride Bible Company, 1999.

Nongbri, Brent. "Brent Nongbri on P52." *rtPanel*, Aug 23, 2005. http://hypotyposeis.org/weblog/2005/08/brent-nongbri-on-p52.html.

———. "The Use and Abuse of P52: Papyrological Pitfalls in the Dating of the Fourth Gospel." www.academia.edu/436092/The_Use_and_Abuse_of_P52_Papyrological_Pitfalls_in_the_Dating_of_the_Fourth_Gospel.

Norton, Andrew. "Ross 128 Mystery Signals Aren't from Aliens. But What Would Happen If They Were?" *Newsweek*, Jul 18, 2017. www.newsweek.com/ross-128-mystery-signals-aliens-what-happens-638172.

Oberhaus, Daniel. "A Brief History of Scientists Searching for Extraterrestrial Life." *Vice*, Dec 4, 2015. www.vice.com/en_us/article/jmaawd/a-brief-history-of-scientists-searching-for-extraterrestrial-life-124.

O'Connell, Cathal. "Alien Megastructure 'Discovery': A Review of the Facts." *Cosmos*, Aug 31, 2016. https://cosmosmagazine.com/space/alien-megastructure-discovery-a-review-of-the-facts.

O'Connell, Jake H. *Jesus' Resurrection and Apparitions: A Bayesian Analysis*. Eugene, OR: Resource, 2017.

———. "Jesus' Resurrection and Collective Hallucinations." *Tyndale Bulletin* 60:1 (2009) 69–105. https://www.tyndalebulletin.org/article/29267-jesus-resurrection-and-collective-hallucinations.pdf.

Ogasa, Nikk. "The Last Vital Ingredient for Life Has Been Discovered on Enceladus." *Science News*, Dec 16, 2022. https://www.sciencenews.org/article/enceladus-phosphorus-life-building-block-saturn-moon.

O'Hear, Anthony. *After Progress: Finding the Old Way Forward*. London: Bloomsbury, 1999.

———. *Jesus for Beginners*. London: Icon, 1993.

———. *Philosophy in the New Century*. London: Continuum, 2001.

Omohundro, John T. "Von Däniken's Chariots: A Primer in the Art of Cooked Science." *Skeptical Inquirer* 1:1 (Fall/Winter 1976) 59–68. https://skepticalinquirer.org/1976/10/von-danikens-chariots-a-primer-in-the-art-of-cooked-science/.

Ortlund, Gavin. "Did Augustine Read Genesis 1 Literally?" Carl F. H. Henry Center for Theological Understanding, Sep 4, 2017. http://henrycenter.tiu.edu/2017/09/did-augustine-read-genesis-1-literally/.

Osborne, Margaret. "Whistleblower Alleges U.S. Government Is Covering Up Alien Life at UFO Hearing." *Smithsonian*, Jul 7, 2023. https://www.smithsonianmag.com/smart-news/whistleblower-alleges-us-government-is-covering-up-alien-life-at-UFO-hearing-180982614/.

Osborn, Peter. *The Assault on Truth: Boris Johnson, Donald Trump and the Emergence of a New Moral Barbarism*. London: Simon & Schuster, 2021.

Overman, Dean L. *A Case for the Divinity of Jesus: Examining the Earliest Evidence*. New York: Rowman & Littlefield, 2009.

Parker, Christopher H., et al. "The Pyrophilic Primate Hypothesis." *Evolutionary Anthropology Issues News and Reviews* 25:2 (Mar 2016) 54–63. https://www.researchgate.net/publication/301252297_The_pyrophilic_primate_hypothesis.

Paroschi, Wilson. "Archaeology and the Interpretation of John's Gospel: A Review Essay." *Journal of the Adventist Theological Society* 20:1–2 (2009) 67–88. https://digitalcommons.andrews.edu/cgi/viewcontent.cgi?article=1132&context=jats.

Patterson, Paige. "James, the Letter." In *Holman Bible Dictionary*, edited by Trent C. Butler. Nashville: Broadman & Holman, 1991. https://www.studylight.org/dictionaries/hbd/j/james-the-letter.html.

Patzia, Arthur G. *The Making of the New Testament: Origin, Collection, Text and Canon*. 2nd ed. Downers Grove, IL: IVP Academic, 2011.

Pearcey, Nancy. *Saving Leonardo*. Nashville: B&H, 2010.

Pemberton, Barbara B. "Are We Really All Hindus Now?" In *Come Let Us Reason: New Essays in Christian Apologetics*, edited by Paul Copan and William Lane Craig, 289–304. Nashville: B&H, 2012.

Pequeño, Antonio IV. "Aliens in Mexico? Not So Fast—Presenters Have History of Being Debunked." *Forbes*, Sep 13, 2023. https://www.forbes.com/sites/antoniopequenoiv/2023/09/13/aliens-in-mexico-not-so-fast-presenters-have-history-of-being-debunked/.

Perina, Kaja. "Alien Abductions: The Real Deal?" *Psychology Today*, Mar 2003. www.psychologytoday.com/articles/200303/alien-abductions-the-real-deal.

Perspectiva. "What Is Metamodernism and Why Does It Matter?" YouTube video, Jun 24, 2022. www.youtube.com/watch?v=qM_71pPO3A0.

Pester, Patrick. "What's the Best Evidence We've Found for Alien Life?" LiveScience, Oct 28, 2023. https://www.livescience.com/space/extraterrestrial-life/whats-the-best-evidence-weve-found-for-alien-life.

The Physics arXiv Blog. "AI Hunt for Extraterrestrial Intelligence Finds 8 Promising Signals." *Discover Magazine*, May 8, 2023. https://www.discovermagazine.com/the-sciences/ai-hunt-for-extraterrestrial-intelligence-finds-8-promising-signals.

Pinker, Steven. *How the Mind Works*. New York: Norton, 1997.

Pinnock, Clark H., ed. *The Grace of God and the Will of Man*. Bloomington, MN: Bethany, 1989.

Pinnock, Clark, and Robert C. Brow. *Unbounded Love*. Downers Grove, IL: InterVarsity, 1994.

Plantinga, Alvin. "Against Materialism." https://andrewmbailey.com/ap/Against_Materialism.pdf.

———. "Augustinian Christian Philosophy." *The Monist* (1992) 296–320. https://andrewmbailey.com/ap/Augustinian_Christian_Philosophy.pdf.

———. "Content and Natural Selection." *Philosophy and Phenomenological Research* 83:2 (Sep 2011) 438–58. https://andrewmbailey.com/ap/Content_Natural_Selection.pdf.

———. "An Evolutionary Argument against Naturalism." Jan 2010. https://www.researchgate.net/publication/227992849_An_Evolutionary_Argument_Against_Naturalism.

———. "Two Dozen (Or So) Theistic Arguments." 206–27. https://appearedtoblogly.files.wordpress.com/2011/05/plantinga-alvin-22two-dozen-or-so-theistic-arguments221.pdf.

———. *Warranted Christian Belief*. Oxford: Oxford University Press, 2000.

———. *Where the Conflict Really Lies: Science, Religion, and Naturalism*. Oxford: Oxford University Press, 2011.

Polkinghorne, John. *Encountering Scripture*. London: SPCK, 2010.

Porter, Stanley E. *How We Got the New Testament: Text, Transmission, Translation*. Grand Rapids, MI: Baker Academic, 2013.

———. "Recent Efforts to Reconstruct Early Christianity on the Basis of Its Papyrological Evidence." In *Early Christianity in Its Hellenistic Context*. Vol. 1, *Christian Origins and Greco-Roman Culture: Social and Literary Contexts for the New Testament*, edited by Stanley E. Porter and Andrew Pitts, 71–84. Leiden: Brill, 2013.

Potter, Doug. "A Revised Approach to Defending New Testament Textual Reliability." 2023. https://www.academia.edu/99525454/A_Revised_Approach_to_Defending_New_Testament_Textual_Reliability?email_work_card=view-paper.

Powell, Mark Allan. *Introducing the New Testament*. Grand Rapids, MI: Baker Academic, 2009.

Powers, Daniel G. *1 and 2 Peter, Jude: A Commentary in the Wesleyan Tradition*. New Beacon Commentary. Kansas City: Beacon Hill, 2010.

Premier Unbelievable? "Is the Death of Judas Iscariot a Bible Contradiction? Bart Ehrman vs Peter J. Williams." YouTube video, Nov 11, 2019. https://www.youtube.com/watch?v=6JTXgYw8_fE.

———. "Peter J Williams vs Bart Ehrman. The Story of Jesus: Are the Gospels Historically Reliable?" YouTube video, Oct 25, 2019. https://www.youtube.com/watch?app=desktop&v=ZuZPPGvF_2I.

Puckett, Joe, Jr. *The Apologetics of Joy: A Case for the Existence of God from C. S. Lewis's Argument from Desire*. London: James Clarke, 2013.

Pultarova, Tereza. "No Hope for Life in Venus Clouds." Live Science, Jun 30, 2021. https://www.livescience.com/venus-clouds-life-not-enough-water.html.

Quarles, Charles L. *Midrash Criticism: Introduction and Appraisal*. Lanham, MD: University Press of America, 1998.

Qureshi, Nabeel. *No God but One: Allah or Jesus? A Former Muslim Investigates the Evidence for Islam and Christianity*. Grand Rapids, MI: Zondervan, 2016.

Ramberg, Bjørn, and Susan Dieleman. "Richard Rorty." *Stanford Encyclopedia of Philosophy*, last updated June 2023. https://plato.stanford.edu/entries/rorty/.

Rapske, Brian Mark. "Exiles, Islands, and the Identity and Perspective of John in Revelation." In *Early Christianity in Its Hellenistic Context*. Vol. 1, *Christian Origins and Greco-Roman Culture: Social and Literary Contexts for the New Testament*, edited by Stanley E. Porter and Andrew Pitts, 311–46. Leiden: Brill, 2013.

Rasmussen, Joshua, and Kevin Vallier, eds. *A New Theist Response to the New Atheism*. London: Routledge, 2021.

Ratzsch, Del. *Science and Its Limits: The Natural Sciences in Christian Perspective*. Leicester: Apollos, 2000.

Rea, Michael, ed. *Evil and the Hiddenness of God*. Boston: Cengage, 2015.

Redford, John. *Born of a Virgin: Proving the Miracle from the Gospels*. London: St Pauls, 2007.

Regis, Ed. "Interstellar Travel as Delusional Fantasy [Excerpt]." *Scientific American*, Oct 3, 2015. www.scientificamerican.com/article/interstellar-travel-as-delusional-fantasy-excerpt/.

Reppert, Victor. "The Argument from Reason." In *The Blackwell Companion to Natural Theology*, edited by William Lane Craig and J. P. Moreland, 344–90. Oxford: Blackwell, 2009. https://appearedtoblogly.wordpress.com/wp-content/uploads/2011/05/the-argument-from-reason.pdf.

———. *C. S. Lewis's Dangerous Idea*. Downers Grove, IL: InterVarsity, 2003.

Reznick, Leibel. "Secret Chambers of the Temple Mount." *Jewish Action*, Spring 1997. https://jewishaction.com/jewish-world/israel/secret-chambers-temple-mount/.

Richards, Jay Wesley. "Divine Simplicity: The Good, the Bad, and the Ugly." In *For Faith and Clarity: Philosophical Contributions to Christian Theology*, edited by James K. Beilby, 157–78. Grand Rapids, MI: Baker Academic, 2006.

Ridpath, Ian. "Flying Saucers Thirty Years On." *New Scientist* (Jul 14, 1977) 79.

Ritmeyer, Leen. "Locating the Original Temple Mount." In *Secrets of Jerusalem's Temple Mount*, by Leen Ritmeyer and Kathleen Ritmeyer, 85. Washington, DC: Biblical Archaeological Society, 1998.

———. *The Quest: Revealing The Temple Mount In Jerusalem*. Jerusalem: Carta/Lamb Foundation, 2015.

Ritmeyer, Kathleen, and Leen Ritmeyer. "Reconstructing Herod's Temple Mount in Jerusalem." *Biblical Archaeological Review* 15:6 (1989). https://www.baslibrary.org/biblical-archaeology-review/15/6/1.

Ritmeyer, Leen, and Kathleen Ritmeyer. *Jerusalem: The Temple Mount*. Jerusalem: Carta, 2015.

———. *Secrets of Jerusalem's Temple Mount*. Washington, DC: Biblical Archaeological Society, 1998.

Roberts, Alexander, et al. *Translations of the Writings of the Fathers down to A.D. 325*. Ante-Nicene Fathers 3. Oak Harbor: Logos, 1997.

Roberts, Alexander, et al., eds. "On the Apostles and Disciples." Translated by J. H. MacMahon. *Ante-Nicene Fathers* 5. Buffalo, NY: Christian Literature, 1886. Rev. and ed. by Kevin Knight for *New Advent*. https://www.newadvent.org/fathers/0524.htm.

Roberts, Mark D. *Can We Trust the Gospels?* Wheaton, IL: Crossway, 2007.

Robinson, J. A. T. *Redating the New Testament*. London: SCM, 1976.

Rojas, Alejandro. "New Survey Shows Nearly Half of Americans Believe in Aliens." *Huffington Post*, Aug 2, 2017. www.huffingtonpost.com/entry/new-survey-shows-nearly-half-of-americans-believe-in_us_59824c11e4b03d0624b0abe4.

Romano, Aja. "The True Story of the Fake Unboxed Aliens Is Wilder Than Actual Aliens." *Vox*, Sep 16, 2023. https://www.vox.com/culture/23875671/aliens-mexican-congress-real-or-hoax-peru-nazca-mummies-jaime-maussan-fraud-scam.

Rorty, Richard. *Philosophy and the Mirror of Nature*. Princeton, NJ: Princeton University Press, 1979.

———. "Untruth and Consequences: A Review of *Killing Time* by Paul Feyerabend." *New Republic* (Jul 31, 1995) 32–36.

Rosenberg, Alex. *The Atheist's Guide to Reality*. New York: Norton, 2013.

Rosenblatt, Helena. "The Christian Enlightenment." In *Enlightenment, Reawakening and Revolution 1660–1815*, edited by Stewart J. Brown and Timothy Tackett. Cambridge University Press, 2006. https://www.cambridge.org/core/books/abs/cambridge-history-of-christianity/christian-enlightenment/DF98D7464B68A39FFF2AB2027DE0F4E5#.

Rosenfeld, Amnon, et al. "The Authenticity of the James Ossuary." *Open Journal of Geology* 4:3 (2014) 69–78.

Ross, Hugh. "Have Astronomers Found Life on Planet K2-18b?" Reasons to Believe, Oct 23, 2023. https://reasons.org/explore/blogs/todays-new-reason-to-believe/have-astronomers-found-life-on-planet-k2-18b.

———. "More Evidence That Planets Orbiting M Dwarf Stars Are Uninhabitable." Reasons to Believe, Nov 20, 2023. https://reasons.org/explore/blogs/todays-new-reason-to-believe/more-evidence-that-planets-orbiting-m-dwarf-stars-are-uninhabitable.

———. "Waterworld Planets Are Acidic, Primordial Earth Was Not." Reasons to Believe, May 14, 2018. https://reasons.org/explore/blogs/todays-new-reason-to-believe/waterworld-planets-are-acidic-primordial-earth-was-not.

Ross, Hugh, and Fazale Rana. *Origins of Life*. Colorado Springs: NavPress, 2004.

Rucker, Philip, and Carol Leonnig. *A Very Stable Genius: Donald J. Trump's Testing of America*. New York: Bloomsbury, 2020.

Rudd, Steve. "Jerusalem Temple Mount: The Charles Wilson and Charles Warren Map Collection with Notes." www.bible.ca/archeology/bible-archeology-jerusalem-temple-mount-charles-wilson-charles-warren.htm.

Rudrum, David. "Note on the Supplanting of 'Post-'." In *Supplanting the Postmodern: An Anthology of Writings on the Arts and Culture of the Early 21st Century*, edited by David Rudrum and Nicholas Stavris, 333–48. London: Bloomsbury Academic, 2015.

Rudrum, David, and Nicholas Stavris. "Introduction to Ihab Hassan." In *Supplanting the Postmodern: An Anthology of Writings on the Arts and Culture of the Early 21st Century*, edited by David Rudrum and Nicholas Stavris. London: Bloomsbury Academic, 2015.

———, eds. *Supplanting the Postmodern: An Anthology of Writings on the Arts and Culture of the Early 21st Century*. London: Bloomsbury Academic, 2015.

Ruloff, Colin, and Peter Horban, eds. *Contemporary Arguments in Natural Theology: God and Rational Belief*. London: Bloomsbury Academic, 2021.

Ruse, Michael. *Atheism: What Everyone Needs to Know*. Oxford: Oxford University Press, 2015.

Russell, Bertrand. "A Free Man's Worship." 1903. https://ia601300.us.archive.org/15/items/Russell_Bertrand_-_Collection_1/Russell_Bertrand_-_Collection_1.pdf.

———. *Religion and Science*. Oxford: Oxford University Press, 1947.

Russell, Calum. "Everything Everywhere All at Once and the Beauty of Nihilism." *Far Out*, Feb 19, 2023. https://faroutmagazine.co.uk/everything-everywhere-all-at-once-the-beauty-of-nihilism/.

Rutt, Jim. "Lene Rachel Andersen on Polymodernity." YouTube video, Jan 31, 2024. *Jim Rutt Show*, episode 220. https://youtu.be/00PKt6bANTs?si=yKA-Ytm2Kb267q2R.

Sanders, John. *No Other Name: Can Only Christians Be Saved?* London: SPCK, 1994.

Sartre, Jean-Paul. "Existentialism Is a Humanism." 1946. https://www.marxists.org/reference/archive/sartre/works/exist/sartre.htm.

Scharping, Nathaniel. "70-Year-Old Astronomy Photos May Be Clues to Alien Visitors—Study." Inverse, Feb 20, 2024. https://www.inverse.com/science/alien-craft-in-old-photos.

Schenkel, Peter. "SETI Requires a Skeptical Reappraisal." *Skeptical Inquirer* 30:3 (May/Jun 2006) 26–30. www.csicop.org/si/show/seti_requires_a_skeptical_reappraisal.

Schmidt, Tom. "The Contribution of 1 Thessalonians 3:11–13 to a Pauline Christology." http://ttschmidt.com/wp-content/uploads/2012/11/1-Thess-3-and-Pauline-Christology.pdf.

SciShow Space. "The Fermi Paradox and Our Search for Alien Life." YouTube video, Jul 14, 2015. https://youtu.be/5tJnuVheDoY.

Scott, Douglas D. *Is Jesus of Nazareth the Predicted Messiah?* Eugene, OR: Wipf & Stock, 2019.

Scott, J. C. "Matthew's Intention to Write History." *Westminster Theological Journal* 47:1 (1985) 68–82. https://www.galaxie.com/article/wtj47-1-04.

Scott, Latayne C. *The Mormon Mirage: A Former Member Looks at the Mormon Church Today*. 3rd ed. Grand Rapids, MI: Zondervan, 2009.

Scrivener, Glen. *The Air We Breathe*. Epsom: Good Book, 2022.

Scruton, Roger. *An Intelligent Person's Guide to Culture*. London: Duckworth, 1998.

———. *Modern Philosophy: An Introduction and Survey*. London: A&C Black, 2012.

Sennett, James F., and Douglas Groothuis, eds. *In Defence of Natural Theology: A Post-Humean Assessment*. Downers Grove, IL: IVP Academic, 2005.

SETI Institute. "The Trouble with M Dwarf Stars and the Search for Habitable Worlds." YouTube video, Feb 9, 2023. https://www.youtube.com/watch?v=Wa2JF1f81KA.

———. "Will Machine Learning Help Us Find Extraterrestrial Life?" *Science Daily*, Jan 30, 2023. https://www.sciencedaily.com/releases/2023/01/230130130512.htm.

Shanks, Hershel. "The James Ossuary Is Authentic." *Biblical Archaeological Review* 38:4 (Jul/Aug 2012). http://members.bib-arch.org/publication.asp?PubID=BSBA&Volume=38&Issue=4&ArticleID=2.

Shanks, Hershel, and Ben Witherington III. *The Brother of Jesus: The Dramatic Story and Meaning of the First Archaeological Link to Jesus and His Family*. San Francisco: Continuum, 2003.

Sheaffer, Robert. "An Examination of the Claims That Extraterrestrial Visitors to Earth Are Being Observed." In *Extraterrestrials: Where Are They?*, edited by Ben Zuckerman and Michael H. Hart, 20–28. Cambridge: Cambridge University Press, 2009.

———. *UFO Sightings: The Evidence*. Amherst, NY: Prometheus, 1998.

Shepherd, Tory. "Alien False Alarm: 'Extraterrestrial' Radio Signals Turn Out to Be Human." *The Guardian*, Oct 25, 2021. https://www.theguardian.com/australia-news/2021/oct/26/alien-false-alarm-extraterrestrial-radio-signals-turn-out-to-be-human.

Sheppard, Si. *The Jewish Revolt AD 66–74*. Oxford: Osprey, 2013.

Short, A. Rendle. *Why Believe?* IVF, 1964.

Shorttle, Oliver, et al. "Distinguishing Oceans of Water from Magma on Mini-Neptune K2-18b." Feb 22, 2024. https://arxiv.org/pdf/2401.05864.

Shostak, Seth. "Whatever Happened to UFO Sightings?" *SFGate*, Sep 2, 2015. www.sfgate.com/science/article/UFO-sightings-down-extraterrestrial-intelligence-6481669.php.

Sider, Ronald J. *The Spiritual Danger of Donald Trump: 30 Evangelical Christians on Justice, Truth, and Moral Integrity*. Eugene, OR: Cascade, 2020.

Siegel, Ethan. "The 5 Possibilities for Life on Mars." *Starts with a Bang!*, Aug 11, 2020. https://medium.com/starts-with-a-bang/the-5-possibilities-for-life-on-mars-4fc1d2495c9c.

Siemion, Andrew P. V., et al. "A 1.1 to 1.9 GHz SETI Survey of the Kepler Field." *Astrophysical Journal* 767:1 (2013). www.researchgate.net/publication/235359333_A_11_to_19_GHz_SETI_Survey_of_the_Kepler_Field_I_A_Search_forNarrow-band_Emission_from_Select_Targets.

Simek, Slater. "A Bayesian Exploration of C. S. Lewis's 'Argument from Desire.'" *Sophia* 61 (2022) 757–73. https://link.springer.com/article/10.1007/s11841-021-00887-9.

Sinnott-Armstrong, Walter. *Think Again: How to Reason and Argue*. London: Pelican, 2018.

Sire, James W. *The Universe Next Door*. 5th ed. Downers Grove, IL: InterVarsity, 2002.

———. *The Universe Next Door—A Basic Worldview Catalog*. 6th ed. Downers Grove, IL: IVP Academic, 2020.

Skeptical Inquirer. "What Is Skepticism?" https://skepticalinquirer.org/what-is-skepticism/.

Smith, Barry D. "James." In *Religious Studies 1023: The New Testament and Its Context*. Atlantic Baptist University.

Smith, Christian. *To Flourish or Destruct: A Personalist Theory of Human Goods. Motivations, Failure, and Evil*. Chicago: University of Chicago Press, 2015.

Smith, D. Moody. *First, Second, and Third John*. Interpretation: A Bible Commentary for Teaching and Preaching. Louisville: John Knox, 1991.

Smith, Mark D. *The Final Days of Jesus: The Thrill of Defeat, the Agony of Victory: A Classical Historian Explores Jesus's Arrest, Trial, and Execution*. Cambridge: Lutterworth, 2018.

Smith, Peter. "Highlights from AP-NORC Poll about the Religiously Unaffiliated in the US." AP News, Oct 4, 2023. https://apnews.com/article/religion-ap-poll-nones-survey-111e9f5bbcaaa47ea522f1aae9c24df9.

Sohn, Rebecca. "Enceladus: Everything You Need to Know about Saturn's Bright, Icy Moon." Space.com, May 22, 2023. https://www.space.com/20543-enceladus-saturn-s-tiny-shiny-moon.html.

Sol Company. "G Stars within 100 Light-Years." 2005. www.solstation.com/stars3/100-gs.htm.

Southwest Research Institute. "Scientists Have Modeled Mars Climate to Understand Habitability." *Science Daily*, May 11, 2020. www.sciencedaily.com/releases/2020/05/200511142150.htm.

Spencer, Nick. *Atheists: The Origin of the Species*. London: Bloomsbury, 2014.

Stannard, Russell. *Science and Wonders*. London: Faber and Faber, 1996.

Stanton, Graham. *The Gospels and Jesus*. Oxford: Oxford University Press, 1990.

Stark, Rodney. *The Triumph of Christianity: How the Jesus Movement Became the World's Largest Religion*. New York: HarperOne, 2011.

Stavris, Nicholas. "The Anxieties of the Present." In *Supplanting the Postmodern: An Anthology of Writings on the Arts and Culture of the Early 21st Century*, edited by David Rudrum and Nicholas Stavris, 349–64. London: Bloomsbury Academic, 2015.

Stecher, Carl. "The Historical Evidence Is Insufficient and Contradictory." In *Resurrection: Faith or Fact? A Scholars' Debate between a Skeptic and a Christian*, 51–79. Durham, NC: Pitchstone, 2019.

———. "Miracle Not Required." In *Resurrection: Faith or Fact? A Scholars' Debate between a Skeptic and a Christian*, 265–78. Durham, NC: Pitchstone, 2019.

Stecher, Carl, et al. *Resurrection: Faith or Fact? A Scholars' Debate between a Skeptic and a Christian*. Durham, NC: Pitchstone, 2019.

Steele, Edward J., et al. "Cause of Cambrian Explosion—Terrestrial or Cosmic?" *Progress in Biophysics and Molecular Biology* 136 (Aug 2018) 3–23. www.sciencedirect.com/science/article/pii/S0079610718300798.

Stein, Robert H. "Criteria for the Gospel's Authenticity." In *Contending with Christianity's Critics*, edited by Paul Copan and William Lane Craig, 88–103. Nashville: B&H Academic, 2009.

Stewart, Aubrey, trans. *The Epitome of S. Eucherius about Certain Holy Places (circ. A.D. 440), and the Breviary or Short Description of Jerusalem (circ. A.D. 530)*. Annotated by Charles W. Wilson. Vol 2. London: Palestine Pilgrim's Text Society, 1890. https://babel.hathitrust.org/cgi/pt?id=uva.x004061612&seq=17.

Stewart, Don. "When Were the Four Gospels Written?" Blue Letter Bible. www.blueletterbible.org/Comm/stewart_don/faq/historical-accuracy-of-the-bible/question10-when-were-the-gospels-written.cfm.

Stewart, Don, and Joseph M. Holden. "Were the New Testament Manuscripts Copied Accurately?" In *The Harvest Handbook of Apologetics*, edited by Joseph M. Holden, 191–98. Eugene, OR: Harvest, 2018.

Stewart, Robert B. "On Habermas's Minimal Facts Argument." In *Raised on the Third Day*, edited by W. David Beck and Michael R. Licona, 1–14. Bellingham, WA: Lexham, 2020.

———, ed. *The Reliability of the New Testament: Bart Ehrman and Daniel Wallace in Dialogue*. Minneapolis: Fortress, 2011.

Stirner, Simone. "Notes on the State of the Subject." *Notes on Metamodernism*, Nov 2, 2011. www.metamodernism.com/2011/11/02/notes-on-the-state-of-the-subject/.

Stonehouse, Ned B. *The Witness of the Synoptic Gospels to Christ*. Grand Rapids, MI: Baker, 1979.

Strobel, Lee. *The Case for Miracles*. Grand Rapids, MI: Zondervan, 2018.

StudyLight.org. "James 2:7: Verse-by-Verse Bible Commentary." www.studylight.org/commentary/james/2-7.html.

Swinburne, Richard. *Evidence for God*. London: Christian Evidence Society, 2012. https://christianevidence.org/wp-content/uploads/2012/09/evidence_for_god.pdf.

———. *The Resurrection of God Incarnate*. Oxford: Clarendon, 2003.

———. *Was Jesus God?* Oxford: Oxford University Press, 2010.

Taliaferro, Charles. *Consciousness and the Mind of God*. Cambridge: Cambridge University Press, 1994.

———. *Philosophy of Religion*. Oxford: OneWorld, 2009.

Talking Jesus. *What People in the UK Think of Jesus, Christians and Evangelism*. Talking Jesus report, 2022. https://www.eauk.org/assets/files/downloads/Talking-Jesus-Report.pdf.

Tallis, Raymond. *Aping Mankind: Darwinitis and the Misrepresentation of Humanity*. London: Routledge, 2014.

Tan, Change Laura, and Rob Stadler. *The Stairway to Life: An Origin-of-Life Reality Check*. Evorevo, 2020.

Taylor, Charles. *A Secular Age*. Cambridge, MA: Belknap, 2007.

Taylor, Marisa. "Heart Disease, Depression and Blindness—The Hazards of Deep Space Travel." *The Guardian*, Jul 29, 2016. www.theguardian.com/lifeandstyle/2016/jul/29/space-travel-side-effects-scott-kelly-nasa-mars-astronauts-ross-3-mins.

Tellis, Nathaniel K., and Geoffrey Marcy. "Search for Laser Emission with Megawatt Thresholds from 5600 FGKM Stars." *The Astronomical Journal* 153:6 (2017). https://iopscience.iop.org/article/10.3847/1538-3881/aa6d12/meta.

———. "A Search for Optical Laser Emission Using Keck HIRES." *Publications of the Astronomical Society of the Pacific* (2015) 127.

Tepper, Yotam. *A Christian Prayer Hall of the Third Century CE at Kefar 'Othnay (legio): Excavations at the Megiddo Prison 2005*. Israel Antiquities Authority, 2006.

Thaxton, Charles B., et al. *The Mystery of Life's Origin: The Continuing Controversy*. Seattle: Discovery Institute, 2020.

Thompson, Marianne Meye. *1–3 John*. IVP New Testament Commentary Series. Downers Grove, IL: IVP Academic, 1992.

Thorne, Kip. *The Science of Interstellar*. New York: Norton, 2014.

Tillman, Nola Taylor. "What Are Wormholes?" Space.com, Mar 5, 2024. www.space.com/20881-wormholes.html.

Timmer, John. "Just How Dangerous Is It to Travel at 20% the Speed of Light?" Ars Technica, Aug 23, 2016. https://arstechnica.com/science/2016/08/could-breakthrough-starshots-ships-survive-the-trip/.

Tingley, Brett. "Pentagon Has 'No Credible Evidence' of Aliens or UFOs That Defy Physics." Space.com, Apr 19, 2023. https://www.space.com/pentagon-aaro-ufo-hearing-april-2023.

Tour, James. "An Open Letter to My Colleagues." *Inference: International Review of Science* 3:2 (Aug 2, 2017). http://inference-review.com/article/an-open-letter-to-my-colleagues.

Turley, Stephen. *Awakening Wonder: A Classical Guide to Truth, Goodness and Beauty*. Camp Hill, PA: Classical Academic, 2014.

Turner, Eric. *The Typology of the Early Codex*. Philadelphia: University of Pennsylvania Press, 1977.

Tzaferis, Vassilios. "Inscribed to "God Jesus Christ": Early Christian Prayer Hall Found in Megiddo Prison." *Biblical Archaeology Review* 33.2 (2007).

Vago, Mike. "Greetings from the UFO Zealots Who Say Aliens Created Life on Earth." AV Club, Jun 24, 2018. www.avclub.com/greetings-from-the-ufo-zealots-who-say-aliens-created-l-1826940199.

Vehlow, Katja. "Michael Meerson and Peter Schäfer, eds. and Trans. *Toledot Yeshu: The Life Story of Jesus - Two Volumes and Database*: Vol. I: Introduction and Translation, Vol. II: Critical Edition (Texts and Studies in Ancient Judaism 159)." *SCJR* 11:1 (2016) 1–3. www.researchgate.net/publication/306127688_Michael_Meerson_and_Peter_Schafer_Eds_and_Trans_Toledot_Yeshu_The_Life_Story_of_Jesus/fulltext/57b3128108aeeob132d8d2e2/Michael-Meerson-and-Peter-Schaefer-Eds-and-Trans-Toledot-Yeshu-The-Life-Story-of-Jesus.pdf.

Vermes, Geza. *The Resurrection*. London: Penguin, 2008.

Vermeulen, Timotheus. "Knock Knock." Digital Bauhaus Summit, Jun 18, 2017. https://vimeo.com/222081144.

Vermeulen, Timotheus, and Robin van den Akker. "Notes on Metamodernism." *Journal of Aesthetics and Culture* 2:1 (2010). https://www.tandfonline.com/doi/full/10.3402/jac.v2i0.5677.

Wahlde, Urban C. von. "Archaeology and John's Gospel." In *Jesus and Archaeology*, edited by James H. Charlesworth, 523–86. Grand Rapids, MI: Eerdmans, 2006.

Walker, Andrew. *Seven Atheisms*. Christian Evidence Society, 2019. https://christianevidence.org/booklet/seven_atheisms/.

Wallace, Daniel B. "John 5,2 and the Date of the Fourth Gospel." *Biblica* 71:2 (1990) 177–205.

———. "John 5:2 and the Date of the Fourth Gospel . . . Again." Bible.org, Nov 6, 2006. https://bible.org/article/john-52-and-date-fourth-gospel-again.

———. "John 5.2 One More Time: A Response to Andreas Köstenberger." Bible.org, Jun 15, 2007. https://bible.org/article/john-52-one-more-time-response-andreas-k%C3%B6stenberger.

Wallace, J. Warner. *Cold Case Christianity: A Homicide Detective Investigates the Claims of the Gospels*. Colorado Springs: David Cook, 2013.

———. "How (and Where) Did Judas Really Die?" Cold Case Christianity, Sep 1, 2003. https://coldcasechristianity.com/writings/how-and-where-did-judas-really-die/.

———. "John's Gospel May Have Been Last, but It Wasn't Late." Cold Case Christianity, Mar 13, 2017. https://coldcasechristianity.com/writings/johns-gospel-may-have-been-last-but-it-wasnt-late/.

Wall, Mike. "If We Find Life on Europa or Enceladus, It Will Probably Be a '2nd Genesis.'" Space.com, Dec 17, 2019. https://www.space.com/alien-life-europa-enceladus-second-genesis.html.

———. "'Interstellar' Science: Is Wormhole Travel Possible?" Space.com, Nov 24, 2014. https://www.space.com/27845-interstellar-movie-wormhole-travel-feasibility.html.

———. "Methane in Plume of Saturn's Moon Enceladus Could Be Sign of Alien Life, Study Suggests." Space.com, Jul 7, 2021. https://www.space.com/methane-plume-enceladus-possible-sign-alien-life.

Walls, Jerry L. *Heaven: The Logic of Eternal Joy*. Oxford: Oxford University Press, 2002.

Walls, Jerry L., and Joseph R. Dongell. *Why I Am Not a Calvinist*. Downers Grove, IL: InterVarsity, 2004.

Walls, Jerry L., and Trent Dougherty. *Two Dozen (Or So) Arguments for God: The Plantinga Project*. Oxford: Oxford University Press, 2018.

Waltham, David. *Lucky Planet: Why Earth Is Exceptional—And What That Means for Life in the Universe*. London: Icon, 2015.

Ward, Keith. "Creatio Ex Nihilo." Encyclopedia.com. https://www.encyclopedia.com/education/encyclopedias-almanacs-transcripts-and-maps/creatio-ex-nihilo.

———. *Evidence for the Virgin Birth*. London: Christian Evidence Society, 2012. http://christianevidence.org/docs/booklets/evidence_for_the_virgin_birth.pdf.

———. *God, Chance and Necessity*. Oxford: OneWorld, 1996.

———. *Is Religion Dangerous?* 2nd ed. Oxford: Lion, 2011.

Ward, Peter C., and Donald Brownlee. *Rare Earth: Why Complex Life Is Uncommon in the Universe*. New York: Springer, 2009.

Wasson, Donald L. "Trajan." *World History Encyclopedia*, May 25, 2013. www.worldhistory.org/trajan/.

Wattles, J. "C. S. Lewis, Peter Kreeft, and the Sequence: Truth, Goodness, and Beauty." 2015. *Universal Family*, 2015. https://universalfamily.org/c-s-lewis-peter-kreeft-and-the-sequence-truth-goodness-and-beauty/.

Watts, Geoff. "Is There Life on Other Planets?" In *Big Questions in Science*, edited by Harriet Swain, 200–203. London: Jonathan Cape, 2002.

Waugh, Rob. "Painting 'Proves Aliens Were Present at Christ's Crucifixion.' UFO Fans Claim." *Metro*, Jul 17, 201. https://metro.co.uk/2017/07/17/painting-proves-aliens-were-present-at-christs-crucifixion-ufo-fans-claim-6784461/.

Webb, Stephen. *Where Is Everybody? Fifty Solutions to the Fermi Paradox and the Problem of Extraterrestrial Life*. Göttingen: Copernicus, 2010.

Weikart, Richard. *From Darwin to Hitler: Evolutionary Ethics, Eugenics and Racism in Germany*. London: Palgrave Macmillan, 2004.

———. *Hitler's Ethic: The Nazi Pursuit of Evolutionary Progress*. London: Palgrave Macmillan, 2009.

Wells, H. G. *The War of the Worlds*. London: Penguin, 2005.

Wenham, John. *Easter Enigma: Are the Resurrection Accounts in Conflict?* 2nd ed. London: Paternoster, 1992.

Wenham, John, and Steve Walton. *Exploring the New Testament: A Guide to the Gospels and Acts*. New Testament 1. 3rd ed. London: SPCK, 2021.

Westcott, Ben. "'No One's Out There': We're Likely Alone in the Milky Way, Says Shaw Prize Astronomy Winner as He Visits Hong Kong for Award Ceremony." *South China Morning Post*, Sep 24, 2015. www.scmp.com/news/hong-kong/health-environment/article/1860781/no-ones-out-there-shaw-prize-astronomy-winner-says.

West, Mick. "Some Thoughts on David Grusch—Alien Whistleblower." YouTube video, Jun 11, 2023. https://www.youtube.com/watch?v=AvhMMhW-JN0.
What Is Metamodern? "About the Authors." https://whatismetamodern.com/about-the-authors/.
———. "Talking Metamodernism with Tim Vermeulen." YouTube video, Oct 25, 2021. www.youtube.com/watch?v=IusoCjpdWwg.
White, Chris. "UFO in the Bible? Ezekiel." YouTube video, Dec 14, 2012. https://youtu.be/gm_6dnptTFA.
White, Michael. *The Science of the X Files*. Hong Kong: Legend, 1996.
White, Peter. *The Past Is Human*. Sydney: Angus and Robertson, 1976.
Wikipedia. "Bargate." Last updated April 2, 2024. https://en.wikipedia.org/wiki/Bargate.
———. "Enceladus." Last updated April 11, 2024. https://en.wikipedia.org/wiki/Enceladus.
———. "James, Brother of Jesus." Last updated March 28, 2024. https://en.wikipedia.org/wiki/James,_brother_of_Jesus#cite_note-16/.
———. "James MacKnight." Last updated August 19, 2023. https://en.wikipedia.org/wiki/James_MacKnight.
———. "Middot (Talmud)." Last updated August 6, 2021. https://en.wikipedia.org/wiki/Middot_(Talmud).
———. "Papias of Hierapolis." Last updated April 1, 2024. https://en.wikipedia.org/wiki/Papias_of_Hierapolis.
Wilcock, Michael. *The Message of Revelation*. Leicester: InterVarsity, 2000.
Wilkins, Michael. "Gospel of Matthew." In *The Gospel and Acts*. The Holman Apologetics Commentary on the Bible, edited by Jeremy Royal Howard, 7–198. Nashville: Holman Reference, 2013.
Wilkinson, David. *Science, Religion, and the Search for Extraterrestrial Intelligence*. Oxford: Oxford University Press, 2017.
Willard, Dallas. *Knowing Christ Today*. New York: HarperOne, 2009.
———. "Knowledge and Naturalism." Dallas Willard Ministries. https://dwillard.org/resources/articles/knowledge-and-naturalism.
———. *Renewing the Christian Mind: Essays, Interviews, and Talks*. New York: HarperOne, 2016.
Williams, Donald T. "The Validity of Lewis's Trilemma." In *Reflections from Plato's Cave: Essays in Evangelical Philosophy*. Monroe, VA: Lantern Hollow, 2012.
Williams, Peter J. *Can We Trust the Gospels?* Wheaton, IL: Crossway, 2018.
Williams, Peter S. "Aliens and UFOs." YouTube playlist. www.youtube.com/playlist?list=PLQhh3qcwVEWiixwhvDhbqSoO3qcIK7zu5.
———. "Ancient Aliens? Rebutting Alien Conspiracy Theories as Popular Alternatives to Biblical History: (ELF 2020)." *The Peter S. Williams Podcast*, May 26, 2020. http://podcast.peterswilliams.com/e/elf-2020-ancient-aliens-rebutting-alien-conspiracy-theories-as-popular-alternatives-to-biblical-history/.
———. *Apologetics in 3D: Essays on Apologetics and Spirituality*. Eugene, OR: Wipf & Stock, 2019.
———. "Archaeology, Jesus and the New Testament." *The Peter S. Williams Podcast*, Nov 2, 2014. http://podcast.peterswilliams.com/e/archaeology-jesus-and-the-new-testament-1415879310/?token=000f381bf8ed408be9f0aee7d7860f7b.

———. "The Argument from Desire." YouTube playlist. https://www.youtube.com/playlist?list=PLQhh3qcwVEWj3nK3TBydEVAFRtdqfrpW2.

———. "A Beginner's Guide to the Theist Argument from Desire." https://www.peterswilliams.com/wp-content/uploads/2021/01/Intro_Lewis_Desire_2019.pdf.

———. "Buddhism." YouTube playlist. https://www.youtube.com/playlist?list=PLQhh3qcwVEWif_IZ4RSdtPpT9PZ6p3O7I.

———. "Can Moral Objectivism Do without God?" Be Thinking, 2011. www.bethinking.org/morality/can-moral-objectivism-do-without-god.

———. *The Case for Angels*. Carlisle, Cumbria: Paternoster, 2003.

———. *The Case for God*. Crowborough: Monarch, 1999.

———. "Christianity and Archaeology." YouTube playlist. https://www.youtube.com/playlist?list=PLQhh3qcwVEWjh9aRRWF1kYZIVCPc5iCcw.

———. "Christianity, Space and Aliens." Be Thinking, 2004. www.bethinking.org/human-life/christianity-space-and-aliens.

———. "Christology." YouTube playlist. www.youtube.com/playlist?list=PLQhh3qcwVEWgjXlj2cVn_ZjOE8Wd9dVbv.

———. "Critical Thinking." YouTube playlist. https://www.youtube.com/playlist?list=PLQhh3qcwVEWjunXM096VWNyJgx-XAn8fp.

———. "C. S. Lewis as a Central Figure in Formulating the Theistic Argument from Desire." *Linguaculture* 2 (2019). https://journal.linguaculture.ro/index.php/home/article/view/149/136.

———. *C. S. Lewis vs. the New Atheists*. Milton Keynes: Paternoster, 2013.

———. "Debating God." YouTube playlist. https://www.youtube.com/playlist?list=PLQhh3qcwVEWiY3UmTAiRdj2OW4SBGoy_W.

———. "Debating the Resurrection." YouTube playlist. https://www.youtube.com/playlist?list=PLQhh3qcwVEWhAPCkcpFsSwEXrYKuBhoaq.

———. "Defending an Early High Christology from Archaeology and the New Testament Letters (with Special Reference to the Epistle of James)." *The Peter S. Williams Podcast*, May 28, 2018. http://podcast.peterswilliams.com/e/european-leadership-forum-2018-defending-an-early-high-christology-from-archaeology-and-new-testament-letters/.

———. "Did Jesus Perform Miracles?" YouTube playlist. https://www.youtube.com/playlist?list=PLQhh3qcwVEWi1yi_tcY-Ptl9nNJzRCeiN.

———. *Digging for Evidence: Archaeology and the Historical Reliability of the New Testament*. London: Christian Evidence Society, 2016. http://christianevidence.org/docs/booklets/digging_for_evidence.pdf.

———. "Discipleship and Spiritual Formation." YouTube playlist. https://www.youtube.com/playlist?list=PLQhh3qcwVEWhGSK1x6H3qeqzefB8hmvvM.

———. "Do Angels Really Exist?" Be Thinking, 2015. https://www.bethinking.org/christian-beliefs/do-angels-really-exist.

———. "ELF 2023: Evidence for Old Testament History: From Abraham to Solomon." *The Peter S. Williams Podcast*, May 30, 2023. http://podcast.peterswilliams.com/e/evidence-for-old-testament-history-from-abraham-to-solomon/.

———. "The Epistle of St. James vs. Evolutionary Christology." *Theofilos* 8:1 (2016) 49–65. https://theofilos.no/wp-content/uploads/2019/09/2c_Academia_Williams_The-Epistle-of-James-vs.-Evolutionary.pdf.

———. "Evidence, Explanation, and Expectation." In *Resurrection: Faith or Fact? A Scholars' Debate between a Skeptic and a Christian*, by Carl Stecher et al., 220–61. Durham, NC: Pitchstone, 2019.

———. "The Existence of Jesus." YouTube playlist. https://www.youtube.com/playlist?list=PLQhh3qcwVEWiCALtjBWyxo78Dxxib4g8E.

———. "Faith and Rationality (Oslo, 2022)." *The Peter S. Williams Podcast*, Oct 14, 2020. http://podcast.peterswilliams.com/e/faith-rationality-oslo-2022/.

———. *A Faithful Guide to Philosophy*. Eugene, OR: Wipf & Stock, 2019.

———. *Getting at Jesus: A Comprehensive Critique of Neo-Atheist Nonsense about the Jesus of History*. Eugene, OR: Wipf & Stock, 2019.

———. "High Christology in the Letter of James." *The Peter S. Williams Podcast*, Nov 16, 2015. http://podcast.peterswilliams.com/e/high-christology-in-the-epistle-of-james/?token=7ca115fe28628cc342112e1267a8271f.

———. "Historical Criteria of Authenticity." YouTube playlist. https://www.youtube.com/playlist?list=PLQhh3qcwVEWg6gh7wSlE4EWoDtTHaq--5.

———. *An Informed Cosmos: Essays on Intelligent Design Theory*. Eugene, OR: Wipf & Stock, 2023.

———. "The Inspiration, Authority and Activity of the Bible." *The Peter S. Williams Podcast*, Sep 20, 2016. http://podcast.peterswilliams.com/e/the-authority-inspiration-and-activity-of-the-bible/.

———. "Intelligent Design." YouTube playlist. www.youtube.com/playlist?list=PLQhh3qcwVEWjckJboK1rfuBKPcHiMFTSO.

———. "An Introduction to *An Informed Cosmos: Essays on Intelligent Design Theory*." *The Peter S. Williams Podcast*, Oct 5, 2023. http://podcast.peterswilliams.com/e/introduction-to-an-informed-cosmos-essays-on-intelligent-design-theory/.

———. "Is Christianity Good for Society?" YouTube playlist. https://www.youtube.com/playlist?list=PLQhh3qcwVEWhEFhLjwAL_Qp4dCzCvwGc-.

———. "Islam." YouTube playlist. https://www.youtube.com/playlist?list=PLQhh3qcwVEWjhD84EBojEG5PswCOcDsmJ.

———. *I Wish I Could Believe in Meaning*. Southampton: Damaris, 2005.

———. "Jesus' Tomb Was Empty." YouTube playlist. www.youtube.com/playlist?list=PLQhh3qcwVEWhqraAeJ8gVcSlbXhZR2R6p.

———. "The 'Lunatic, Liar or Lord' Argument." YouTube playlist. https://www.youtube.com/playlist?list=PLQhh3qcwVEWiCA7mwy67RLgGt_2n4j7ra.

———. "Memory Implantation." YouTube playlist. www.youtube.com/playlist?list=PLQhh3qcwVEWjoBnrBC8UZrQuIoMR5Hsq7&disable_polymer=true.

———. "The 'Minimal Facts' Approach to the Resurrection." YouTube playlist. https://www.youtube.com/playlist?list=PLQhh3qcwVEWibeo-6SuXmjOkmFE_4C8Vx.

———. "Miracles." YouTube playlist. https://www.youtube.com/playlist?list=PLQhh3qcwVEWjIqwpnQZQfCxB-ZWLXNvh-.

———. "Mormonism." YouTube playlist. www.youtube.com/playlist?list=PLQhh3qcwVEWjOn4gyNXipluUzVuNsJjjI.

———. "Mormonism—An Introductory Critique." *The Peter S. Williams Podcast*, Feb 29, 2016. http://podcast.peterswilliams.com/?s=Mormonism.

———. "Mythology." In *Dictionary of Christianity and Science*, edited by Paul Copan et al., 459–60. Grand Rapids, MI: Zondervan, 2017.

———. "The Nativity." *The Peter S. Williams Podcast*. http://peterswilliams.podbean.com/mf/feed/rh7ek3/rf_nativity.mp3.

———. "The Nativity." YouTube playlist. www.youtube.com/playlist?list=PLQhh3qcwVEWjXCwcSr2FYzpj5-uQrLKIR.

———. "Natural Theology." YouTube playlist. https://www.youtube.com/playlist?list=PLQhh3qcwVEWiDA8QN4h8wLrrbm49fLzPN.

———. "The Nature of Faith." YouTube playlist. https://www.youtube.com/playlist?list=PLQhh3qcwVEWgaKjEEuPC-ziv9pbReCFHD.

———. "The 'New Atheism.'" YouTube playlist. https://www.youtube.com/playlist?list=PLQhh3qcwVEWifP3P_gIS8MMsRXLOGDiG_.

———. "The New Testament Canon." YouTube playlist. https://www.youtube.com/playlist?list=PLQhh3qcwVEWgB1baV-0QrZ3foJRkj74hM.

———. "New Testament Criticism and Jesus the Exorcist." *Quodlibet Journal of Christian Theology and Philosophy* 4:1 (Winter 2002). www.peterswilliams.com/2016/02/09/jesus-the-exorcist/.

———. "The Origin of Life." YouTube playlist. www.youtube.com/playlist?list=PLQhh3qcwVEWggFeEP9H7k1LyccfxzvoSr.

———. *Outgrowing God? A Beginners' Guide to Richard Dawkins and the God Debate.* Eugene, OR: Cascade, 2020.

———. "Pantheism/New Age Spirituality." YouTube playlist. https://www.youtube.com/playlist?list=PLQhh3qcwVEWhcBAtPezM2sCyMVv7K_NRJ.

———. "The Particular and Exclusive Christ." *The Peter S. Williams Podcast.* http://peterswilliams.podbean.com/mf/feed/zr36r9/Exclusivism_2017.mp3.

———. "Physical Preconditions of Science and Technology." YouTube playlist. www.youtube.com/playlist?list=PLQhh3qcwVEWiEbtcuD5f8bKoDHH31Lg6Y.

———. "President Trump and Nationalism." YouTube playlist. https://www.youtube.com/playlist?list=PLQhh3qcwVEWhnWWAGk-Deg3llMcmjNUQB.

———. "The Problem of Evil." YouTube playlist. https://www.youtube.com/playlist?list=PLQhh3qcwVEWjSOz8xsGXuS_VahByzSzhe.

———. "Problems with Materialism/Metaphysical Naturalism." YouTube playlist. www.youtube.com/playlist?list=PLQhh3qcwVEWgolWsfZnhQvzNfRT_jHLJA.

———. "Problems with the Problem of Evil (Trondheim University, 2018)." *The Peter S. Williams Podcast.* http://peterswilliams.podbean.com/mf/feed/jpz78a/Trondheim_2018_Problems_With_Evil.mp3.

———. "Raelians Successfully Clone Naturalism." 2003. www.arn.org/docs/williams/pw_raeliansclonenaturalism.htm.

———. "The Rare Earth Hypothesis." YouTube playlist. https://www.youtube.com/playlist?list=PLQhh3qcwVEWiLU4H5kBr2JzSAzfIlTRst.

———. "Reading Culture in 3D: From Pre-Modernism to Metamodernism." *The Peter S. Williams Podcast*, Oct 3, 2023. http://podcast.peterswilliams.com/e/reading-culture-in-3d-from-pre-modernism-to-metamodernism/.

———. "Re-Defending Arguments from Desire: A Second Response to Gregory Bassham." Sep 2016. https://www.peterswilliams.com/wp-content/uploads/2016/11/In-Defence-of-Arguments-from-Desire-1.pdf.

———. *"Resurrection: Faith or Fact? Miracle Not Required?" Theofilos* 11:2 (2019) 209–31. https://theofilos.no/wp-content/uploads/2020/03/Theofilos-vol.-11-nr.-2-2019-Forum-3-Arkiv.pdf.

———. "The Resurrection of Jesus." YouTube playlist. https://www.youtube.com/playlist?list=PLQhh3qcwVEWjF0VbpQ9sPUUivlyF5nowB.

———. "Scientific Rebuttals to Ancient Alien Conspiracy Theories as Popular Alternatives to Biblical History." *The Peter S. Williams Podcast*, Oct 24, 2018. http://podcast.peterswilliams.com/e/scientific-rebuttals-to-ancient-alien-conspiracy-theories-as-popular-alternatives-to-biblical-history/.

———. "Scientific Rebuttals to 'Ancient Aliens' as Popular Alternatives to Biblical History." *Theofilos* 12:1 (2020) 85–111. https://theofilos.no/wp-content/uploads/2020/12/Theofilos-vol-12-nr-1-2020-Supplement-academia-6.pdf.

———. "Scientism." YouTube playlist. https://www.youtube.com/playlist?list=PLQhh3qcwVEWiIgrCwkM8Y-RoqU1TmYK8R.

———. "Sorting the Chaff from the Wheat: A Review of Julian Baggini's *Atheism: A Very Short Introduction* (Oxford, 2003)." http://arn.org/docs/williams/pw_chafffromwheat.htm.

———. "Textual Reliability of the New Testament." YouTube playlist. https://www.youtube.com/playlist?list=PLQhh3qcwVEWhx61s1CiNf9_CATxat5bn8.

———. "The Theological Roots of Science." YouTube playlist. https://www.youtube.com/playlist?list=PLQhh3qcwVEWh3jDVYqFFzWSnTbtlUeCg3.

———. "Thinking in 3D: Spirituality, Rhetoric and Transcendental Values." *The Peter S. Williams Podcast*, Sep 29, 2023. http://podcast.peterswilliams.com/e/thinking-in-3d-spirituality-rhetoric-transcendental-values/.

———. "The Trinity." YouTube playlist. https://www.youtube.com/playlist?list=PLQhh3qcwVEWhlDMYNYyenLkqdEQMMtMY0.

———. *Understanding Jesus: Five Ways to Spiritual Enlightenment*. Leicester: Paternoster, 2013.

———. "Understanding the Trinity." Be Thinking, 2012. https://www.bethinking.org/god/understanding-the-trinity.

———. "Understanding Worldviews." YouTube playlist. https://www.youtube.com/playlist?list=PLQhh3qcwVEWhCn7rqlW7UsvFNRjQ9wx0H.

———. "Undesigned Coincidences in the Gospels." YouTube playlist. https://www.youtube.com/playlist?list=PLQhh3qcwVEWgZ_2TLqaPchdovuItTyZll.

———. *A Universe from Someone*. Eugene, OR: Wipf & Stock, 2022.

———. "Was Jesus' Claim to Be God an Invention? Examining Ehrman's Arguments." *Premier Christian Radio*, Dec 10, 2019. www.premierunbelievable.com/topics/was-jesus-claim-to-be-god-an-invention-examining-ehrmans-arguments/11728.article.

———. "Young Earth Creationism." YouTube playlist. www.youtube.com/playlist?list=PLQhh3qcwVEWitFuSuMLz5fmhRGBHR8-_O.

Williams, Rowan. *What Is Christianity? A Little Book of Guidance*. London: SPCK, 2015.

Witherington, Ben, III. *The Christology of Jesus*. Minneapolis: Fortress, 1990.

———. "James Ossuary." Restitutio, Oct 26, 2015. http://restitutio.org/2015/10/26/james-ossuary/.

Wofford, Lynnette. "When Was Homer's Iliad Written?" https://www.enotes.com/topics/iliad/questions/when-was-homers-iliad-written-658281.

Wogan, Nicholas F., et al. "JWST Observations of k2-18b Can Be Explained by a Gas-Rich Mini-Neptune with No Habitable Surface." *Astrophysical Journal Letters*, 963:1 (2024). https://iopscience.iop.org/article/10.3847/2041-8213/ad2616.

Wolchover, Natalie. "Newfound Wormhole Allows Information to Escape Black Holes." *Quanta*, Oct 23, 2017. https://www.quantamagazine.org/newfound-wormhole-allows-information-to-escape-black-holes-20171023/.

Wolf, C. Umhau. "Introduction." *The Onomasticon of Eusebius of Caesarea*. 1971. https://www.tertullian.org/fathers/eusebius_onomasticon_01_intro.htm.
Woods, Amanda. "Half of Humans Believe in Alien Life, Study Says." *New York Post*, Dec 8, 2017. https://nypost.com/2017/12/08/half-of-humans-believe-in-alien-life-study-says/.
Woodward, Bob. *Rage*. London: Simon & Schuster, 2021.
Wright, Jason. "Avi Loeb and 'Oumuamua. Why the Controversy?" *EarthSky*, Sep 24, 2023. https://earthsky.org/human-world/avi-loeb-oumuamua-controversy/.
Wright, N. T. *The Resurrection of the Son of God*. London: SPCK, 2003.
———. *Simply Christian*. New York: HarperOne, 2018.
Wright, N. T., and Michael F. Bird. *The New Testament in Its World: An Introduction to the History, Literature, and Theology of the First Christians*. London: SPCK, 2019.
Yarborough, Robert W. *1–3 John*. Baker Exegetical Commentary on the Bible. Grand Rapids, MI: Baker Academic, 2008.
———. "The Date of Papias: A Reassessment." *Journal of the Evangelical Theological Society* 26:2 (Jun 1983) 181–91. https://etsjets.org/wp-content/uploads/2010/08/files_JETS-PDFs_26_26-2_26-2-pp181-191_JETS.pdf.
Young, Chris. "China's FAST Telescope Did Detect Intelligent Life. But It Was 'Very Likely' Humans." Interesting Engineering, Jun 20, 2022. https://interestingengineering.com/science/china-fast-telescope-alien-life-humans.
Zackrisson, Erik, et al. "Extragalactic SETI: The Tully–Fisher Relation as a Probe of Dysonian Astroengineering in Disk Galaxies." *The Astrophysical Journal* 810:23 (Sep 1, 2015) 1–12. http://iopscience.iop.org/article/10.1088/0004-637X/810/1/23/pdf.
Zaske, Sara. "Study Finds Organic Molecules Discovered by Curiosity Rover Consistent with Early Life on Mars." *WSU Insider*, Mar 5, 2020. https://news.wsu.edu/2020/03/05/study-finds-organic-molecules-discovered-curiosity-rover-consistent-early-life-mars/.
Zondervan Academic Blog. "Who Wrote the Book of Hebrews?" https://zondervanacademic.com/blog/who-wrote-the-book-of-hebrews.
Zondervan NIV Archaeology Study Bible. Grand Rapids, MI: Zondervan, 2005.

www.ingramcontent.com/pod-product-compliance
Lightning Source LLC
Chambersburg PA
CBHW070232230426
43664CB00014B/2276